Why Do You Need This New Edition?

If you're wondering why you should buy this new edition of *Guide to College Reading,* here are eight good reasons!

1. The world of reading is changing. Now you are expected not only to focus on words, but images as well. *Guide to College Reading* will help you develop and improve your **visual literacy skills** as it explains how to read and benefit from visuals in textbooks. Every chapter provides valuable practice with visuals that accompany exercises (many presented with related questions or comments in a bubble format); additional practice opportunities can be found in the "Reading Visually" sections after longer readings.

2. **Chapter 2 (The Basics of College Textbook Reading),** introduces the theme of visual literacy; explains how you can use textbook features to study more efficiently; introduces and provides strategies for collaborative learning, an approach that will improve your comprehension and study skills; and teaches the basics of summarizing.

3. A new insert, **Troubleshooting Guide: Solutions to the Top 10 Reading and Study Problems,** addresses the most common reading and study problems that entering college students face. In each of ten main categories, it briefly outlines the problems you might experience and offers a range of possible solutions to them.

4. Chapter 2 includes a section titled **Using Writing to Help You Learn.** Writing is essential to thinking about and learning from what you read. This new feature explores the value of writing as a learning and critical thinking tool and will teach you the basics of writing an effective summary.

5. Knowing how to write a clear, concise summary is a crucial skill for success in every academic discipline. A new **summary-writing feature** is included in each chapter. To guide you through the steps, in early chapters the summaries start as outlines for you to complete and they become progressively less guided until you are confidently writing summaries on your own by the end of the book.

6. Working together with your peers helps you understand and actively learn from what you read. New collaborative exercises titled **Working Together** have been added to each chapter and are designed to take you beyond the textbook to apply your reading skills to other genres such as newspapers, magazines, editorials, movie reviews, photos, and so on.

7. Within the Fiction Mini-Reader, **a new section on how to read novels** has been added. Using an excerpt from the best seller *Water for Elephants,* by Sara Gruen, this section provides useful guidelines for reading full length fiction.

8. To ensure you have up-to-date, informative, and interesting material to practice with, **130 reading passages, sample paragraphs, and examples have been replaced** in this edition. There are also **ten full-length reading selections.** New topics include music piracy, compulsive gambling, neuroprosthetics, sleep deprivation, multitasking, environmentally friendly college campuses, voter turnout, and computer scammers.

Guide to College Reading

NINTH EDITION

Kathleen T. McWhorter
Niagara County Community College

Longman

Boston Columbus Indianapolis New York San Francisco Upper Saddle River
Amsterdam Cape Town Dubai London Madrid Milan Munich Paris Montréal Toronto
Delhi Mexico City São Paulo Sydney Hong Kong Seoul Singapore Taipei Tokyo

Editor-in-Chief: Eric Stano
Senior Acquisitions Editor: Kate Edwards
Senior Development Editor: Gillian Cook
Senior Supplements Editor: Donna Campion
Senior Media Producer: Stefanie Liebman
Marketing Manager: Thomas DeMarco
Production Manager: Ellen MacElree
Project Coordination, Text Design, and Electronic Page Makeup: PreMediaGlobal
Cover Design Manager/Cover Designer: John Callahan
Cover Images: © claudiobaba/iStockphoto (second from top),
Losevsky Pavel/Shutterstock (bottom)
Photo Researcher: Connie Gardner
Senior Manufacturing Buyer: Roy L. Pickering, Jr.
Printer and Binder: Quad/Graphics

Cover Printer: Lehigh Phoenix
For permission to use copyrighted material, grateful acknowledgment is made to the
copyright holders on pp. 518–530, which are hereby made part of this copyright page.

1 2 3 4 5 6 7 8 9 10—QGT—14 13 12 11

Longman
is an imprint of

www.pearsonhighered.com

Student Edition ISBN-13: 978-0-205-82324-6
Student Edition ISBN-10: 0-205-82324-6
Annotated Instructor's Edition ISBN-13: 978-0-205-01347-0
Annotated Instructor's Edition ISBN-10: 0-205-01347-3

Brief Contents

Detailed Contents

Preface

Guide to College Reading, Ninth Edition, is written to equip students of widely different backgrounds with the basic textbook reading and critical thinking skills they need to cope with the demands of academic work.

NEW TO THE NINTH EDITION

Numerous changes and additions have been made in this ninth edition in response to changing student needs.

1. **New! Emphasis on visual literacy.** The world of reading is changing. The focus remains on words but is now expanding to include images as well. Changes in the content and presentation of recently published college textbooks in a range of disciplines confirm this new focus.

   A new visual literacy theme is presented in *Guide to College Reading* in three ways. First, Chapter 2 presents an introduction to visual literacy and discusses ways textbooks have become more visual. Second, each chapter includes several visuals that accompany practice exercises. Many of these are accompanied by a question or comment in bubble format to help students explore the purpose of the visual or examine how it contributes to meaning. Third, most full-length reading selections include at least one visual. A new section titled "Reading Visually" has been added to the apparatus of each selection.

2. **New! Chapter 2: "The Basics of College Textbook Reading."** This chapter starts with a discussion of the textbook as a learning tool and explains how students can use its features (headings, typographical aids, vocabulary lists, review questions, etc.) to study more efficiently. It also introduces visual literacy and demonstrates the various visual features textbooks contain. In addition, collaborative learning is presented, and students are given strategies for participating in collaborative projects. Finally, the chapter discusses writing as a method of learning, and students learn the basics of summarizing.

3. New! Troubleshooting Guide: Solutions to the Top Ten Reading and Study Problems. This insert identifies the most common reading and study problems that beginning students face and offers helpful solutions. The guide begins with a brief index, identifying the following categories: (1) focus, motivation, and concentration; (2) retention of reading material; (3) background knowledge and vocabulary; (4) reading and understanding graphics; (5) exams and assignments; (6) reading speed; (7) critical reading and thinking; (8) pulling ideas together; (9) working with other students; and (10) course-specific concerns. Arranged in tabular form, the guide concisely states problems in each category and offers a range of possible solutions. It is placed after Part Three for easy reference and is identified by yellow page banding.

4. New! Numerous passages, reading selections, and examples. More than 130 reading passages, sample paragraphs, and examples have been replaced throughout the book to provide relevant and current reading material. Ten full-length reading selections (Mastery Test 3) have been replaced. New topics include music piracy, compulsive gambling, advanced prosthetics, sleep deprivation, multitasking, environmentally friendly college campuses, voter turnout, post-traumatic stress disorder, conversational dilemmas, and choosing a college major. The Contemporary Issues Minireader contains three new selections on the topics of genetic testing, cyberbullying, and the negative effects of texting.

5. New! Emphasis on writing about reading. To emphasize the reading-writing connection in the text, a signature McWhorter feature, Chapter 2 includes a section titled "Using Writing to Learn." This new feature explores the value of writing as a learning and critical thinking tool and introduces students to summarizing.

6. New! Working Together collaborative activities. Because instructors recognize the need to actively engage students to promote learning, many use collaborative activities in their courses. New collaborative exercises have been added to each chapter and are designated with an icon and labeled "Working Together." Many take the student beyond the textbook to apply reading skills to other genres such as newspaper headlines, movie reviews, and so on.

7. New! Summary-writing exercises. A new summary-writing feature is included in each chapter in Mastery Test 3 (the chapter's full-length reading). A scaffolding method of instruction is used. In early chapters the summaries start as skeletal outlines for students to complete, and they become progressively less guided until students are writing complete summaries on their own by the end of the book.

8. New! Expanded emphasis on critical thinking. The apparatus for each full-length reading now includes a section titled "Thinking Critically About the Reading." These questions may be used as journal writing prompts or as writing activities.

9. New! Introduction to reading novels. Within the Fiction Minireader, a new section on reading novels has been added. Using an excerpt from *Water for Elephants*, by Sara Gruen, this section offers guidelines for reading full-length fiction. A new short story, "Little Brother," by Bruce Holland Rogers, has also been added to the minireader.

THE PURPOSE OF THIS TEXT

Guide to College Reading, Ninth Edition, addresses the learning characteristics, attitudes, and motivational levels of college students. It is intended to equip them with the skills they need to handle the diverse reading demands of college coursework. Specifically, the book guides students in becoming active learners and critical thinkers. Using an encouraging, supportive, nonthreatening voice, the text provides clear instruction and a variety of everyday examples and extensive exercises that encourage students to become involved and apply the skills presented.

The chapters are divided into numerous sections; exercises are frequent but brief and explicit. The language and style are simple and direct; explanations are clear and often presented in step-by-step form. Reading topics and materials have been chosen carefully to relate to students' interests and background, while broadening their range of experience. Many students have compensated for poor reading skills with alternate learning styles; they have become visual and auditory learners. To capitalize on this adaptation, a visual approach to learning is used throughout. The importance of visual literacy in today's world is emphasized by numerous photographs—many with bubble captions designed to provoke thought about how the visuals are used to enhance and add meaning to text—drawings, diagrams, and other visual aids used to illustrate concepts.

CONTENT OVERVIEW

The text is organized into seven major sections, following the logical progression of skill development from vocabulary development to reading paragraphs, articles, essays, and chapters. It also proceeds logically from literal comprehension to critical interpretation and response. An opening chapter focuses on student success strategies, including such topics as attitudes toward college, concentration, learning styles, and comprehension monitoring.

- Part One presents the basics for success in college reading.
- Part Two teaches students basic approaches to vocabulary development. It includes contextual aids, analysis of word parts, pronunciation, and the use of a dictionary and other reference sources.
- Part Three helps students develop literal comprehension skills. It emphasizes prereading techniques that prepare and enable the student to comprehend and to recall content. Previewing, activating background knowledge, and using guide questions are emphasized. The unit provides extensive instruction and practice with paragraph comprehension and recognition of thought patterns. An entire chapter is now devoted to stated and implied main ideas; another entire chapter focuses on supporting details and transitions.
- Part Four teaches students textbook reading skills. Topics include ways to read graphics and technical material, reading and evaluating Internet sources, and methods of organizing and retaining course content.
- Part Five introduces critical reading and thinking skills. It presents skills that enable students to interact with and evaluate written material, including material on the Internet. Topics include making inferences, identifying the author's purpose, recognizing assumptions, and distinguishing between fact and opinion.
- Part Six, "A Fiction Minireader," offers a brief introduction to reading fiction. An introductory section discusses the essential elements of a short story, using Chopin's "The Story of an Hour" as an example. Two additional short stories with accompanying apparatus are also included, as well as an introduction to reading novels.
- Part Seven, "A Contemporary Issues Minireader," contains six articles on contemporary issues. Each reading is prefaced by an interest-catching introduction, prereading questions, and a vocabulary preview. Literal and critical thinking questions as well as a words-in-context exercise, vocabulary review, summary exercise, and writing exercises follow each selection.

SPECIAL FEATURES

The following features enhance the text's effectiveness and directly contribute to students' success:

- Integration of reading and writing. The text integrates reading and writing skills. Students respond to exercises by writing sentences and paragraphs. Each reading selection is followed by "Thinking Critically about the Reading" questions, which encourage composition. A writing exercise accompanies each reading selection in Part Seven.

- **Reading as thinking.** Reading is approached as a thinking process—a process in which the student interacts with textual material and sorts, evaluates, and reacts to its organization and content. For example, students are shown how to define their purpose for reading, ask questions, identify and use organization and structure as a guide to understanding, make inferences, and interpret and evaluate what they read.

- **Comprehension monitoring.** Comprehension monitoring is also addressed within the text. Through a variety of techniques, students are encouraged to be aware of and to evaluate and control their level of comprehension of the material they read.

- **Skill application.** Chapters 2 through 12 conclude with three mastery tests that enable students to apply the skills taught in each chapter and to evaluate their learning.

BOOK-SPECIFIC ANCILLARY MATERIALS

- **Annotated Instructor's Edition**
  The Annotated Instructor's Edition is identical to the student text but includes all answers printed directly on the pages where questions, exercises, or activities occur. (ISBN: 0-205-01347-3)

- **Instructor's Manual**
  An Instructor's Manual, including an Answer Key, accompanies the text. The manual describes in detail the basic features of the text and offers suggestions for structuring the course, for teaching nontraditional students, and for approaching each section of the text. (ISBN: 0-205-01348-1)

- **Test Bank**
  This supplement features two sets of chapter quizzes and a mastery test for each chapter. It is printed in an 8½ × 11 format that allows for easy photocopying and distribution. (ISBN: 0-205-82447-1)

- **PowerPoint Presentations**
  For the lab or electronic classroom, a PowerPoint presentation is available for each chapter of *Guide to College Reading*. Each chapter's presentation consists of approximately 15–20 slides highlighting key concepts from the text, as well as additional activities. Download the presentations from our Web site at http://www.ablongman.com/mcwhorter.

- **Expanding Your Vocabulary.** Instructors may choose to shrink-wrap *Guide to College Reading* with a copy of *Expanding Your Vocabulary*. This book, written by Kathleen McWhorter, works well as a supplemental text by providing additional instruction and practice in vocabulary. Students can work through the book independently, or units may be incorporated into weekly lesson plans. Topics covered include methods of vocabulary learning, contextual aids, word parts, connotative meanings, idioms, euphemisms, and many more fun and interesting topics. The book concludes with vocabulary lists and exercises representative of 11 academic disciplines. To preview the book, contact your Longman sales consultant for an examination copy.

THE LONGMAN BASIC SKILLS PACKAGE

Longman is pleased to offer a variety of support materials to help make teaching developmental reading easier for teachers and to help students excel in their course work. Visit http://www.ablongman.com or contact your local Longman sales representative for a detailed listing of our supplements package or for more information on pricing and how to create a package.

ACKNOWLEDGMENTS

I wish to express my gratitude to my reviewers for their excellent ideas, suggestions, and advice on this and previous editions of this text: Alfradene Armstrong, Tougaloo College; Carla Bell, Henry Ford Community College; Michelle Biferie, Palm Beach Community College; Dorothy Booher, Florida Community College at Jacksonville, Kent Campus; Diane Bosco, Suffolk County Community College; Sharon Cellemme, South Piedmont Community College; Beth Childress, Armstrong Atlantic University; Pam Drell, Oakton Community College, Des Plaines Campus; Deborah Paul Fuller, Bunker Hill Community College; Shirley Hall, Middle Georgia College; Pam Hallene, Community College of Rhode Island; Kevin Hayes, Essex County College; Peggy Hopper, Walters State Community College; Danica Hubbard, College of DuPage; Suzanne E. Hughes, Florida Community College at Jacksonville; Jacqueline Jackson, Art Institute of Philadelphia; Arlene Jellinek, Palm Beach Community College; Mahalia H. Johnson, Greenville Technical College; Jeanne Keefe, Belleville Area College; Patti Levine-Brown, Florida Community College at Jacksonville; Wendy McBride, Kishwaukee Community College; Anne Mueller, Kishwaukee Community College; Sharyn Neuwirth, Montgomery College, Tacoma Park Campus; Alice Nitta, Leeward Community College; Pauline Noznick, Oakton Community College; Jean Olsen, Oakton Community College; Catherine Packard, Southeastern Illinois College; Elizabeth Parks, Kishwaukee Community College; Kathy Purswell, Frank Phillips College; Regina Rochford, Queensborough Community College,

CUNY; Diane Schellack, Burlington County College; Marilyn Schenk, San Diego Mesa College; Jackie Stahlecker, St. Phillips College; Cynthia Taber, Schenectady County Community College, SUNY; Marie Ulmen, Harrisburg Area Community College; Pam Walsh, Schenectady County Community College, SUNY; Mary Wolting, Indiana University—Purdue University at Indianapolis; and Nora Yaeger, Cedar Valley College.

I am particularly indebted to Gillian Cook, my development editor, for her energetic guidance and valuable advice and to Kate Edwards, senior acquisitions editor, for her enthusiastic support of this project.

KATHLEEN T. McWHORTER

CHAPTER

1

Successful Attitudes toward Reading and Learning

Looking at …
College Success

LEARNING OBJECTIVES

*This chapter will
show you how to:*

OBJECTIVE **1** Understand what is expected in college

OBJECTIVE **2** Start with a positive attitude

OBJECTIVE **3** Build your concentration

OBJECTIVE **4** Understand learning style

OBJECTIVE **5** Analyze your learning style

OBJECTIVE **6** Monitor your comprehension

OBJECTIVE **7** Strengthen your comprehension

Your first semester of college is often the most difficult because you don't know what to expect. The classes you have selected are challenging and your instructors are demanding. This chapter will help you discover how to learn most effectively and help you approach the reading and study demands of your courses successfully.

1

College is very different from any other type of educational experience. It is different from high school, job training programs, adult education, and technical training programs. New and different types of learning are demanded, and you need new skills and techniques to meet these demands. This chapter offers you ways to become a successful student. You will discover what is expected of you in college, learn how to improve your concentration, analyze how you learn, and strengthen your comprehension.

UNDERSTAND WHAT IS EXPECTED IN COLLEGE

Following is a list of statements about college. Treat them like a quiz, if you wish. Decide whether each statement is true or false, and write *T* for true or *F* for false in the space provided. Each statement will make you think about the reading and study demands of college. Check your answers by reading the paragraph following each item. As you work through this quiz, you will find out a little about what is expected of you in college. You will see whether or not you have an accurate picture of what college work involves. You will also see how this text will help you to become a better, more successful student.

_____   1. For every hour I spend in class, I should spend one hour studying outside of class.

Many students feel that even one hour for each class (or 15 hours per week for students carrying a 15 credit-hour load) is a lot. Actually, the rule of thumb used by many instructors is two hours of study for each class hour. So you can see that you are expected to do a great deal of reading, studying, and learning on your own time. The purpose of this text is to help you read and learn in the easiest and best way for you.

_____   2. I should expect to read about 80 textbook pages per week in each of my courses.

A survey of freshman courses at one college indicated that the average course assignment was roughly 80 pages per week. This may seem like a lot of reading—and it is. You will need to build your reading skills to handle this task. To help you do this, techniques for understanding and remembering what you read, improving your concentration, and handling difficult reading assignments will be suggested throughout this book.

_____   3. There are a lot of words I do not know, but my vocabulary is about as good as it needs to be.

For each college course you take, there will be new words to learn. Some will be everyday words; others will be specialized or technical. Part Two of this book will show you how to develop your vocabulary by learning new words, figuring out words you do not know, and using reference sources.

_____ 4. College instructors will tell me exactly what to learn for each exam.

College instructors seldom tell you exactly what to learn or review. They expect you to decide what is important and to learn that information. In Part Three of this text you will learn how to identify what is important in sentences and paragraphs and how to follow authors' thought patterns.

_____ 5. The more facts I memorize, the higher my exam grades will be.

Learning a large number of facts is no guarantee of a high grade in a course. Some instructors and the exams they give are concerned with your ability to see how facts and ideas fit together, or to evaluate ideas, make comparisons, and recognize trends. Parts Three and Four of this text will help you to do this by showing you how to read textbook chapters, use graphic aids, and organize and remember information.

_____ 6. The only assignments that instructors give are readings in the textbook.

Instructors often assign readings in a variety of sources including periodicals, newspapers, reference and library books, and online sources. These readings are intended to add to the information presented in your text and by your instructor. The six reading selections contained in Part Seven will give you the opportunity to practice and apply your skills to readings taken from a variety of sources. These selections are similar to the outside readings your instructors will assign.

_____ 7. Rereading a textbook chapter is the best way to prepare for an exam on that chapter.

Rereading is actually one of the poorest ways to review. Besides, it is often dull and time-consuming. In Chapter 10, you will learn about four more-effective alternatives: _highlighting and marking, outlining, mapping,_ and _summarizing._

_____ 8. College instructors expect me to react to, evaluate, and criticize what I read.

Beyond understanding the content of textbooks, articles, and essays, students need to be able to criticize and evaluate ideas.

To help you read and think critically, Part Five of this text will show you how to interpret what you read, find the author's purpose, and ask critical questions.

_____ 9. The best way to read a textbook assignment is to turn to the correct page, start reading, and continue until you reach the end of the assignment.

There are numerous things you can do before you read, while you read, and after you read that can improve your comprehension and retention. These techniques for improving your comprehension and recall are presented throughout this text. For example, later in this chapter you will learn techniques for building your concentration. In Chapter 5 you will be shown how to preview, think about what you will read, and use questions to guide your reading. Chapter 10 focuses on techniques to use after you read to strengthen comprehension and recall.

_____ 10. You can never know whether you have understood a textbook reading assignment until you take an exam on the chapter.

As you read, it is possible and important to keep track of and evaluate your level of understanding. You will learn how to keep track of your comprehension, recognize comprehension signals, and strengthen your comprehension.

By analyzing the above statements and the correct responses, you can see that college is a lot of work, much of which you must do on your own. However, college is also a new, exciting experience that will acquaint you with new ideas and opportunities.

This text will help you to get the most out of college and to take advantage of the opportunities it offers. Its purpose is to equip you with the reading and learning skills necessary for academic success.

The opportunity of college lies ahead of you. The skills you are about to learn, along with plenty of hard work, will make your college experience a meaningful and valuable one. The remainder of this chapter will help you take four important steps to becoming a successful student. You will learn to develop a positive attitude, control your concentration, strengthen your comprehension, and analyze how you learn.

START WITH A POSITIVE ATTITUDE

Reading and studying are keys to college success and, later, to success on the job. In fact, many employers identify reading, thinking, and communicating as three essential skills for the workplace.

Becoming a Successful Student

Here are a few approaches that will help you become a successful college student:

Success Strategies

1. **Be confident: send yourself positive messages.** Tell yourself that college is something you want and can do. Negative messages such as "I might not be able to do this" or "What if I fail?" will only get in the way. In fact, there is substantial evidence to suggest that negative thinking interferes with performance. In other words, you may be limiting your success by thinking negatively. Instead, send yourself positive messages such as "I can do this" or "I've studied hard, and I'm going to pass this test."

2. **Accept responsibility for your own learning.** Think of your instructors as guides. Fishing guides take you to where you are likely to catch fish, but they do not catch them for you. Similarly, your college instructors will lead you to the information you need to learn, but they will not learn for you. You must choose the strategies and techniques necessary to learn from your textbooks and college lectures.

3. **Visualize success.** Close your eyes and imagine yourself completing a long or difficult assignment or passing an upcoming exam. Just as athletes prepare for a competition by visualizing themselves finishing a marathon in record time or completing a difficult ski run, you should visualize yourself successfully working through challenging tasks.

4. **Set long-term goals for yourself.** You will feel more like working on assignments if you have things you are working toward. Goals such as "to get my own apartment," "to be able to quit my job at Kmart," or "to become a registered nurse" will help you focus and stick with daily tasks.

Becoming a Successful Reader

Reading can open up worlds of new ideas, show you different ways of looking at things, and provide a welcome escape from day-to-day problems. It is an opportunity to visit new places, meet new people and ideas, and broaden your experience. You will spend a great deal of time in college reading your textbooks and other assignments. Think of reading in a positive way. Here are a few approaches that will make reading work for you:

Positive Approaches to Reading

1. **Stick with a reading assignment.** If an assignment is troublesome, experiment with different methods of completing it. Consider highlighting, outlining, testing yourself, preparing vocabulary cards, or

drawing diagrams, for example. You will learn these methods in later chapters.

2. **Plan on spending time.** Reading is not something you can rush through. The time you invest will pay off in increased comprehension.

3. **Actively search for key ideas as you read.** Try to connect these ideas with what your instructor is discussing in class. Think of reading as a way of sifting and sorting out what you need to learn from the less important information.

4. **Think of reading as a way of unlocking the writer's message to you, the reader.** Look for clues about the writer's personality, attitudes, opinions, and beliefs. This will put you in touch with the writer as a person and help you understand his or her message. Part Five of this book will offer suggestions to help you do this.

BUILD YOUR CONCENTRATION

myreadinglab

To practice your concentration skills, go to
▼ STUDY PLAN
  ▼ READING SKILLS
    ▼ MEMORIZATION AND CONCEN-TRATION

Do you have difficulty concentrating? If so, you are like many other college students who say that lack of concentration is the main reason they cannot read or study effectively. Building concentration involves two steps: (1) controlling your surroundings, and (2) focusing your attention.

Controlling Your Surroundings

Poor concentration is often the result of distractions caused by the time and place you have chosen to study. Here are a few ideas to help you overcome poor concentration:

Controlling Distractions

1. **Choose a place to read where you will not be interrupted.** If people interrupt you at home or in the dormitory, try the campus library.

2. **Find a place that is relatively free of distractions and temptations.** Avoid places with outside noise, friends, a television set, or an interesting project close at hand.

3. **Silence your cell phone and shut off instant messaging.** If left on, these will break your concentration and cost you time.

4. **Read in the same place each day.** Eventually you will get in the habit of reading there, and concentration will become easier, almost automatic.

5. **Do not read where you are too comfortable.** It is easy to lose concentration, become drowsy, or fall asleep when you are too relaxed.

6. **Choose a time of day when you are mentally alert.** Concentration is easier if you are not tired, hungry, or drowsy.

Focusing Your Attention

Even if you follow these suggestions, you may still find it difficult to become organized and stick with your reading. This takes self-discipline, but the following suggestions may help:

Strengthening Your Comprehension

1. **Set goals and time limits for yourself.** Before you begin a reading assignment, decide how long it should take, and check to see that you stay on schedule. Before you start an evening of homework, write down what you plan to do and how long each assignment should take. Sample goals for an evening are shown in Figure 1-1.

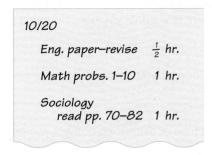

10/20

Eng. paper—revise $\frac{1}{2}$ hr.

Math probs. 1–10   1 hr.

Sociology
    read pp. 70–82 1 hr.

Figure 1-1   Goals and time limits

2. **Choose and reserve blocks of time each day for reading and study.** Write down what you will study in each time block each day or evening. Working at the same time each day establishes a routine and makes concentration a bit easier.

3. **Vary your reading.** For instance, instead of spending an entire evening on one subject, work for one hour on each of three subjects.

4. **Reward yourself for accomplishing things as planned.** Delay entertainment until after you have finished studying. Use such things as ordering a pizza, calling a friend, or watching TV as rewards after you have completed several assignments.

5. **Plan frequent breaks.** Do this at sensible points in your reading— between chapters or after major chapter divisions.

6. **Keep physically as well as mentally active.** Try highlighting, underlining, or making summary notes as you read (see Chapter 10). These activities will focus your attention on the assignment.

EXERCISE 1-1   ## Analyzing Your Level of Concentration

Directions: Answer each of the following questions as honestly as you can. They will help you analyze problems with concentration. Discuss your answers with others in your class.

1. Where do you read and study? _____

   What interruptions, if any, occur there? _____

2. Do you need to find a better place? _____

   If so, list a few alternatives. _____

3. What is the best time of day for you to read? (If you do not know, experiment with different times until you begin to see a pattern.)

   _____

4. How long do you normally read without a break?

   _____

5. What type of distraction bothers you the most?

   _____

6. On average, how many different assignments do you work on in one evening?

   _____

7. What types of rewards might work for you?

   _____

EXERCISE 1-2   ## Identifying Distractions

Directions: As you read your next textbook assignment, either for this course or another, be alert for distractions. Each time your mind wanders, try to identify the source of the distraction. List in the space provided the cause of each break in your concentration and a way to eliminate each, if possible.

_____

_____

_____

EXERCISE 1-3 Setting Goals

Directions: Before you begin your next study session, make a list in the space provided of what you intend to accomplish and how long you should spend on each task.

	Assignment	**Time**
1.	_____	_____
2.	_____	_____
3.	_____	_____

ANALYZE YOUR LEARNING STYLE

Reading assignments are the primary focus of many college classes. Instructors give daily or weekly textbook assignments. You are expected to read the material, learn it, and pass tests on it. Class lectures and discussions are often based on textbook assignments. An important part of many college classes, then, is completing reading assignments.

Reading and understanding an assignment, however, does not mean you have learned it. In fact, if you have read an assignment once, you probably have *not* learned it. You need to do more than read to learn an assignment. Your question, then, is "What else should I do?" The answer is not a simple one.

Not everyone learns in the same way. In fact, everyone has his or her own individual way of learning, which is called *learning style*. The following section contains a brief Learning Style Questionnaire that will help you analyze how you learn and prepare an action plan for learning what you read.

LEARNING STYLE QUESTIONNAIRE

Directions: Each item presents two choices. Select the alternative that best describes you. In cases in which neither choice suits you, select the one that is closer to your preference. Write the letter of your choice in the space provided.

Part One

_____ 1. I would prefer to follow a set of
   a. oral directions.
   b. print directions.

_____ 2. I would prefer to
   a. attend a lecture given by a famous psychologist.
   b. read an online article written by the psychologist.

_____ 3. When I am introduced to someone, it is easier for me to remember the person's
    a. name.
    b. face.

_____ 4. I find it easier to learn new information using
    a. language (words).
    b. images (pictures).

_____ 5. I prefer classes in which the instructor
    a. lectures and answers questions.
    b. uses PowerPoint illustrations and videos.

_____ 6. To follow current events, I would prefer to
    a. listen to the news on the radio.
    b. read the newspaper.

_____ 7. To learn how to repair a flat tire, I would prefer to
    a. listen to a friend's explanation.
    b. watch a demonstration.

Part Two

_____ 8. I prefer to
    a. work with facts and details.
    b. construct theories and ideas.

_____ 9. I would prefer a job involving
    a. following specific instructions.
    b. reading, writing, and analyzing.

_____ 10. I prefer to
    a. solve math problems using a formula.
    b. discover why the formula works.

_____ 11. I would prefer to write a term paper explaining
    a. how a process works.
    b. a theory.

_____ 12. I prefer tasks that require me to
    a. follow careful, detailed instructions.
    b. use reasoning and critical analysis.

_____ 13. For a criminal justice course, I would prefer to
    a. discover how and when a law can be used.
    b. learn how and why it became law.

_____ 14. To learn more about the operation of a high-speed computer printer, I would prefer to
   a. work with several types of printers.
   b. understand the principles on which they operate.

Part Three

_____ 15. To solve a math problem, I would prefer to
   a. draw or visualize the problem.
   b. study a sample problem and use it as a model.

_____ 16. To best remember something, I
   a. create a mental picture.
   b. write it down.

_____ 17. Assembling a bicycle from a diagram would be
   a. easy.
   b. challenging.

_____ 18. I prefer classes in which I
   a. handle equipment or work with models.
   b. participate in a class discussion.

_____ 19. To understand and remember how a machine works, I would
   a. draw a diagram.
   b. write notes.

_____ 20. I enjoy
   a. drawing or working with my hands.
   b. speaking, writing, and listening.

_____ 21. If I were trying to locate an office on an unfamiliar campus, I would prefer
   a. a map.
   b. print directions.

Part Four

_____ 22. For a grade in biology lab, I would prefer to
   a. work with a lab partner.
   b. work alone.

_____ 23. When faced with a difficult personal problem, I prefer to
   a. discuss it with others.
   b. resolve it myself.

_____ 24. Many instructors could improve their classes by
   a. including more discussion and group activities.
   b. allowing students to work on their own more frequently.

_____ 25. When listening to a lecturer or speaker, I respond more to the
      a. person presenting the idea.
      b. ideas themselves.

_____ 26. When on a team project, I prefer to
      a. work with several team members.
      b. divide the tasks and complete those assigned to me.

_____ 27. I prefer to shop and do errands
      a. with friends.
      b. by myself.

_____ 28. A job in a busy office is
      a. more appealing than working alone.
      b. less appealing than working alone.

Part Five

_____ 29. To make decisions, I rely on
      a. my experiences and gut feelings.
      b. facts and objective data.

_____ 30. To complete a task, I
      a. can use whatever is available to get the job done.
      b. must have everything I need at hand.

_____ 31. I prefer to express my ideas and feelings through
      a. music, song, or poetry.
      b. direct, concise language.

_____ 32. I prefer instructors who
      a. allow students to be guided by their own interests.
      b. make their expectations clear and explicit.

_____ 33. I tend to
      a. challenge and question what I hear and read.
      b. accept what I hear and read.

_____ 34. I prefer
      a. essay exams.
      b. objective exams.

_____ 35. In completing an assignment, I prefer to
      a. figure out my own approach.
      b. be told exactly what to do.

To score your questionnaire, record the total number of *a*'s you selected and the total number of *b*'s for each part of the questionnaire. Record your totals in the scoring grid provided at the top of the next page.

Scoring Grid

Parts	Choice A Total	Choice B Total
Part One	_____	_____
	Auditory	Visual
Part Two	_____	_____
	Applied	Conceptual
Part Three	_____	_____
	Spatial	Verbal
Part Four	_____	_____
	Social	Independent
Part Five	_____	_____
	Creative	Pragmatic

Now, circle your higher score for each part of the questionnaire. The word below the score you circled indicates a strength of your learning style. The next section explains how to interpret your scores.

Interpreting Your Scores

The questionnaire was divided into five parts; each part identifies one aspect of your learning style. Each of these five aspects is explained below.

Part One: Auditory or Visual Learners   This score indicates whether you learn better by listening (auditory) or by seeing (visual). If you have a higher auditory than visual score, you tend to be an auditory learner. That is, you tend to learn more easily by hearing than by reading. A higher visual score suggests strengths with visual modes of learning—reading, studying pictures, reading diagrams, and so forth.

Part Two: Applied or Conceptual Learners   This score describes the types of learning tasks and learning situations you prefer and find easiest to handle. If you are an applied learner, you prefer tasks that involve real objects and situations. Practical, real-life examples are ideal for you. If you are a conceptual learner, you prefer to work with language and ideas; you do not need practical applications for understanding.

Part Three: Spatial or Verbal (Nonspatial) Learners   This score reveals your ability to work with spatial relationships. Spatial learners are able to visualize or mentally see how things work or how they are positioned in space. Their strengths may include drawing, assembling, or repairing things. Verbal learners lack skills in positioning things in space. Instead they rely on verbal or language skills.

Part Four: Social or Independent Learners   This score reveals whether you like to work alone or with others. If you are a social learner, you prefer to work with others—both classmates and instructors—closely and directly. You tend to be people oriented and enjoy personal interaction. If you are an independent learner, you prefer to work alone and study alone. You tend to be self-directed or self-motivated and are often goal oriented.

Part Five: Creative or Pragmatic Learners   This score describes the approach you prefer to take toward learning tasks. Creative learners are imaginative and innovative. They prefer to learn through discovery or experimentation. They are comfortable taking risks and following hunches. Pragmatic learners are practical, logical, and systematic. They seek order and are comfortable following rules.

Evaluating Your Scores

If you disagree with any part of the Learning Style Questionnaire, go with your own instincts rather than the questionnaire results. The questionnaire is just a quick assessment; trust your knowledge of yourself in areas of dispute.

Developing a Learning Action Plan

Now that you know more about *how* you learn, you are ready to develop an action plan for learning what you read. Suppose you discovered that you are an auditory learner. You still have to read your assignments, which is a visual task. However, to learn the assignment you should translate the material into an auditory form. For example, you could repeat aloud, using your own words, information that you want to remember, or you could record key information and play it back. If you also are a social learner, you could work with a classmate, testing each other out loud.

Table 1-1 lists each aspect of learning style and offers suggestions for how to learn from a reading assignment. To use the table

1. **Circle the five aspects of your learning style in which you received the highest scores.** Disregard the others.
2. **Read through the suggestions that apply to you.**

TABLE 1-1   Learning Styles and Reading/Learning Strategies

If your learning style is . . .	Then the reading/learning strategies to use are . . .
Auditory	• discuss/study with friends • talk aloud when studying • record self-testing questions and answers
Visual	• draw diagrams, charts, tables (Chapter 10) • try to visualize events • use films and videos, when available • use computer-assisted instruction, if available
Applied	• think of practical situations to which learning applies • associate ideas with their application • use case studies, examples, and applications to cue your learning
Conceptual	• organize materials that lack order • use outlining (Chapter 10) • focus on organizational patterns (Chapter 8)
Spatial	• use mapping (Chapter 10) • use outlining (Chapter 10) • draw diagrams, make charts and sketches • use visualization
Verbal (Nonspatial)	• translate diagrams and drawings into language • record steps, processes, procedures in words • write summaries (Chapters 2 and 10) • write your interpretation next to textbook drawings, maps, graphics
Social	• form study groups • find a study partner • interact with your instructor • work with a tutor
Independent	• use computer-assisted instruction, if available • purchase review workbooks or study guides, if available
Creative	• ask and answer questions • record your own ideas in margins of textbooks
Pragmatic	• study in an organized environment • write lists of steps, procedures, and processes

3. **Place a check mark in front of suggestions that you think will work for you.** Choose at least one from each category.
4. **List the suggestions that you chose in the box labeled Action Plan for Learning below.**

Action Plan for Learning

Learning Strategy 1 _____

_____

Learning Strategy 2 _____

_____

Learning Strategy 3 _____

_____

Learning Strategy 4 _____

_____

Learning Strategy 5 _____

_____

Learning Strategy 6 _____

_____

In the Action Plan for Learning box you listed five or more suggestions to help you learn what you read. The next step is to experiment with these techniques, one at a time. (You may need to refer to chapters listed in parentheses in Table 1-1 to learn or review how a certain technique works.) Use one technique for a while, and then move to the next. Continue using the techniques that seem to work; work on revising or modifying those that do not. Do not hesitate to experiment with other techniques listed in the table as well. You may find other techniques that work well for you.

Developing Strategies to Overcome Limitations

You should also work on developing styles in which you are weak. Your learning style is not fixed or unchanging. You can improve areas in which you scored lower. Although you may be weak in auditory learning, for example, many of your professors will lecture and expect you to take notes. If you work on improving your listening and note-taking skills, you can learn to handle lectures effectively. Make a conscious effort to work on improving areas of weakness as well as taking advantage of your strengths.

EXERCISE 1-4   Evaluating Learning Strategies

Directions: Write a brief evaluation of each learning strategy you listed in your Action Plan for Learning. Explain which worked; which, if any, did not; and what changes you have noticed in your ability to learn from reading.

EXERCISE 1-5   Learning Styles I

Directions: Form several small groups (three to five students), each of which consists of people who are either predominantly visual learners or predominantly auditory learners. Each group should discuss and outline strategies for completing each of the following tasks:

- Task 1: reading a poem for a literature class
- Task 2: revising an essay for a writing class
- Task 3: reviewing an economics textbook chapter that contains numerous tables, charts, and graphs

Groups should report their findings to the class and discuss how visual and auditory learners' strategies differ.

EXERCISE 1-6   Learning Styles II

Directions: Form several small groups (three to five students), each of which consists of people who are either predominantly social learners or predominantly independent learners. Each group should discuss and outline strategies for completing each of the following tasks:

- Task 1: reading a sociology textbook chapter that contains end-of-chapter study and review questions
- Task 2: working on sample problems for a math class
- Task 3: reading a case study (a detailed description of a criminal case) for a criminal justice class

Groups should report their findings to the class and discuss how social and independent learners' strategies differ.

PAY ATTENTION TO COMPREHENSION SIGNALS

Think for a moment about how you feel when you read material you can easily understand. Now compare that with what happens when you read something difficult and complicated. When you read easy material, does it seem that everything "clicks"? That is, do ideas seem to fit together and make sense? Is that "click" noticeably absent in difficult reading?

Read each of the following paragraphs. As you read, be aware of how well you understand each of them.

Paragraph 1

The **spinal cord** is actually an extension of the brain. It runs from the base of the brain down the center of the back, protected by a column of bones. The cord acts as a sort of bridge between the brain and the parts of the body below the neck. But the spinal cord is not merely a bridge. It also produces some behaviors on its own, without any help from the brain. These behaviors, called spinal **reflexes**, are automatic, requiring no conscious effort. For example, if you accidentally touch a hot iron, you will immediately pull your hand away, even before the brain has had a chance to register what has happened. Nerve impulses bring a message to the spinal cord (HOT!), and the spinal cord immediately sends out a command via other nerve impulses, telling muscles in your arm to contract and pull your hand away from the iron. (Reflexes above the neck, such as sneezing and blinking, involve the lower part of the brain rather than the spinal cord.)

—Wade and Tavris, *Psychology*, p. 82

Paragraph 2

Diluted earnings per share (EPS) are calculated under the assumption that all contingent securities that would have dilutive effects are converted and exercised and are therefore common stock. They are found by adjusting basic EPS for the impact of converting all convertibles and exercising all warrants and options that would have dilutive effects on the firm's earnings. This approach treats as common stock all contingent securities. It is calculated by dividing earnings available for common stockholders (adjusted for interest and preferred stock dividends that would not be paid, given assumed conversion of all outstanding contingent securities that would have dilutive effects) by the number of shares of common stock that would be outstanding if all contingent securities that would have dilutive effects were converted and exercised.

—Gitman, *Principles of Managerial Finance*, p. 733

Did you feel comfortable and confident as you read Paragraph 1? Did ideas seem to lead from one to another and make sense? How did you feel while reading Paragraph 2? Most likely you sensed its difficulty and felt confused. Some words were unfamiliar, and you could not follow the flow of ideas.

As you read Paragraph 2, did you know that you were not understanding it? Did you feel lost and confused? Table 1-2 lists and compares some common signals that are useful in monitoring your comprehension. Not all signals appear at the same time, and not all signals work for everyone. As you study the list, identify those positive signals you sensed as you read Paragraph 1 on the spinal cord. Then identify those negative signals that you sensed when reading about diluted earnings per share.

Once you are able to recognize negative signals while reading, the next step is to take action to correct the problem. Specific techniques are given in the last section of this chapter.

TABLE 1-2 Comprehension Signals

Positive Signals	Negative Signals
Everything seems to fit and make sense; ideas flow logically from one to another.	Some pieces do not seem to belong; the ideas do not fit together or make sense.
You are able to understand what the author is saying.	You feel as if you are struggling to stay with the author.
You can see where the author is leading.	You cannot think ahead or predict what will come next.
You are able to make connections among ideas.	You are unable to see how ideas connect.
You read at a regular, comfortable pace.	You often slow down or lose your place.
You understand why the material was assigned.	You do not know why the material was assigned and cannot explain why it is important.
You can understand the material after reading it once.	You need to reread sentences or paragraphs frequently.
You recognize most words or can figure them out from context.	Many words are unfamiliar.
You can express the key ideas in your own words.	You must reread and use the author's language to explain an idea.
You feel comfortable with the topic; you have some background knowledge.	The topic is unfamiliar; you know nothing about it.

Monitoring Your Comprehension

Directions: Read the following excerpt from a biology textbook on the theory of continental drift. It is intended to be difficult, so do not be discouraged. As you read, monitor your comprehension. After reading, answer the questions that follow.

In 1912, Alfred Wegener published a paper that was triggered by the common observation of the good fit between South America's east coast and Africa's west coast. Could these great continents ever have been joined? Wegener coordinated this jigsaw-puzzle analysis with other ecological and climatological data and proposed the theory of continental drift. He suggested that about 200 million years ago, all of the earth's continents were joined together into one enormous land mass, which he called Pangaea. In the ensuing millennia, according to Wegener's idea, Pangaea broke apart, and the fragments began to drift northward (by today's compass orientation) to their present location.

Wegener's idea received rough treatment in his lifetime. His geologist contemporaries attacked his naivete as well as his supporting data, and his theory was neglected until about 1960. At that time, a new generation of geologists revived the idea and subjected it to new scrutiny based on recent findings.

The most useful data have been based on magnetism in ancient lava flows. When a lava flow cools, metallic elements in the lava are oriented in a way that provides permanent evidence of the direction of the earth's magnetic field at the time, recording for future geologists both its north-south orientation and its latitude. From such maps, it is possible to determine the ancient positions of today's continents. We now believe that not only has continental drift occurred, as Wegener hypothesized, but that it continues to occur today. . . .

The disruption of Pangaea began some 230 million years ago in the Paleozoic era. By the Mesozoic era, the Eurasian land mass (called Laurasia) had moved away to form the northernmost continent. Gondwanaland, the mass that included India and the southern continents, had just begun to divide. Finally, during the late Mesozoic era, after South America and Africa were well divided, what was to be the last continental separation began, with Australia and Antarctica drifting apart. Both the North and South Atlantic oceans would continue to widen considerably up to the Cenozoic era, a trend that is continuing today. So we see that although the bumper sticker "Reunite Gondwanaland" has a third-world, trendy ring to it, it's an unlikely proposition.

—Wallace, *Biology*, p. 185

1. How would you rate your overall comprehension? What positive signals did you sense? Did you feel any negative signals?

2. Test the accuracy of your rating in Question 1 by answering the following questions based on the material you read.

a. Explain Wegener's theory of continental drift.

b. Which two continents led Wegener to develop his theory?

c. What recent finding has supported Wegener's theory?

d. Describe the way in which Pangaea broke up and drifted to become the continents we know today.

3. In which sections was your comprehension strongest?

4. Did you feel at any time that you had lost, or were about to lose, comprehension? If so, go back to that paragraph now. What made that paragraph difficult to read?

5. Would it have been useful to refer to a world map?

6. Underline any difficult words that interfered with your comprehension.

WORK ON IMPROVING YOUR COMPREHENSION

At times, you will realize that your comprehension is poor or incomplete. When this occurs, take immediate action. Identify as specifically as possible the cause of the problem. Do this by answering the following question: "Why is this not making sense?" Determine if it is difficult words, complex ideas, organization, or your lack of concentration that is bothering you. Next, make changes in your reading to correct or compensate for the problem. Table 1-3 below lists common problems and offers strategies to correct them.

TABLE 1-3   How to Improve Your Comprehension

Problems	Strategies
Your concentration is poor.	1. Take limited breaks. 2. Tackle difficult material when your mind is fresh and alert. 3. Choose an appropriate place to study. 4. Focus your attention.
Words are difficult or unfamiliar.	1. Use context and analyze word parts. 2. Skim through material before reading. Mark and look up meanings of difficult words. Jot meanings in the margin. 3. Refer to the vocabulary preview list, footnotes, or glossary.

Problems	Strategies
Sentences are long or confusing.	1. Read aloud. 2. Locate the key idea(s). 3. Check difficult words. 4. Express each sentence in your own words.
Ideas are hard to understand, complicated.	1. Rephrase or explain each in your own words. 2. Make notes. 3. Locate a more basic text that explains ideas in simpler form. 4. Study with a classmate; discuss difficult ideas.

Ideas are new and unfamiliar; you have little or no knowledge about the topic, and the writer assumes you do.	1. Make sure you didn't miss or skip introductory information.
	2. Get background information by referring to
	   a. an earlier section or chapter in the book.
	   b. an encyclopedia.
	   c. a more basic text.

The material seems disorganized or poorly organized.	1. Pay more attention to headings. 2. Read the summary, if available. 3. Try to discover organization by writing an outline or drawing a map as you read (see Chapter 10).
You do not know what is and is not important.	1. Preview. 2. Ask and answer guide questions. 3. Locate and underline topic sentences (see Chapter 6).

EXERCISE 1-8   **Monitoring Your Comprehension**

Directions: Read each of the following difficult paragraphs, monitoring your comprehension as you do so. After reading each passage, identify and describe any problems you experienced. Then indicate what strategies you would use to correct them.

A.   A word about food—in the simplest of terms, there are two kinds of organisms: those that make their own food, usually by photosynthesis (autotrophs, "self-feeders") and those that depend upon an outside-the-cell food source (heterotrophs, "other-feeders"). The autotrophs include a few kinds of bacteria, some one-celled eukaryotes (protistans), and all green plants. The heterotrophs encompass most bacteria, many protistans, all fungi, and all animals. Because this chapter is about animal nutrition, attention first will be given to examining the nature of food, then to how food is made available to cells.

—Norstog and Meyerricks, *Biology,* p. 193

Problem: _____

Strategies: _____

B.   The vestibular apparatus in the inner ear has two distinct components: the semi-circular canals (three mutually perpendicular, fluid-filled tubes that contain hair cells connected to nerve fibers), which are sensitive to angular acceleration of the head; and the otolith organs (two sacs filled with calcium carbonate crystals embedded in a gel), which respond to linear acceleration. Because movement of the crystals in the otoliths generates the signal of acceleration to the brain and because the laws of physics relate that acceleration to a net force, gravity is always implicit in the signal. Thus, the otoliths have been referred to as gravity receptors. They are not the only ones. Mechanical receptors in the muscles, tendons and joints—as well as pressure receptors in the skin, particularly on the bottom of the feet—respond to the weight of limb segments and other body parts.

—White, "Weightlessness and the Human Body," *Scientific American Online,* p. 2

Problem: _____

Strategies: _____

C.   The objective of some tariffs is to protect an industry that produces goods vital to a nation's defense. In the case of a strategic industry, productive efficiency relative to that of other nations may not be an important consideration. The domestic industry— oil, natural gas, shipping, or steel, for example—may require protection because of its importance to national defense. Without protection, such industries might be weakened by foreign competition. Then, in an international crisis, the nation might find itself in short supply of products essential to national defense.

—Chisholm and McCarty, *Principles of Economics,* p. 443

Problem: _____

Strategies: _____

EXERCISE 1-9   **Analyzing Difficult Readings**

Directions: Bring to class a difficult paragraph or brief excerpt. Working in groups, each student should read each piece, and then, together, members should (1) discuss why each piece was difficult and (2) compare the negative and positive signals they received while reading them (refer to Table 1-2). Each student should then select strategies to overcome the difficulties he or she experienced.

LEARNING STYLE TIPS

If you are a(n) . . .	Then improve your comprehension by . . .
Auditory learner	Reading aloud
Visual learner	Visualizing paragraph organization
Applied learner	Thinking of real-life situations that illustrate ideas in the passage
Conceptual learner	Asking questions

SELF-TEST SUMMARY

OBJECTIVE 1 **What is expected of you in college?**	You are expected to take control of your learning by reading and studying effectively and efficiently.
OBJECTIVE 2 **How can you develop a positive attitude toward reading?**	You can begin to develop a positive attitude if you think of reading as an active process of looking for important ideas and unlocking a writer's message, and if you realize to do this successfully you cannot rush through it.
OBJECTIVE 3 **What can you do to control your concentration?**	Building concentration involves two steps: 1. Control your surroundings by wisely choosing your time and place of study and avoiding distractions. 2. Focus your attention on the assignment by setting goals and rewarding yourself for achieving them by working in planned, small time blocks with frequent breaks, and by getting actively involved in the assignment.
OBJECTIVE 4 **What is learning style?**	Learning style refers to your profile of relative strengths as a learner. Its five components are: 1. Auditory or visual learner 2. Applied or conceptual learner 3. Spatial or verbal learner 4. Social or independent learner 5. Creative or pragmatic learner
OBJECTIVE 5 **How can knowing your learning style make you a better student?**	Discovering what type of learner you are can help you find out what strategies work best for you in reading and studying. It will also help you to recognize your limitations so that you can work on overcoming them.
OBJECTIVE 6 **How can you monitor your comprehension?**	Pay attention to whether you sense positive or negative signals while reading.

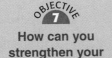 **How can you strengthen your comprehension?**	If you sense poor or incomplete comprehension, take immediate action to identify the source of the problem. Determine whether lack of concentration, difficult words, complex ideas, or confusing organization is causing the problem.

GOING ONLINE

1. Index of Learning Styles Questionnaire

    http://www.engr.ncsu.edu/learningstyles/ilsweb.html

    Try another learning style assessment at this site from North Carolina State University. Compare your results with those from the assessment in this book. How do online tests differ from those on paper? Which do you prefer? Is this a result of your learning style?

2. Improving Your Concentration

    http://www.k-state.edu/counseling/topics/career/concentr.html

    Kansas State University offers some interesting ideas for keeping your mind from wandering, being distracted, and much more! Try some of these techniques, and keep track of what works (and what does not) for you.

3. College Readiness

    http://www.bhc.edu/DocumentView.aspx?DID=1165

    Examine this chart comparing the educational systems of high school and college. Is there anything on here that surprises you? What could be added? What do you think are the most challenging aspects of college?

 To check your progress in meeting chapter objectives, log in to **http://www.myreadinglab.com**, click on the Study Plan tab, and then click on the Reading Skills tab. Choose Memorization and Concentration from the list of subtopics. Read and view the information in the Review Materials section, and then complete the Practices and Tests in the Activities section. You can check your scores by clicking on the Gradebook tab.

MASTERY TEST 1 Reading Selection

Name _____ Section _____

Date _____ Number right _____ × 10 points = Score _____

ASSESSMENT READING SELECTION

This reading and the questions that follow are intended to help you assess your current level of skill. Read the article and then answer the questions that measure your comprehension. You may refer back to the reading in order to answer them. Compute your score by filling in the score grid above.

Stop Asking Me My Major

Scott Keyes

In this essay, which originally appeared in *The Chronicle of Higher Education*, the author explains what is most important for college students to focus on when choosing a major.

> **Vocabulary Preview**
> **render** (par. 4) cause to be
> **cultivate** (par. 5) develop
> **hindering** (par. 7) interfering with
> **perpetuates** (par. 8) continues
> **realm** (par. 9) area
> **prominent** (par. 9) important or well known
> **lucrative** (par. 13) profitable

Scott Keyes, a recent college graduate, advises against gearing one's study concentration to fickle job prospects. Instead, he says, follow your intellectual passion.

1   One of my best friends from high school, Andrew, changed majors during his first semester at college. He and I had been fascinated by politics for years, sharing every news story we could find and participating in the Internet activism that was exploding into a new political force. Even though he was still passionate about politics, that was no longer enough. "I have to get practical," he messaged me one day, "think about getting a job after graduation. I mean, it's like my mom keeps asking me: What can you do with a degree in political science anyway?"

2   I heard the same question from my friend Jesse when students across campus were agonizing about which major was right for them. He wasn't quite sure what he wanted to study, but every time a field sparked his interest, his father would

pepper him with questions about what jobs were available for people in that discipline. Before long, Jesse's dad had convinced him that the only way he could get a job and be successful after college was to major in pre-med.

3   My friends' experiences were not atypical.

4   Choosing a major is one of the most difficult things students face in college. There are two main factors that most students consider when making this decision. First is their desire to study what interests them. Second is the fear that a particular major will render them penniless after graduation and result in that dreaded post-college possibility: moving back in with their parents.

5   All too often, the concern about a major's practical prospects are pushed upon students by well-intentioned parents. If our goal is to cultivate students who are happy and successful, both in college as well as in the job market, I have this piece of advice for parents: Stop asking, "What can you do with a degree in (fill in the blank)?" You're doing your children no favors by asking them to focus on the job prospects of different academic disciplines, rather than studying what interests them.

6   It is my experience, both through picking a major myself and witnessing many others endure the process, that there are three reasons why parents (and everyone else) should be encouraging students to focus on what they enjoy studying most, rather than questioning what jobs are supposedly available for different academic concentrations.

7   The first is psychological. For his first two years of college, Jesse followed his dad's wishes and remained a pre-med student. The only problem was that he hated it. With no passion for the subject, his grades slipped, hindering his chances of getting into medical school. As a result his employability, the supposed reason he was studying medicine in the first place, suffered.

8   The second reason to stop asking students what they can do with a major is that it perpetuates the false notion that certain majors don't prepare students for the workplace. The belief that technical majors such as computer science are more likely to lead to a job than a major such as sociology or English is certainly understandable. It's also questionable. "The problem," as my friend José explained to me, "is that even as a computer-science major, what I learned in the classroom was outdated by the time I hit the job market." He thought instead that the main benefit of his education, rather than learning specific skills, was gaining a better way of thinking about the challenges he faced. "What's more," he told me, "no amount of education could match the specific on-the-job training I've received working different positions."

9   Finally, it is counterproductive to demand that students justify their choice of study with potential job prospects because that ignores the lesson we were all taught in kindergarten (and shouldn't ignore the closer we get to employment): You can grow up to be whatever you want to be. The jobs people work at often fall within the realm of their studies, but they don't have to. One need look no further than some of the most prominent figures in our society to see illustrations. The TV chef Julia Child studied English in college. Author Michael Lewis, whose best sellers focus on sports and the financial industry, majored in art history. Matt Groening, creator of The Simpsons, got his degree in philosophy, as did the

former Hewlett Packard chief executive Carly Fiorina. Jeff Immelt, chief executive of General Electric, focused on mathematics. Indeed, with the Department of Labor estimating that on average people switch careers (not just jobs) two or three times in their lives, relying on a college major as career preparation is misguided.

10   I'm not saying any applicant can get any job. Job seekers still need marketable skills if they hope to be hired. However, in a rapidly changing economy, which majors lead to what jobs is not so clear cut. Many employers look for applicants from a diverse background—including my friend who has a degree in biochemistry but was just hired at an investment consulting firm.

11   That doesn't mean that majors no longer matter. It is still an important decision, and students are right to seek outside counsel when figuring out what they want to study. But questioning how a particular major will affect their employability is not necessarily the best approach. Although parents' intentions may be pure—after all, who doesn't want to see their children succeed after graduation?—that question can hold tremendous power over impressionable freshmen. Far too many of my classmates let it steer them away from what they enjoyed studying to a major they believed would help them get a job after graduation.

12   One of those friends was Andrew. He opted against pursuing a degree in political science, choosing instead to study finance because "that's where the jobs are." Following graduation, Andrew landed at a consulting firm. I recently learned with little surprise that he hates his job and has no passion for the work.

13   Jesse, on the other hand, realized that if he stayed on the pre-med track, he would burn out before ever getting his degree. During his junior year he changed tracks and began to study engineering. Not only did Jesse's grades improve markedly, but his enthusiasm for the subject recently earned him a lucrative job offer and admission to a top engineering master's program.

14   Andrew and Jesse both got jobs. But who do you think feels more successful?

Scott Keyes is a 2009 graduate of Stanford University, where he majored in political science.

MASTERY TEST SKILLS CHECK

Directions: Select the choice that best completes each of the following statements.

Checking Your Comprehension

_____ 1. The main point of this selection is that
   a. on-the-job training is more valuable than studying a particular major.
   b. college students should choose a major based on its job potential.
   c. parents should question how a particular major will lead to employment.
   d. college students should choose a major based on what interests them.

_____ 2. The word *atypical* in paragraph 3 means
   a. uncommon.
   b. advisable.
   c. normal.
   d. uncomfortable.

_____ 3. The main point of paragraph 4 is that
a. most parents are well intentioned.
b. choosing a major is a difficult decision.
c. most students are focused on job prospects.
d. students often dread moving back in with their parents.

_____ 4. According to the author, people should stop asking students about the job prospects of different majors because
a. it creates psychological consequences for the student.
b. it promotes the mistaken belief that certain majors do not prepare students for the workplace.
c. it ignores the fact that people often work in jobs outside the realm of their studies.
d. all of the above.

_____ 5. The author's friend José believes that the main benefit of his education was gaining
a. specific, technical skills for the workplace.
b. information about what jobs were available in his discipline.
c. a better way of thinking about the challenges he faced.
d. training for a variety of different types of jobs.

_____ 6. According to the author, the kindergarten lesson that should not be ignored is:
a. Hard work pays off.
b. You can grow up to be whatever you want to be.
c. Never stop learning.
d. Be willing to try new things.

_____ 7. All of the following people were named in the article as examples of prominent figures with jobs outside the realm of their studies _except_
a. Julia Child.
b. Matt Groening.
c. Bill Gates.
d. Carly Fiorina.

_____ 8. The word _counterproductive_ in paragraph 9 means
a. against one's purpose.
b. worthwhile.
c. extremely useful.
d. practical.

_____ 9. The main point of paragraph 11 is that
a. majors no longer matter.
b. students should not seek outside advice when choosing a major.
c. job seekers need marketable skills to be hired.
d. questioning the job prospects of a particular major is not helpful.

_____ 10. The author's friend who found success after changing his major to follow his own interests was
a. Andrew.   c. José.
b. Jesse.   d. Michael.

For more practice, ask your instructor for an opportunity to work on the mastery tests that appear in the Test Bank.

2

The Basics of College Textbook Reading

Looking at . . .
College Textbooks

LEARNING OBJECTIVES

*This chapter will
show you how to:*

OBJECTIVE 1 Use textbooks as a learning tool

OBJECTIVE 2 Analyze photographs and other textbook graphics

OBJECTIVE 3 Work with and learn from classmates

OBJECTIVE 4 Use writing to help you learn

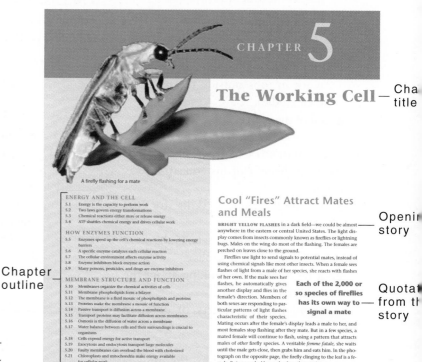

CHAPTER 5

The Working Cell —Cha title

A firefly flashing for a mate

ENERGY AND THE CELL
5.1   Energy is the capacity to perform work
5.2   Two laws govern energy transformations
5.3   Chemical reactions either store or release energy
5.4   ATP shuttles chemical energy and drives cellular work

HOW ENZYMES FUNCTION
5.5   Enzymes speed up the cell's chemical reactions by lowering energy barriers
5.6   A specific enzyme catalyzes each cellular reaction
5.7   The cellular environment affects enzyme activity
5.8   Enzyme inhibitors block enzyme action
5.9   Many poisons, pesticides, and drugs are enzyme inhibitors

MEMBRANE STRUCTURE AND FUNCTION
5.10 Membranes organize the chemical activities of cells
5.11 Membrane phospholipids form a bilayer
5.12 The membrane is a fluid mosaic of phospholipids and proteins
5.13 Proteins make the membrane a mosaic of function
5.14 Passive transport is diffusion across a membrane
5.15 Transport proteins may facilitate diffusion across membranes
5.16 Osmosis is the diffusion of water across a membrane
5.17 Water balance between cells and their surroundings is crucial to organisms
5.18 Cells expend energy for active transport
5.19 Exocytosis and endocytosis transport large molecules
5.20 Faulty membranes can overload the blood with cholesterol
5.21 Chloroplasts and mitochondria make energy available for cellular work

Chapter outline —

Cool "Fires" Attract Mates and Meals

BRIGHT YELLOW FLASHES in a dark field—we could be almost anywhere in the eastern or central United States. The light display comes from insects commonly known as fireflies or lightning bugs. Males on the wing do most of the flashing. The females are perched on leaves close to the ground.

Fireflies use light to send signals to potential mates, instead of using chemical signals like most other insects. When a female sees flashes of light from a male of her species, she reacts with flashes of her own. If the male sees her flashes, he automatically gives another display and flies in the female's direction. Members of both sexes are responding to particular patterns of light flashes characteristic of their species. Mating occurs after the female's display leads a male to her, and most females stop flashing after they mate. But in a few species, a mated female will continue to flash, using a pattern that attracts males of *other* firefly species. A veritable *femme fatale*, she waits until the male gets close, then grabs him and eats him. In the photograph on the opposite page, the firefly clinging to the leaf is a female dining on a luckless male of another species.

Each of the 2,000 or so species of fireflies has its own way to signal a mate. Some flash more often than others or during

Each of the 2,000 or so species of fireflies has its own way to signal a mate

Openi story

Quota from th story

This page from an introductory biology textbook is an example of a chapter opener. Chapter openers are designed to stimulate your interest in the topics covered in the chapter. The learning tools in this example include a chapter outline, a photograph of a firefly with a caption, an opening story/example, and a quotation to highlight an interesting part of the story.

Guide to College Reading also features openers for each chapter. Flip through this book and get a sense of the chapter openers. What do they include? How will they help you learn?

TEXTBOOKS AS LEARNING TOOLS

myreadinglab

To practice using textbooks effectively, go to

▼ STUDY PLAN
  ▼ READING SKILLS
    ▼ READING
       TEXTBOOKS

While textbooks may seem to be long and impersonal, they are actually carefully crafted teaching and learning systems. They are designed to work with your instructor's lecture to provide you with reliable and accurate information and to help you practice your skills.

Why Buy and Study Textbooks?

Chapter 1 discussed the importance of having a positive attitude toward reading. This positive attitude should extend to your textbooks. Did you know the following?

- **Nearly all textbook authors are college teachers.** They work with students daily and understand students' needs.
- **Along with your instructor, your textbook is the single best source of information for the subject you are studying.**
- **The average textbook costs only about $7 a week.** For the price of a movie ticket, you are getting a complete learning system that includes not only a textbook but also a companion Web site and other study materials.
- **Your textbook can be a valuable reference tool in your profession.** For example, many nursing majors keep their textbooks and refer to them often when they begin their career.

Textbooks are an investment in your education and in your future. A textbook is your ally—your partner in learning.

EXERCISE 2-1   **Examining Your Textbook**

Directions: Use your copy of *Guide to College Reading* to complete the following tasks.

1. An additional online resource available with *Guide to College Reading* is MyReadingLab, which can be found at http://www.myreadinglab.com. Go to that Web site and list four features that you would like to use.

_____

_____

2. At what college does the author of *Guide to College Reading* teach? (*Hint*: Look at the title page, early in the book.)

_____

Using Textbook Organization to Your Advantage

Have you ever walked into an unfamiliar supermarket and felt lost? How did you finally find what you needed? Most likely, you looked for the signs hanging over the aisles indicating the types of products shelved in each section. Walking along the aisle, you no doubt found that similar products were grouped together. For example, all the cereal was in one place, all the meat was in another, and so forth.

You can easily feel lost or intimidated when beginning to read a textbook chapter, too. It may seem like a huge collection of unrelated facts, ideas, and numbers that have to be memorized. Actually, a textbook chapter is much like a supermarket. It, too, has signs that identify what is located in each section. These signs are the major **headings** that divide the chapter into topics. Underneath each heading, similar ideas are grouped together, just as similar products are grouped together in a supermarket aisle. In most cases, several paragraphs come under each heading.

Sometimes headings are further divided into **subheadings** (usually set in smaller type than the main heading or indented or set in a different color). Using headings and subheadings, chapters take a major idea, break it into its important parts, and then break those parts into smaller parts, so you can learn it one step a time.

A typical textbook chapter might have an organization that looks like the diagram on the right. Notice that this diagram shows a chapter divided into four major headings, and the first major heading is divided into eight subheadings. The number of major headings and subheadings and the number of paragraphs under each will vary from chapter to chapter in a book.

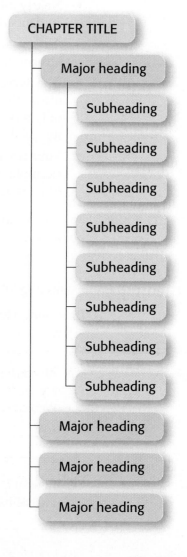

Once you know how a chapter is organized, you can use this knowledge to guide your reading. Once you are familiar with the organization, you will also begin to see how ideas are connected. The chapter will then seem orderly, moving from one idea to the next in a logical fashion.

Look at the following partial list of headings and subheadings from a chapter of a sociology textbook.

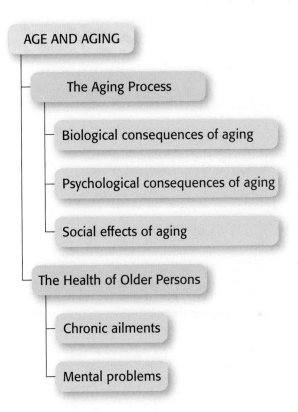

In this chapter on age and aging, "The Aging Process" and "The Health of Older Persons" are the first two major topics. The topic "The Aging Process" is broken into three parts: biological consequences, psychological consequences, and social effects. "The Health of Older Persons" is divided into two parts: chronic ailments and mental problems.

The titles and headings, taken together, form a brief outline of a chapter. Later, in Chapter 10, you will see how these headings can help you make a more complete outline of a chapter. For now, think of headings as guides that direct you through a chapter one step at a time.

EXERCISE 2-2   **Analyzing Chapter Organization**

Directions: Complete the following diagram of headings and subheadings for this chapter of *Guide to College Reading*.

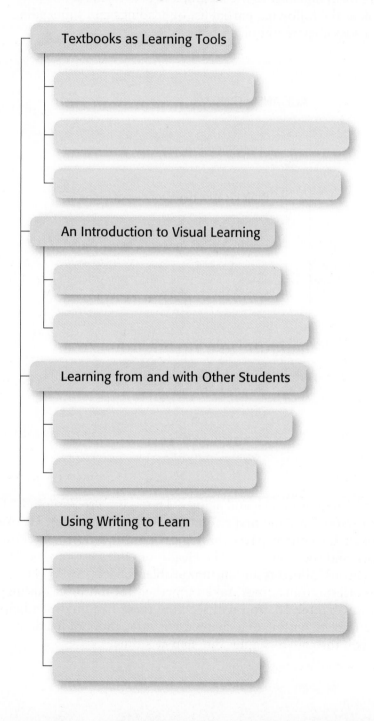

Textbooks as Learning Tools

An Introduction to Visual Learning

Learning from and with Other Students

Using Writing to Learn

EXERCISE 2-3   Analyzing a Chapter Opener

Directions: Refer to the chapter opener on page 30 (from the introductory biology text-book) to answer the following questions.

1. The biology textbook's chapter opener includes an outline that summarizes all the headings in that chapter. How many major headings are included in the chapter? _____

2. How many subheadings are found in the second section, titled "How Enzymes Function"? _____

3. What is the purpose of the photograph? _____

_____

EXERCISE 2-4   Drawing an Organizational Diagram

Directions: Choose a textbook that you are using for another course. Select a chapter you have already read. On a separate sheet of paper, draw an organizational diagram of its contents. Use the diagram on page 32 as a guide.

Textbook Learning Aids and How to Use Them

Textbooks contain numerous features to help you learn. Features vary from book to book and from discipline to discipline, but most textbooks contain the following:

- Preface
- To the Student
- Table of contents
- Opening chapter
- Typographical aids
- Chapter exercises and questions

- Boxes and case studies
- Vocabulary lists
- Chapter summary
- Glossary
- Index

Preface   The preface is the author's introduction to the text. It presents information you should know before you begin reading Chapter 1. It may contain such information as:

- Why and for whom the author wrote the text
- How the text is organized

- Purpose of the text
- References and authorities consulted
- Major points of emphasis
- Learning aids included and how to use them
- Special features of the text
- New materials included since the book's last update

The last point is particularly important. Knowledge is not static; it is ever-changing. Textbooks must include this new information, as well as new *perspectives*, or ways of looking at the subject. As an example, for many years most of the art shown in art history textbooks was created by male artists. In the last decade, however, art history textbooks have included more works by female artists.

To the Student   Some textbooks contain a section titled "To the Student." This section is written specifically for you. It contains practical information about the text. It may, for example, explain textbook features and how to use them, or it may offer suggestions for learning and studying the text. Often, a "To the Instructor" section precedes or follows "To the Student" and contains information useful to your instructor.

EXERCISE **2-5**   **Analyzing a Preface**

Directions: Use the Preface to *Guide to College Reading* to answer the following questions.

1. You are using the ninth edition of this textbook. Name three items that are new to this edition.

   _____

   _____

   _____

2. Look at the book's content overview (pp. xv–xvi). In what part of the book are vocabulary skills discussed? _____ Which part of the book is devoted to developing your critical reading skills? _____

3. Name three special features of *Guide to College Reading* that are designed to enhance the text's effectiveness. (*Hint*: Look for the heading titled "Special Features.")

   _____

   _____

EXERCISE 2-6   ## Analyzing "To the Student"

Directions: Read the "To the Student" section in a textbook from one of your other courses and answer the following questions.

1. What is the purpose of the text?

   _____

   _____

2. How is the textbook organized?

   _____

   _____

3. What learning aids does the book contain? How useful have you found them?

   _____

   _____

Table of Contents   The **table of contents** is an outline of a text found at the beginning of the book. It lists all the important topics and subtopics covered. Glancing through a table of contents will give you an overview of a text and suggest its organization.

Before beginning to read a chapter, refer to the table of contents. Although chapters are intended to be separate parts of a book, it is important to see how they fit together as parts of the whole—the textbook itself.

A table of contents can be a useful study aid when preparing for exams. To review the material on which you will be tested, read through the table of contents listings for chapters covered on the exam. This review will give you a sense of which topics you are already familiar with and which topics you have yet to learn about.

EXERCISE 2-7   ## Analyzing the Table of Contents

Directions: Use the table of contents for this book to answer the following questions.

1. This textbook includes not only a *detailed* table of contents (pp. vii–xii) but also a *brief* table of contents (p. v). What is the difference between the two?

   _____

   _____

2. What value do you see in the brief table of contents?

_____

_____

3. In which chapter will you learn about stated and implied main ideas? _____

4. Name two of the authors whose work is represented in the Fiction Minireader.

_____

Opening Chapter The first chapter of a textbook is one of the most important and deserves close attention. Here the author sets the stage for what is to follow. More important, it defines the discipline, explains basic principles, and introduces terminology that will be used throughout the text.

Typically, you can expect to find as many as 20 to 50 new words introduced and defined in the first chapter. These words are the language of the course, so to speak. To be successful in any new subject area, you must learn to read and speak its language. (Chapters 3 and 4 of this text will help you develop your vocabulary skills.)

EXERCISE 2-8 **Analyzing Chapter 1**

Directions: Refer to Chapter 1 of *Guide to College Reading*. List at least two techniques or features the author uses to get students involved with and interested in the material.

_____

_____

_____

Typographical Aids Textbooks contain various **typographical aids** (arrangements or types of print) that make it easy to pick out what is important to learn and remember. These include the following:

1. **Different types of font.** Italic type (*slanted print*) and boldfaced type (**dark print**) are often used to call attention to a particular word or phrase. Often new terms are printed in italics or boldface in the sentence in which they are defined. For example:

> The term *drive* is used to refer to internal conditions that force an individual to work toward some goal.

> **Animism** is the belief that inanimate objects, such as trees, rocks, and rivers, possess souls.

Note: Colored print is sometimes used to emphasize important ideas or definitions.

2. **Enumeration. Enumeration** refers to the numbering or lettering of facts and ideas within a paragraph. It is used to emphasize key ideas and make them easy to locate.

> Consumer behavior and the buying process involve five mental states: (1) awareness of the product, (2) interest in acquiring it, (3) desire or perceived need, (4) action, and (5) reaction or evaluation of the product.

3. **Listing. Bulleted lists** and **numbered lists** provide important information in a list format. (A bullet looks like this: •). These lists are typically indented, which makes them easy to find as you read and review the chapter.

> Sigmund Freud defined three parts of the human psyche:
>
> 1. Id
> 2. Ego
> 3. Superego

> North America is sometimes divided into eight distinctive regions:
>
> • New England and the Atlantic Provinces
> • Quebec
> • The Old Economic Core
> • The American South (The Southeast)
> • The Great Plains Breadbasket
> • The Continental Interior
> • The Pacific Northwest
> • Southern California and the Southwest

EXERCISE 2-9   **Evaluating Typographical Aids**

Directions: Bring a textbook from one of your other courses to class. With a partner or in a small group, point out the typographical aids used in the book. Discuss how each can help you learn.

Chapter Exercises and Questions   Exercises and questions fall into several categories.

1. *Review questions* **cover the factual content of the chapter.**

   - **In-chapter review questions appear at the end of a major section.** They allow you to test your mastery of the material before you move on to the next section.
   - **End-of-chapter review questions appear at the end of the chapter.** They test your comprehension of the entire chapter.

   Here are some examples of review questions from a marketing textbook:

   - List some product characteristics that are of concern to marketers.
   - Distinguish between a trademark and a brand name.
   - What are two characteristics of a good brand name?

2. *Discussion questions* **deal with interpretations of content.** These are often meant to be jumping-off points for discussion in the classroom or with other students. Here are some examples of discussion questions from the marketing textbook:

   - What do you think is the future of generic products?
   - How has the downturn in the economy affected American consumers' buying habits?

3. *Application questions* **ask you to apply your knowledge to the world around you or to a real-life situation.** Many students like these questions because they help prepare them for their chosen career. Here are some sample application questions:

   - Go to your local grocery store and look at the ways the products are packaged. Find three examples of packages that have value in themselves. Find three examples of packages that promote the products' effectiveness.
   - How would you go about developing a brand name for a new type of soft drink?

4. *Critical thinking questions* **ask you to think deeply about a topic or issue.** These questions require close attention and are often asked on exams. Here are two sample critical thinking questions:

   - There is much controversy about the issue of warning labels on products. Outline the pros and cons of putting warning labels on products.
   - How is advertising good for society? How is it bad for society?

5. *Problem questions* **are usually mathematical in nature**. You are given an equation to solve, or you are given a problem in words and asked to use mathematical concepts to find the solution. Working with problems is one of the most important parts of any math, science, or technical course. Here are two sample problems:

- If $x = 6$, $4x + 5 = $?
- If a microwave oven costs the retailer $325 and the markup is 35%, find the selling price of the microwave.

Boxes and Case Studies   Many textbooks include boxed inserts or case studies that are set off from the text. Generally, these "boxes" contain interesting information or extended examples to illustrate text concepts. Boxes are sometimes a key to what the author considers important. For example, a business textbook may contain boxes in each chapter about green business practices. From the presence of these boxes, you can assume that the author is interested in how business practices can be changed to help preserve the environment. (Note that the word *green* here refers to the movement to preserve Planet Earth.)

Case studies usually follow the life history of a person, or the business practices of a particular company. These are valuable applications of the textbook concepts to the real world.

Vocabulary Lists   Textbooks usually contain a list of new terms introduced in each chapter. This list may appear at the beginning or end of the chapter. Sometimes they include page numbers that identify where the term is defined.

Regardless of where they appear, vocabulary lists are a valuable study aid. Here is a sample vocabulary list (sometimes called a **key terms list**) from a financial management textbook:

Key Terms

assets	liabilities
budget	money market fund
cash flow statement	net worth
fixed disbursements	

Notice that the author identifies the terms but does not define them. In such cases, mark the new terms as you come across them in the chapter. (The key terms are often printed in boldfaced type, so pay close attention whenever you see boldface.) After you have finished the chapter, review each marked item and its definition. To learn the terms, use the index card system suggested in Chapter 4 ("A System for Learning New Words," p. 128).

Creating a List of Key Terms

Directions: If a textbook does not contain a key terms list, you should make one of your own for each chapter. Using boldfaced terms as your guide, create a key terms list for this chapter of *Guide to College Reading*.

Chapter Summary   In most textbooks, each chapter ends with a **chapter summary** that reviews all the chapter's key points. While the summary is sometimes in paragraph form, it is more often formatted as a numbered list. If you are having difficulty extracting the main points from the chapter, the summary is an excellent resource.

This text features a "Self-Test Summary" at the end of each chapter. For an example, see page 60. Note how the summary is provided in a question-and-answer format to help you quiz yourself on the concepts.

Glossary   Usually found at the end of the book, a **glossary** is a mini-dictionary that lists alphabetically the important vocabulary used in the book. Because it is built into the textbook, a glossary is faster and more convenient than a dictionary. It does not list all the common meanings of a word, as a dictionary does, but instead gives only the meaning used in the text.

Glossary entries are usually focused and specific. Sometimes the glossary includes the page numbers on which the vocabulary words are defined. Here is an excerpt from the glossary of a health textbook:

latent functions   unintended beneficial consequences of people's actions

leadership styles   ways in which people express their leadership

leader   someone who influences other people

leisure   time not taken up by work or necessary activities

—Henslin, *Sociology*, p. G4

In some textbooks, a key term is defined in the text, and the term and its definition are repeated in the margin. Many students say that a **marginal glossary** is one of the most useful textbook features.

Index   Suppose you are studying for a final exam and want to review a vocabulary term, but you can't remember where it's located in your textbook. The book's **index**, found at the end of the book, is an alphabetical listing of all the topics in the book. It includes not only key terms, but also topics, names of authors, and titles of texts or readings. Next to each entry you will find the page number(s) on which the topic is discussed.

Here is an excerpt taken from the index of an English handbook:

namely, punctuation with, 311
names of persons
  abbreviating, 415
  capitalizing, 409
  titles before and after, 196, 410–11, 415

narration
  in paragraph development, 124
  in visual images, 62
narrators, of literary works, 170
nationalities, capitalizing, 410

—McWhorter and Aaron, *The Successful Writer's Handbook,* p. 572

If you were looking in this handbook for rules regarding the capitalizing of nationalities, you would find that information on page 410. Note that some subjects are covered on multiple pages (for example, titles before and after the names of persons).

EXERCISE 2-11   **Evaluating Textbook Learning Aids**

Directions: With a partner or in a small group, choose a textbook from one of your other courses. Each person in the group should take turns answering the following questions and showing examples.

1. What learning aids does the book contain? Does it contain any special features not listed in this section? If so, what are they and what is their function? Which of these features do you expect to use most often?

    _____

    _____

2. How is the information given in the preface important?

    _____

    _____

3. Look at the opening chapter. What is its function?

    _____

    _____

4. Review the table of contents. What are its major parts?

    _____

    _____

AN INTRODUCTION TO VISUAL LEARNING

Visual aids, such as photographs, graphs, and illustrations, are very common in college textbooks, so it's important to understand how they can help you learn chapter content.

Reading and Analyzing Photographs

An old saying goes, "A picture is worth a thousand words." In some cases, a photograph will substitute for words, but photos in textbooks are typically used *in addition to* words. Photographs are used to

- Spark interest
- Provide perspective
- Draw out an emotional response
- Introduce new ideas
- Offer examples
- Give students an opportunity to write, either formally or in writing journals

Use these suggestions when studying the photographs in your textbooks.

Tips for Studying Photographs

1. **Read the caption and title.** The **caption** is the text that accompanies the photo. It is usually placed above, below, or to the side of the photo. The caption will usually explain how the photo fits into the textbook discussion. When a title is provided, read it before examining the photo.

2. **Ask: What is my first overall impression?** Because photos can be so powerful, they are often chosen to elicit a strong reaction. Analyze your response to the photo, which can help you discover why the author chose to include it.

3. **Examine the details.** Look closely at the picture, examining both the foreground and the background. Details can provide clues regarding the date the photograph was taken and its location. For example, people's hairstyles and clothing often give hints as to the year or decade. Landmarks help point to location. If you saw a photo of a smiling couple with the Eiffel Tower in the background, you would know that the photo was taken in Paris, France.

4. **Look for connections to the textbook, society, or your life.** As you view the photograph and read the caption, ask yourself how the photo works with the textbook concepts. Putting the image in context will help you learn the textbook materials *and* help you prepare for exams.

Here's an example of how to apply the above suggestions using the photograph from a geography textbook shown in Figure 2-1. Sample student responses are provided for each question.

Figure 2-1   A favela in Rio de Janeiro. Shantytowns are very common in South American countries, where they often develop in close proximity to wealthy neighborhoods in big cities with large populations. These shantytowns are called *favelas, barrios, colonias,* or *barriadas.* The people who live in favelas sometimes organize themselves to press the government for social services.

1. **What did you learn from reading the caption?** The photo was taken in Rio de Janeiro, Brazil. key vocabulary terms like *favelas, barrios, colonias, and barriadas.*

2. **What are your first impressions?** This is clearly a densely settled area. There are many houses built very close together on a steep hill. There are a few trees.

3. **What does the photograph tell you about the income level of the people who live in this favela?** It suggests the people who live here are probably poor, perhaps with limited access to electricity or other utilities like running water.

4. **Compare the way poor people live in South America to the way poor people live in the United States. How is this favela similar to low-income neighborhoods in U.S. cities?** It is similar as many people who live in low-income neighborhoods in U.S. live in crowed conditions and receive poor services and experience social problems.

EXERCISE **2-12**   **Analyzing Photographs**

Directions: Analyze the photos below and answer the accompanying questions.

Photo from a business textbook. European labor unions trace their origins back to medieval days, but unionism in the United States started to become a major force in the mid-1840s. Today more than 16 million Americans belong to a union. The chief goal of unions is to provide better working conditions and fair pay for their members. When union members feel mistreated, a strike can result.

1. How many Americans currently belong to a labor union?

   _____

2. Today the average workweek is 40 hours. What does this photo tell you about the length of the workweek when the photo was taken?

   _____

3. Notice the hairstyles and clothing of the women in this black-and-white photo. What do these details suggest about the date/year the photo was taken?

   _____

   _____

   _____

4. Have you ever seen workers on strike? How would you feel about crossing a picket line? Do you belong to a union, or do you have any friends or family members who are part of a union?

Photo from an advertising textbook. In a society as culturally diverse as the United States, companies try to ensure that their advertising is appealing to as many people as possible.

1. What does the term *culturally diverse society* mean?

   _____

   _____

2. Which culturally diverse groups are represented in this photo?

   _____

   _____

3. What do the hairstyles and clothing of the people in the photo tell you about their income level? (Also notice the type of car being driven.)

   _____

   _____

4. What audience do you think the advertiser is trying to reach with this photo? For example, is this ad trying to appeal to senior citizens? To college students? To recent college graduates?

   _____

   _____

A General Approach to Reading Graphics

In addition to photographs, you will encounter many other types of graphics in college textbooks. These include:

- Tables
- Pictograms
- Cartoons
- Diagrams
- Flowcharts
- Maps
- Graphs

Each type of graphic will be discussed in more detail in Chapter 9, but because you'll be seeing graphics throughout this text, it is important to have a general awareness of how to work with them now. Read the Step-by-Step Guide to Reading Graphics on the facing page, and as you read it, apply each step to the graph shown below in Figure 2-2.

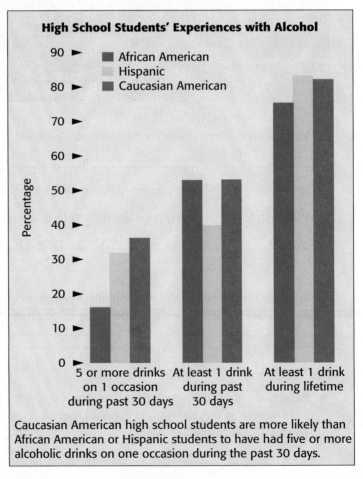

Figure 2-2   A sample graph.

—Fabes and Martin, Exploring Child Development, p. 454

Step-by-Step Guide to Reading Graphics

1. **Look for the references in the text.** The textbook authors will refer you to specific graphics. When you see a reference in a text, finish reading the sentence, then look at the graphic.

2. **Read the title and caption.** The title identifies the subject, and the caption provides important information about what appears in the graphic, sometimes specifying the key take-away point.

3. **Examine how the graphic is organized.** Read column headings and labels, which are sometimes turned sideways as in Figure 2-2. Labels tell you what topics or categories are being discussed, and they are important. For example, if Figure 2-2 did not specify "Percentage," you might incorrectly think the numbers along the left side refer to *numbers* of students instead of *percentage* of students.

4. **Look at the legend.** The **legend** is the guide to the colors, terms, and symbols in a graphic. In Figure 2-2, the legend appears at the top and shows green for African Americans, yellow for Hispanics, and orange for Caucasian Americans. In maps, the legend usually contains a **scale** explaining how measurements should be read, for example, one inch on a map may represent one mile.

5. **Analyze the graphic.** Based on what you see, determine the graphic's key purpose. Is its purpose to show change over time, describe a process, or present statistics? In Figure 2-2 the purpose is to compares high school students of three ethnic groups in terms of their alcohol consumption.

6. **Study the data to identify trends or patterns.** Note changes, unusual statistics, or unexplained variations. For instance, note that while Caucasian American students are much more likely than African American students to have had *five or more* alcoholic drinks once during the past thirty days, they are equally like to have had at least *one* drink during the past thirty days.

7. **Make a brief summary note.** In the margin, jot a brief note summarizing the trend or pattern emphasized by the graphic. It will help you understand the idea and be useful for reviewing. A summary note of Figure 2-2 might read, "Most adolescents have had some experience with alcohol, and about one-third have engaged in heavy consumption in the last month."

Now read the following graphics, and answer the study questions that relate to them.

A **table** lists factual information (often numbers) in an organized manner, usually in rows and columns.

Human Population Trends, 1900–2100					
	Population (Millions)				
	1900	1950	2000	2025	2100
Developing regions (total)	1,070	1,681	4,837	6,799	8,748
Africaᵃ	133	224	872	1,617	2,591
Asia	867	1,292	3,419	4,403	4,919
Latin America	70	165	546	779	1,238
Developed regions (total)	560	835	1,284	1,407	1,437
Europe, USSR, Japan, Oceaniaᵇ	478	669	987	1,062	1,055
Canada, United States	82	166	297	345	382
World total	1,630	2,516	6,121	8,206	10,185

ᵃExcludes Japan.
ᵇIncludes Australia and New Zealand.

—Mix, Farber, and King, *Biology: The Network of Life*, p. 165

Figure 2-3   A sample table

Study Questions

1. Which region will have the largest population in 2100? _____

2. In which region is Australia located? _____

A **cartoon** expresses an idea and makes a point with humor.

Frank and Ernest

Figure 2-4   A sample cartoon

Study Questions

1. What message or main point does the cartoon make?

_____

2. Why might this cartoon be included in a sociology textbook chapter?

_____

A **flowchart** shows a process from beginning to end.

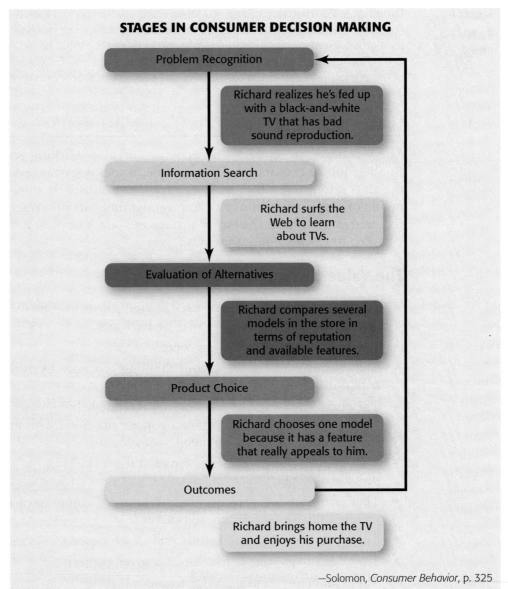

STAGES IN CONSUMER DECISION MAKING

Problem Recognition

Richard realizes he's fed up with a black-and-white TV that has bad sound reproduction.

Information Search

Richard surfs the Web to learn about TVs.

Evaluation of Alternatives

Richard compares several models in the store in terms of reputation and available features.

Product Choice

Richard chooses one model because it has a feature that really appeals to him.

Outcomes

Richard brings home the TV and enjoys his purchase.

—Solomon, *Consumer Behavior*, p. 325

Figure 2-5   A sample flowchart

Study Questions

1. What example does the author use to illustrate the stages in consumer decision making? _____

2. In which stage does the consumer look for information about available products?

   _____

EXERCISE 2-13   **Analyzing Photographs**

Directions: Form groups of four students. Each student should look through various magazines and choose three photos to bring to class. Discuss each photo and caption as a group. What concept is the photo trying to illustrate? What is your reaction to each one? Think about the other courses you are taking this term. Do you see any elements of the photograph that could illustrate concepts you are learning in those courses?

LEARNING FROM AND WITH OTHER STUDENTS

Many college assignments and activities involve working with a partner or small group of classmates. For example, a sociology professor might divide the class into groups and ask each group to brainstorm solutions to the economic or social problems of recent immigrants. Group presentations may be required in a business course, or groups in your American history class might be asked to research and present a topic.

The Value of Working with Classmates

Group, or *collaborative*, projects are designed to help students learn from one another. Consider the benefits of group projects:

- They help you meet other students.
- They allow you to develop your thinking processes by evaluating the contributions of the group's members.
- They take advantage of your strengths while helping you compensate for your weaknesses. For example, if you are not good with numbers, you can ask one of your group members for help.
- They bring a variety of perspectives to the task. Multiple perspectives provide a deeper, richer understanding of the course content.
- They encourage you to develop interpersonal communication skills that will be valuable in your chosen career.
- They can motivate you to study and stay focused.
- They can lower your workload on a given project.
- They can help you prepare for exams.

In short, group projects are excellent learning opportunities. Throughout this text you will notice that some exercises are labeled "Working Together." These are intended to give you experience working with classmates. Look for this icon:

Tips for Working with Classmates

Some students are reluctant to work in groups. They are shy, or they dislike having their grade depend on the performance of others. Use the following suggestions to help your group function effectively.

How to Work Effectively as a Group

1. **Select alert, energetic classmates** if you are permitted to choose group members.

2. **Create a roster of group members with all contact information** (phone, e-mail, and so forth). Get to know your group members. It is always easier to work together when you know something about your collaborators.

3. **Approach each activity seriously.** Save joking and socializing until the group work has been completed.

4. **Be an active, responsible participant.** Accept your share of the work and ask others to do the same.

5. **Choose a leader who will keep the group focused.** The leader should direct the group in analyzing the assignment, organizing a plan of action, distributing the assignments, and establishing deadlines.

6. **Take advantage of individual strengths.** For instance, a person who has strong organizational skills might be assigned the task of recording the group's findings. A person with strong communication skills might be chosen to present group results to the class.

7. **Treat others as you would like to be treated.** Offer praise when it is deserved. Listen to others, but be willing to disagree with them if doing so is in the group's best interests.

8. **If the group is not functioning effectively or if one or more members are not doing their share, take action quickly.** The box on the next page lists a few common complaints about working with others in groups and possible solutions for each.

TABLE 2-1   Improving Group Dynamics

If a Group Member . . .	You Might Want to Say . . .
Hasn't begun the work he or she has been assigned	"You've been given a difficult part of the project. How can we help you get started?"
Complains about the workload	"We all seem to have the same amount of work to do. Is there some way we might lessen your workload?"
Seems confused about the assignment	"This is an especially complicated assignment. Would it be useful to summarize each member's job?"
Is uncommunicative and doesn't share information	"Since we are all working from different angles, let's each make an outline of what we've done so far, so we can plan how to proceed from here."
Misses meetings	"To ensure that we all meet regularly, would it be helpful if I called everyone the night before to confirm the day and time?"
Seems to be making you or other members do all the work	Make up a chart before the meeting with each member's responsibilities. Give each member a copy and ask, "Is there any part of your assignment that you have questions or concerns about? Would anyone like to change his or her completion date?" Be sure to get an answer from each member.

EXERCISE **2-14**   **Analyzing a Group Project**

Directions: Imagine that your psychology instructor has assigned a group project on the elderly in America. You must choose two classmates to be part of your group. The project has three components: (1) Read a chapter from the textbook and prepare a brief written overview of the problems facing the elderly. (2) Interview three people over age 80 and provide transcripts of those interviews. (3) Prepare a multimedia presentation of photographs, music, and video to accompany your presentation.

1. Which of these three tasks best suits you? Which task suits you least?

2. Take a show of hands. Ask students who are interested in component (1) to raise their hands: then do the same for components (2) and (3). Based on the results, everyone in class should choose two teammates.

3. With your teammates, discuss why you have chosen your specific activity. Did your choice have anything to do with your learning style(s)? Why did you *not* choose the other two activities?

USING WRITING TO LEARN

Do you read with a pen or pencil in hand? Do you write notes in the margin of your textbook and take notes while your instructors lecture? If so, you have already discovered that writing is one of the best ways to learn. Taking notes as you read makes the process more active. The act of writing out key points and important vocabulary helps cement the information in your brain. It also develops your writing skills, which are valuable in all careers.

Why Write?

You may have noticed that the exercises and tests in this book fall into two categories: (1) multiple-choice questions and (2) questions that require you to write out your answer. Both formats reflect the type of questions you will encounter in your college courses.

Multiple-choice questions are common on exams, especially in courses with high enrollments, and on *exit exams* (the tests a student must take to move out of a particular course and onto higher areas of study). Several strategies are available for answering multiple-choice questions correctly. For more information, see section 5a of the Troubleshooting Guide (p. 308).

Writing questions are common on essay exams. In addition, most college courses require written essays or term papers.

Working with Writing Exercises and Assignments

Some students don't like to write because they feel their command of grammar and spelling is not perfect. But grammar is easily learned, and reference tools (such as dictionaries) can help you check your spelling. If you are using a computer program such as Word to write, you can use the program's spell-check and grammar-check features to help you analyze your mistakes and correct them.

Remember that good writing is as much about *ideas* as it is about grammar. Writing exercises and assignments are designed to help you work with information and think deeply about the material.

The following tips can help you approach writing exercises and assignments in the right frame of mind.

> ### Tips for Doing Well on Writing Assignments
>
> 1. **Do the reading before working on the writing assignment.** Do not attempt to answer questions until the reading assignment is complete!

2. **Take notes while reading.** Underline key points and take notes in the margin. Doing so will help you focus on the reading and retain the information. For specific note-taking skills, see Chapter 10 "Organizing and Remembering Information."

3. **Read the writing assignment carefully.** Most writing assignments or questions ask for specific information. If you read the question too quickly, you may not provide the correct answer.

4. **Answer the question with specific information and examples.** The key to good writing is making a point and then supporting it with examples.

5. **Determine the correct length of the answer/response.** Students sometimes write everything they know instead of just the answer to the question. Not all answers require a paragraph or essay; sometimes one sentence is enough.

6. **In writing assignments, "Yes" or "No" is not a complete answer.** Some writing exercises will ask you a "yes or no" or "agree or disagree" question. It is important to include the *reasons* for your answer because the assignment is really asking you how you arrived at your opinion.

7. **Write complete sentences.** On most writing assignments and essay exams, it is important to write in complete sentences. Examine the question to determine when it is acceptable to provide a briefer answer. For example, fill-in-the-blank questions usually require you to write only key words or phrases, not whole sentences.

EXERCISE 2-15 **Analyzing Exam Questions**

Directions: For each of the essay exam/writing questions that follow, determine whether the best answer would be a single sentence, a paragraph, or a complete essay.

1. Define the term *monopoly* as it is used by economists. _____

2. Compare and contrast the work of William Thackeray and Charles Dickens, making specific reference to at least two books by each novelist. _____

3. Do you agree with the idea of decriminalizing marijuana use in the United States? Why or why not? _____

4. List four of Freud's defense mechanisms, providing a definition of

   each. _____

5. Provide a brief summary of the public reception to Pablo Picasso's famous painting

   Guernica. _____

6. What is the difference between fiction and nonfiction? _____

An Introduction to Summarizing

readinglab

practice summarizing,
to
STUDY PLAN
▼ READING SKILLS
  ▼ OUTLINING AND
     SUMMARIZING

A **summary** is a brief review of the major idea(s) of something you have read. Its purpose is to record the reading's most important ideas in a condensed form.

Summarizing is an extremely valuable skill because it forces you to identify a reading's key points. It is quite helpful in many college writing situations, such as

- Answering essay questions on exams
- Reviewing a film
- Recording the results of a lab experiment
- Summarizing the plot (main events) of a short story

Understanding how to write a good summary requires an understanding of main ideas (Chapter 6) and details (Chapter 7). Complete directions for summary writing are provided in Chapter 10, "Organizing and Remembering Information."

Every chapter in this book includes a summary writing exercise. In early chapters, the summaries are provided in a fill-in-the-blank format that asks you to fill in missing words. In later chapters, you'll be writing complete sentences and more complete summaries.

Here is a reading passage, followed by a sample summary.

On Visiting An Art Museum

It is a mistake to enter a museum with the belief that you should like everything you see—or even that you should see everything that is there. Without selective viewing, the visitor to a large museum is likely to come down with a severe case of museum exhaustion.

It makes sense to approach an art museum the way a seasoned traveler approaches a city for a first visit: Find out what there is to see. In the museum, inquire about the schedule of special shows, then see those exhibitions and outstanding works that interest you.

If you are visiting without a specific exhibition in mind, follow your interests and instincts. Browsing can be highly rewarding. Zero in on what you feel are the highlights, savoring favorite works and unexpected discoveries.

Don't stay too long. Take breaks. Perhaps there is a garden or café in which you can pause for a rest. The quality of your experience is not measured by the amount of time you spend in the galleries or how many works you see. The most rewarding experiences can come from finding something that "speaks" to you, then sitting and enjoying it in leisurely contemplation.

—adapted from Preble and Preble, *Artforms*, p. 100

Summary
When you are visiting an art museum, you should practice selective viewing. Find out what the museum has to offer. Decide what special exhibitions and outstanding works appeal to you. Follow your instincts and focus on the highlights. Don't stay too long, and take breaks. Find art that speaks to you and take time to enjoy it.

Note that the summary goes one step beyond recording what the writers say. It pulls together the writers' ideas by condensing and grouping them together.

EXERCISE 2-16   **Writing a Summary**

Directions: Read the passage, and then complete the summary that follows.

What can you do if you have trouble sleeping? Several techniques may help. Restrict your sleeping hours to the same nightly pattern. Avoid sleeping late in the morning, napping longer than an hour, or going to bed earlier than usual, all of which will throw off your schedule, creating even more sleep difficulties. Use your bed only for sleep (don't read or watch TV in bed). Avoid ingesting substances with stimulant properties. Don't smoke cigarettes or drink beverages with alcohol or caffeine in the evening. Alcohol may cause initial drowsiness, but it has a "rebound effect" that leaves many people wide awake in the middle of the night. Don't drink water close to bedtime; getting up to use the bathroom can lead to poor sleep. Consider meditation or progressive muscle relaxation. Either technique can be helpful, if used regularly.

—adapted from Kosslyn and Rosenberg, *Fundamentals of Psychology*, pp. 368–369

Summary

To get a good night's sleep, go to bed at the same _____ every night and get up at the same time every _____. Don't do anything in your bed except _____. Don't smoke or drink beverages with _____ or _____ in the evening, and don't drink _____ before bedtime. Try _____ or progressive muscle relaxation.

LEARNING STYLE TIPS

If you tend to be a(n) . . .	Then work with textbooks and visuals by . . .
Auditory or social learner	Discussing textbook content with friends or a study group
Independent learner	Using the textbook's companion Web site frequently
Verbal learner	Translating photos, diagrams, and drawings into language
Visual learner	Drawing your own diagrams, charts, and tables

SELF-TEST SUMMARY

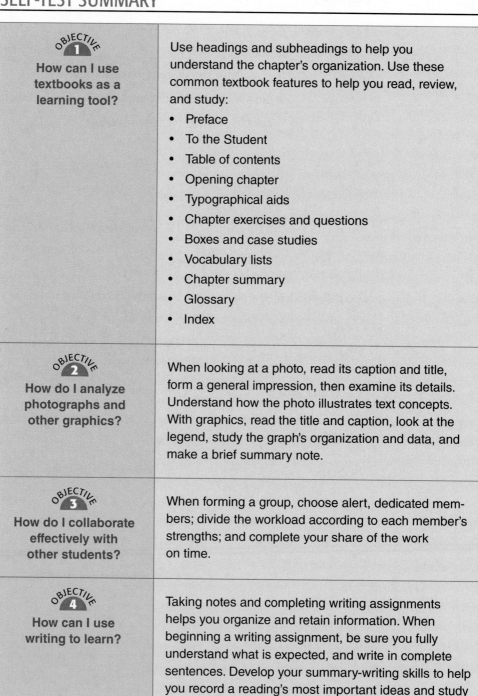

OBJECTIVE 1 How can I use textbooks as a learning tool?	Use headings and subheadings to help you understand the chapter's organization. Use these common textbook features to help you read, review, and study: • Preface • To the Student • Table of contents • Opening chapter • Typographical aids • Chapter exercises and questions • Boxes and case studies • Vocabulary lists • Chapter summary • Glossary • Index
OBJECTIVE 2 How do I analyze photographs and other graphics?	When looking at a photo, read its caption and title, form a general impression, then examine its details. Understand how the photo illustrates text concepts. With graphics, read the title and caption, look at the legend, study the graph's organization and data, and make a brief summary note.
OBJECTIVE 3 How do I collaborate effectively with other students?	When forming a group, choose alert, dedicated members; divide the workload according to each member's strengths; and complete your share of the work on time.
OBJECTIVE 4 How can I use writing to learn?	Taking notes and completing writing assignments helps you organize and retain information. When beginning a writing assignment, be sure you fully understand what is expected, and write in complete sentences. Develop your summary-writing skills to help you record a reading's most important ideas and study for exams.

GOING ONLINE

1. Teamwork Skills for Group Projects

   http://www.iamnext.com/academics/groupproject.html

   Use these tips for your next group project. Keep track of what works well; add your own suggestions based on the experience you have in your own group.

2. Study Skills: Group Projects

   http://duguides.drury.edu/content.php?pid=932&sid=3688

   Use this guide to figure out what roles you tend to play in group work situations. Evaluate your participation in the group. What do you do well? Are there ways you could improve? Write a paragraph describing yourself as a group member.

3. Group Work Peer Assessment

   http://www.phy.ilstu.edu/pte/399content/careers/Group_Work_Peer_

   Assessment.pdf

   Sometimes instructors ask group members to evaluate one another's contribution to the group. Look at this example of a peer assessment. What do you think of the categories and grading system? Do you think anything could be added to this assessment? How would your group members perform? How do you think they would grade you? What are the advantages and disadvantages of using a form like this?

4. Reading Your Textbooks Effectively and Efficiently

   http://www.dartmouth.edu/~acskills/success/reading.html

   Dartmouth College offers several online documents designed to help students read textbooks more effectively and efficiently. Two featured documents are "Six Reading Myths" and "Harvard Report on Reading." Read them over and discuss with your classmates how these documents apply to your current experiences. Offer each other suggestions for improving reading skills.

To check your progress in meeting chapter objectives, log in to **http://www.myreadinglab.com**, click on the Study Plan tab, and then click on the Reading Skills tab. Choose Reading Textbooks and Outlining and Summarizing from the list of subtopics. Read and view the information in the Review Materials section, and then complete the Practices and Tests in the Activities section. You can check your scores by clicking on the Gradebook tab.

MASTERY TEST 1 Working with Textbook Features

Name _____ Section _____

Date _____ Number right _____ × 20 points = Score _____

Directions: Read the following excerpt from a communication textbook. Then answer the questions that follow.

UNDER-THE-RADAR ADVERTISING

Inundated with advertisements, 6,000 a week on network television, double since 1983, many people tune out. The problem is ad clutter. Advertisers are trying to address the clutter in numerous ways, including stealth ads. Although not hidden or subliminal, stealth ads are subtle—even covert. You might not know you're being pitched unless you're really attentive.

- **Stealth ads.** So neatly can *stealth ads* fit into the landscape that people may not recognize they're being pitched. Consider the Bamboo lingerie company, which stenciled messages on a Manhattan sidewalk: "From here it looks like you could use new underwear." Sports stadiums like FedEx Field outside of Washington, D.C., work their way into everyday dialogue, subtly reinforcing product identity.
- **Product placement.** In the 1980s advertisers began wiggling brand-name placements into movie scripts, creating an additional minor revenue stream for filmmakers. The practice, *product placement*, stirred criticism about artistic integrity, but it gained momentum. For the 2005 release of *The Green Hornet*, Miramax was seeking an automaker willing to pay at least $35 million for its products to be written into the script.
- **Infomercials.** Less subtle is the *infomercial*, a program-length television commercial dolled up to look like a newscast, a live-audience participation show, or a chatty talk show. With the proliferation of 24-hour television service and of cable channels, airtime is so cheap at certain hours that advertisers of even offbeat products can afford it.

—adapted from Vivian, *The Media of Mass Communication*, pp. 336–338

_____ 1. The reading selection uses all of the following typographical aids *except*
a. boldfaced type.
b. numbered list.
c. bulleted list.
d. italic type.

_____ 2. The key terms list for this selection would most likely include which set of terms?
a. radar, stealth, product placement
b. advertising, filmmakers, cable channels
c. Bamboo, FedEx, Miramax
d. stealth ad, product placement, infomercial

_____ 3. What does the heading "Under-the-Radar Advertising" mean?
a. sneaky advertising
b. television advertising
c. creative advertising
d. movie advertising

_____ 4. Which is the best example of a critical thinking question based on the reading?
a. What is stealth advertising?
b. What are the three types of under-the-radar advertising?
c. What are two examples of stealth advertising at work?
d. What ethical issues are involved with stealth advertising?

_____ 5. Which of the following would be the best glossary entry for **infomercial**?
a. **infomercial:** a form of stealth advertising
b. **infomercial:** a common and inexpensive type of cable TV advertising
c. **infomercial:** a program-length TV commercial made to look like a newscast, audience participation show, or talk show
d. **infomercial:** stealth advertising used by companies to sell products

MASTERY TEST 2 Analyzing Photographs

Name _____ Section _____

Date _____ Number right _____ × 20 points = Score _____

Directions: Analyze the following photos from a sociology textbook along with the title and caption. Then answer the questions that follow.

(a)

(b)

Japanese Lunch: Bento Boxes

A bento is a boxed lunch very common in Japan. Traditional bentos usually include fish or meat, rice, and vegetables. While bentos are available almost everywhere in Japan, from convenience stores to train stations, many homemakers spend considerable time and energy preparing elegant bentos for their spouse and children. Other countries in which boxed lunches like the bento are common include India, Taiwan, Korea, and the Philippines. In (a), the ingredients include fried chicken, pasta, broccoli, and quail eggs. The pigs' ears and snouts are made from fish sausage. In (b), the bento maker has made a cat's face out of seaweed placed on bed of rice and added beans, carrots, and other vegetables.

_____ 1. What is the best synonym for *bento*? (A synonym is a word with the same meaning as another word.)
   a. fish
   b. rice
   c. Japanese
   d. boxed lunch

_____ 2. All of the following ingredients are used in the pictured bentos *except*
   a. sardines.
   b. fish sausage.
   c. quail eggs.
   d. nuts.

_____ 3. The bento in photo (a) was most likely prepared for
   a. the president of a company.
   b. a grandparent.
   c. a child.
   d. a spouse.

_____ 4. These photos appeared in a sociology textbook chapter on culture, in a section titled "Food: Ingredients, Preparation, and Mealtime Traditions." Most likely, these photos were included in the chapter to
   a. show the foods most commonly eaten in Korea.
   b. illustrate the way lunches are often served in Japan.
   c. provide photos of interest to vegetarians.
   d. demonstrate how food can be arranged to resemble animals.

_____ 5. Boxed lunches are common in all of the following countries *except*
   a. the Philippines.
   b. Korea.
   c. China.
   d. India.

MASTERY TEST 3 Reading Selection

Name _____ Section _____

Date _____ Number right* _____ × 10 points = Score _____

Conversational Dilemmas

Shelley D. Lane

This selection, taken from the communication textbook *Interpersonal Communication: Competence and Context*, explores the difficult communication encounters known as conversational dilemmas.

> **Vocabulary Preview**
>
> **dilemmas** (par. 1) situations which require a choice between two equally undesirable options
>
> **tactful** (par. 1) polite or diplomatic
>
> **competent** (par. 3) capable
>
> **optimality** (par. 3) the best or most desirable outcome
>
> **subterfuge** (par. 5) deception
>
> **collaborator** (par. 7) partner or colleague

1   There are times when our conversations are difficult and challenging, even though most of our conversations are likely to be successful. Occasionally we may experience conversations during which we feel that we can't say anything right; whatever we say creates a problem or some sort of undesirable outcome. Such types of difficult communication encounters are called **conversational dilemmas**. Conversational dilemmas need not accompany or result from rule violations, yet as illustrated in the "Baby Blues" comic, they create negative feelings such as embarrassment and defensiveness when we realize that we may be trapped in one. Examples of conversational dilemmas include:

- being caught in a lie
- saying something we shouldn't
- being judged as not saying anything right
- feeling torn between telling the truth (even if it is hurtful) and lying to be factful

2   Suppose a friend wants to marry someone you don't particularly like. How will you respond if your friend asks whether he or she should marry the future bride or groom? Even though people caught in conversational dilemmas can

---

*To calculate the number right, use items 1–10 under "Mastery Test Skills Check."

BABY BLUES   **By Rick Kirkman and Jerry Scott**

A conversational dilemma

Source: © Baby Blues—Baby Blues Partnership. King Features Syndicate

use various strategies to cope with such situations, conversational dilemmas are difficult to resolve. There are six categories of responses to conversational dilemmas:

1. **Direct responses**—this category includes blunt talk (e.g., "I'd never marry someone like the person you want to marry") or honest but tactful communication (e.g.,"I'll probably look for someone with a different sort of personality when I want to get married.")

2. **Indirect responses**—included in this category are strategic ambiguity, vagueness, or subtlety to avoid directly stating the truth, as well as sarcasm, hints, humor, and nonverbal cues (e.g., "Hah! You're asking me about who to marry? I'll never get married so don't ask me 'marriage questions'!")

3. **Deception**—this category involves a direct misrepresentation of the truth (e.g., "I think the person you're engaged to will make a good spouse.")

4. **Impression management**—this category includes apologies, excuses, explanations, and reassurances (e.g., "I'm sorry but I can't answer your question; I'm not a good judge of character. However, everything I've seen tells me that your future spouse will make a good one.")

5. **Pleasing the other**—included in this category are compromises and giving in to avoid conflict or additional awkwardness (e.g., "OK, OK, I'll answer your question, but don't blame me if you get married and you regret your decision or don't get married and regret your decision.")

6. **Soliciting the other's help**—asking for more information and/or asking the other's cooperation to resolve the dilemma (e.g., "Well, first tell me why you want to marry this person. It's difficult to answer such a question when I don't know what you're looking for in a spouse.")

3   Researchers have discovered that communicatively competent individuals are able to extricate themselves from conversational dilemmas in a manner that saves face for self and the other. Such individuals tend to choose more sophisticated and effective responses than people who aren't communicatively competent. However, we cannot label certain tactics as more beneficial than others. "What determines optimality is a complex issue that demands consideration of such things as the others involved in the exchange, the context within which the exchange occurs, and the goals of each interactant. With some people one response is preferred over another; in some settings one response is more appropriate than another; and sometimes it is important to a person to be sophisticated, and sometimes it is not."

Knowledge Power

I Can't Win!

4   Review the four types of conversational dilemmas and six categories of responses to conversational dilemmas. Think about a past conversation when you felt trapped. To which type of conversational dilemma does your example relate? To which response to a conversational dilemma does your example correspond? With a partner or in a group, share your conversational dilemma, and tell your partner or group how you attempted to resolve the dilemma. Ask your partner or the group to assess your effectiveness and appropriateness and (if warranted) to suggest other tactics for dealing with the dilemma.

A Case Study in Ethics

Cell Phone Subterfuge

5   Competent communication includes an ethical dimension of well-based standards of right and wrong. To help us make decisions and select communication strategies that are effective and appropriate, we can ask ourselves a series of questions: Have I practiced any virtues today (e.g., have I demonstrated integrity, trustworthiness, honesty, and responsibility)? Have I done more good than harm (e.g., have I shown appreciation and gratitude to others)? Have I treated people with dignity and respect? Have I been fair and just? Have I made my community stronger because of my actions? Read the following case study about cell phone subterfuge and consider whether staged phone calls, alibi clubs, and fake noises are ethical ways to engage in conversations with others.

6   James E. Katz, professor of communication at Rutgers University, suggests that some people use cell phones to indirectly communicate with people who surround them. For example, some people stage fake phone calls as explanations for their behavior, such as scolding a pretend child for invading a wallet when they find themselves without cash in a checkout line. Others pretend to be talking on their cell phone when they are actually trying to get a good angle to take a photo on it. Still

others create fake phone calls for reasons of safety. Loudly saying, "I'll meet you in a few minutes!" may be helpful when we think we're being followed.

7   In addition to using cell phones to stage fake phone calls, some people, with the help of other cell phone users, use their cell phones to lie. "Cell phone alibi clubs" are flourishing in many parts of the globe as a way to help callers make excuses and hide their whereabouts. People pay a fee to join a club and are subsequently linked to thousands of members to whom they can send text messages en masse that ask for help. When a potential collaborator indicates her or his willingness to phone a "victim," the caller and collaborator create a lie, and the collaborator phones with the excuse. Similar to alibi clubs, companies offer audio recordings that can be played in the background of such phone calls. Sounds such as honking horns, a dentist's drill, and ambulance sirens can be used to make a phone call sound realistic.

8   Although fake cell phone calls, cell phone alibi clubs, and background audio recordings may reflect questionable ethics, some individuals find nothing wrong with their use. Harry Kargman, founder of a company that sells audio background sounds, says that using background sounds is "not necessarily malicious or nefarious," Michelle Logan, founder of an alibi club based in San Diego, suggests that such clubs spare others' feelings with "white lies."

9   *Do you think it's ethical to stage fake phone calls? Is it ethical to use alibi clubs and/or background audio recordings? Do you agree with Michelle Logan that alibi clubs spare others' feelings?*

MASTERY TEST SKILLS CHECK

Directions: Select the choice that best completes each of the following statements.

Checking Your Comprehension

_____ 1. The purpose of this selection is to
   a. compare different communication styles.
   b. identify the qualities of highly effective communicators.
   c. describe conversational dilemmas and responses to those dilemmas.
   d. discuss strategies for overcoming communication challenges.

_____ 2. Conversational dilemmas can best be defined as
   a. communication difficulties that result from rule violations.
   b. difficult conversations in which whatever you say causes problems.
   c. dishonest and unethical forms of communication.
   d. communication strategies that are ineffective and inappropriate.

_____ 3. The main point of paragraph 2 is that
   a. conversational dilemmas are impossible to resolve.
   b. there are six categories of responses to conversational dilemmas.
   c. most strategies for responding to conversational dilemmas involve deception.
   d. honest responses are the best way to cope with conversational dilemmas.

_____ 4. The category of responses that includes apologies, excuses, explanations, and reassurances is known as
   a. direct responses.
   b. deception.
   c. impression management.
   d. pleasing the other.

_____ 5. The main point of paragraph 3 is that
   a. most people find it easy to get out of conversational dilemmas.
   b. the best response to a conversational dilemma depends on several factors.
   c. certain tactics for coping with conversational dilemmas are always better than others.
   d. communicatively competent people choose the best responses to conversational dilemmas.

Applying Your Skills

_____ 6. The purpose of the bulleted list (p. 66) is to
   a. illustrate successful ways to begin conversations.
   b. show how to avoid conversational dilemmas.
   c. list examples of conversational dilemmas.
   d. suggest strategies for responding to conversational dilemmas.

_____ 7. The "Baby Blues" cartoon on page 67 illustrates the type of conversational dilemma that occurs when we
   a. are caught in a lie.
   b. perceive that we can't say anything right.

c. feel torn between telling the truth and lying.

d. use nonverbal cues to communicate.

_____ 8. The numbered list on page 67 includes all of the following categories of responses to conversational dilemmas *except*

a. direct and indirect responses.

b. deception.

c. consideration of context.

d. impression management.

_____ 9. In the KNOWLEDGE power "I Can't Win!" box on page 68, students are asked to recall their own experience with a conversational dilemma and

a. write an essay about their experience.

b. find a person who has responded differently to the same dilemma.

c. have their response to the dilemma evaluated by a partner or group.

d. ask the teacher for better ways to deal with the dilemma.

_____ 10. The main purpose of the Case Study in Ethics box (p. 68) is to

a. describe companies that specialize in creating audio recordings for cell phone users.

b. encourage people to use cell phones to communicate indirectly with those around them.

c. defend the use of cell phone alibi clubs as a way to make excuses or hide a person's whereabouts.

d. explore the ethics of fake phone calls, alibi clubs, and background audio recordings.

Studying Words

_____ 11. The word *ambiguity* (par. 2) means

a. category.

b. unclear meaning.

c. criticism.

d. truthfulness.

_____ 12. The word *soliciting* (par. 2) means

a. lying.

b. asking.

c. excusing.

d. avoiding.

_____ 13. The word *extricate* (par. 3) means

a. include.

b. cooperate.

c. disengage.

d. delay.

_____ 14. The word in paragraph 3 that means the same as *strategies* is

a. consideration

b. interactant

c. responses

d. tactics.

_____ 15. The word *beneficial* (par. 3) means

a. helpful.

b. useless.

c. harmful.

d. artificial.

Summarizing the Reading

Directions: Complete the following summary of the reading by filling in the blanks.

Conversational _____ occur when whatever we say leads to a _____ or an undesirable _____. Conversational dilemmas include being caught in a _____, saying something we shouldn't, being _____ as not saying anything right, and feeling torn between being _____ but hurtful or being dishonest but _____. Six categories of responses to conversational dilemmas are direct responses, _____ responses, deception, _____ management, pleasing the other, and soliciting the other's _____.

Reading Visually

1. Why is the KNOWLEDGE Power box included? What is its purpose?

   _____

2. Why would the "Baby Blues" cartoon be included in an interpersonal communication textbook chapter?

   _____

   _____

3. What types of visual aids are included in this selection?

   _____

Thinking Critically about the Reading

WRITE IN YOUR
JOURNAL

1. Make a connection between the textbook and your own life by rereading the KNOWLEDGE Power box. Use one of your own past conversational dilemmas to answer the questions in the box. After reading this selection, can you think of other ways you could have resolved your dilemma?

2. Is it ethical to fake a phone call, use an alibi club, or play background noises on a cell phone? Why or why not? Describe any situations in which you think "cell phone subterfuge" is acceptable.

CHAPTER

3

Using Context Clues

Looking at …
Context Clues

LEARNING OBJECTIVES

This chapter will show you how to:

OBJECTIVE **1** Understand context clues

OBJECTIVE **2** Use five types of context clues

OBJECTIVE **3** Understand the limitations of context clues

Suppose you saw this photograph in a psychology textbook. Why is the photo confusing? The top half of the photo does not fit with the bottom half. No doubt you would have trouble understanding and explaining the photograph. What is missing is its context—the information surrounding the image shown in the photo. However, if you read the chapter opener and learned that the chapter is about the aging process, then you would be able to grasp its meaning and purpose.

WHAT IS CONTEXT?

Try to figure out what is missing in the following brief paragraph. Write the missing words in the blanks provided.

> Most Americans can speak only one _____. Europeans, however, _____ several. As a result, Europeans think _____ are unfriendly and unwilling to communicate with them.

Did you insert the word *language* in the first blank, *speak* or *know* in the second blank, and *Americans* in the third blank? Most likely, you correctly identified all three missing words. You could tell from the sentence which word to put in. The words around the missing words—the sentence context—gave you clues as to which word would fit and make sense. Such clues are called **context clues.**

While you probably will not find missing words on a printed page, you will often find words that you do not know. Context clues can help you to figure out the meanings of unfamiliar words.

Example

Phobias, such as fear of heights, water, or confined spaces, are difficult to eliminate.

From the sentence, you can tell that *phobia* means "fear of specific objects or situations."

Here is another example:

> The couple finally **secured** a table at the popular, crowded restaurant.

You can figure out that *secured* means "got" or "took ownership of" the table.

TYPES OF CONTEXT CLUES

There are five types of context clues to look for: (1) definition, (2) synonym, (3) example, (4) contrast, and (5) inference.

Definition Clues

Many times a writer defines a word immediately following its use. The writer may directly define a word by giving a brief definition or a synonym (a word that has the same meaning). Such words and phrases as *means, is, refers to,* and *can be defined as* are often used. Here are some examples:

> **Corona** refers to the outermost part of the sun's atmosphere.
>
> A **soliloquy** is a speech made by a character in a play that reveals his or her thoughts to the audience.

At other times, rather than formally define the word, a writer may provide clues or synonyms. Punctuation is often used to signal that a definition clue to a word's meaning is to follow. Punctuation also separates the meaning clue from the rest of the sentence. Three types of punctuation are used in this way. In the examples below, notice that the meaning clue is separated from the rest of the sentence by punctuation.

1. Commas

   > An **oligopoly,** *control of a product by a small number of companies,* exists in the long-distance phone market.
   >
   > **Equity,** *general principles of fairness and justice,* is used in law when existing laws do not apply or are inadequate.

2. Parentheses

   > A leading cause of heart disease is a diet with too much **cholesterol** (*a fatty substance made of carbon, hydrogen, and oxygen*).

3. Dashes

   > Ancient Egyptians wrote in **hieroglyphics**—*pictures used to represent words.*
   >
   > **Facets**—*small flat surfaces at different angles*—bring out the beauty of a diamond.

EXERCISE 3-1 **Using Definition Context Clues**

Directions: Read each sentence and write a definition or synonym for each boldfaced word or phrase. Use the definition context clue to help you determine word meaning.

1. **Glog,** a Swedish hot punch, is often served at holiday parties.

   _____

2. The judge's **candor**—his sharp, open frankness—shocked the jury.

   _____

3. A **chemical bond** is a strong attractive force that holds two or more atoms together.

   _____

4. **Lithium** (an alkali metal) is so soft it can be cut with a knife.

   _____

5. Hearing, technically known as **audition,** begins when a sound wave reaches the outer ear.

   _____

6. Five-line rhyming poems, or **limericks,** are among the simplest forms of poetry.

   _____

7. Our country's **gross national product**—the total market value of its national output of goods and services—is increasing steadily.

   _____

8. A **species** is a group of animals or plants that share similar characteristics and are able to interbreed.

   _____

9. Broad, flat noodles that are served covered with sauce or butter are called **fettuccine.**

   _____

10. Many diseases have **latent periods,** periods of time between the infection and the first appearance of a symptom.

   _____

Synonym Clues

At other times, rather than formally define the word, a writer may provide a synonym—a word or brief phrase that is close in meaning. The synonym may appear in the same sentence as the unknown word.

> The author purposely left the ending of his novel **ambiguous,** or _unclear,_ so readers would have to decide for themselves what happened.

Other times, it may appear anywhere in the passage, in an earlier or later sentence.

> After the soccer match, a **melee** broke out in the parking lot. Three people were injured in the *brawl,* and several others were arrested.

EXERCISE 3-2   Using Synonym Context Clues

Directions: Read each sentence and write a definition or synonym for each boldfaced word or phrase. Use the synonym context clue to help you determine word meaning.

1. The mayor's assistant was accused of **malfeasance,** although he denied any wrongdoing. _miscanduct, misdoing_

2. The words of the president seemed to excite and **galvanize** the American troops, who cheered enthusiastically throughout the speech. _charge, excite, turn on_

3. Venus and Serena Williams' superior ability and **prowess** on the tennis court have inspired many girls to become athletes. _bracy, courageousness, daring_ _skill_

4. Many gardeners improve the quality of their soil by **amending** it with organic compost. _to enhance, to improve,_

5. Eliminating salt from the diet is a **prudent,** sensible decision for people with high blood pressure. _wise, intelligent, (well advised)_

6. The **cadence,** or rhythm, of the Dixieland band had many people tapping their feet along with the music. _beat, rhythm_

7. Edgar Allan Poe is best known for his **macabre** short stories and poems. His eerie tale "The Fall of the House of Usher" was later made into a horror movie starring Vincent Price. _horrible, dreadful, awful, frightful_

8. While she was out of the country, Greta authorized me to act as her **proxy,** or agent, in matters having to do with her business and her personal bank accounts. _delegate, representative_

9. The **arsenal** of a baseball pitcher ideally includes several different kinds of pitches. From this supply of pitches, he or she needs to have at least one that can fool the batter. _store, depot, dump (collection)_

10. A **coalition** of neighborhood representatives formed to fight a proposed highway through the area. The group also had the support of several local businesses.
    party, joint group, body, combination

Example Clues

Writers often include examples that help to explain or clarify a word. Suppose you do not know the meaning of the word *toxic,* and you find it used in the following sentence:

> **Toxic** materials, such as arsenic, asbestos, pesticides, and lead, can cause bodily damage.

This sentence gives four examples of toxic materials. From the examples given, which are all poisonous substances, you could conclude that *toxic* means "poisonous."

Examples

Forest floors are frequently covered with **fungi**—molds, mushrooms, and mildews.

Legumes, such as peas and beans, produce pods.

Arachnids, including tarantulas, black widow spiders, and ticks, often have segmented bodies.

Newsmagazines, like *Time* or *Newsweek,* provide more details about news events than newspapers because they focus on only a few stories.

EXERCISE 3-3 | **Using Example Context Clues**

Directions: Read each sentence and write a definition or synonym for each boldfaced word or phrase. Use the example context clue to help you determine meaning.

1. Many **pharmaceuticals,** including morphine and penicillin, are not readily available in some countries. <u>drugs, medicines</u>

2. The child was **reticent** in every respect; she would not speak, refused to answer questions, and avoided looking at anyone. <u>silent, uncommunicative</u>

3. Most **condiments,** such as pepper, mustard, and catsup, are used to improve the flavor of foods. <u>seasoning</u>

4. Instructors provide their students with **feedback** through test grades and comments on papers. <u>return</u>

5. **Physiological needs**—hunger, thirst, and sex—promote survival of the human species. <u>factors, characteristic</u>

6. Clothing is available in a variety of **fabrics,** including cotton, wool, polyester, and linen. _cloth, textile_

7. In the past month, we have had almost every type of **precipitation**—rain, snow, sleet, and hail. _haste, hurry, rush (water)_

8. **Involuntary reflexes,** like breathing and beating of the heart, are easily measured. _unintentional, unintended (unconcious)_

9. The student had a difficult time distinguishing between **homonyms**—words such as *see* and *sea, wore* and *war,* and *deer* and *dear.* _words spelled and pronounced alike but different in meaning_

10. Abstract paintings often include such **geometrics** as squares, cubes, and triangles. _form, figure, shape_

Contrast Clues

It is sometimes possible to determine the meaning of an unknown word from a word or phrase in the context that has an opposite meaning. If a single word provides a clue, it is often an **antonym**—a word opposite in meaning to the unknown word. Notice, in the following sentence, how a word opposite in meaning to the boldfaced word provides a clue to its meaning:

> One of the dinner guests **succumbed** to the temptation to have a second piece of cake, but the others resisted.

Although you may not know the meaning of *succumbed*, you know that the one guest who succumbed was different from the others who resisted. The word *but* suggests this. Since the others resisted a second dessert, you can tell that one guest gave in and had a piece. Thus, *succumbed* means the opposite of *resist*; that is, "to give in to."

Examples

The professor **advocates** testing on animals, *but* many of her students feel it is cruel.

Most of the graduates were **elated,** *though* a few felt sad and depressed.

The old man acted **morosely,** *whereas* his grandson was very lively.

The gentleman was quite **portly,** *but* his wife was thin.

EXERCISE 3-4   **Using Contrast Context Clues**

Directions: Read each sentence and write a definition or synonym for each boldfaced word. Use the contrast clue to help you determine meaning.

1. Some city dwellers are **affluent;** others live in or near poverty.

    _____ rich _____

2. I am certain that the hotel will hold our reservation; however, if you are **dubious,** call to make sure. _____ doubtful, suspicious _____

3. Although most experts **concurred** with the research findings, several strongly disagreed. ____ agree , coincide _____

4. The speaker **denounced** certain legal changes while praising other reforms.

    ___ condemn, accuse, proclaim _____

5. The woman's parents **thwarted** her marriage plans though they liked her fiancé.

    ___ frustrate, to oppose _____

6. In medieval Europe, **peasants** led difficult lives, whereas the wealthy landowners lived in luxury. ___ low social status people, poor _____

7. When the couple moved into their new home they **revamped** the kitchen and bathroom but did not change the rest of the rooms. ___ make-over, remake, change __

8. The young nurse was **bewildered** by the patient's symptoms, but the doctor realized she was suffering from a rare form of leukemia. ___ puzzled, perplexed __

9. Despite my husband's **pessimism** about my chances of winning the lottery, I was certain I would win. ___ unhopeful, negative _____

    _____

10. The mayoral candidate praised the town council, while the mayor **deprecated** it.

    ___ belittle, disapproved , put-down, _____

Inference Clues

Many times you can figure out the meaning of an unknown word by using logic and reasoning skills. For instance, look at the following sentence:

> Bob is quite **versatile;** he is a good student, a top athlete, an excellent car mechanic, and a gourmet cook.

You can see that Bob is successful at many different types of activities, and you could reason that *versatile* means "capable of doing many things competently."

Examples

When the customer tried to pay with Mexican **pesos,** the clerk explained that the store accepted only U.S. dollars.

The potato salad looked so plain that I decided to **garnish** it with parsley and paprika to give it some color.

We had to leave the car and walk up because the **incline** was too steep to drive.

Since Reginald was nervous, he brought his rabbit's foot **talisman** with him to the exam.

EXERCISE 3-5 ## Using Inference Context Clues

Directions: Read each sentence and write a definition or synonym for each boldfaced word. Try to reason out the meaning of each word using information provided in the context.

1. The **wallabies** at the zoo looked like kangaroos. _____

2. The foreign students quickly **assimilated** many aspects of American culture.
   _____ comprize, absorb, incorporated, internalize _____

3. On hot, humid summer afternoons, I often feel **languid.**
   _____ weak, slow, sluggish, listless, _____

4. Some physical fitness experts recommend jogging or weight lifting to overcome the effects of a **sedentary** job. _doing much sitting, not physically active_

5. The legal aid clinic was **subsidized** by city and county funds.
   _____ financed, funded _____

6. When the bank robber reached his **haven,** he breathed a sigh of relief and began to count his money. _refuge, a place of safety_

7. The teenager was **intimidated** by the presence of a police officer walking the beat and decided not to spray-paint the school wall. _bully, to make timid, fearful_

8. The vase must have been **jostled** in shipment because it arrived with several chips in it. _crash, push, squeeze_

9. Although she had visited the fortune-teller several times, she was not sure she believed in the **occult.** _blot out, hide, cover, mask_

10. If the plan did not work, the colonel had a **contingency** plan ready.
case, event, possibility

EXERCISE 3-6   **Using Context Clues**

Directions: Read each sentence and write a definition or synonym for each boldfaced word. Use the context clue to help you determine meaning.

1. The economy was in a state of continual **flux;** inflation increased one month and decreased the next. _change,_

2. The grand jury **exonerated** the police officer of any possible misconduct or involvement in illegal activity. _acquit, clear_

3. Art is always talkative, but Ed is usually **taciturn.** _silent_

4. Many **debilities** of old age, including poor eyesight and loss of hearing, can be treated medically. _weakness,_

5. Police **interrogation,** or questioning, can be a frightening experience.
ask, inquire, question

6. The soap opera contained numerous **morbid** events: the death of a young child, the suicide of her father, and the murder of his older brother.
depressing, loresome, miserable, gloomy

7. After long hours of practice, Xavier finally learned to type; Riley's efforts, however, were **futile.** _useless, of no avail, not worth_

8. Although the farm appeared **derelict,** we discovered that an elderly man lived there.
abandoned,

9. The newspaper's error was **inadvertent;** the editor did not intend to include the victim's name. _unintentional, accidental, incidental_

10. To save money, we have decided to **curtail** the number of DVDs we buy each month. _shorten, cut back_

11. Steam from the hot radiator **scalded** the mechanic's hand.
burned, scorch

12. The businesswoman's **itinerary** outlined her trip and listed Cleveland as her next stop. _____ route _____

13. **Theologies,** such as Catholicism, Buddhism, and Hinduism, are discussed at great length in the class. _____ study of religious faith _____

14. Sven had a very good **rapport** with his father but was unable to get along well with his mother. _____ relation, fellowship, communion _____

15. The duchess had a way of **flaunting** her jewels so that everyone could see and envy them. _____ display, show _____

EXERCISE 3-7   Using Context Clues

Directions: Read each of the following passages and use context clues to figure out the meaning of each boldfaced word or phrase. Write a synonym or brief definition for each in the space provided.

A.   Some **visionaries** say that we can **transform** nursing homes into warm, inviting places. They started with a clean piece of paper and asked how we could redesign nursing homes so they **enhance** or maintain people's quality of life. The model they came up with doesn't look or even feel like a nursing home. In Green Houses, as they are called, elderly people live in a homelike setting. Instead of a **sterile** hallway lined with rooms, 10 to 12 residents live in a carpeted ranch-style house. They receive medical care suited to their personal needs, share meals at a **communal** dining table, and, if they want to, they can cook together in an open kitchen. They can even play **virtual** sports on plasma televisions. This home-like setting **fosters** a sense of community among residents and staff.

—adapted from Henslin, *Sociology: A Down-To-Earth Approach*, p. 386

> This photograph is a visual context clue for one of the terms used in the paragraph. Find the clue and circle it.

1. visionaries _creative, imaginative_

2. transform _____ change _____

3. enhance _____ improve _____

4. sterile _____ infruitful, barren _____

5. communal _____ common, combine _____

6. virtual _____ real _____

7. fosters _____ encourage, nourish, nurture, promote _____

B.   Marketers and consumers **coexist** in a complicated, two-way relationship. It's often hard to tell where marketing efforts leave off and "the real world" begins. One result of these **blurred** boundaries is that we are no longer sure (and perhaps we don't care) where the line separating this **fabricated** world from reality begins and ends. Sometimes, we **gleefully** join in the illusion. A story line in a Wonder Woman comic book featured the usual out-of-this-world **exploits** of a **vivacious** superhero. But it also included the real-world proposal of the owner of a chain of comic book stores, who persuaded DC Comics to let him **woo** his beloved in the issue.

—Solomon, *Consumer Behavior*, p. 19

1. coexist _____live_____   5. exploits _feat, adventure, activity_

2. blurred _distortion, unclear_   6. vivacious _lively, cheerful_

3. fabricated _invented, untrue, false, fake_   7. woo _persuade, pursue_

4. gleefully _happily_

C.   Rising tuition; roommates who bug you; social life drama; too much noise; no privacy; long lines at the bookstore; pressure to get good grades; never enough money; worries about the economy, terrorism, and natural disaster all add up to: STRESS! You can't run from it, you can't hide from it, and it can affect you in **insidious** ways that you aren't even aware of. When we try to sleep, it **encroaches** on our **psyche** through outside noise or internal worries over all the things that need to be done. While we work at the computer, stress may interfere in the form of noise from next door, strain on our eyes, and **tension** in our back. Even when we are out socializing with friends, we feel guilty, because there is just not enough time to do what needs to be accomplished. The **precise** toll that stress exacts from us over a lifetime is unknown, but increasingly, stress is recognized as a major threat to our health.

—Donatelle, *Health: The Basics*, p. 57

1. insidious _gradual, sneaky_   4. tension _stress, pressure_

2. encroaches _intrude, trespass, invade_   5. precision _accuracy, exact_

3. psyche _mind, personality_

EXERCISE 3-8   **Working with Context Clues**

Directions: Bring a brief textbook excerpt, editorial, or magazine article that contains difficult vocabulary to class. Working with another student, locate and underline at least three words in the article that your partner can define by using context clues. Work together in reasoning out each word, checking a dictionary to verify meanings.

EXERCISE 3-9

Using Context Clues

Bring to class three sentences, each containing a word whose meaning is suggested by the context of the sentence. The sentences can come from textbooks or other sources, or you can write them yourself. Underline the words, and write each one on a separate index card.

Form groups of three to five students. Each student should create a definition sheet to record meanings.

Pass the index cards around the group. For each card, each student should list the word and write its meaning on the definition sheet. When everyone has read each card, compare meanings.

EXERCISE 3-10

A Nonsense Words Activity

Directions: Each student should write five sentences, each containing a nonsense word whose meaning is suggested by the context of the sentence. Here is an example:

> Before I went out to pick up a pizza, I put on my purplut. I buttoned up my purplut and went outside, glad that it was filled with down.

> (Can you figure out the meaning of a purplut?)

Form groups of three to five students. Students should take turns reading aloud their sentences as group members guess the meanings of the nonsense words.

THE LIMITATIONS OF CONTEXT CLUES

OBJECTIVE 3

There are two limitations to the use of context clues. First, context clues seldom lead to a complete definition. Second, sometimes a sentence does not contain clues to a word's meaning. In these cases you will need to draw on other vocabulary skills. Chapter 4 will help you with these skills.

LEARNING STYLE TIPS

If you tend to be a(n) . . .	Then use context by . . .
Auditory learner	Reading the context aloud
Visual learner	Visualizing the context

SELF-TEST SUMMARY

OBJECTIVE 1 **What are context clues used for?**	They are used to figure out the meaning of an unknown word used in a sentence or paragraph.
OBJECTIVE 2 **What are the five types of context clues?**	The five types of context clues are: • Definition—a brief definition of or synonym for a word • Synonym—a word or phrase that is similar in meaning to the unknown word • Example—specific instances or examples that clarify a word's meaning • Contrast—a word or phrase of opposite meaning • Inference—the use of reasoning skills to figure out word meanings
OBJECTIVE 3 **What are the limitations of context clues?**	Context clues usually do not offer a complete definition. Context clues are not always provided.

GOING ONLINE

1. Context Clues

   http://www.mdc.edu/Kendall/collegeprep/documents2/ CONTEXT%20CLUESrev8192.pdf

   Practice figuring out more word meanings with these exercises. Use a dictionary to check your work.

2. Context Clues Quiz

   http://www.quia.com/pop/35971.html

   Try this short online vocabulary quiz using context clues to figure out the answers. How did you do? Were there any surprising words?

3. Using Context Clues

   http://www.tv411.org/lessons/cfm/reading.cfm?str=reading&num=7&act=1

   Here is another online tutorial with a quiz about using context clues to figure out new vocabulary. Compare your experience with this exercise with those in activities 1 and 2 above.

 To check your progress in meeting chapter objectives, log in to **http://www.myreadinglab.com**, click on the Study Plan tab, and then click on the Reading Skills tab. Choose Vocabulary from the list of subtopics. Read and view the information in the Review Materials section, and then complete the Practices and Tests in the Activities section. You can check your scores by clicking on the Gradebook tab.

MASTERY TEST 1 Vocabulary Skills

Name _____ Section _____

Date _____ Number right _____ × 20 points = Score _____

Directions: For each of the following statements, select the answer that correctly defines the bold-faced word.

_____C_____ 1. In the past two hundred years, many species of whales have been hunted almost to the point of extinction. In response to worldwide concern over whales, the International Whaling Commission (IWC) declared a **moratorium** on commercial whaling in 1986.
a. promotion
b. proposition
c. stopping of activity
d. competition

_____B_____ 2. After months of declining profits, the company president declared that he would cut his salary to $1 until business improved. His announcement was intended to restore trust in the company and **avert** panic in its stockholders.
a. repair   c. inspire
b. prevent   d. ignore

_____D_____ 3. Although Lillian was 94 years old, she was healthy and mentally sharp. As she had done for most of her life, she insisted on living in her own apartment, buying her own groceries and paying her own bills, taking care of herself and making her own decisions—it was clear that she valued her **autonomy** above all else.
a. social life
b. family support
c. loneliness
d. independence

_____B_____ 4. Our idea of the perfect vacation includes first-class airline tickets, a deluxe hotel room, and 24-hour room service, whereas Anne and Neil prefer something much more **rustic.** The last place they stayed didn't even have indoor plumbing!
a. elegant
b. simple
c. comfortable
d. active

_____C_____ 5. The third-grade teacher marveled at the physical **disparities** among her students. Some were the size of kindergartners while others were almost as tall as she was.
a. dislikes
b. attitudes
c. differences
d. appearances

MASTERY TEST 2 Vocabulary Skills

Name _____ Section _____

Date _____ Number right _____ × 20 points = Score _____

> What information do this photograph and caption provide that the passage does not?

Directions: Read the following passage and choose the answer that best defines each boldfaced word from the passage.

At home, children learn attitudes and values that match their family's situation in life. At school, they learn a broader **perspective** that helps prepare them to take a role in the world beyond the family. At home, a child may have been the almost **exclusive** focus of **doting** parents, but in school, the child learns *universality*—that the same rules apply to everyone, regardless of who their parents are or how special they may be at home. These new values and ways of looking at the world sometimes even replace those the child learns at home.

Sociologists have also identified a hidden **curriculum** in our schools. This term refers to values that, although not **explicitly** taught, are part of a school's "cultural message." For example, the stories and examples that are used to teach math and English may bring with them lessons in patriotism, democracy, justice, and honesty.

—adapted from Henslin, *Sociology: A Down-To-Earth Approach*, p. 83

Schools are one of the primary agents of socialization. One of their chief functions is to sort young people into the adult roles thought appropriate for them, and to teach them attitudes and skills that match these roles. What sorts of attitudes, motivations, goals, and adult roles do you think this child is learning?

_D_ 1. perspective
    a. education   c. system
    b. skill   d. point of view

_B_ 2. exclusive
    a. unfriendly   c. restricted
    b. sole   d. selective

_C_ 3. doting
    a. harmless   c. devoted
    b. elderly   d. uncomfortable

_A_ 4. curriculum
    a. program   c. replacement
    b. appearance   d. classroom

_B_ 5. explicitly
    a. importantly   c. rudely
    b. openly   d. typically

Name _____ Section _____

Date _____ Number right* _____ × 10 points = Score _____

disease
(2)

Compulsive or Pathological Gambling
Rebecca J. Donatelle *feeling*

This selection from the health textbook, *Access to Health, Green Edition*, describes the characteristics and consequences of the disorder known as compulsive gambling.

> **Vocabulary Preview**
> **pathological** (par. 2) caused by or related to a disease

1   Gambling is a form of recreation and entertainment for millions of Americans. Most people who gamble do so casually and moderately to experience the excitement of anticipating a win.

2   However, over 2 million Americans are **compulsive (pathological) gamblers**, *obsessive* and 6 million more are considered at risk for developing a gambling addiction. The American Psychiatric Association (APA) recognizes pathological gambling as a mental disorder and lists ten characteristic behaviors, including preoccupation with gambling, unsuccessful efforts to cut back or quit, using gambling to escape problems, and lying to family members to conceal the extent of involvement.

3   Gamblers and drug addicts describe many similar cravings and highs. A recent study supports what many experts believe to be true: that compulsive gambling is like drug addiction. Compulsive gamblers in this study were found to have decreased blood flow to a key section of the brain's reward system. Much as with people who abuse drugs, it is thought that compulsive gamblers compensate for this deficiency in their brain's reward system by

DIDyouKNOW?

The average tuition for a 4-year public university in 2007–2008 was $6,185. If you gamble and lose an average of $120 per week for a full year, you'll have spent your entire year's tuition!

Source: Trends in College Pricing, 2007. The College Board, New York.

*To calculate the number right, use items 1–10 under "Mastery Test Skills Check."

overdoing it and getting hooked. Most compulsive gamblers state that they seek excitement even more than money. They place progressively larger bets to obtain the desired level of exhilaration.

4   Gambling problems are more prevalent among men than among women. Gambling prevalence is also higher among lower-income individuals, those who are divorced, African Americans, older adults, and people residing within 50 miles of a casino. Residents in Southern states, where opportunities to gamble have increased significantly over the past 20 years, also have higher gambling rates?

5   Among students, gambling is on the rise on college campuses across the nation. Since 2002, the University of Pennsylvania's Annenburg Public Policy Center has been conducting a tracking survey of gambling among young people aged 14 to 22. Their survey reported that in 2005, 15.5 percent of college students reported gambling once a week, up from 8.3 percent in 2002, an 87 percent increase. Men dominated the gambling scene, with 26 percent reportedly doing it each week, whereas 5.5 percent of women reported gambling weekly.

6   What accounts for this trend? College students have easier access to gambling opportunities than ever before, with the advent of online gambling, a growing number of casinos, scratch tickets, lotteries, and sports-betting networks. In particular, the largest boost has been from the increasing popularity of poker. Access to poker on the Internet and poker tournaments that are frequently televised have revived the game, causing many young people to spend an unhealthy amount of time and money participating in online poker tournaments.

7   Other characteristics associated with gambling among college students include spending more time watching TV and using computers for nonacademic purposes, spending less time studying, earning lower grades, participating in intercollegiate athletics, engaging in heavy episodic drinking, and using illicit drugs in the past year. See the Health Headlines box on page 92 for more on college students and gambling.

8   Whereas casual gamblers can stop anytime they wish and are capable of understanding why they need to stop, compulsive gamblers are unable to control the urge to gamble even in the face of devastating consequences: high debt, legal problems, and the loss of everything meaningful, including homes, families, jobs, health, and even their lives. Gambling can also have a detrimental effect on health: cardiovascular problems affect 38 percent of compulsive gamblers, and their suicide rate is 20 times higher than that of the general population.

Health Headlines

Gambling and College Students

9   Although many people gamble occasionally without it ever becoming a problem, many otherwise "model" students can find themselves caught up in the rush of making big bets and winning even bigger money. Consider the story of John,* a Lehigh University sophomore, who is the son of a Baptist minister, a fraternity member, a cellist in the university orchestra, and the sophomore class president—the epitome of a responsible student active in the community and serving as a role model to the student body. When John was arrested for allegedly robbing the Wachovia Bank branch in Allentown, Pennsylvania, making off with $2,781, many wondered why such a good kid would be driven to such an act. According to the Associated Press, his lawyer stated that his client had run up about $5,000 in debt playing online poker. In a desperate move to feed his compulsive gambling addiction, John turned to bank robbery.

10   Compulsive gambling on college campuses has become a big concern for college administrators as gambling grows ever more popular among students. The National Collegiate Athletic Association (NCAA) estimates that each year during March Madness (the men's college basketball tournament), there are over 1.2 million active gambling pools, with over 2.5 billion dollars gambled. More and more of these dollars come from the pockets of college students. There is growing evidence, in fact, that betting on college campuses is interfering with students' financial and academic futures. In a recent survey, approximately 60 percent of students reported they had gambled, and almost 13 percent reported a significant loss of time and 12 percent a significant loss of money. Consider the following:

- Almost 53 percent of college students have participated in most forms of gambling, including casino gambling, lottery tickets, racing, and sports betting in the past month.
- At least 78 percent of youths have placed a bet by the age of 18.
- An estimated 18 percent of men and 4 percent of women on college

*Not his real name

campuses could be classified as problem gamblers.

- The three most common reasons college students give for gambling are risk, excitement, and the chance to make money.

11   Although most college students who gamble are able to do so without developing a problem, warning signs of problem gambling include the following:

- Frequent talk about gambling
- Spending more time or money on gambling than can be afforded

- Borrowing money to gamble
- Encouraging or challenging others to gamble
- Selling sports-betting cards or organizing sports pools
- Possession of gambling paraphernalia such as lottery tickets or poker items
- Missing or being late for school, work, or family activities due to gambling
- Feeling sad, anxious, fearful, or angry about gambling losses

MASTERY TEST SKILLS CHECK

Directions: Select the best answer for each of the following questions.

Checking Your Comprehension

_____ 1. The purpose of this selection is to
   a. compare different forms of recreation and entertainment.
   b. identify treatment options for people with addictions.
   c. describe compulsive gambling and its effects.
   d. discuss popular trends on college campuses.

_____ 2. The main point of paragraph 3 is that
   a. compulsive gambling is similar to drug addiction.
   b. compulsive gamblers often become addicted to drugs.
   c. drug addicts have decreased blood flow to the brain's reward system.
   d. gamblers and drug addicts crave excitement.

_____ 3. The largest boost to college gambling has come from the increasing popularity of
   a. lotteries.
   b. sports-betting networks.
   c. scratch tickets.
   d. poker.

_____ 4. Gambling rates are higher among all of the following groups *except*
   a. divorced people.
   b. women.
   c. residents in Southern states.
   d. people living within 50 miles of a casino.

_____ 5. Paragraph 8 is primarily about
   a. casual gamblers' legal problems.
   b. the causes of addictive behavior.
   c. health problems among gamblers.
   d. the negative consequences of compulsive gambling.

Applying Your Skills

_____ 6. In paragraph 2, the word that is given as a synonym clue for *compulsive* is
   a. pathological.
   b. psychiatric.
   c. mental.
   d. unsuccessful.

_____ 7. In paragraph 3, the synonym for the word *exhilaration* is
   a. addiction.
   b. compulsive.
   c. excitement.
   d. cravings.

_____ 8. In paragraph 4, inference clues indicate that the word *prevalent* means
   a. unusual or rare.
   b. widespread or common.
   c. decreasing in popularity.
   d. expensive.

_____ 9. In paragraph 8, the examples of "high debt, legal problems, and the loss of everything meaningful" indicate that the word *devastating* means
   a. unimportant.
   b. rewarding.
   c. pleasant.
   d. crushing.

_____ 10. In paragraph 8, the meaning of the word *detrimental* is indicated by which of the following types of context clues?
   a. contrast
   b. example
   c. definition
   d. inference

Studying Words

_____ 11. The word *deficiency* (par. 3) means
   a. similarity.
   b. shortage.
   c. creation.
   d. approach.

_____ 12. In the sentence "Men dominated the gambling scene" (par. 5), the word *dominated* means
   a. took command.
   b. were powerful.
   c. were larger in number.
   d. looked down on.

_____ 13. The word *advent* (par. 6) means
   a. arrival.
   b. average.
   c. ending.
   d. advertisement.

_____ 14. The word *nonacademic* (par. 7) means
   a. published.
   b. studious.
   c. not harmful.
   d. not educational.

_____ 15. The word *epitome* (par. 9 in the Health Headlines box) means
   a. opponent.
   b. model.
   c. message.
   d. delivery.

For more practice, ask your instructor for an opportunity to work on the mastery tests that appear in the Test Bank.

Summarizing the Reading

Directions: Complete the following summary of the reading by filling in the blanks.

Over 2 million Americans are _compulsive_ or pathological gamblers, and 6 million more may develop a gambling _addiction_. The American _Psychiatric_ Association recognizes pathological gambling as a _mental disorder_ with ten characteristic behaviors. Compulsive gambling is similar to _drug addiction_. Gambling problems are more _prevalent_ ~~common~~ among men, and gambling rates are higher among several groups. Gambling is increasing among _college students_, a trend related to students' easy access to gambling opportunities and especially to the revival of _poker_. In contrast to _casual_ gamblers, compulsive gamblers cannot _control_ the urge to gamble despite facing harmful _consequences_ for their financial, emotional, and physical health.

Reading Visually

1. What concept does the "Did You Know?" box on p. 90 illustrate or correspond to in the reading?

   120 per week for a full year, cost entire years' tuition

2. What is your overall impression of the photograph in the Health Headlines box on page 92? How does the photograph contrast with the information that is discussed in the box?

   _____

   _____

   _____

Thinking Critically about the Reading

WRITE IN YOUR JOURNAL

1. How big a problem do you think gambling is at your school or among the people you know? Were the statistics in the selection surprising to you?

2. Reread the warning signs of problem gambling in the Health Headlines box. Could those warning signs apply to any of your own habits or behaviors? Try replacing the word *gambling* with another word or phrase such as *shopping*, *texting*, or *video gaming*.

3. Why did the author include the story about John (par. 9 in the Health Headlines box)? What does his story contribute to the selection?

Using Word Parts and Learning New Words

Looking at …
Word Parts

This ingredients label is taken from a can of rice pudding. How many of the ingredients and terms are familiar? Do you know what monosaturates, acidity regulators, and sodium carbonate are? If not, how could you figure out the meanings?

This chapter shows you how to use your knowledge of word parts to figure out the meanings of words you do not know, how to use a dictionary and thesaurus, and how to use an index card system to learn and remember new words.

LEARNING PREFIXES, ROOTS, AND SUFFIXES

OBJECTIVE 1

Many students build their vocabulary word by word: if they study ten new words, then they have learned ten new words. If they study 30 words, they can recall 30 meanings. Would you like a better and faster way to build your vocabulary?

By learning the meanings of the parts that make up a word, you will be able to figure out the meanings of many more words. For example, if you learn that *pre-* means "before," then you can begin to figure out hundreds of words that begin with *pre-* (*premarital, premix, preemployment*).

In this chapter you will learn about compound words and about the beginnings, middles, and endings of words called prefixes, roots, and suffixes.

Suppose that you came across the following sentence in a human anatomy textbook:

> Trichromatic plates are used frequently in the text to illustrate the position of body organs.

If you did not know the meaning of *trichromatic,* how could you determine it? There are no clues in the sentence context. One solution is to look up the word in a dictionary. An easier and faster way is to break the word into parts and analyze the meaning of each part. Many words in the English language are made up of word parts called **prefixes, roots,** and **suffixes.** These word parts have specific meanings that, when added together, can help you determine the meaning of the word as a whole.

The word *trichromatic* can be divided into three parts: its *prefix, root,* and *suffix*.

Prefix	+	Root	+	Suffix	=	New word
tri	+	chrom	+	atic	=	trichromatic

Meaning ⟶ three + color + characteristic of = having three colors

You can see from this analysis that *trichromatic* means "having three colors."

Here are a few other examples of words that you can figure out by using prefixes, roots, and suffixes:

The parents thought the child was **unteachable.**

un- = not

teach = help someone learn

-able = able to do something

unteachable = not able to be taught

The student was a **nonconformist.**

non- = not

conform = go along with others

-ist = one who does something

nonconformist = someone who does not go along with others

The first step in using the prefix-root-suffix method is to become familiar with the most commonly used word parts. The prefixes and roots listed in Tables 4-1 (p. 100) and 4-2 (p. 105) will give you a good start in determining the meanings of thousands of words without looking them up in the dictionary. For instance, more than ten thousand words can begin with the prefix *non-*. Not all these words are listed in a collegiate dictionary, but they would appear in an unabridged dictionary. Another common prefix, *pseudo-*, is used in more than four hundred words. A small amount of time spent learning word parts can yield a large payoff in new words learned.

Before you begin to use word parts to figure out new words, there are a few things you need to know:

1. **In most cases, a word is built upon at least one root.**
2. **Words can have more than one prefix, root, or suffix.**
    a. Words can be made up of two or more roots (geo/logy).
    b. Some words have two prefixes (in/sub/ordination).
    c. Some words have two suffixes (beauti/ful/ly).
3. **Words do not always have a prefix and a suffix.**
    a. Some words have neither a prefix nor a suffix (read).
    b. Others have a suffix but no prefix (read/ing).
    c. Others have a prefix but no suffix (pre/read).
4. **The spelling of roots may change as they are combined with suffixes.** Some common variations are included in Table 4-2.

5. **Different prefixes, roots, or suffixes may have the same meaning.** For example, the prefixes *bi-*, *di-*, and *duo-* all mean "two."

6. **Sometimes you may identify a group of letters as a prefix or root but find that it does not carry the meaning of that prefix or root.** For example, the letters *mis* in the word *missile* are part of the root and are not the prefix *mis-*, which means "wrong, bad."

Prefixes

Prefixes appear at the beginning of many English words: they alter the meaning of the root to which they are connected. For example, if you add the prefix *re-* to the word *read*, the word *reread* is formed, meaning "to read again." If *pre-* is added to the word *reading*, the word *prereading* is formed, meaning "before reading." If the prefix *post-* is added, the word *postreading* is formed, meaning "after reading." In Table 4-1 (p. 100), more than 40 common prefixes are grouped according to meaning.

EXERCISE 4-1   **Using Prefixes**

Directions: Using the list of common prefixes in Table 4-1, match each word in Column A with its meaning in Column B. Write the letter of your choice in the space provided.

	Column A	Column B
f	1. misplaced	a. half of a circle
D	2. postgraduate	b. build again
I	3. dehumidify	c. tiny duplicate of printed material
A	4. semicircle	d. continuing studies past graduation
H	5. nonprofit	e. not fully developed
B	6. reconstruct	f. put in the wrong position
J	7. triathlete	g. build up electrical power again
C	8. microcopy	h. not for making money
G	9. recharge	i. to remove moisture from
E	10. immature	j. one who participates in three-part sporting events

TABLE 4-1 Common Prefixes

Prefix	Meaning	Sample Word
Prefixes referring to amount or number		
mono/uni	one	monocle/unicycle
bi/di/du	two	bimonthly/divorce/duet
tri	three	triangle
quad	four	quadrant
quint/pent	five	quintet/pentagon
deci	ten	decimal
centi	hundred	centigrade
milli	thousand	milligram
micro	small	microscope
multi/poly	many	multipurpose/polygon
semi	half	semicircle
equi	equal	equidistant
Prefixes meaning "not" (negative)		
a	not	asymmetrical
anti	against	antiwar
contra	against, opposite	contradict
dis	apart, away, not	disagree
in/il/ir/im	not	incorrect/illogical/irreversible/impossible
mis	wrongly	misunderstand
non	not	nonfiction
pseudo	false	pseudoscientific
un	not	unpopular
Prefixes giving direction, location, or placement		
ab	away	absent
ad	toward	adhesive
ante/pre	before	antecedent/premarital
circum/peri	around	circumference/perimeter
com/col/con	with, together	compile/collide/convene
de	away, from	depart
dia	through	diameter
ex/extra	from, out of, former	ex-wife/extramarital
hyper	over, excessive	hyperactive
inter	between	interpersonal
intro/intra	within, into, in	introduction/intramural
post	after	posttest
re	back, again	review
retro	backward	retrospect
sub	under, below	submarine
super	above, extra	supercharge
tele	far	telescope
trans	across, over	transcontinental

EXERCISE 4-2   **Using Prefixes**

Directions: Use the list of common prefixes in Table 4-1 to determine the meaning of each of the following words. Write a brief definition or synonym for each. If you are unfamiliar with the root, you may need to check a dictionary.

1. interoffice: _____

2. supernatural: _more than_ _____

3. nonsense: _no_ _____

4. introspection: _inside_ _____

5. prearrange: _get ready._ _____

6. reset: _____

7. subtopic: _____

8. transmit: _to send_ _____

9. multidimensional: _many_ _____

10. imperfect: _not_ _____

EXERCISE 4-3   **Using Prefixes to Write Brief Definitions**

Directions: Write a brief definition for each word in boldfaced type.

1. an **atypical** child: _unusual_ _____

2. to **hyperventilate**: _above_ _____

3. an **extraordinary** request: _outside uncommon_ _____

4. **semisoft** cheese: _not complete_ _____

5. **antisocial** behavior: _____

6. to **circumnavigate** the globe: _around_ _____

7. a **triweekly** publication: _____three weeks_____ 3 in 1 week

8. an **uneventful** weekend: _____bountie_____

9. a **disfigured** face: _____

10. to **exhale** smoke: _____breathe out_____

EXERCISE 4-4   Using Prefixes

Directions: Read each of the following sentences. Use your knowledge of prefixes to fill in the blank to complete the word.

1. A person who speaks two languages is ___bi___ **lingual.**

2. A letter or number written beneath a line of print is called a ___sub___ **script.**

3. The new sweater had a snag, and I returned it to the store because it was ___im___ **perfect.**

4. The flood damage was permanent and ___ir___ **reversible.**

5. I was not given the correct date and time; I was ___mis___ **informed.**

6. People who speak several different languages are ___mutil___ **lingual.**

7. A musical ___inter___ **lude** was played between the events in the ceremony.

8. I decided the magazine was uninteresting, so I ___dis___ **continued** my subscription.

9. Merchandise that does not pass factory inspection is considered ___sub___ **standard** and sold at a discount.

10. The tuition refund policy approved this week will apply to last year's tuition as well; the policy will be ___retro___ **active** to January 1 of last year.

11. The elements were ___re___ **acting** with each other when they began to bubble and their temperature rose.

12. ___Contra___ **ceptives** are widely used to prevent unwanted pregnancies.

13. All of the waitresses were required to wear the restaurant's ___uni___ **form.**

HW Pp03~114

14. The ___*in*___ **viewer** asked the presidential candidates unexpected questions about important issues.

15. The draperies were ___*dis*___ **colored** from long exposure to the sun.

EXERCISE 4-5   ## Using Prefixes

Directions: Use your knowledge of prefixes to supply the missing word in each sentence. Write the word in the space provided.

1. Our house is a duplex. The one next door with three apartments is a ___*triplex*___.

2. A preparation applied to the skin to reduce or prevent perspiration is called an ___*antiperspirant*___.

3. A person who cannot read or write is ___*illibterate*___.

4. I did not use my real name; instead I gave a ___*pseudonym*___.

5. If someone seems to have greater powers than do normal humans, he or she might be called ___*superhuman*___.

6. If you plan to continue to take college courses after you graduate, you will be taking ___*postgraduate*___ courses.

7. Substances that fight bacteria are known as ___*anti*___ drugs.

8. The branch of biology that deals with very small living organisms is ___*microbiology*___.

9. In the metric system a ___*centimetre*___ is one one-hundredth of a meter.

10. One one-thousandth of a second is called a ___*millisecond*___.

EXERCISE 4-6   ## Using Prefixes

Directions: Working in teams of two, list as many words as you can think of for two of the following prefixes: *multi-, mis-, trans-, com-, inter-*. Then share your lists with the class.

Roots

Roots carry the basic or core meaning of a word. Hundreds of root words are used to build words in the English language. More than thirty of the most common and most useful are listed in Table 4-2. Knowledge of the meanings of these roots will enable you to unlock the meanings of many words. For example, if you know that the root *dic/dict* means "tell or say," then you would have a clue to the meanings of such words as *dictate* (to speak for someone to write down), *diction* (wording or manner of speaking), or *dictionary* (book that "tells" what words mean).

EXERCISE 4-7 **Using Roots**

Directions: Using the list of common roots in Table 4-2, match each word in Column A with its meaning in Column B. Write the letter of your choice in the space provided.

Column A

_____ G 1. benediction

_____ I 2. audible

_____ H 3. missive

_____ J 4. telemarketing

_____ A 5. mortician

_____ D 6. intervene

_____ B 7. reverted

_____ E 8. aqueduct

_____ C 9. photoactive

_____ F 10. vocalize

Column B

a. undertaker

b. went back to

c. able to respond to light

d. come between two things

e. channel or pipe that brings water from a distance

f. use the voice

g. blessing

h. letter or message

i. can be heard

j. selling a product by phone

TABLE 4-2   Common Roots

Common Root	Meaning	Sample Word
aster/astro	star	astronaut
aud/audit	hear	audible
bene	good, well	benefit
bio	life	biology
cap	take, seize	captive
chron/chrono	time	chronology
cog	to learn	cognitive
corp	body	corpse
cred	believe	incredible
dict/dic	tell, say	predict
duc/duct	lead	introduce
fact/fac	make, do	factory
geo	earth	geophysics
graph	write	telegraph
log/logo/logy	study, thought	psychology
mit/miss	send	permit/dismiss
mort/mor	die, death	immortal
path	feeling	sympathy
phono	sound, voice	telephone
photo	light	photosensitive
port	carry	transport
scop	seeing	microscope
scrib/script	write	inscription
sen/sent	feel	insensitive
spec/spic/spect	look, see	retrospect
tend/tens/tent	stretch or strain	tension
terr/terre	land, earth	territory
theo	god	theology
ven/vent	come	convention
vert/vers	turn	invert
vis/vid	see	invisible/video
voc	call	vocation

EXERCISE 4-8   **Using Roots**

Directions: Use the list of common roots in Table 4-2 to determine the meanings of the following words. Write a brief definition or synonym for each, checking a dictionary if necessary.

1. dictum: _dic / pronouncement_

2. biomedicine: _bio / bio science applied to medicine_

3. photocopy: _photo / copy_

4. porter: _gate keeper_

5. visibility: _distance, view_

6. credentials: _identification_

7. speculate: _consider, wonder to risk_

8. terrain: _land_

9. audition: _test, interview, trial_

10. sentiment: _feeling, emotion_

11. astrophysics: _physical science, astronomy_

12. capacity: _volume, size_

13. chronicle: _record, history_

14. corporation: _company, business, firm_

15. facile: _superficial_

16. autograph: _signature_

17. sociology: _study of society_

18. phonometer: _____

19. sensation: _feeling_

20. vocal: _spoken, verbal_

EXERCISE 4-9   **Completing Sentences**

Directions: Complete each of the following sentences with one of the words listed below.

apathetic	dictated	graphic	scriptures	tendon
captivated	extensive	phonics	spectators	verdict
deduce	extraterrestrial	prescribed	synchronized	visualize

1. The jury brought in its _____verdict_____ after one hour of deliberation.

2. Religious or holy writings are called _____scriptures_____ .

3. She closed her eyes and tried to _____visualize_____ the license plate number.

4. The _____spectators_____ watching the football game were tense.

5. The doctor _____prescribed_____ two types of medication.

6. The list of toys the child wanted for his birthday was _____extensive_____ .

7. The criminal appeared _____apathetic_____ when the judge pronounced the sentence.

8. The runners _____synchronized_____ their watches before beginning the race.

9. The textbook contained numerous _____graphic_____ aids, including maps, charts, and diagrams.

10. The study of the way different parts of words sound is called _____phonics_____ .

11. The athlete strained a(n) _____tendon_____ and was unable to continue training.

12. The movie was about a(n) _____extraterrestrial_____ , a creature not from earth.

13. The district manager _____dictated_____ a letter to her secretary, who then typed it.

14. Through his attention-grabbing performance, he _____captivated_____ the audience.

15. By putting together the clues, the detective was finally able to _____deduce_____ who committed the crime.

EXERCISE 4-10   Using Roots

Directions: List two words for each of the following roots: *dict/dic, spec/spic/spect, fact/fac, phono, scrib/script.*

Suffixes

Suffixes are word endings that often change the part of speech of a word. For example, adding the suffix -*y* to the noun *cloud* forms the adjective *cloudy*. Accompanying the change in part of speech is a shift in meaning (*cloudy* means "resembling clouds; overcast with clouds; dimmed or dulled as if by clouds").

Often, several different words can be formed from a single root word by adding different suffixes.

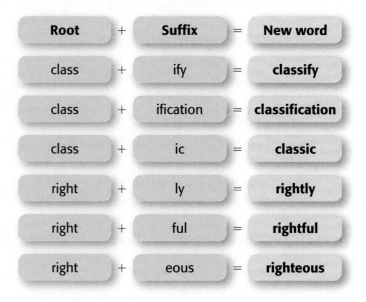

Root	+	Suffix	=	New word
class	+	ify	=	classify
class	+	ification	=	classification
class	+	ic	=	classic
right	+	ly	=	rightly
right	+	ful	=	rightful
right	+	eous	=	righteous

If you know the meaning of the root word and the ways in which different suffixes affect the meaning of the root word, you will be able to figure out a word's meaning when a suffix is added. A list of common suffixes and their meanings appears in Table 4-3.

You can expand your vocabulary by learning the variations in meaning that occur when suffixes are added to words you already know. When you find a word that you do not know, look for the root. Then, using the sentence the word is in (its context; see Chapter 3), figure out what the word means with the suffix added. Occasionally you may find that the spelling of the root word has been changed. For instance, a final *e* may be dropped, a final consonant may be doubled, or a final *y* may be changed to *i*. Consider the possibility of such changes when trying to identify the root word.

The article was a **compilation** of facts.

root + suffix

compil(e) + -ation = something that has been compiled, or put together into an orderly form

We were concerned with the **legality** of our decision to change addresses.

root + suffix

legal + -ity = something pertaining to legal matters

Our college is one of the most **prestigious** in the state.

root + suffix

prestig(e) + -ious = having prestige or distinction

TABLE 4-3   Common Suffixes

Suffix	Sample Word
Suffixes that refer to a state, condition, or quality	
able	touchable
ance	assistance
ation	confrontation
ence	reference
ible	tangible
ion	discussion
ity	superiority
ive	permissive
ment	amazement
ness	kindness
ous	jealous
ty	loyalty
y	creamy
Suffixes that mean "one who"	
an	Italian
ant	participant
ee	referee
eer	engineer
ent	resident
er	teacher
ist	activist
or	advisor
Suffixes that mean "pertaining to or referring to"	
al	autumnal
ship	friendship
hood	brotherhood
ward	homeward

EXERCISE 4-11   Using Suffixes

Directions: For each suffix shown in Table 4-3, write another example of a word you know that has that suffix.

EXERCISE 4-12   Creating New Words by Adding Suffixes

Directions: For each of the words listed, add a suffix so that the word will complete the sentence. Write the new word in the space provided. Check a dictionary if you are unsure of the spelling.

1. converse

   Our phone ___conversation___ lasted ten minutes.

2. assist

   The medical ___assistant___ labeled the patient's blood samples.

3. qualify

   The job applicant outlined his ___qualification___ to the interviewer.

4. intern

   The doctor completed her ___internship___ at Memorial Medical Center.

5. eat

   We did not realize that the blossoms of the plant could be ___eatable___ eaten.

6. audio

   She spoke so softly that her voice was not ___audible___.

7. season

   It is usually very dry in July, but this year it has rained constantly. The weather is not very ___seasonal___.

8. permit

   The professor granted her ___permission___ to miss class.

9. instruct

   The lecture on Freud was very ___instructive___.

10. remember

The wealthy businessman donated the building in ___remembrance___ of his deceased father.

11. mortal

The ___mortality___ rate in Ethiopia is very high.

12. president

The ___presidential___ race held many surprises.

13. feminine

She called herself a ___feminine___, although she never actively supported the movement for equal rights for women.

14. hazard

The presence of toxic waste in the lake is ___hazardous___ to health.

15. destine

The young man felt it was his ___destiny___ to become a priest.

EXERCISE 4-13   Adding Suffixes

Directions: Working with a classmate, for each word listed below, write as many new words as you can create by adding suffixes. Share your findings with the class.

1. compare: _____comparison_____

2. adapt: _____adaptation_____

3. right: _____righteous_____

4. identify: _____identification_____

5. will: _____willing_____

6. prefer: _____preferable_____

7. notice: _____noticeable_____

8. like: _____likeable   dislike_____

9. pay: _____ *Payable* _____

10. promote: _____ *promotion* _____

How to Use Word Parts

Think of roots as being at the root or core of a word's meaning. There are many more roots than are listed in Table 4-2. You already know many of these because they are used in everyday speech. Think of prefixes as word parts that are added before the root to qualify or change its meaning. Think of suffixes as add-ons that make the word fit grammatically into the sentence in which it is used.

When you come upon a word you do not know, keep the following pointers in mind:

Using Word Parts

1. **First, look for the root.** Think of this as looking for a word inside a larger word. Often a letter or two will be missing.

un/utter/able	defens/ible
inter/colleg/iate	re/popular/ize
post/operat/ive	non/adapt/able
im/measur/ability	non/commit/tal

2. **If you do not recognize the root, then you will probably not be able to figure out the word.** The next step is to check its meaning in a dictionary. For tips on locating words in a dictionary rapidly and easily, see "Using a Dictionary" page 120.

3. **If you did recognize the root word, look for a prefix.** If there is one, determine how it changes the meaning of the word.

un/utterable	un- = not
post/operative	post- = after

4. **Locate the suffix.** Determine how it further adds to or changes the meaning of the root word.

unutter/able	-able = able to
postoperat/ive	-ive = state or condition

5. **Next, try out the meaning in the sentence in which the word was used.** Substitute your meaning for the word, and see whether the sentence makes sense.

> Some of the victim's thoughts were **unutterable** at the time of the crime.
>
> unutterable = cannot be spoken
>
> My sister was worried about the cost of **postoperative** care.
>
> postoperative = describing state or condition after an operation

EXERCISE 4-14   ## Identifying Roots and Writing Definitions

Directions: Use the steps listed previously to determine the meaning of each boldfaced word. Underline the root in each word, and then write a brief definition of the word that fits its use in the sentence.

1. The doctor felt the results of the X-rays were **indisputable**

   unquestionable

2. The **dissimilarity** among the three brothers was surprising.

   unlike

3. The **extortionist** demanded two payments of $10,000 each, threatening physical harm if it was not paid ontime.

   a person who engages in extortion

4. It is **permissible** to camp in most state parks.

   allowable

5. The student had an unusually **retentive** memory.

   having power, property

6. The **traumatic** event changed the child's attitude toward animals.

   an injury, emotional upset

7. We were surprised by her **insincerity**.

   not sincere

8. The child's **hypersensitivity** worried his parents.

   excessively   sensitive   overly

9. The English instructor told Peter that he had written a **creditable** paper.

   praiseworthy belief

10. The rock group's agent hoped to **repopularize** their first hit song.

    to make   popular

11. The gambler was filled with **uncertainty** about the horse race.

    doubt

12. The **nonenforcement** of the speed limit led to many deaths.

    not enforce

13. The effects of the disease were **irreversible**.

    not   reversible

14. The mysterious music seemed to **foretell** the murder of the movie's heroine.

    predict

15. The **polyphony** filled the concert hall.

    music   polyhol

16. Sailors used to think the North Sea **unnavigable**.

17. She received a **dishonorable** discharge from the Marines.

    lack of   honor /integrity

18. The criminal was **unapologetic** to the judge about the crimes he had committed.

    not sorry,   not apologize

19. A systems analysis revealed that the factory was **underproductive**.

    less   productive

20. He rotated the dial **counterclockwise**.

    opposite   direction

EXERCISE 4-15   **Using Word Parts**

Directions: Read each of the following paragraphs and determine the meaning of each boldfaced word. Write a brief definition for each in the space provided.

> What is the purpose of this photo and caption?

A. The values and norms of most **subcultures** blend in with mainstream society. In some cases, however, some of the group's values and norms place it at odds with the dominant culture. **Sociologists** use the term **counterculture** to refer to such groups. To better see this distinction, consider motorcycle enthusiasts and motorcycle gangs. Motorcycle **enthusiasts**—who emphasize personal freedom and speed and **affirm** cultural values of success through work or education—are members of a subculture. In contrast, the Hell's Angels, Pagans, and Bandidos not only stress freedom and speed but also value dirtiness and contempt toward women, work, and education. This makes them a counterculture. Countercultures do not have to be negative, however. Back in the 1800s, the Mormons were a counterculture that challenged the dominant culture's core value of **monogamy**.

—Henslin, *Sociology: A Down-to-Earth Approach*, p. 52

1. subcultures

   an ethnic, social group exhibiting characteristic patterns of behaviour sufficient to distinguish it from others

2. sociologists

   who studies society, social relationships

3. counterculture

   a culture of values & mores that run counter to those of established society

Why is professional dancing a subculture and not a counterculture?
Source: Bonnie Kamin/Photo Edit, Inc.

4. enthusiasts

   are who tends to become absorb in an interest

5. affirm

   confirm, validate support. agree with

6. monogamy

   married only once

B. Our **perception** of the richness or quality of the material in clothing, bedding, or upholstery is linked to its "feel," whether rough or smooth, flexible or **inflexible**. We **equate** a smooth fabric, such as silk, with luxury, whereas we consider denim to be practical and **durable**. Fabrics composed of **scarce** materials or that require a high degree of processing to achieve their smoothness or fineness tend to be more expensive and thus we assume they are of a higher class.

—adapted from Solomon, *Consumer Behavior*, pp. 62–63

1. perception

   observation, concept understanding.

2. inflexible

   unyielding stubborn

3. equate

   equalize

4. durable

   lasting

5. scarce 缺乏

   not abundant

C. The college years mark a critical **transition** period for young adults as they move away from families and establish themselves as **independent** adults. The transition to independence will be easier for those who have successfully accomplished earlier developmental tasks, such as learning how to solve problems, make and evaluate decisions, define and **adhere** to personal values, and establish both casual and **intimate** relationships. People who have not fulfilled these earlier tasks may find their lives interrupted by **recurrent** "crises" left over from earlier stages. For example, if they did not learn to trust others in childhood, they may have difficulty establishing intimate relationships as adults.

—Donatelle, *Health: The Basics*, p. 34

1. transition

   change

2. independent

   not dependent not reli

3. adhere

   to give support.

4. intimate

   affectionate close

5. recurrent

   repeating frequently

D.   The **biosphere**, which extends from the atmosphere several kilometers above the Earth to the depths of the oceans, is all of the Earth that is **inhabited** by life. It encompasses a **multitude** of wildly diverse environments, some **hospitable** to life and others so hostile that the presence of any organism is surprising.

—Campbell et al., *Biology: Concepts & Connections*, p. 680

1. biosphere

   part of earth's crust, water & atmosphere that supports life

2. inhabited

   occupied

3. multitude

   great number

4. hospitable

   courteous, cordial, friendly   supportly

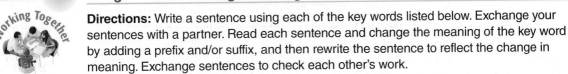

EXERCISE **4-16**

Using Prefixes to Change Meaning

Directions: Write a sentence using each of the key words listed below. Exchange your sentences with a partner. Read each sentence and change the meaning of the key word by adding a prefix and/or suffix, and then rewrite the sentence to reflect the change in meaning. Exchange sentences to check each other's work.

Key Words: allow   interest   regular   agree   direct

LEARNING NEW WORDS

OBJECTIVE 2

Most people think they have just one level of vocabulary and that this can be characterized as large or small, strong or weak. Actually, everyone has at least four levels of vocabulary, and each varies in strength:

1.   Words you use in everyday speech or writing

   Examples: decide, death, daughter, damp, date

2.   Words you know but seldom or never use in your own speech or writing

   Examples: rebuke, bleak, literate, originality, orient

3. Words you have heard or seen before but cannot fully define

> **Examples:** denounce, deficit, decadent, deductive, decisive

4. Words you have never heard or seen before

> **Examples:** doggerel, dogma, denigrate, deleterious, diatropism

In the spaces provided, list five words that fall under each of these four categories. It will be easy to think of words for Category 1. Words for Categories 2–4 may be taken from the following list:

contort	garbanzo	voluntary	impertinent
continuous	logic	resistance	delicacy
credible	connive	alien	impartial
activate	congruent	meditate	delve
deletion	demean	fraught	attentive
focus	liberate	gastronome	osmosis
manual	heroic	havoc	

Category 1	Category 2	Category 3	Category 4
_____	_____	_____	_____
_____	_____	_____	_____
_____	_____	_____	_____
_____	_____	_____	_____
_____	_____	_____	_____

To build your vocabulary, try to shift as many words as possible from a less familiar to a more familiar category. Use the following steps:

1. Start by noticing words.
2. Question, check, and remember their meanings.
3. Record new words and their meanings in a log, notebook, or computer file.
4. Use these new words often in your speech and writing.

SELECTING AND USING A DICTIONARY

Every writer needs to use a dictionary, not only to check spellings, but also to check meanings and the appropriate usage of words.

Print Dictionaries

You should have a desk or collegiate dictionary plus a pocket dictionary that you can carry with you to classes. Widely used dictionaries include:

> *The American Heritage Dictionary of the English Language*
> *Merriam-Webster's Collegiate Dictionary*
> *Webster's New World Dictionary of the American Language*

Online Dictionaries

Several dictionaries are available online. Two of the most widely used are *Merriam-Webster Online* (http://www.m-w.com) and *The American Heritage Dictionary* (http://yourdictionary.com/index.shtml)

Online dictionaries have several important advantages over print dictionaries.

- **Audio component.** Some online dictionaries such as Merriam-Webster and American Heritage feature an audio component that allows you to hear how the word is pronounced.

- **Multiple dictionary entries.** Some sites, such as Dictionary.com, display entries from several dictionaries at once for a particular word.

- **Misspellings.** If you aren't sure of how a word is spelled or you mistype it, several suggested words will be returned.

By permission. From MERRIAM-WEBSTER'S ONLINE DICTIONARY, © 2010 by Merriam-Webster, Incorporated. (www.Merriam-Webster.com)

If you have difficulty with spelling, a misspeller's dictionary is another valuable reference tool. It can help you locate correct spellings easily. Two commonly used sources are *Webster's New World Misspeller's Dictionary* and *How to Spell It: A Handbook of Commonly Misspelled Words*.

ESL Dictionaries

If you are an ESL student, be sure to purchase an ESL dictionary. Numerous ones are available in paperback editions, including *The Longman Advanced American Dictionary*.

Subject Area Dictionaries

Many subject areas have specialized dictionaries that list most of the important words used in that field. These dictionaries give specialized meanings for words and suggest how and when to use them. For the field of nursing, for instance, there is *Taber's Cyclopedic Medical Dictionary*. Other subject area dictionaries include *A Dictionary of Anthropology*, *The New Grove Dictionary of Music and Musicians*, and *A Dictionary of Economics*.

Using a Dictionary

The first step in using your dictionary is to become familiar with the kinds of information it provides. Here is a brief review of the information a dictionary entry contains. As you read, refer to the sample dictionary entry below.

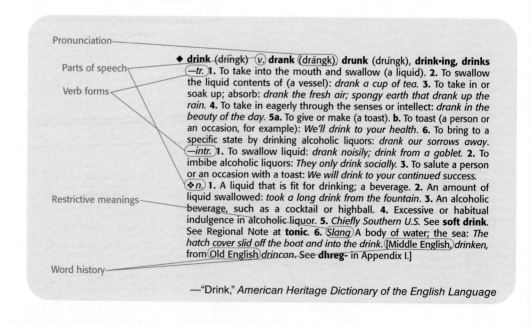

Pronunciation

Parts of speech

Verb forms

♦ **drink** (drĭngk) (*v.*) **drank** (drăngk) **drunk** (drŭngk), **drink·ing**, **drinks**
—tr. **1.** To take into the mouth and swallow (a liquid). **2.** To swallow the liquid contents of (a vessel): *drank a cup of tea.* **3.** To take in or soak up; absorb: *drank the fresh air; spongy earth that drank up the rain.* **4.** To take in eagerly through the senses or intellect: *drank in the beauty of the day.* **5a.** To give or make (a toast). **b.** To toast (a person or an occasion, for example): *We'll drink to your health.* **6.** To bring to a specific state by drinking alcoholic liquors: *drank our sorrows away.*
—intr. **1.** To swallow liquid: *drank noisily; drink from a goblet.* **2.** To imbibe alcoholic liquors: *They only drink socially.* **3.** To salute a person or an occasion with a toast: *We will drink to your continued success.*

Restrictive meanings

❖ *n.* **1.** A liquid that is fit for drinking; a beverage. **2.** An amount of liquid swallowed: *took a long drink from the fountain.* **3.** An alcoholic beverage, such as a cocktail or highball. **4.** Excessive or habitual indulgence in alcoholic liquor. **5.** *Chiefly Southern U.S.* See **soft drink**. See Regional Note at **tonic**. **6.** *Slang* A body of water; the sea: *The hatch cover slid off the boat and into the drink.* [Middle English, *drinken*, from Old English *drincan*. See **dhreg-** in Appendix I.]

Word history

—"Drink," *American Heritage Dictionary of the English Language*

1. **Pronunciation** The pronunciation of the word is given in parentheses. Symbols are used to indicate the sounds letters make within specific words. Refer to the pronunciation key printed on each page or on alternate pages of your print dictionary.

2. **Grammatical information** The part of speech is indicated, as well as information about different forms the word may take. Most dictionaries include

   - spelling of word variations.
   - principal forms of verbs (both regular and irregular).
   - plural forms of irregular nouns.
   - comparative and superlative forms of adjectives and adverbs.

3. **Meanings** Meanings are numbered and are usually grouped by the part of speech they represent.

4. **Restrictive meanings** Meanings that are limited to special situations are labeled. Some examples are:

   - *Slang*—casual language used only in conversation.
   - *Biol.*—words used in specialized fields, in this case biology.
   - *Regional*—words used only in certain parts of the United States.

5. **Synonyms** Words with similar meanings may be listed.

6. **Word history** The origin of the word (its etymology) is described. (Not all dictionaries include this feature.)

Beyond definitions, a dictionary contains a wealth of other information as well. For example, in the *American Heritage Dictionary*, Third Edition, you can find the history of the world *vampire*, the population of Vancouver, and an explanation of the New England expression "Vum!" Consider your dictionary a helpful and valuable resource that can assist you in expressing your ideas more clearly and correctly.

7. **Usage Notes** Some collegiate dictionaries contain a usage note or synonym section of the entry for words that are close in meaning to others. For example, a usage note for the word *indifferent* may explain how it differs in meaning from *unconcerned*, *detached*, and *uninterested*.

8. **Idioms** An idiom is a phrase that has a meaning other than what the common definitions of the words in the phrase indicate. For example, the phrase *wipe the slate clean* is not about slates. It means "to start over." Most idiomatic expressions are not used in academic writing because they are considered trite or overused.

EXERCISE 4-17   Using a Dictionary

Directions: Use a dictionary to answer the following questions:

1. How many meanings are listed for the word *fall*?

   ① To drop or sink due to gravity ② Experience a drop

2. How is the word *phylloxera* pronounced? (Record is phonetic spelling.)

   fillak seera.

3. Can the word *protest* be used other than as a verb? If so, how?   *this*

   N: 1. declaration or demostration of objection   V: 1. object, disagree
   3. assert formally

4. The word *prime* can mean first or original. List some of its other meanings.

   top, superlative, premier, main

5. What does the French expression *savoir faire* mean?

   know how to respond appropriately to any situation

6. List three meanings for the word *fault*.

   error, defect, blunder

7. List several words that are formed using the word *dream*.

8. What is the plural spelling of *addendum*?

   addenda

9. Explain the meaning of the idiom *turn over a new leaf.*

   change for the better

10. Define the word *reconstituted* and write a sentence using the word.

    bring something back to original state

    Ex: In the Phil, most people drink reconstituted milk.

Finding the Right Meaning

Most words have more than one meaning. When you look up the meaning of a new word, you must choose the meaning that fits the way the word is used in the sentence context. The meanings are often grouped by part of speech and are numbered consecutively in each group. Generally, the most common meanings of the word are listed first, with more specialized, less-common meanings appearing toward the end of the entry.

Here are a few suggestions for choosing the correct meaning from among those listed in an entry:

Finding Correct Meanings

1. **If you are familiar with the parts of speech, try to use these to locate the correct meaning.** For instance, if you are looking up the meaning of a word that names a person, place, or thing, you can save time by reading only those entries given after *n* (noun).

2. **For most types of college reading, you can skip definitions that give slang and colloquial (abbreviated *colloq.*) meanings.** Colloquial meanings refer to informal or spoken language.

3. **If you are not sure of the part of speech, read each meaning until you find a definition that seems correct.** Skip over restrictive meanings that are inappropriate.

4. **Test your choice by substituting the meaning in the sentence with which you are working.** Substitute the definition for the word and see whether it makes sense in the context (see Chapter 3).

Suppose you are looking up the word *oblique* to find its meaning in this sentence:

My sister's oblique answers to my questions made me suspicious.

Oblique is used in the above sentence as an adjective. Looking at the entries listed after *adj.* (adjective) below, you can skip over the definition under the heading *Geometry*, as it would not apply here. Definition 4a (indirect, evasive) best fits the way *oblique* is used in the sentence.

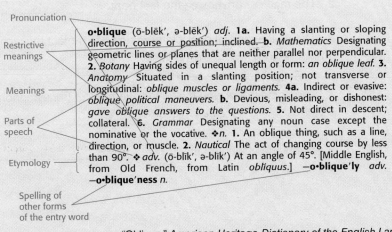

—"Oblique," *American Heritage Dictionary of the English Language*

EXERCISE 4-18   Finding Multiple Meanings

Directions: The following words have two or more meanings. Look them up in your dictionary, and write two sentences with different meanings for each word.

1. culture: _Culture_ _____ = arts collectively etc; Civilization; ① Understanding of literature, art, hum...
   Asian _____ = beliefs   ② Rearing of animals;

2. perch: _____ (put something high) ① To alight or take a position ② To be located (to land on perch)

3. surge: _____ (sudden increase) (move like wave) ① sudden power increase ② strong rolling movement ③ increase sudden ④ move forward stro...

4. apron: ① garment worn over the front of the body to protect the clothes ② area at an airport or hangar for manoeuvring and loading aircraft. ③ part of a stage in front of the curtain.

5. irregular: ① Not regular ② Contrary to rules or custom ③ Uneven

EXERCISE 4-19   Finding the Right Meaning

Directions: Use a dictionary to help you write an appropriate meaning for the boldfaced word in each of the following sentences.

1. The last contestant did not have a **ghost** of a chance: _trace_

2. The race car driver won the first **heat:** _Preliminary round_

3. The police took all possible **measures** to protect the witness.
   action taken

4. The orchestra played the first **movement** of the symphony.
   section of musical work

5. The plane stalled on the **apron:** _paved area at airport_

PRONOUNCING UNFAMILIAR WORDS

At one time or another, we come across words that we are unable to pronounce. To pronounce an unfamiliar word, sound it out syllable by syllable. Here are a few simple guidelines for dividing words into syllables:

1. **Divide compound words between the individual words that form the compound word.**

house/broken	house/hold	space/craft
green/house	news/paper	sword/fish

2. **Divide words between prefixes (word beginnings) and roots (base words) and/or between roots and suffixes (word endings).**

   Prefix + Root

pre/read	post/pone	anti/war

   Root + Suffix

sex/ist	agree/ment	list/ing

3. **Each syllable is a separate, distinct speech sound.** Pronounce the following words and try to hear the number of syllables in each.

expensive	ex/pen/sive = 3 syllables
recognize	rec/og/nize = 3 syllables
punctuate	punc/tu/ate = 3 syllables
complicated	com/pli/cat/ed = 4 syllables

4. **Each syllable has at least one vowel and usually one or more consonants.** (The letters *a, e, i, o, u,* and sometimes *y* are vowels. All other letters are consonants.)

as/sign	re/act	cou/pon	gen/er/al

5. **Divide words before a single consonant, unless the consonant is the letter *r*.**

hu/mid	re/tail	fa/vor	mor/on

6. **Divide words between two consonants appearing together.**

> pen/cil   lit/ter   lum/ber   sur/vive

7. **Divide words between two vowel sounds that appear together.**

> te/di/ous   ex/tra/ne/ous

These rules will prove helpful but, as you no doubt already know, there will always be exceptions.

EXERCISE 4-20   ## Syllabication

Directions: Use vertical marks (|) to divide each of the following words into syllables.

1. polka

2. pollute

3. ordinal

4. hallow

5. judicature

6. innovative

7. obtuse

8. germicide

9. futile

10. extol

11. tangelo

12. symmetry

13. telepathy

14. organic

15. hideous

16. tenacity

17. mesmerize

18. intrusive

19. infallible

20. fanaticism

Using a Thesaurus

A thesaurus is a dictionary of synonyms. It groups words with similar meanings together. A thesaurus is particularly useful when you want to do the following:

- locate the precise term to fit a particular situation
- find an appropriate descriptive word

- replace an overused or unclear word
- convey a more specific shade of meaning

Suppose you are looking for a more precise word for the expression *tell us about* in the following sentence:

> In class today, our chemistry instructor will **tell us about** our next assignment.

A thesaurus lists the following synonyms for "tell–explain":

10 explain, explicate, expound, exposit; give the meaning, tell the meaning of; spell out, unfold; account for, give reason for; clarify, elucidate, clear up; make clear, make plain; simplify, popularize; illuminate, enlighten, shed *or* throw light upon; rationalize, euhemerize, demythologize, allegorize; tell *or* show how, show the way; demonstrate, show, illustrate, exemplify; decipher, crack, unlock, find the key to, unravel, solve; explain oneself; explain away.

11 comment upon, commentate, remark upon; annotate, gloss; edit, make an edition.

12 translate, render, transcribe, transliterate, put *or* turn into, transfuse the sense of; construe; English.

13 paraphrase, rephrase, reword, restate, rehash; give a free *or* loose translation.

Read the entry above and underline words or phrases that you think would be more descriptive than *tell about*. You might underline words and phrases such as *comment upon, illustrate, demonstrate,* and *spell out*.

The most widely used thesaurus is *Roget's Thesaurus*. Inexpensive paperback editions are available in most bookstores; you can also access thesauruses online.

EXERCISE 4-21   **Using a Thesaurus**

Directions: Using a thesaurus, replace the boldfaced word or phrase in each sentence with a more precise or descriptive word. Write the word in the space provided. Rephrase the sentence, if necessary.

1. Although the movie was **good,** it lasted only an hour.

   _____

2. The judge **looked at** the criminal as she pronounced the sentence.

   _____

3. The accident victim was awarded a **big** cash settlement.

   _____

4. The lottery winner was **happy** to win the $100,000 prize, but he was surprised to learn that a sizable portion had already been deducted for taxes.

_____

5. On the first day of class, the instructor **talked to** the class about course requirements.

_____

EXERCISE 4-22   **Pronouncing Words**

Working Together

Directions: Locate ten words that you find difficult to pronounce. Sources may be a dictionary, a textbook, or one of the reading selections in Part Seven of this book. Write each of the ten words on a separate index card, and then create a list of the words and how they are pronounced. Your instructor will form groups. Pass the cards around the group. Each student should attempt a pronunciation. The student who pronounces the word correctly keeps the card. Make a note of words that you were unable to pronounce; check their pronunciation in your dictionary.

A SYSTEM FOR LEARNING NEW WORDS

OBJECTIVE 5

As you read textbook assignments and reference sources and while listening to your instructors' class presentations, you are constantly exposed to new words. Unless you make a deliberate effort to remember and use these words, many of them will probably fade from your memory. One of the most practical and easy-to-use systems for expanding your vocabulary is the index card system. It works like this:

1. **Whenever you hear or read a new word that you intend to learn, jot it down in the margin of your notes or mark it some way in the material you are reading.**

2. **Later, write the word on the front of an index card.** Then look up its meaning and write it on the back of the card. Also, record a phonetic key for the word's pronunciation, its part of speech, other forms the word may take, and a sample sentence or example of how the word is used. Your cards should look like the one in Figure 4-1.

3. **Once a day, take a few minutes to go through your pack of index cards.** For each card, look at the word on the front and try to recall its meaning on the back. Then check the back of the card to see whether you were correct. If you were unable to recall the meaning or if you confused the word with another word, retest yourself. Shuffle the cards after each use.

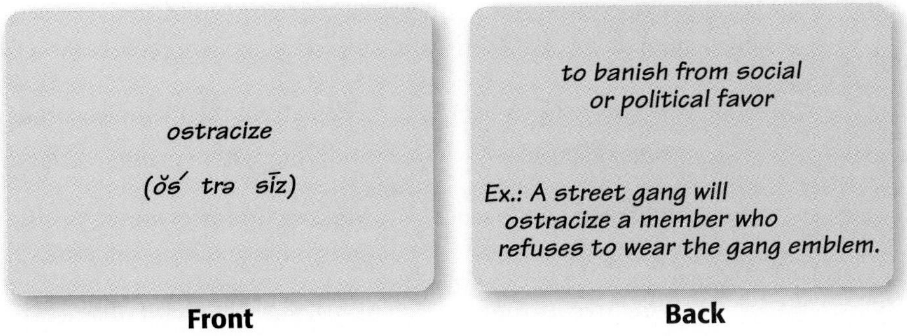

ostracize

(ŏs′ trə sīz)

Front

to banish from social
or political favor

Ex.: A street gang will
ostracize a member who
refuses to wear the gang emblem.

Back

Figure 4-1   Sample index card

4. After you have gone through your pack of cards several times, sort the cards into two piles—words you know and words you have not learned. Then, putting the known words aside, concentrate on the words still to be learned.

5. Once you have learned the entire pack of words, review them often to refresh your memory.

This index card system is effective for several reasons. First, you can review the cards in the spare time that is often wasted waiting for a class to begin, riding a bus, and so on. Second, the system enables you to spend time learning what you do *not* know rather than wasting time studying what you already know. Finally, the system overcomes a major problem that exists in learning information that appears in list form. If the material to be learned is presented in a fixed order, you tend to learn it in that order and may be unable to recall individual items when they appear alone or out of order. By shuffling the cards, you scramble the order of the words and thus avoid this problem.

EXERCISE 4-23   **Using the Index Card System**

Directions: Make a set of at least 20 word cards, choosing words from one of your textbooks or from one of the reading selections in Part Six of this book. Then study the cards using the method described in this chapter.

LEARNING STYLE TIPS

If you tend to be a . . .	Then strengthen your vocabulary by . . .
Social learner	Studying with a group of classmates
Independent learner	Making up review tests, or asking a friend to do so, and practice taking the tests
Creative learner	Experimenting with new words in both speech and writing
Pragmatic learner	Creating lists or computer files of words you need to learn and use

SELF-TEST SUMMARY

OBJECTIVE 1 **What are prefixes, roots, and suffixes and why are they useful?**	Prefixes are beginnings of words, roots are middles of words, and suffixes are endings of words. They unlock the meanings of thousands of English words.
OBJECTIVE 2 **What reference sources are useful in building a strong vocabulary?**	Collegiate and unabridged dictionaries, online dictionaries, ESL dictionaries, subject area dictionaries, and the thesaurus are all useful in building a strong vocabulary.
OBJECTIVE 3 **How do you pronounce unfamiliar words?**	To pronounce unfamiliar words, use the pronunciation key in your dictionary and apply the seven rules listed in this chapter.
OBJECTIVE 4 **Explain the index card system.**	The index card system is a method of learning vocabulary. Write a word on the front of an index card and its meaning on the back. Study the cards by sorting them into two piles—known and unknown words.

P130~142 HW
ch 8

GOING NLINE

1. Learn a Word a Day

   http://www.wordsmith.org/awad/index.html

   Sign up to receive a word a day in your e-mail or read a newsletter about words at this interesting language lovers' site. Use the new words in your writing and speech.

2. Word Families

   http://www.rit.edu/ntid/rate/sea/wordknowledge/wordkn06guided_6.html

   Complete this exercise that shows how roots combine with various prefixes and suffixes to form different parts of speech.

3. Take Our Word for It

   http://www.takeourword.com/theory.html

   Learn about the different ways words have come into our language. Come up with an example of each method that is listed.

4. Practice Quiz on Vocabulary with Greek and Latin Roots

   http://english.glendale.edu/roots.html

   Try this quiz on vocabulary with Greek and Latin roots. Write down some of the new words you learn.

5. Sports Idioms

   http://www.englishclub.com/vocabulary/idioms-sports.htm

   The English language uses many phrases in daily speech that have a sports association. Look over this list and see how many of these you hear on a regular basis. Are there any that are new to you? Try the quiz at the end.

 To check your progress in meeting chapter objectives, log in to **http://www.myreadinglab.com**, click on the Study Plan tab, and then click on the Reading Skills tab. Choose Vocabulary from the list of subtopics. Read and view the information in the Review Materials section, and then complete the Practices and Tests in the Activities section. You can check your scores by clicking on the Gradebook tab.

MASTERY TEST 1 Vocabulary Skills

Name _____ Section _____

Date _____ Number right _____ × 10 points = Score _____

Part A

Directions: For each of the following statements, select the answer that provides the correct prefix, root, or suffix that makes sense in the blank next to the boldfaced word.

_____ 1. Students who attend ethnically diverse schools are often exposed to a variety of foreign languages. One suburban Atlanta elementary school, for instance, has students whose native languages are Spanish, Vietnamese, Romanian, and Sudanese. Parents and school administrators in this school speak in glowing terms about their _____**lingual** student population.
   a. mono
   b. tri
   c. multi
   d. semi

_____ 2. Samuel L. Clemens was born in 1835 in Hannibal, Missouri. Using the _____**nym** Mark Twain, he drew upon his childhood experiences along the Mississippi River to write *Tom Sawyer* and *The Adventures of Huckleberry Finn*.
   a. anti
   b. pseudo
   c. poly
   d. retro

_____ 3. Melanie's father and grandfather are both police officers, so it was not surprising that she decided to pursue a career in law enforcement. She has already enrolled at the community college where she plans to major in criminal justice and take classes in **crimino**_____ in order to learn more about crime, criminals, and criminal behavior.
   a. graphy
   b. scopy
   c. pathy
   d. logy

_____ 4. The portion of the earth that is inhabited by living things is known as the earth's _____**sphere.** It includes the atmosphere and the oceans to specified heights and depths, as well as lakes and rivers.
   a. bio
   b. astro
   c. geo
   d. chrono

_____ 5. Our composition instructor always asked us to exchange our essays with each other in class in order to get another person's feedback on our work. He allowed us to give only **construct**_____ criticism, encouraging us to keep in mind how we would want our own work to be reviewed.
   a. ent
   b. ible
   c. ive
   d. or

Part B

Directions: Using your knowledge of roots, prefixes, and suffixes, choose the correct definition for each of the boldfaced words from the following passage.

> What additional information does this graphic contribute to the passage?

In the U.S. legal system, the family has traditionally been defined as a unit consisting of a heterosexual married couple and their child or children. Many scholars have a more flexible definition of "family," taking into account the **extended** family of grandparents, aunts and uncles, and cousins, and sometimes even people who are not related by blood at all.

Class, race, and ethnicity are important factors to consider as we define what makes a family. The traditional, middle-class Caucasian family with lots of cheerful children depicted in many classic movies has always been a **projection** of the class that produced it rather than a reality. Not only is U.S. society a **composite** of many different economic statuses, but it is also made up of different races and an increasing variety of ethnicities that are in turn mixing to create **interracial** and **multiethnic** families.

—adapted from Kunz, *Think: Marriages and Families*, pp. 278–279

Percentage of Americans Approving of Marriage Between African-Americans and Whites

Percentage of Americans Approving of Marriage Between African-Americans and Whites

_____ 6. extended
   a. limited
   b. larger
   c. artificial
   d. unrelated

_____ 7. projection
   a. difference
   b. advertisement
   c. vision
   d. mistake

_____ 8. composite
   a. property
   b. complex
   c. division
   d. mixture

_____ 9. interracial
   a. away from races
   b. between races
   c. against races
   d. equal races

_____ 10. multiethnic
   a. not ethnic
   b. one ethnicity
   c. many ethnicities
   d. beyond ethnicity

CHAPTER 4

MASTERY TEST 2 Dictionary Skills

Name _____ Section _____

Date _____ Number right _____ × 10 points = Score _____

Part A

Directions: Each numbered sentence below is followed by a dictionary entry for the boldfaced word. Use this entry to select the choice that best fits the meaning of the word as it is used in the sentence.

_____ 1. At the entrance to the international exhibition hall, visitors are greeted by a **panoply** of flags representing every nation in the world.

pan•o•ply (păn′ə-plē) *n., pl.* **-plies 1.** A splendid or striking array: *a panoply of colorful flags.* See synonyms at **display. 2.** Ceremonial attire with all accessories: *a portrait of the general in full panoply.* **3.** Something that covers and protects: *a porcupine's panoply of quills.* **4.** The complete arms and armor of a warrior. [Greek *panopliā: pan-,* pan- + *hopla,* arms, armor, pl. of *hoplon,* weapon.]

—"Panoply," *American Heritage Dictionary of the English Language,* p. 1270

a. the complete arms and armor of a warrior
b. ceremonial attire with all accessories
c. something that covers and protects
d. a splendid and striking array

_____ 2. At the town meeting, several citizens **ventilated** their concerns about the proposed increase in property taxes.

ven•ti•late (věn′tl-āt′) *tr.v.* **-lat•ed, -lat•ing, -lates 1.** To admit fresh air into (a mine, for example) to replace stale or noxious air. **2.** To circulate through and freshen: *A sea breeze ventilated the rooms.* **3.** To provide with a vent, as for airing. **4.** To expose (a substance) to the circulation of fresh air, as to retard spoilage. **5.** To expose to public discussion or examination: *The students ventilated their grievances.* **6.** To aerate or oxygenate (blood). [Middle English *ventilaten,* to blow away, from Latin *ventilāre, ventilāt-,* to fan, from *ventulus,* diminutive of *ventus,* wind. See **wē-** in Appendix I.]

—"Ventilate," *American Heritage Dictionary of the English Language,* p. 1909

a. to admit fresh air in order to replace stale or noxious air
b. to circulate through and freshen
c. to expose to the circulation of fresh air, as to retard spoilage
d. to expose to public discussion or examination

_____ 3. Many people with coronary artery disease do not **manifest** symptoms until they have their first heart attack.

man•i•fest (măn′ə-fěst′) *adj.* Clearly apparent to the sight or understanding; obvious. See synonyms at **apparent.** ❖ *tr.v.* **-fest•ed, -fest•ing, -fests 1.** To show or demonstrate plainly; reveal: *"Mercedes . . . manifested the chaotic abandonment of hysteria"* (Jack London). **2.** To be evidence of; prove. **3a.** To record in a ship's manifest. **b.** To display or present a manifest of (cargo). ❖ *n.* **1.** A list of cargo or passengers carried on a ship or plane. **2.** An invoice of goods carried on a truck or train. **3.** A list of railroad cars according to owner and location. [Middle English *manifeste*, from Old French, from Latin *manufestus, manifest-sus,* caught in the act, blatant, obvious. See g^whedh- in Appendix I.] —**man′i•fest′ly** *adv.*

— "Manifest," *American Heritage Dictionary of the English Language,* p. 1064

   a. clearly apparent to the sight or understanding; obvious

   b. to show or demonstrate plainly; reveal

   c. to be evidence of; prove

   d. to record in a ship's manifest

_____ 4. After moving halfway across the country for his new job, Kerry was **besieged** by rumors that the company was going out of business.

be•siege (bĭ-sēj′) *tr.v.* -sieged, -sieg•ing, -sieg•es 1. To surround with hostile forces. 2. To crowd around; hem in. 3. To harass or importune, as with requests: *Reporters besieged the winner for interviews.* 4. To cause to feel distressed or worried: *She was besieged by problems.* [Middle English *besegen,* probably *assegen,* from Old French *assegier,* from Vulgar Latin* *assedicāre:* Latin *ad-,* ad- + Vulgar Latin* *sedicāre,* to sit; see SIEGE.] —**be•siege′ment;** *n.*—**be•sieg′er** *n.*

— "Besiege," *American Heritage Dictionary of the English Language,* p. 172

Synonyms besiege, beleaguer, blockade, invest, siege. These verbs mean to surround with hostile forces: *besiege a walled city; the enemy beleaguered the enclave; blockaded the harbor; investing a fortress; a castle sieged by invaders.*

   a. to cause to feel distressed or worried

   b. to crowd around; hem in

   c. to harass or importune, as with requests

   d. to surround with hostile forces

_____ 5. The student task force obviously did not spend much time considering the problem of the limited number of parking spaces on campus; its **facile** solution to the problem disappointed all of us.

fac•ile (făs′əl) *adj.* **1.** Done or achieved with little effort or difficulty; easy. See Synonyms at **easy. 2.** Working, acting, or speaking with effortless ease and fluency. **3.** Arrived at without due care, effort, or examination; superficial: *proposed a facile solution to a complex problem.* **4.** Readily manifested, together with an aura of insincerity and lack of depth: *a facile slogan devised by politicans.* **5.** *Archaic* Pleasingly mild, as in disposition or manner. [Middle English, from Old French, from Latin *facilis.* See dhe- in Appendix I.] —**fac′ile•ly** *adv.* —**fac′ile•ness** *n.*

— "Facile," *American Heritage Dictionary of the English Language,* p. 633.

   a. done or achieved with little effort or difficulty; easy

   b. working, acting, or speaking with effortless ease and fluency

   c. arrived at without due care, effort, or examination; superficial

   d. pleasingly mild, as in disposition or manner

Part B

Directions: Use a dictionary to select the best answer for each of the following questions.

_____ 6. The definition of the word *ligature* is
   a. legal suit
   b. relief
   c. coal
   d. bond

_____ 7. The most accurate phonetic spelling for the word *neuropathy* is
a. nyu ro path e
b. nyur o path e
c. nyu rop a the
d. nyu rop a te

_____ 8. What part of speech is the word *tole*?
a. noun
b. verb
c. adjective
d. adverb

_____ 9. What is the origin of the word *hirsute*?
a. French
b. German
c. Latin
d. Middle English

_____ 10. The correct syllabication of the word *marsupial* is
a. mar sup i al
b. mar su pi al
c. mars up ial
d. mar su pial

MASTERY TEST 3 Reading Selection

Name _____ Section _____

Date _____ Number right* _____ × 10 points = Score _____

A Step Beyond Human

Andy Greenberg

This selection first appeared in a December 2009 issue of *Forbes* magazine. Read the article to find out how and why one man is working to transform the field of artificial limbs.

Cyborg Evangelist: Herr wears a pair of his disability-defying PowerFoot devices

Vocabulary Preview

biomechatronics (par. 3) an applied science combining elements of biology, mechanics, and electronics, as well as robotics and neuroscience

crampons (par. 4) spikes attached to shoes for ice climbing

inertia (par. 5) in physics, the tendency of a body to maintain its state of rest or uniform motion unless acted upon by an external force

Paralympic (par. 12) relating to an international competition for athletes with disabilities

1   On his way to a lunch meeting a few years ago Hugh Herr was running late. So he parked his Honda Accord in a handicapped parking spot, sprang out of the car and jogged down the sidewalk. Within seconds a policeman called out, asking to see his disability permit. When Herr pointed it out on his dashboard, the cop eyed him suspiciously. "What's your affliction?" he asked dryly.

2   Herr, a slim and unassuming 6-footer with dark, neatly parted hair, took a step toward the officer and responded in an even tone: "I have no [expletive] legs."

3   Blurring the boundaries of disability is a trick that Herr, director of the biomechatronics group at MIT's Media Lab, has spent the last 27 years perfecting. At age 17 both of Herr's legs were amputated 6 inches below the knee after a rock

_____
*To calculate the number right, use items 1–10 under "Mastery Test Skills Check."

climbing trip ended in severe frostbite. Today he's one of the world's preeminent prosthetics experts. His goal: to build artificial limbs that are superior to natural ones. His favorite test subject: himself. "I like to say that there are no disabled people," says Herr, 45. "Only disabled technology."

4   Herr swaps his feet out to suit his needs. He generally walks on flat carbon-fiber springs inside his shoes but sometimes replaces them with longer carbon bows for jogging. When he goes rock climbing—often scaling cliffs of expert-level difficulty—he switches to one of multiple pairs of climbing legs he's built himself, including small, rubber feet on aluminum poles that stretch his height beyond 7 feet, spiked aluminum claws that replace crampons for ice climbing or tapered polyethylene hatchets that wedge into crevices. "The fact that I'm missing lower limbs is an opportunity," he says. "Between my residual limb and the ground, I can create anything I want. The only limits are physical laws and my imagination."

5   Over the last several years that imagination has been working overtime. Late next year iWalk, a company Herr founded in 2006, plans to release the Power-Foot One, the world's most advanced robotic ankle and foot. Most prosthetic feet are fixed at a clumsy 90 degrees. The PowerFoot, equipped with three internal microprocessors and 12 sensors that measure force, inertia and position, automatically adjusts its angle, stiffness and damping 500 times a second. Employing the same sort of sensory feedback loops that the human nervous system uses, plus a library of known patterns, the PowerFoot adjusts for slopes, dips its toe naturally when walking down stairs, even hangs casually when the user crosses his or her legs.

6   The PowerFoot is the only foot and ankle in the world that doesn't depend on its wearer's energy. With a system of passive springs and a half-pound rechargeable lithium iron phosphate battery, the foot—made of aluminum, titanium, plastic and carbon fiber—provides the same 20-joule push off the ground that human muscles and tendons do. It automatically adjusts the power to the walker's speed, but users can also dial that power up or down with a Bluetooth-enabled phone. (And soon, Herr says, with an iPhone application.) One test subject told Herr that his nonamputated leg often tires before his prosthetic-enhanced one. "This is the first time that the prosthesis is driving the human, instead of the other way around," says Herr.

7   Herr frequently wears a pair of his new creations. The next to try the PowerFoot will be the Department of Defense, which is looking for prostheses for the nearly 1,000 soldiers who have lost limbs in Iraq and Afghanistan. The Veterans Administration and the Army are among the investors who funded his MIT research. Veterans, he argues, also make the perfect early adopters, given their athletic, active lifestyles. "These are remarkable people," says Herr. "If the PowerFoot can work for them, it can work for anyone." iWalk hopes to put the PowerFoot on the general market in 2010, priced in the low five figures. The startup has raised $10.2 million from investors, including General Catalyst Partners and WFD Ventures.

8   Herr's motives extend beyond profit. In 1982 he and a friend climbed Mount Washington in New Hampshire, a place infamous for its unpredictable and nasty weather. They were caught in a snowstorm, losing their way in a near-complete whiteout and subzero temperatures. After three and a half days of crawling along a frozen river, Herr's lower legs were practically destroyed by cold. A member of the rescue team sent after them, 28-year-old Albert Dow, was killed in an avalanche. "I feel a responsibility to use my intellect and resources to do as much as I can to help people. That's Albert Dow's legacy for me," says Herr.

9   Within three months of his amputations Herr was rock climbing with simple prosthetics. Within six months he was in a machine shop, building new feet, using the skills he'd learned at a vocational high school in Lancaster, Pa., where he grew up.

10   While he had previously focused on merely working a trade, Herr became a nearly obsessive student, earning a master's in mechanical engineering at MIT and a Ph.D. in biophysics at Harvard. Once, when his hands suffered from repetitive stress disorder while he was writing his doctoral thesis, he attached a pencil to a pair of sunglass frames and typed with his head. "He's driven to the point of exhaustion, physical degradation," says Rodger Kram, a professor of integrative physiology at the University of Colorado at Boulder, who worked with Herr at Harvard. "Every step he takes, he's forced to think about making prosthetics better."

11   Herr wants to transform how people define disability. Last year he sat on a panel of scientists that confirmed that Oscar Pistorius, a South African sprinter with no legs below the knee, should be allowed to compete in the Olympics. Herr helped discredit arguments that Pistorius got a metabolic advantage from his carbon-fiber legs. (Pistorius missed qualifying by a fraction of a second.)

12   Herr has tasted athletic discrimination, too. Because he uses special climbing prosthetics, many dispute his claim to be the second in the world to free-climb a famously challenging pitch near Index Mountain, Wash. "When amputees participate in sports, they call it courageous," he says. "Once you become competitive, they call it cheating." Herr even believes that in the coming decades Paralympic athletes will regularly outperform Olympic athletes. We may need special disability laws for humans who decline to have their bodies mechanically enhanced, he says.

13   "Disabled people today are the test pilots for technology that will someday be pervasive," Herr explains. "Eliminating disability and blurring man and machine will be one of the great stories of this century."

MASTERY TEST SKILLS CHECK

Directions: Select the choice that best completes each of the following statements.

Checking Your Comprehension

_____ 1. The focus of this selection is on Hugh Herr's
   a. ice and rock climbing trips.
   b. athletic achievements.
   c. work with prosthetics.
   d. research at MIT.

_____ 2. The main point of paragraph 4 is that Herr
   a. uses flat springs in his shoes for walking.
   b. has built his own pair of artificial legs.
   c. has created special prosthetics for ice climbing.
   d. uses different prosthetics for different tasks.

_____ 3. The PowerFoot One has all of the following characteristics *except*
   a. it adjusts for slopes.
   b. it is equipped with microprocessors and sensors.
   c. it is fixed at a 90-degree angle.
   d. users can adjust its power using a Bluetooth-enabled phone.

_____ 4. Herr's lower legs were amputated because of
   a. a war injury.
   b. severe frostbite.
   c. a car accident.
   d. bone disease.

_____ 5. The main point of paragraph 12 is that Herr
   a. has faced discrimination because of his use of prosthetics.
   b. wants to compete in the Paralympics.
   c. claims to be second in the world to climb Index Mountain.
   d. does not want special disability laws to be enacted.

Applying Your Skills

_____ 6. Context clues indicate that the word *prosthetics* (par. 3) means
   a. boundaries.
   b. disabilities.
   c. artificial limbs.
   d. technology.

_____ 7. The root of the word *unpredictable* (par. 8) means
   a. before.
   b. tell.
   c. send.
   d. light.

_____ 8. The prefix in the word *subzero* (par. 8) means
   a. through.
   b. excessive.
   c. below.
   d. not.

_____ 9. The root of the word *discredit* (par. 11) means
   a. see.
   b. write.
   c. carry.
   d. believe.

_____ 10. The suffix in the word *amputees* (par. 12) means
    a. again.
    b. one who.
    c. hundred.
    d. away from.

Studying Words

_____ 11. The word *affliction* (par. 1) means
    a. hurry.
    b. disability.
    c. purpose.
    d. approach.

_____ 12. The word *preeminent* (par. 3) means
    a. top.
    b. difficult.
    c. unknown.
    d. worst.

_____ 13. The word *residual* (par. 4) means
    a. automatic.
    b. remaining.
    c. unlimited.
    d. nonworking.

_____ 14. The word *vocational* (par. 9) refers to
    a. a competition.
    b. an occupation or calling.
    c. a degree.
    d. an investor.

_____ 15. The word *pitch* as it is used in paragraph 12 refers to
    a. a throw.
    b. a sales talk.
    c. a steep piece of ground.
    d. an element of sound.

For more practice, ask your instructor for an opportunity to work on the mastery tests that appear in the Test Bank.

Summarizing the Reading

Directions: Complete the following summary of the reading by filling in the blanks.

As a young man, Hugh Herr's lower legs were _____ because of _____

_____. This experience led to his work in prosthetics, earn-

ing a _____ at MIT and a _____ at Harvard.

Herr has become a world-renowned expert in _____ and is director of

_____ at MIT. His goal is to build _____ limbs that are

superior to _____ limbs. Herr frequently tests his _____ on himself and

has built _____ for different uses. In 2006, Herr founded a

_____, which will soon release the _____, the

world's most advanced _____ the Department of _____ is con-

sidering the _____ for _____. Herr wants to change

how _____ is defined; he believes _____ should be able to

compete using prosthetic limbs.

Reading Visually

1. What does the photograph of Herr contribute to the reading?
2. What illustrations or photographs do you think would enhance this selection?
3. Explain how the title of this article relates to the subject. Can you think of another title that would also work for this selection?

Thinking Critically about the Reading

1. Why did the author begin by telling about the incident with the handicapped parking spot? Explain how this brief story contributes to your understanding of what kind of person Herr is. Based on the entire selection, what words would you use to describe Herr?
2. How would you describe Herr's feelings toward veterans who have lost limbs and Paralympians?
3. How does Herr's attitude toward his own disability make him especially well suited to his work?

CHAPTER

5

Reading as Thinking

Looking at…
Reading as Thinking

LEARNING OBJECTIVES

This chapter will show you how to:

OBJECTIVE
1 Preview before reading

OBJECTIVE
2 Develop questions to guide your reading

OBJECTIVE
3 Read for meaning

OBJECTIVE
4 Test your recall as you read

OBJECTIVE
5 Review after reading

OBJECTIVE
6 Use the SQ3R system

If you were searching for a new vacation spot to visit, the materials shown above would be useful. However, would you read every brochure to find what you need? Most likely not. Instead, you would check to see how each is organized and locate the travel destination you had in mind. In much the same way that you become familiar with these everyday materials before delving into them, you should think ahead and plan your approach to a textbook chapter before you begin reading it.

Rhonda is taking an anatomy and physiology course, one required in nursing. She reads all the assignments and spends long hours studying. She rereads the assignments, and rereads them again before each quiz. When the instructor returns the weekly quiz, Rhonda is always surprised and disappointed. She thinks she has done well but receives a failing grade. She cannot understand why she fails the quizzes, since she has read the material.

Rhonda decides to visit the college's learning center. The first thing the instructor asks her to do is to locate the correct answer to each quiz item in her textbook. When Rhonda has difficulty doing this, the instructor questions her on portions of the textbook. The instructor realizes that Rhonda has not thought about what she has read, so he asks Rhonda several questions about how she read the chapters and discovers that she simply read and reread them. Rhonda did nothing before beginning to read a chapter to sharpen her mind and make reading easier. She read mechanically, from beginning to end, and she did not check her understanding of the material. She did not realize her comprehension was poor or incomplete, and she did not review what she had read. She was reading, but she was not thinking about what she was reading. The instructor then suggests five strategies to help Rhonda get involved with what she is reading, and shows her how to keep track of her level of comprehension.

In this chapter you will learn to approach reading as a thinking process. You will learn five strategies that, when combined, lead to a systematic, effective method of reading called SQ3R. You will also learn how to keep track of your level of understanding and what to do if it is poor or incomplete.

PREVIEW

Would you cross a city street without checking for traffic first? Would you pay to see a movie you had never heard of and knew nothing about? Would you buy a car without test-driving it or checking its mechanical condition?

Most likely you answered "no" to each of these questions. Now answer a related question, one that applies to reading: Should you read an article or textbook chapter without knowing what it is about or how it is organized? You can probably guess that the answer is "no." This section explains a technique called previewing.

Previewing is a way of quickly familiarizing yourself with the organization and content of written material *before* beginning to read it. It is an easy method to use and will make a dramatic difference in how effectively you read.

How to Preview

When you preview, try to (1) find only the most important ideas in the material, and (2) note how they are organized. To do this, look only at the parts that state these important ideas and skip the rest. Previewing is a fairly rapid technique. You should take only a few minutes to preview a 15- to 20-page textbook chapter. The parts to look at in previewing a textbook chapter are listed here:

How to Preview Textbook Chapters

1. **The title and subtitle** The title is a label that tells what the chapter is about. The subtitle, if there is one, suggests how the author approaches the subject. For example, an article titled "Brazil" might be subtitled "The World's Next Superpower." In this instance, the subtitle tells which aspects of Brazil the article discusses.

2. **Chapter introduction** Read the entire chapter introduction if it is brief. If it is lengthy, read only the first few paragraphs.

3. **The first paragraph** The first paragraph, or introduction, of each section of the chapter may provide an overview of the section and/or offer clues about its organization.

4. **Boldfaced headings** Headings, like titles, serve as labels and identify the topic of the material. By reading each heading, you will be reading a list of the important topics the chapter covers. Together, the headings form a mini-outline of the chapter.

5. **The first sentence under each heading** The first sentence following the heading often further explains the heading. It may also state the central thought of the entire selection. If the first sentence is purely introductory, read the second as well.

6. **Typographical aids** Typographical aids are those features of a page that help to highlight and organize information. These include *italics*, **boldfaced type**, marginal notes, colored ink, underlining, and enumeration (listing). A writer frequently uses typographical aids to call attention to important key words, definitions, and facts.

7. **Graphs, charts, and pictures** Graphs, charts, and pictures will point you toward the most important information. Glance at these to determine quickly what information is being emphasized or clarified.

8. **The final paragraph or summary** The final paragraph or summary will give a condensed view of the chapter and help you identify key ideas. Often, a summary outlines the key points of the chapter.

9. **End-of-chapter material** Glance through any study or discussion questions, vocabulary lists, or outlines that appear at the end of the chapter. These will help you decide what in the chapter is important.

Demonstration of Previewing

The following article was taken from a chapter of a communications textbook on nonverbal messages. It discusses four major functions of eye communication and has been included to demonstrate previewing. Everything that you should look at or read has been shaded. Preview this excerpt now, reading only the shaded portions.

Functions of Eye Communication

From Ben Jonson's poetic observation "Drink to me only with thine eyes, and I will pledge with mine" to the scientific observations of contemporary researchers, the eyes are regarded as the most important nonverbal message system. Researchers note four major functions of eye communication.

To Seek Feedback

You frequently use your eyes to seek feedback from others. In talking with someone, you look at her or him intently,* as if to say, "Well, what do you think?" As you might predict, listeners gaze at speakers more than speakers gaze at listeners. Research shows that the percentage of interaction time spent gazing while listening was between 62 and 75 percent. However, the percentage of time spent gazing while talking was between 38 and 41 percent.

Women make eye contact more and maintain it longer (both in speaking and in listening) than do men. This holds true whether the woman is interacting with other women or with men. This difference in eye behavior may result from women's tendency to display their emotions more than men; eye contact is one of the most effective ways of communicating emotions. Another possible explanation is that women have been conditioned more than men to seek positive feedback from others. Women may thus use eye contact in seeking this visual feedback.

To Regulate the Conversation

A second function of eye contact is to regulate the conversation and particularly to pass the speaking turn from one person to another. You use eye contact, for example, to tell the listener that you are finished with your thought and that you would now like to assume the role of listener and hear what the other person has to say. Or, by maintaining a steady eye contact while you plan your next sentence, you tell the other person that although you are now silent, you don't want to give up your speaking turn. You also see this in the college classroom when the instructor asks a question and then locks eyes with a student—without saying anything, the instructor clearly communicates the desire for that student to say something.

To Signal the Nature of the Relationship

Eye contact is also used to signal the nature of the relationship between two people— for example, a focused attentive glance indicates a positive relationship, but avoiding eye contact shows one of negative regard. You may also signal status relationships with your eyes. This is particularly interesting because the same movements of the eyes may signal either subordination or superiority. The superior individual, for example, may stare at the subordinate or may glance away. Similarly, the subordinate may look directly at the superior or perhaps at the floor.

Eye movements may also signal whether the relationship between two people is amorous, hostile, or indifferent. Because some of the eye movements expressing these different relationships are so similar, you often use information from other areas, particularly the rest of the face, to decode the message before making any final judgments.

To Compensate for Increased Physical Distance

Last, eye movements may compensate for increased physical distance. By making eye contact you overcome psychologically the physical distance between you and the other individual. When you catch someone's eye at a party, for example, you become psychologically close even though separated by a large physical distance. Not surprisingly, eye contact and other expressions of psychological closeness, such as self-disclosure, are positively related; as one increases, so does the other.

—Devito, *Messages*, p. 146

Although you may not realize it, you have gained a substantial amount of information from the minute or so that you spent previewing. You have become familiar with the key ideas in this section. To demonstrate, read each of the following statements and mark them *T* for "true" or *F* for "false" based on what you learned by previewing.

_____ 1. The most important nonverbal message system involves the eyes.

_____ 2. We can obtain feedback from others by using just our eyes.

_____ 3. Eye movements cannot compensate for physical distances.

_____ 4. The relationship between two people can be signaled through eye contact.

_____ 5. Eye contact regulates conversations.

This quiz tested your recall of some of the more important ideas in the article. Check your answers by referring back to the article. Did you get most or all of the above items correct? You can see, then, that previewing acquaints you with the major ideas contained in the material before you read it.

EXERCISE 5-1   **Practicing Previewing**

Directions: Preview Chapter 6 in this book. After you have previewed it, complete the items below.

1. What is the subject of Chapter 6?

   _____

2. List the three major topics Chapter 6 covers.

   a. _____

   b. _____

   c. _____

EXERCISE 5-2   **Previewing Your Textbooks**

Directions: Preview a chapter from one of your other textbooks. After you have previewed it, complete the items below.

1. What is the chapter title?

   _____

   _____

2. What subject does the chapter cover?

   _____

   _____

3. List some of the major topics covered.

   _____

   _____

Previewing Articles and Essays

Previewing works on articles and essays, as well as textbook chapters. However, you may have to make a few changes in the steps listed on page 145. Here are some guidelines:

How to Preview Articles and Essays

1. **Check the author's name.** If you recognize the author's name, you may have an idea of what to expect in the article or essay. For example, you would expect humor from an article by Dave Barry but more serious material from an article written by the governor of your state.

2. **Check the source of the article.** Where was it originally published? The source may suggest something about the content or slant of the article. (For more about sources see Chapter 12.)

3. **If there are no headings, read the first sentence of a few paragraphs throughout the essay.** These sentences will usually give you a sense of what the paragraph is about.

EXERCISE 5-3 **Previewing a Reading Selection**

Directions: Preview the article that appears at the end of this chapter, "Body Piercing and Tattooing." Then answer the following questions.

1. What is the purpose of the article?

   _____

2. The article offers advice to those considering tattoos or body piercing. Which can you recall?

   _____

LEARNING STYLE TIPS

If you tend to be a(n) . . .	Then strengthen your prereading skills by . . .
Auditory learner	Asking and answering guide questions aloud or recording them
Visual learner	Writing guide questions and their answers

Discover What You Already Know

After you have previewed an assignment, take a moment to discover what you already know about the topic. Regardless of the topic, you probably know *something* about it. We will call this your **background knowledge.** Here is an example.

A student was about to read an article titled "Growing Urban Problems" for a sociology class. At first she thought she knew very little about urban problems, since she lived in a small town. Then she began thinking about her recent trip to a nearby city. She remembered seeing homeless people and overcrowded housing. Then she recalled reading about drug problems, drive-by shootings, and muggings.

Now let us take a sample chapter from a business textbook titled *Small Business Management.* The headings are listed below. Spend a moment thinking about each one; then make a list of things you already know about each.

- Characteristics of Small Businesses
- Small-Business Administration
- Advantages and Disadvantages of Small Businesses
- Problems of Small Businesses

Discovering what you already know is useful for three important reasons. First, it makes reading easier because you have already thought about the topic. Second, the material is easier to remember because you can connect the new information with what you already know. Third, topics become more interesting if you can link them to your own experiences. You can discover what you know by using one or more of the following techniques:

How to Activate Your Background Knowledge

1. **Ask questions and try to answer them.** For the above business textbook headings, you might ask and try to answer questions such as: Would I want to own a small business or not? What problems could I expect?

2. **Draw upon your own experience.** For example, if a chapter in your business textbook is titled "Advertising: Its Purpose and Design," you might think of several ads you have seen on television, in magazines, and in newspapers and analyze the purpose of each and how it was constructed.

LEARNING STYLE TIPS

If you are a(n) . . .	Then improve your comprehension by . . .
Applied learner	Thinking of real-life situations that illustrate ideas in the passage
Conceptual learner	Asking questions

TEST YOUR RECALL AS YOU READ

Many students read an assignment from beginning to end without stopping. Usually, this is a mistake. Instead, it is best to stop frequently to test yourself to see if you are remembering what you are reading. You can do this easily by using your guide questions. If you write guide questions in the textbook margin next to the section to which they correspond, you can easily use them as test questions after you have read the section. Cover the textbook section and try to recall the answer. If you cannot, reread the section. You have not yet learned the material. Depending on your learning style, you might either repeat the answer aloud (auditory style) or write it (verbal style).

REVIEW AFTER YOU READ

Once you have finished reading, it is tempting to close the book, take a break, and move on to your next assignment. If you want to be sure that you remember what you have just read, take a few moments to go back through the material, looking things over one more time.

You can review using some or all of the same steps you followed to preview (see page 145). Instead of viewing the assignment *before* reading, you are viewing it again *after* reading. Think of it as a "re-view." Review will help you pull ideas together as well as help you retain them for later use on a quiz or exam.

EXERCISE 5-11   **Practicing Reviewing**

Directions: Work with a partner to choose a chapter in this book that you have already read. Review the chapter, previewing for the important information listed in the box on page 145. Next, each student should write five questions on the chapter content. Test each other's recall of the chapter content by taking turns asking and answering your questions.

BUILDING A SYSTEM: SQ3R

Each of the five techniques presented in this chapter, (1) previewing, (2) asking guide questions, (3) reading for meaning, (4) testing yourself, and (5) reviewing will make a difference in how well you comprehend and remember what you read. While each of these makes a difference by itself, when you use all five together you will discover a much bigger difference. Because these five techniques do work together, numerous researchers and psychologists have put them together into a reading-learning system. One of the most popular systems is called SQ3R. The steps in the system are listed below. You will see that the steps are just other names for what you have already learned in this chapter.

SQ3R

S	Survey	(Preview)
Q	Question	(Ask Guide Questions)
R	Read	(Read for Meaning)
R	Recite	(Test Yourself)
R	Review	(Review After You Read)

Be sure to use SQ3R on all your textbook assignments. You will find that it makes an important difference in the amount of information you can learn and remember.

EXERCISE 5-12   Using SQ3R

Directions: Read the following excerpt from a chapter on digestion in a nutrition textbook (pp. 157–160), following the steps listed above.

1. Preread the excerpt. Write a sentence describing what the excerpt will be about.

   _____

   _____

2. Form several questions that you want to answer as you read. Write them in the space provided.

   _____

   _____

3. Read the excerpt, and on a separate sheet, answer your guide questions.

4. Review the excerpt immediately after you finish reading.

What Happens to the Fats We Eat?

Because fats are not soluble in water, they cannot enter our bloodstream easily from the digestive tract. Thus, fats must be digested, absorbed, and transported within the body differently from carbohydrates and proteins, which are water **soluble**.

The digestion and absorbtion of fat is shown in Figure A. Dietary fats usually come mixed with other foods in our diet, which we chew and then swallow. Salivary enzymes have a limited role in the breakdown of fats, and so they reach the stomach intact (Figure A, step 1, p. 158). The primary role of the stomach in fat di-

Foods containing fats, such as bread, can spoil quickly.

gestion is to mix and break up the fat into droplets. Because they are not soluble in water, these fat droplets typically float on top of the watery digestive juices in the stomach until they are passed into the small intestine (Figure A, step 2).

The Gallbladder, Liver, and Pancreas Assist in Fat Breakdown

Because fat is not soluble in water, its digestion requires the help of digestive enzymes from the pancreas and mixing compounds from the gallbladder. Recall that the gallbladder is a sac attached to the underside of the liver, and the pancreas is an oblong-shaped organ sitting below the stomach. Both have a duct connecting them to the small intestine. As fat enters the small intestine from the stomach, the gallbladder contracts and releases a substance called bile (Figure A, step 3). Bile is produced in the liver from cholesterol and is stored in the gallbladder until needed. You can think of bile acting much like soap, breaking up the fat into smaller and smaller droplets. At the same time, lipid-digesting enzymes produced in the pancreas travel through the pancreatic duct into the small intestine. Once bile has broken the fat into small droplets, these pancreatic enzymes take over, breaking some of the fatty acids away from the glycerol backbone. Each triglyceride molecule is thus broken down into two free fatty acids and one *monoglyceride,* which is the glycerol backbone with one fatty acid still attached.

Most Fat Is Absorbed in the Small Intestine

The free fatty acids and monoglycerides next need to be transported to the cells that make up the wall of the small intestine (Figure A, step 4), so that they can be absorbed into the body. This trip requires the help *of micelles,* spheres of bile and phospholipids that surround the free fatty acids and monoglycerides and transport them to the intestinal cell wall. Once there, shorter fatty acids can pass directly across the intestinal cell membrane. Longer fatty acids first bind to a special carrier protein and then are absorbed.

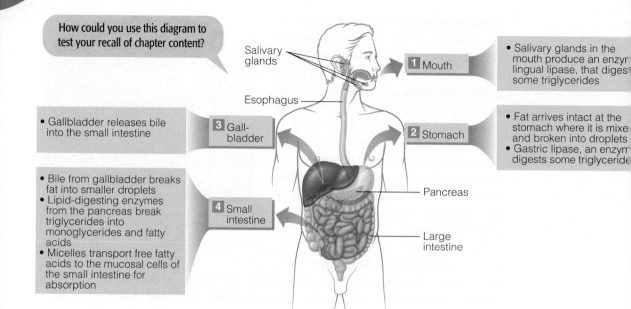

How could you use this diagram to test your recall of chapter content?

- Salivary glands in the mouth produce an enzyme lingual lipase, that digests some triglycerides

- Gallbladder releases bile into the small intestine

- Fat arrives intact at the stomach where it is mixed and broken into droplets
- Gastric lipase, an enzyme digests some triglyceride

- Bile from gallbladder breaks fat into smaller droplets
- Lipid-digesting enzymes from the pancreas break triglycerides into monoglycerides and fatty acids
- Micelles transport free fatty acids to the mucosal cells of the small intestine for absorption

Salivary glands
Esophagus
1 Mouth
2 Stomach
3 Gall-bladder
4 Small intestine
Pancreas
Large intestine

Figure A   The process of fat digestion.

lipoprotein

A spherical compound in which fat clusters in the center and phospholipids and proteins form the outside of the sphere.

chylomicron

A lipoprotein produced in the mucosal cell of the intestine; transports dietary fat out of the intestinal tract.

After absorption into the small intestine, the shortest fatty acids cross unassisted into the bloodstream and are then transported throughout the body. In contrast, the longer fatty acids and monoglycerides are reformulated back into triglycerides. As you know, triglyceride molecules don't mix with water, so they can't cross independently into the bloodstream. Once again, their movement requires special packaging, this time in the form of lipoproteins. A **lipoprotein** is a spherical compound in which triglycerides cluster deep in the center and phospholipids and proteins, which are water soluble, form the surface of the sphere (Figure B). The specific lipoprotein that transports fat from a meal is called a **chylomicron.** Packaged as chylomicrons, dietary fat finally arrives in your blood.

Fat Is Stored in Adipose Tissues for Later Use

The chylomicrons, which are filled with the fat you just ate, now begin to circulate through the blood looking for a place to unload. There are three primary fates of this dietary fat: (1) If your body needs the fat for energy, it will be quickly transported into your cells and used as fuel. (2) If the fat is not needed for immediate energy, it can be used to make lipid-containing compounds such as certain hormones and bile. (3) Alternatively, it can be stored in your muscles or adipose tissue for later use. If you are physically active, your body will preferentially store this extra fat in the muscle tissue first, so the next time you go out for a run, the fat is

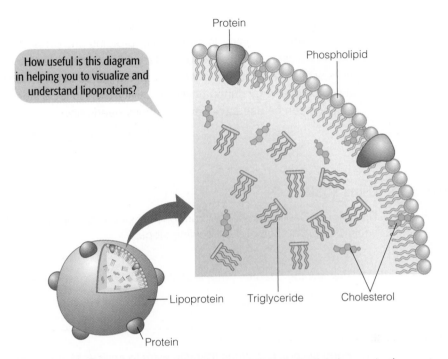

How useful is this diagram in helping you to visualize and understand lipoproteins?

Figure B   Structure of a lipoprotein. Notice that the fat clusters in the center of the molecule and the phospholipids and proteins, which are water soluble, form the outside of the sphere. This enables lipoproteins to transport fats in the bloodstream.

readily available for energy. That is why people who engage in regular physical activity are more likely to have extra fat stored in the muscle tissue and to have less adipose tissue—something many of us would prefer. Of course, fat stored in the adipose tissue can also be used for energy during exercise, but it must be broken down first and then transported to the muscle cells.

Recap: Fat digestion begins when fats are broken into droplets by bile. Enzymes from the pancreas subsequently digest the triglycerides into two free fatty acids and one monoglyceride. These end products of digestion are then transported to the intestinal cells with the help of micelles. Once inside the intestinal

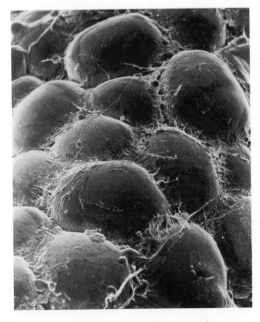

During times of weight gain, excess fat consumed in the diet is stored in adipose tissue.

cells, triglycerides are re-formed and packaged into lipoproteins called chylomicrons. Their outer layer is made up of proteins and phospholipids, which allows
them to dissolve in the blood. Dietary fat is transported by the chylomicrons to
cells within the body that need energy. Fat stored in the muscle tissue is used as
a source of energy during physical activity. Excess fat is stored in the adipose tissue and can be used whenever the body needs energy.

—Thompson and Manore, *Nuitrition for Life*, pp. 109–11.

EXERCISE 5-13   Using SQ3R

Directions: Choose a chapter from one of your textbooks, or use a later chapter in this
book. Complete each of the following steps.

1. Preview the chapter. Write a sentence describing what the chapter will be about.

   _____

   _____

2. Form several questions that you want to answer as you read. Write them in the
   space provided.

   _____

   _____

3. Read the first section (major heading) of the chapter, and highlight the important
   information.

4. Review the section immediately after you finish reading and highlighting.

5. On a separate sheet, write a brief outline or draw a map of the major ideas in the
   section of the chapter that you read.

SELF-TEST SUMMARY

OBJECTIVE **1** **What is previewing?**	Previewing is a method of becoming familiar with the content and organization of written material before reading.
OBJECTIVE **2** **What are guide questions?**	Guide questions focus your attention on what you need to learn and remember.
OBJECTIVE **3** **How can you read for meaning?**	Highlight answers to your guide questions. Also, highlight important information in each paragraph.
OBJECTIVE **4** **How can you test your recall as you read?**	Cover the text and try to recall answers to each of your guide questions.
OBJECTIVE **5** **How can you review after you read?**	Use the steps you followed to preview the assignment.
OBJECTIVE **6** **What is the SQ3R system?**	SQ3R is a system that enables you to learn as you read (Survey, Question, Read, Recite, and Review).

GOING ONLINE

1. Practice Reading Comprehension Test
   http://www.gsu.edu/~wwwrtp/pracread.htm
   Try this practice test from the Georgia State University Board of Regents. Questions are answered and scored online. You can even take an instructional version that explains the right and wrong answers.

2. Preview-Read-Recall

   **http://www.utexas.edu/student/utlc/learning_resources/reading/
   Preview_Read_Recall.pdf**

   Print out these tips for reading more effectively, and follow them while you read a short selection from a textbook, newspaper, or magazine. How effective are these suggestions?

3. Study Skills Checklist

   http://www.oakton.edu/learn/readsvy.htm

   Take this self-evaluation on study skills. What are the results? Where do you need to focus to improve your reading?

To check your progress in meeting chapter objectives, log in to **http://www.myreadinglab.com**, click on the Study Plan tab, and then click on the Reading Skills tab. Choose Reading as Thinking from the list of subtopics. Read and view the information in the Review Materials section, and then complete the Practices and Tests in the Activities section. You can check your scores by clicking on the Gradebook tab.

Name _____ Section _____

Date _____ Number right _____ × 20 points = Score _____

Indoor Air Pollution

1   Combating the problems associated with air pollution begins at home. Indoor air can be 10 to 40 times more hazardous than outdoor air. There are between 20 and 100 potentially dangerous chemical compounds in the average American home. Indoor air pollution comes primarily from six sources: woodstoves, furnaces, asbestos, formaldehyde, radon, and household chemicals.

WOODSTOVE SMOKE

2   Woodstoves emit significant levels of particulates and carbon monoxide in addition to other pollutants, such as sulfur dioxide. If you rely on wood for heating, you should make sure that your stove is properly installed, vented, and maintained. Burning properly seasoned wood reduces the amount of particulates released into the air.

FURNACE EMISSIONS

3   People who rely on oil- or gas-fired furnaces also need to make sure that these appliances are properly installed, ventilated, and maintained. Inadequate cleaning and maintenance can lead to a buildup of carbon monoxide in the home, which can be deadly.

ASBESTOS

4   **Asbestos** is another indoor air pollutant that poses serious threats to human health. Asbestos is a mineral that was commonly used in insulating materials in buildings constructed before 1970. When bonded to other materials, asbestos is relatively harmless, but if its tiny fibers become loosened and airborne, they can embed themselves in the lungs and cannot be expelled. Their presence leads to cancer of the lungs, stomach, and chest lining, and is the cause of a fatal lung disease called mesothelioma.

FORMALDEHYDE

5   **Formaldehyde** is a colorless, strong-smelling gas present in some carpets, draperies, furniture, particle board, plywood, wood paneling, countertops, and many adhesives. It is released into the air in a process called *outgassing*. Outgassing is highest in new products, but the process can continue for many years.

6   Exposure to formaldehyde can cause respiratory problems, dizziness, fatigue, nausea, and rashes. Long-term exposure can lead to central nervous system disorders and cancer.

163

RADON

7   **Radon** is one of the most serious forms of indoor air pollution. This odorless, colorless gas is the natural by-product of the decay of uranium and radium in the soil. Radon penetrates homes through cracks, pipes, sump pits, and other openings in the foundation. An estimated 30,000 cancer deaths per year have been attributed to radon, making it second only to smoking as the leading cause of lung cancer.

HOUSEHOLD CHEMICALS

8   When you use cleansers and other cleaning products, do so in a well-ventilated room, and be conservative in their use. All other caustic chemicals that zap mildew, grease, and other household annoyances cause a major risk to water and the environment. Avoid buildup. Regular cleanings will reduce the need to use potentially harmful substances. Cut down on dry cleaning, as the chemicals used by many cleaners can cause cancer. If your newly cleaned clothes smell of dry-cleaning chemicals, either return them to the cleaner or hang them in the open air until the smell is gone. Avoid the use of household air freshener products containing the carcinogenic agent *dichlorobenzene*.

—Donatelle and Davis, *Access to Health*, pp. 560–561

Directions: Select the choice that best completes each of the following statements.

_____ 1. The typographical aids in this passage include
   a. boldfaced headings.
   b. italics.
   c. underlined phrases.
   d. a and b only.

_____ 2. The most useful guide question for the first heading would be
   a. How are woodstoves constructed?
   b. How do woodstoves contribute to indoor pollution?
   c. What types of wood produce the most heat?
   d. How is woodstove smoke different from furnace emissions?

_____ 3. The most useful guide question for the last heading would be
   a. Which household chemicals cause indoor pollution?
   b. Why do people use household chemicals?
   c. How are household chemicals manufactured?
   d. Which household chemicals are safest for children?

_____ 4. Which sentence in the first paragraph best describes what the remainder of the passage will discuss?
   a. Sentence 1   c. Sentence 3
   b. Sentence 2   d. Sentence 4

_____ 5. The best way to review this passage would be to
   a. brainstorm about the topic.
   b. reread the entire passage.
   c. reread the first and last paragraphs only.
   d. reread the headings.

MASTERY TEST 2 Thinking Skills

Name _____ Section _____

Date _____ Number right _____ × 10 points = Score _____

Directions: Preview the following selection by reading only the title, first paragraph, headings, first sentence of each paragraph, and last paragraph. *Do not read* the entire selection. Then select the choice that best completes each of the statements that follow.

Health Today

TAMING TECHNOSTRESS

1   Are you "twittered out"? Is all that texting causing your thumbs to seize up in protest? If so, you're not alone. Like millions of others, you may find that all of the pressure for contact is more than enough stress for you! Known as *technostress*, this bombardment is defined as stress created by a dependence on technology and the constant state of being plugged in or wirelessly connected.

> What negative effect of technology does this photograph illustrate?

Technology may keep you in touch, but it can also add to your stress.

2   There is much good that comes from all that technological wizardry; however, for some, technomania can become obsessive—a situation in which people would rather hang out online, talking to strangers, than study, talk to friends, socialize in person, or generally connect in the real world. Although technology can allow us to multitask, work on the go, and communicate in new and different ways, there are some clear downsides to all of that "virtual" interaction.

3   • **Distracted driving.** Exact numbers are hard to come by, but some sources estimate that as much as 25 percent of distracted driving is the result of people either talking or texting on their cell phones or manipulating music devices. About 90 percent of the U.S. population, more than 270 million people, have cell phones and at any given moment, 11 percent of them are using those phones while driving. Because research indicates that doing so puts people at risk, more than 250 cities and several states have passed laws or are considering legislation that would either prohibit or restrict the use of cell phones by drivers.

4   • **Practice Safe Text!** This catchy website title emerged in 2008 and brought international attention to the repetitive stress injury (RSI) known as *Blackberry thumb*. If you are one of a growing number of persons who have this malady, you already know that it refers to a problem experienced by too much thumb use on today's personal digital assistant (PDA) devices. It causes pain, swelling,

or numbness of the thumb. The best advice is to avoid the malady by stretching thumb muscles before texting and keeping messaging to a minimum.

5 • **Other repetitive stress injuries.** Sitting in front of a computer screen set at the wrong height, or working hunched over a laptop for hours can result in stressed muscles, ligaments, and tendons, often with painful consequences. Back pain, neck cramps, and carpal tunnel syndrome are all possible outcomes. Keeping sessions short, stretching muscles frequently, and getting an ergonomic check of your work station can all help prevent future problems.

6 • **Social distress.** Authors Michell Weil and Larry Rosen describe *technosis*, a very real syndrome in which people become so immersed in technology that they risk losing their own identity. Worrying about checking your voice mails, constantly switching to e-mail or Facebook to see who has left a message or is online, perpetually posting to Twitter, and so on can keep you distracted and take important minutes or hours from your day.

7 To avoid technosis and to prevent technostress, set time limits on your technology usage, and make sure that you devote at least as much time to face-to-face interactions with people you care about as a means of nurturing your relationships. Screen your contacts, especially when you are in public or engaged in face-to-face communication with someone. You don't always need to answer your phone or respond to a text or e-mail immediately. Leave your devices at home or turn them off when you are out with others or on vacation. *Tune in* to your surroundings, your loved ones and friends, your job, and your classes by shutting off your devices.

Sources: AAA Foundation for Traffic Safety, "Safety Culture: Cell Phones and Driving: Research Update," 2008, www.aaafoundation.org/pdf/CellPhonesandDrivingFS.pdf; M. Weil and L Rosen, "Technostress: Are You a Victim?" 2007, www.technostress.com.

—Donatelle, *Health: The Basics, Green Edition*, p. 66.

_____ 1. The title of this selection is
  a. "Stress and Technology."
  b. "Stress-Related Injuries."
  c. "Taming Technostress."
  d. "Technomania."

_____ 2. The selection focuses mainly on stress related to
  a. technology.
  b. social networking.
  c. driving.
  d. relationships.

_____ 3. Which sentence in the first paragraph best describes what the rest of the selection will be about?
  a. Sentence 1   c. Sentence 4
  b. Sentence 2   d. Sentence 5

_____ 4. Technostress is defined in the selection as stress created primarily by
  a. a repetitive injury.
  b. a dependence on technology.
  c. an obsession with online relationships.
  d. real-world interactions.

_____ 5. According to the selection, what percentage of distracted driving is the result of people using cell phones or manipulating music devices?
  a. 1 percent
  b. 5 percent
  c. 10 percent
  d. 25 percent

_____ 6. The heading "Practice Safe Text!" refers to
  a. driving while texting.
  b. avoiding a repetitive stress injury.
  c. calling instead of texting.
  d. multitasking at work.

_____ 7. The best guide question for the heading before paragraph 5 is
  a. How can repetitive stress injuries be avoided?
  b. Is technology related to repetitive stress?
  c. Can anyone get a repetitive stress injury?
  d. Is repetitive stress a physical malady?

_____ 8. The best guide question for the heading before paragraph 6 is
  a. Does technology cause social distress?
  b. Is social distress a serious problem?
  c. How can technology lead to social distress?
  d. What should be done about social distress?

_____ 9. At the end of the selection, the author makes all of the following recommendations _except_
  a. set time limits on your technology usage.
  b. always respond to texts and e-mails immediately.
  c. spend time engaging in face-to-face interactions.
  d. turn off your devices when you are on vacation.

_____ 10. The author's purpose in writing this selection is to
  a. complain and criticize.
  b. entertain and amuse.
  c. inform and advise.
  d. persuade and promote.

Name _____ Section _____

Date _____ Number right* _____ × 10 points = Score _____

Body Piercing and Tattooing: Risks to Health

Rebecca J. Donatelle

Tattoos and body piercings are showing up almost everywhere these days. This selection discusses the growing popularity of "body art" as well as the health risks associated with it.

> **Vocabulary Preview**
>
> **enclaves** (par. 1) distinct groups or communities
> **medium** (par. 2) a means of conveying something
> **elitism** (par. 2) pride in being a member of a superior group
> **transmitters** (par. 5) things that carry or spread germs
> **exacerbates** (par. 6) makes worse
> **adverse** (par. 6) unfavorable

1   One look around college campuses and other enclaves for young people reveals a trend that, while not necessarily new, has been growing in recent years. We're talking, of course, about body piercing and tattooing, also referred to as "body art." For decades, tattoos appeared to be worn only by motorcyclists, military guys, and general roughnecks; and in many people's eyes, they represented the rougher, seedier part of society. Body piercing, on the other hand, was virtually nonexistent in our culture except for pierced ears, which didn't really appear until the latter part of the twentieth century. Even then, pierced ears were limited, for the most part, to women.

2   Various forms of body art, however, can be traced throughout human history when people "dressed themselves up" to attract attention or be viewed as acceptable by their peers. Examinations of cultures throughout the world, both historical and contemporary, provide evidence of the use of body art as a medium of self- and cultural expression. Ancient cultures often used body piercing as a mark of royalty or elitism. Egyptian pharaohs underwent rites of passage by piercing their navels. Roman soldiers demonstrated manhood by piercing their nipples.

---

*To calculate the number right, use items 1–10 under "Mastery Test Skills Check."

THE POPULARITY OF BODY ART

3   But why the surge in popularity of body art in current society, particularly among young people? Today, young and old alike are getting their ears and bodies pierced in record numbers in such places as the eyebrows, tongues, lips, noses, navels, nipples, genitals, and just about any place possible. Many people view the trend as a fulfillment of a desire for self-expression, as this University of Wisconsin–Madison student points out:

The nipple [ring] was one of those things that I did as a kind of empowerment, claiming my body as my own and refuting the stereotypes that people have about me. . . . The tattoo was kind of a lark and came along the same lines and I like it too. . . . [T]hey both give me a secret smile.

4   Whatever the reason, tattoo artists are doing a booming business in both their traditional artistry of tattooing as well as in the "art" of body piercing. Amidst the "oohing" and "aahing" over the latest artistic additions, however, the concerns over health risks from these procedures have been largely ignored. Despite warnings from local health officials and federal agencies, the popularity of piercings and tattoos has grown.

COMMON HEALTH RISKS

5   The most common health-related problems associated with tattoos and body piercing include skin reactions, infections, and scarring. The average healing times for piercings depend on the size of the insert, location, and the person's overall health. Facial and tongue piercings tend to heal more quickly than piercings of areas not commonly exposed to open air or light and which are often teeming with bacteria, such as the genitals. Because the hands are great germ transmitters, "fingering" of pierced areas poses a significant risk for infection.

6   Of greater concern, however, is the potential transmission of dangerous pathogens that any puncture of the human body exacerbates. The use of unsterile needles—which can cause serious infections and can transmit HIV, hepatitis B and C, tetanus, and a host of other diseases—poses a very real risk. Body piercing and tattooing are performed by body artists, unlicensed "professionals" who generally have learned their trade from other body artists. Laws and policies regulating body piercing and tattooing vary greatly by state. While some states don't allow tattoo and body-piercing parlors, others may regulate them carefully, and still others provide few regulations and standards by which parlors have to abide. Standards for safety usually include minimum age of use, standards of sanitation, use of aseptic techniques, sterilization of equipment, informed risks, instructions for skin care, record keeping, and recommendations for dealing with adverse reactions. Because of this varying degree of standards regulating the business and the potential for transmission of dangerous pathogens, anyone who receives a tattoo, body piercing, or permanent makeup tattoo cannot donate blood for one year.

Important Advice

7   Anyone who does opt for tattooing or body piercing should remember the following points:

- Look for clean, well-lit work areas, and ask about sterilization procedures.
- Before having the work done, watch the artist at work. Tattoo removal is expensive and often undoable. Make sure the

tattoo is one you can live with.
- Right before piercing or tattooing, the body area should be carefully sterilized and the artist should wear new latex gloves and touch nothing else while working.
- Packaged, sterilized needles should be used only once and then discarded. A piercing gun should not be used because it cannot be sterilized properly.
- Only jewelry made of noncorrosive metal, such as surgical stainless steel, niobium, or solid 14-karat gold, is safe for new piercing.
- Leftover tattoo ink should be discarded after each procedure.
- If any signs of pus, swelling, redness, or discoloration persist, remove the piercing object and contact a physician.

—Donatelle, "Body Piercing and Tattooing" from
Access to Health, pp. 470–471

MASTERY TEST SKILLS CHECK

Directions: Select the choice that best completes each of the following statements.

Checking Your Comprehension

_____ 1. The primary purpose of this selection is to
   a. discuss the use of body art throughout history.
   b. promote the use of body art as a form of self-expression.
   c. explain the popularity of body art.
   d. describe the health risks associated with body art.

_____ 2. The selection focuses on the trend in body piercing and tattooing among
   a. women.
   b. ancient cultures.
   c. young people.
   d. people in the military.

_____ 3. According to the selection, anyone who has received a tattoo or body piercing must wait a year before
   a. donating blood.
   b. getting another tattoo.
   c. getting another piercing.
   d. having a tattoo removed.

_____ 4. One of the greatest health risks from body piercing and tattooing results from
a. leftover ink.
b. unsterile needles.
c. allergic reactions.
d. overexposure to air or light.

_____ 5. The laws and policies regulating body piercing and tattooing can best be described as
a. strict in every state.
b. moderate in every state.
c. completely nonexistent.
d. varying from state to state.

_____ 6. In paragraph 3, which of the following sentences answers the question asked in the first sentence?
a. second sentence
b. third sentence
c. fourth sentence
d. fifth sentence

Applying Your Skills

_____ 7. The only typographical aid used in this selection is
a. italics to emphasize key terms.
b. boldfaced type to announce important ideas.
c. listing of key points.
d. underlining of key ideas.

_____ 8. The most useful guide question for this selection would be
a. What does "body art" mean?
b. What are the health risks of body piercing and tattooing?
c. Which is more popular among young people, body piercing or tattooing?
d. What is the average healing time for piercings?

_____ 9. Which of the following techniques would be most helpful in connecting the reading to your own experience?
a. Rereading the reading.
b. Thinking of people you know who have tattoos or body piercing.
c. Highlighting key information in the reading.
d. Locating and reading another article on the same topic.

_____ 10. In previewing this article, you should read all of the following _except_
a. the title.
b. the first paragraph.
c. the entire second paragraph.
d. the first sentence of each paragraph.

Studying Words

_____ 11. The word _seedier_ (par. 1) means
a. healthier.   c. shabbier.
b. stronger.   d. more remote.

_____ 12. The best synonym for the word _contemporary_ (par. 2) is
a. outdated.
b. extraordinary.
c. distant.
d. modern.

_____ 13. What is the best definition of the word _teeming_ as it is used in paragraph 5?
a. filled with
b. producing
c. emptying or pouring out
d. enriched by

_____ 14. What is the correct pronunciation of the word _exacerbates_ (par. 6)?
a. EX ace ur bates
b. ex ACE ur bates
c. ex ASS ur bates
d. ex ACK ur bates

_____ 15. If _septic_ means "containing germs that cause disease," then the word _aseptic_ (par. 6) means
a. not containing germs.
b. containing thousands of germs.
c. containing one type of germ.
d. moving toward having germs.

Summarizing the Reading

Directions: Complete the following summary of the reading by filling in the blanks.

Body piercing and tattooing, also known as _____, are a growing trend among _____. Body art has appeared in _____, both _____, as a means of _____. The most common health risks associated with _____ include _____ _____. Average healing times for piercings depend on _____. The use of _____ can cause _____ and can transmit many diseases including _____. Body artists are _____ and regulation of the body art business _____. Because of _____ and _____, anyone who _____ _____ cannot _____.

Reading Visually

1. Describe your reaction to the photo that accompanies this passage. What details in the photo correspond to the author's written descriptions of people who give and get tattoos?
2. Why do you think the author included the "Important Advice" box with this passage? Consider who her audience might be and why the information might be important for this audience.
3. How do the headings contribute to the passage overall? How do the other visual elements support or enhance the passage?

Thinking Critically about the Reading

WRITE IN YOUR
JOURNAL

1. Do you agree that the popularity of body art is related to a desire for self-expression? Why or why not? What other reasons might explain the trend?
2. Do you think most people who choose to get body art are aware of the health risks? How would the information in this passage influence your decision to get a tattoo or piercing?
3. How would standardization of laws and policies regulating body piercing and tattooing change the body art business?

For more practice, ask your instructor for an opportunity to work on the mastery tests that appear in the Test Bank.

CHAPTER

6

Understanding Paragraphs:
Topics and Main Ideas

Looking at . . .
Topics and Main Ideas

LEARNING OBJECTIVES

This chapter will show you how to:

OBJECTIVE **1** Understand general and specific ideas

OBJECTIVE **2** Identify topics

OBJECTIVE **3** Identify stated main ideas in paragraphs

OBJECTIVE **4** Recognize topic sentences

OBJECTIVE **5** Understand implied main ideas

The newspaper headlines and book title above announce what the articles and book are about. Each suggests the main point the author wants to make about the topic. Paragraphs work the same way. Each is built around a topic—the one thing the paragraph is about—and each paragraph presents a main point—or main idea—about the topic. This chapter will show you how to identify topics and main ideas.

Understanding a paragraph is a step-by-step process. The first thing you need to know is what the paragraph is about. Then you have to understand what each sentence is saying. Next, you have to see how the sentences relate to one another. Finally, to understand the main point of the paragraph, you have to consider what all the sentences, taken together, mean.

The one subject the whole paragraph is about is called the **topic**. The point that the whole paragraph makes is called the **main idea**. The sentences that explain the main idea are called **details**. To connect their ideas, writers use words and phrases known as **transitions**.

A paragraph, then, is a group of related sentences about a single topic. It has four essential parts: (1) topic, (2) main idea, (3) details, and (4) transitions. To read paragraphs most efficiently, you will need to become familiar with each part of a paragraph and be able to identify and use these parts as you read.

This chapter concentrates on understanding main ideas, both stated and implied. The next chapter, Chapter 7, focuses on supporting details, transitions, and expressing paragraph ideas in your own words.

GENERAL AND SPECIFIC IDEAS

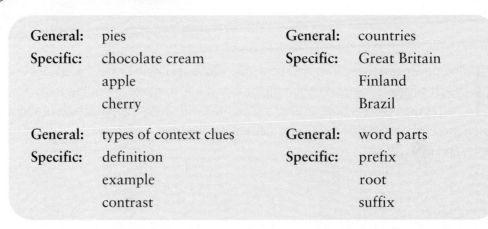

To identify topics and main ideas in paragraphs, it will help you to understand the difference between **general** and **specific**. A general idea is a broad idea that applies to a large number of individual items. The term *clothing* is general because it refers to a large collection of individual items—pants, suits, blouses, shirts, scarves, and so on. A specific idea or term is more detailed or particular. It refers to an individual item. The word *scarf*, for example, is a specific term. The phrase *red plaid scarf* is even more specific.

General:	pies	General:	countries
Specific:	chocolate cream	Specific:	Great Britain
	apple		Finland
	cherry		Brazil
General:	types of context clues	General:	word parts
Specific:	definition	Specific:	prefix
	example		root
	contrast		suffix

EXERCISE **6-1**   **Analyzing General and Specific Ideas**

Directions: Read each of the following items and decide what term(s) will complete the group. Write the word(s) in the spaces provided.

1. General: college courses
   Specific: math

   _____

   _____

2. General: _____

   Specific: roses

   tulips

   narcissus

3. General: musical groups
   Specific: _____

   _____

4. General: art
   Specific: sculpture

   _____

   _____

5. General: types of movies
   Specific: comedies

   _____

   _____

EXERCISE **6-2**   **Identifying General Ideas**

Directions: For each set of specifics, select the general idea that best describes it.

_____ 1. Specific ideas: Michelle Obama, Laura Bush, Nancy Reagan
   a. famous twentieth-century women
   b. famous American parents
   c. wives of American presidents
   d. famous wives

_____ 2. Specific ideas: touchdown, home run, 3-pointer, 5 under par
  a. types of errors in sports
  b. types of activities
  c. types of scoring in sports
  d. types of sports

_____ 3. Specific ideas: for companionship, to play with, because you love animals
  a. reasons to visit the zoo
  b. reasons to feed your cat
  c. reasons to get a pet
  d. ways to solve problems

_____ 4. Specific ideas: taking a hot bath, going for a walk, watching a video, listening to music
  a. ways to relax
  b. ways to help others
  c. ways to listen
  d. ways to solve problems

_____ 5. Specific ideas: listen, be helpful, be generous, be forgiving
  a. ways to get a job
  b. ways to keep a friend
  c. ways to learn
  d. ways to appreciate a movie

EXERCISE 6-3   **Identifying General Terms**

Directions: Underline the most general term in each group of words.

1. pounds, ounces, kilograms, weights

2. soda, coffee, beverage, wine

3. soap operas, news, TV programs, sports specials

4. home furnishings, carpeting, drapes, wall hangings

5. sociology, social sciences, anthropology, psychology

Applying General and Specific to Paragraphs

Now we will apply the idea of general and specific to paragraphs. The main idea is the most general statement the writer makes about the topic. Pick out the most general statement among the following sentences:

1. People differ according to height.
2. Hair color distinguishes some people from others.
3. People differ in a number of ways.
4. Each person has his or her own personality.

Did you choose item 3 as the most general statement? Now we will change this list into a paragraph by rearranging the sentences and adding a few facts.

> People differ in a number of ways. They differ according to physical characteristics, such as height, weight, and hair color. They also differ in personality. Some people are friendly and easygoing. Others are more reserved and formal.

In this brief paragraph, the main idea is expressed in the first sentence. This sentence is the most general statement expressed in the paragraph. All the other statements are specific details that explain this main idea.

EXERCISE 6-4   ## Identifying General Statements

Directions: For each of the following groups of sentences, select the most general statement the writer makes about the topic.

_____ 1. a. Brightly colored annuals, such as pansies and petunias, are often used as seasonal accents in a garden.
   b. Most gardens feature a mix of perennials and annuals.
   c. Some perennials prefer shade, while others thrive in full sun.
   d. Butterfly bushes are a popular perennial.

_____ 2. a. Hiring a housepainter is not as simple as it sounds.
   b. You should try to obtain a cost estimate from at least three painters.
   c. Each painter should be able to provide reliable references from past painting jobs.
   d. The painter must be able to work within the time frame you desire.

_____ 3. a. Flaxseed is an herbal treatment for constipation.
       b. Some people use Kava to treat depression.
       c. Gingko biloba is a popular remedy for memory loss.
       d. A growing number of consumers are turning to herbal remedies to treat certain ailments.

_____ 4. a. Many students choose to live off-campus in apartments or rental houses.
       b. Most colleges and universities offer a variety of student housing options.
       c. Sororities and fraternities typically allow members to live in their organization's house.
       d. On-campus dormitories provide a convenient place for students to live.

_____ 5. a. Try to set exercise goals that are challenging but realistic.
       b. Increase the difficulty of your workout gradually.
       c. Several techniques contribute to success when beginning an exercise program.
       d. Reduce soreness by gently stretching your muscles before you exercise.

IDENTIFYING THE TOPIC

OBJECTIVE 2

The **topic** is the subject of the entire paragraph. Every sentence in a paragraph in some way discusses or explains this topic. If you had to choose a title for a paragraph, the one or two words you would choose are the topic.

To find the topic of a paragraph, ask yourself: What is the one thing the author is discussing throughout the paragraph?

Now read the following paragraph with that question in mind:

Asthma is caused by inflammation of the airways in the lungs, leading to wheezing, chest tightness, shortness of breath, and coughing. In most people, asthma is brought on by allergens or irritants in the air; some people also have exercise-induced asthma. People with asthma can generally control their symptoms through the use of inhaled medications, and most asthmatics keep a "rescue" inhaler of medication on hand to use in case of a flare-up.

—adapted from Donatelle, *Health: The Basics*, p. 424

What causes asthma?

Hw   P179~198   Sep. 13.

In this example, the author is discussing one topic—asthma—throughout the paragraph. Notice that the word *asthma* is used several times. Often the repeated use of a word can serve as a clue to the topic.

EXERCISE 6-5   Identifying the Topic

Directions: Read each of the following paragraphs and then select the topic of the paragraph from the choices given.

___C___ 1.   People have been making glass in roughly the same way for at least 2,000 years. The process involves melting certain Earth materials and cooling the liquid quickly before the atoms have time to form an orderly crystalline structure. This is the same way that natural glass, called obsidian, is generated from lava. It is possible to produce glass from a variety of materials, but most commercial glass is produced from quartz sand and lesser amounts of carbonate minerals.

—Lutgens et al., *Essentials of Geology*, p. 62

    a. Earth
    b. atoms
    c. glass
    d. lava

___C___ 2.   The large majority of shoplifting is not done by professional thieves or by people who genuinely need the stolen items. About 2 million Americans are charged with shoplifting each year, but analysts estimate that for every arrest, 18 unreported incidents occur. About three-quarters of those caught are middle- or high-income people who shoplift for the thrill of it or as a substitute for affection. Shoplifting is also common among adolescents. Research evidence indicates that teen shoplifting is influenced by factors such as having friends who also shoplift.

—Solomon, *Consumer Behavior*, p. 35

    a. professional thieves
    b. shopping
    c. shoplifting
    d. adolescents

___C___ 3.   Kidney transplants are performed when the kidneys fail due to kidney disease. The kidneys are a pair of bean-shaped organs located under the rib cage by the small of the back. Each kidney is a little smaller than a fist and functions as a filter to remove toxins and wastes from the blood. When kidneys fail, waste products build up in the blood, which can be toxic.

—adapted from Belk and Maier, *Biology: Science for Life with Physiology*, p. 438

a. organ transplants
b. organ disease
c. kidneys
d. toxins

_C_ 4.   In order to survive, hunting and gathering societies depend on hunting animals and gathering plants. In some groups, the men do the hunting, and the women the gathering. In others, both men and women (and children) gather plants, the men hunt large animals, and both men and women hunt small animals. Hunting and gathering societies are small, usually consisting of only 25 to 40 people. These groups are nomadic. As their food supply dwindles in one area, they move to another location. They place high value on sharing food, which is essential to their survival.

—adapted from Henslin, *Sociology: A Down-to-Earth Approach*, p. 149

a. hunters
b. food supplies
c. hunting and gathering societies
d. survival

_B_ 5.   People who call themselves **freegans** are modern-day scavengers who live off discards as a political statement against corporations and consumerism. They forage through supermarket trash and eat the slightly bruised produce or just-expired canned goods that we routinely throw out, and obtain surplus food from sympathetic stores and restaurants. Freegans dress in castoff clothes and furnish their homes with items they find on the street. They get the word on locations where people are throwing out a lot of stuff by checking out postings at freecycle.org and at so-called *freemeets* (flea markets where no one exchanges money),

—adapted from Solomon, *Consumer Behavior*, p. 392–393

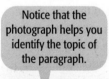

Notice that the photograph helps you identify the topic of the paragraph.

a. scavengers
b. freegans
c. recycling
d. freemeets

EXERCISE 6-6   **Identifying the Topic**

Directions: Read each of the following paragraphs and then write the topic of the paragraph in the space provided.

A.   The word **locavore** has been coined to describe people who eat only food grown or produced locally, usually within close proximity to their homes. Locavores rely on farmers' markets, homegrown foods, or foods grown by independent farmers. Locavores prefer these foods because they are thought to be fresher, more environmentally friendly, and require far fewer resources to get them to market and keep them fresh for longer periods of time. Locavores believe that locally grown organic food is preferable to large corporation- or supermarket-based organic foods, as local foods have a smaller impact on the environment.

                                      —adapted from Donatelle, *Health: The Basics*, p. 282

Topic: _____ lo cavore _____

B.   A monopoly exists when an industry or market has only one producer (or else is so dominated by one producer that other firms cannot compete with it). A sole supplier enjoys nearly complete control over the prices of its products. Its only constraint is a decrease in consumer demand due to increased prices or government regulation. In the United States, laws forbid many monopolies and regulate prices charged by natural monopolies—industries in which one company can most efficiently supply all needed goods or services. Many electric companies are natural monopolies because they can supply all the power needed in a local area.

                                      —adapted from Ebert and Griffin, *Business Essentials*, p. 12

Topic: _____ monopoly _____

C.   Values represent cultural standards by which we determine what is good, bad, right, or wrong. Sometimes these values are expressed as proverbs or sayings that teach us how to live. Do you recognize the phrase, "Life is like a box of chocolates—you never know what you're going to get"? This modern-day saying is popular among those who embrace life's unpredictability. Cultures are capable of growth and change, so it's possible for a culture's values to change over time.

                                      —Carl, *Think Sociology*, p. 51

Topic: _____ cultural values _____

D.   They go by many different names—capsule hotels, modular hotels, and pod hotels—but they all have one thing in common: very efficient use of space in a small footprint. The concept of modular hotels was pioneered by the Japanese, but the idea is sweeping across the world. Priced well below most competitors, these small, 75- to 100-square-foot rooms don't waste any space. Most modular units include the basics: private bathrooms, beds that are designed for two, flat-screen televisions, and a small work space. Weary travelers looking for nothing more than a place to sleep are finding that modular hotels "fit the bill."

—adapted from Cook et al., *Tourism: The Business of Travel*, p. 347

Topic: <u>Modular   Hotels</u>

E.   Television commercials provide a rich source of material to analyze. Begin by asking, "What reasons am I being given to lead me to want to buy this product?" Often, commercials do not overtly state the reasons; instead, they use music, staging, gestures, and visual cues to suggest the ideas they want us to have. We probably will not find a commercial that comes right out and says that buying someone a bottle of perfume or piece of jewelry will lead to a fulfilling love life, but several holiday commercials certainly imply as much.

—adapted from Facione, *Think Critically*, p. 90

Topic: <u>TV com. adv.</u>

FINDING THE STATED MAIN IDEA

The **main idea** of a paragraph is the most important idea; it is the idea that the whole paragraph explains or supports. Usually it is expressed in one sentence called the **topic sentence**. To find the main idea, use the following suggestions.

Locate the Topic

You have learned that the topic is the subject of a paragraph. The main idea is the most important thing the author wants you to know about the topic. To find the main idea, ask yourself, "What is the one most important thing to know about the topic?" Read the following paragraph and then answer this question.

Rather than traveling for rest and relaxation, more and more of the world's population is traveling for sport-related reasons. Sport tourism has exploded in the last ten years and is now seen as a major form of special-interest tourism. Sport tourism is travel away from home to play sport, watch sport, or to visit a sport attraction including both competitive and noncompetitive activities. Think of the vast array of travel that is included in this definition. Sport team members traveling to out-of-town tournaments are included; booster and alumni clubs trekking to "bowl" games are included; golf fans traveling to the British Open are included; a snowboard/ski club traveling to the Rockies for spring break is included!

—Cook et al., *Tourism: The Business of Travel*, p. 52

In this example, the topic is sport tourism. The most important point the author is making is that sport tourism has become a popular form of travel.

Locate the Most General Sentence

The most general sentence in the paragraph expresses the main idea. This sentence is called the topic sentence. This sentence must be broad enough to include or cover all the other ideas (details) in the paragraph. In the paragraph on the previous page, the first sentence makes a general statement about sport tourism—that it is becoming more and more popular. The rest of the sentences provide specifics.

Study the Rest of the Paragraph

The main idea must connect, draw together, and make meaningful the rest of the paragraph. You might think of the main idea as the one that all the details, taken together, add up to, explain, or support. In the paragraph on the previous page, sentence one serves as an introductory sentence. Sentence three offers a definition of sports tourism. Sentences four and five provide examples.

EXERCISE 6-7 | **Writing Main Ideas**

Directions: Bring to class a list of bumper sticker or T-shirt messages you have recently seen. Form groups of three or four students. Each group should select three messages. For each, identify the topic and write a sentence that states its main idea. Groups should share their work with the class. The class may choose to select the most fun, innovative, or effective message and corresponding main idea.

IDENTIFYING TOPIC SENTENCES

OBJECTIVE 4

The topic sentence can be located anywhere in the paragraph. However, there are several positions where it is most likely to be found.

Topic Sentence First

Most often the topic sentence is placed first in the paragraph. In this type of paragraph, the author first states his or her main point and then explains it.

Topic Sentence

Detail

Detail

Detail

> D.W. Griffith, among the first "star" directors, paved the way for future filmmakers. Griffith refined many of the narrative techniques that are still used, including varied camera distances, close-up shots, multiple story lines, fast-paced editing, and symbolic imagery. His major work, *The Birth of a Nation* (1915), was a controversial three-hour Civil War epic. Although considered a technical masterpiece, the film naively glorified the Ku Klux Klan and stereotyped southern blacks. It is nevertheless the movie that triggered Hollywood's eighty-year fascination with long narrative movies. By 1915, more than 20 percent of films were feature-length (around two hours), and *The Birth of a Nation,* which cost a filmgoer a record $2 admission to see, ran for a year on Broadway.
>
> —Campbell, *Media and Culture*, p. 196

Here the writer first states that D. W. Griffith paved the way for future filmmakers. The rest of the paragraph explains how he did this.

Topic Sentence Last

The second most likely place for a topic sentence to appear is last in the paragraph. When using this arrangement, a writer leads up to the main point and then directly states it at the end.

Detail
Detail
Detail
Topic Sentence

> Art can inform, embellish, inspire, arouse, awaken, and delight us. Art can challenge us to think and see in new ways, and help each of us to develop a personal sense of beauty and truth. It can also deceive, humiliate, and anger us. A given work of art may serve several functions all at once.
>
> —Frank, *Prebles' Artforms*, p. 5

This paragraph first describes the positive effects that art can have on us, then describes other effects that are more negative. The paragraph ends with a general statement about the many functions of art.

Topic Sentence in the Middle

If it is placed neither first nor last, then the topic sentence appears somewhere in the middle of the paragraph. In this arrangement, the sentences before the topic sentence lead up to or introduce the main idea. Those that follow the main idea explain or describe it.

Detail
Detail
Topic Sentence
Detail
Detail

If a person won the lottery or invested in the right stocks, his or her social class could change in an upward direction in an instant. Likewise, the mortgage crisis and corporate downsizing have sent many middle-class families plummeting into poverty. <u>Social mobility is a term that describes social class change, either upward or downward.</u> Wherever we are in life, then, there's always the chance that something could happen to us that would change our status. If social class is a ladder, social mobility occurs when we are moved either up or down it.

—adapted from Carl, *Think Sociology*, p. 128

In this paragraph, the author begins with examples of upward as well as downward mobility. He then states his main point and follows it with a general statement about status.

Topic Sentence First and Last

Occasionally the main idea will appear at the beginning of a paragraph and again at the end. Writers may use this organization to emphasize an important idea or to explain an idea that needs clarification.

Topic Sentence

Detail

Detail

Detail

Topic Sentence

<u>Modeling, or learning behaviors by watching others perform them, is one of the most effective strategies for changing behavior.</u> For example, suppose that you have trouble talking to people you don't know very well. One of the easiest ways to improve your communication skills is to select friends whose social skills you envy. Observe them. Do they talk more or listen more? How do people respond to them? Why are they such good communicators? <u>If you observe behaviors you admire, you can model the steps of your behavior-change technique on a proven success.</u>

—adapted from Donatelle, *Health: The Basics*, p. 18

The first and last sentences both state, in slightly different ways, that modeling can be an effective way to change behavior.

EXERCISE 6-8 | **Identifying Topic Sentences**

Directions: Underline the topic sentence in each of the following paragraphs.

A. Sociologists have several different ways of defining poverty. *Transitional poverty* is a temporary state that occurs when someone loses a job for a short time. *Marginal poverty* occurs when a person lacks stable employment (for example, if your job is lifeguarding at a pool during the summer season, you might experience marginal poverty when the season ends). The next, more serious level, *residual poverty*, is chronic and multigenerational. A person who experiences *absolute poverty* is so poor that he or she doesn't have resources to survive. *Relative poverty* is a state that occurs when we compare ourselves with those around us.

—adapted from Carl, *Think Sociology*, p. 122

B. With so many people participating in social networking sites and keeping personal blogs, it's increasingly common for a single disgruntled customer to wage war online against a company for poor service or faulty products. Unhappy customers have taken to the Web to complain about broken computers or poor customer service. Individuals may post negative reviews of products on blogs, upload angry videos outlining complaints on YouTube, or join public discussion forums where they can voice their opinion about the good and the bad. In the same way that companies celebrate the viral spread of good news, they must also be on guard for online backlash that can damage a reputation.

—adapted from Ebert and Griffin, *Business Essentials*, p. 161

C. Elections serve a critical function in American society. They make it possible for most political participation to be channeled through the electoral process rather than bubbling up through demonstrations, riots, or revolutions. Elections provide regular access to political power, so that leaders can be replaced without being overthrown. This is possible because elections are almost universally accepted as a fair and free method of selecting political leaders. Furthermore, by choosing who is to lead the country, the people—if they make their choices carefully—can also guide the policy direction of the government.

—adapted from Edwards et al., *Government in America*, p. 306

D. Animals obtain food in a great many ways. Some animals are "generalists," whereas others are "specialists." Crows, for instance, are extreme generalists; they will eat just about anything that is readily available—plant or animal, alive or dead. In sharp contrast, the koala of Australia, an extreme feeding specialist, eats only the leaves of a few species of eucalyptus trees. Most animals are somewhere in between crows and koalas in the range of their diet.

—adapted from Campbell et al., *Biology: Concepts & Connections*, p. 712

E.   People have not limited themselves to investigating nature. To try to understand life, they have also developed fields of science that focus on the social world. The social sciences examine human relationships. Just as the natural sciences attempt to understand the world of nature, the social sciences attempt to understand the social world. Just as the world of nature contains relationships that are not obvious but must be discovered through controlled observations, so the relationships of the human or social world are not obvious and must be revealed by means of repeated observations.

—adapted from Henslin, *Sociology: A Down-to-Earth Approach*, p. 6

F.   Darwin hypothesized sexual selection as an explanation for differences between males and females within a species. For instance, the enormous tail on a male pea-cock results from female peahens that choose mates with showier tails. Because large tails require so much energy to display and are more conspicuous to their pred-ators, peacocks with the largest tails must be both physically strong and smart to survive. Peahens can use the size of the tail, therefore, as a measure of the "quality" of the male. When a peahen chooses a male with a large tail, she is making sure that her offspring will receive high-quality genes. Sexual selection explains the differ-ences between males and females in many species.

—adapted from Belk and Maier, *Biology: Science for Life with Physiology*, p. 305

G.   In Japan, it's called *kuroi kiri* (black mist); in Germany, it's *schmiergeld* (grease money), whereas Mexicans refer to *la mordida* (the bite), the French say *pot-de-vin* (jug of wine), and Italians speak of the *bustarella* (little envelope). They're all talking about *baksheesh*, the Middle Eastern term for a "tip" to grease the wheels of a trans-action. Giving "gifts" in exchange for getting business is common and acceptable in many countries, even though this may be frowned on elsewhere.

—adapted from Solomon, *Consumer Behavior*, p. 21

H.   Ocean predators often hunt by looking up, searching for a silhouette of their prey above them. Can an animal hide its silhouette? The answer is yes, if it turns on the lights. For instance, the deep-sea firefly squid has light-producing organs that emit a soft glow to match the light filtering down from above. During the day, when the squid remain in deep, cold water, they glow blue to match the blue light that penetrates into deeper water. As night approaches, the squid come closer to the warmer surface, and their glow turns to green, again matching the light. Many marine animals and fishes avoid their predators by producing light to hide their silhouettes.

—adapted from Campbell et al., *Biology: Concepts & Connections*, p. 73

I. ⌠The standards of our peer groups tend to dominate our lives.⌡ If your peers, for example, listen to rap, rock and roll, country, or gospel, it is almost inevitable that you also prefer that kind of music. In high school, if your friends take math courses, you probably do too. It is the same for clothing styles and dating standards. Peer influences also extend to behaviors that violate social norms. If your peers are college-bound and upwardly striving, that is most likely what you will be; but if they use drugs, cheat, and steal, you are likely to do so too.

—adapted from Henslin, *Sociology: A Down-to-Earth Approach*, p. 85

J. ⌠In the western and southwestern United States, sedimentary rocks often exhibit a brilliant array of colors.⌡ In the walls of Arizona's Grand Canyon we can see layers that are red, orange, purple, gray, brown, and buff. Some of the sedimentary rocks in Utah's Bryce Canyon are a delicate pink color. Sedimentary rocks in more humid places are also colorful but they are usually covered by soil and vegetation.

—Lutgens et al., *Essentials of Geology*, p. 144

Does this photograph help you find the main idea of the paragraph?

LEARNING STYLE TIPS

If you tend to be a . . .	Then find topic sentences by . . .
Creative learner	Looking away from the paragraph and stating its main point in your own words. Find a sentence that matches your statement.
Pragmatic learner	Reading through the paragraph, sentence by sentence, evaluating each sentence.

EXERCISE 6-9   **Writing Main Ideas**

Directions: Form groups of three students. Each group writes a topic on the top of a sheet of paper. Groups exchange papers and each group then writes a topic sentence based on the topic. Groups continue to exchange papers and write topic sentences until every group has written a topic sentence for each topic, and then papers are returned to the groups that wrote the original topic. Groups then read aloud the topic and suggested topic sentences. The class evaluates the topic sentences and selects the most effective ones for each topic.

IMPLIED MAIN IDEAS

When you **imply** something, you suggest an idea, but you do not state it out-right. Study the cartoon below. The point the cartoonist is making is clear—relationships change quickly. Notice, however, that this point is not stated directly. To get the cartoonist's point, you had to study the details and read the signs in the cartoon, and then reason out what the cartoonist is trying to say. You need to use the same reasoning process when reading paragraphs that lack a topic sentence. You have to study the details and figure out what all the details mean when considered together. This chapter will show you how to figure out main ideas that are suggested (implied) but not directly stated in a paragraph.

What Does Implied Mean?

Suppose your favorite shirt is missing from your closet and you know that your roommate often borrows your clothes. You say to your roommate, "If that blue plaid shirt is back in my closet by noon, I'll forget that it was missing." Now, you did not directly accuse your roommate of borrowing your shirt, but your message was clear—return my shirt! Your statement implied, or suggested, that your roommate had borrowed it and should return it. Your roommate, if he understood your message, inferred (reasoned out) that you suspected that he had borrowed your shirt and that you want it back.

Speakers and writers imply ideas. Listeners and readers must make inferences in order to understand them. Here are two important terms you need to know:

| Imply | means | to suggest an idea but not state it directly. |
| Infer | means | to reason out something based on what has been said. |

Here is another statement; what is the writer implying?

I wouldn't feed that cake to my dog.

No doubt you inferred that the writer dislikes the cake and considers it inedible, but notice that the writer did not say that.

EXERCISE **6-10**   **Identifying Implications**

Directions: For each of the following statements, select the choice that best explains what the writer is implying but has not directly stated.

_____ 1. Jane's hair looks as if she just came out of a wind tunnel.
   a. Jane's hair needs rearranging.
   b. Jane's hair is messy.
   c. Jane's hair needs styling.
   d. Jane's hair needs coloring.

_____ 2. I would not recommend Professor Wright's class to my worst enemy.
   a. The writer likes Professor Wright's class.
   b. The writer dislikes Professor Wright's class.
   c. Professor Wright's class is popular.
   d. Professor Wright's class is unpopular.

_____ 3. The steak was overcooked and tough; the mashed potatoes were cold; the green beans were withered; and the chocolate pie was mushy.
   a. The dinner was tasty.
   b. The dinner was prepared poorly.
   c. The dinner was nutritious.
   d. The dinner was served carelessly.

_____ 4. Professor Rodriguez assigns three 5-page papers, gives weekly quizzes, and requires both a midterm and final exam. In addition to weekly assigned

chapters in the text, we must read three to four journal articles each week. It is difficult to keep up.
   a. Professor Rodriguez's course is demanding.
   b. Professor Rodriguez is not a good teacher.
   c. Professor Rodriguez likes to give homework.
   d. Professor Rodriguez's course is unpopular.

_____ 5. It was my favorite time of year. The lilacs were blooming—finally!—and even though we still wore sweaters, the breeze held the promise of warm days to come.
   a. It was autumn.
   b. It was springtime.
   c. It was summertime.
   d. There was a storm coming.

_____ 6. When Alton got the estimate for repairing his car, he knew he had a tough decision to make.
   a. Alton was going to repair his own car.
   b. Alton would have to find another car repair shop.
   c. Alton's car repairs were going to be inexpensive.
   d. Alton would have to decide whether to repair the car or buy a different one.

_____ 7. Charlie limped over to the couch and lay down. He put his foot up on a pillow and carefully placed the ice pack on his ankle.
   a. Charlie is getting ready to take a nap.
   b. Charlie has an injured ankle.
   c. Charlie has the flu.
   d. Charlie has been running.

_____ 8. After the girls' sleepover party last Saturday, it looked like a bomb had gone off in the basement.
   a. The sleepover party was too loud.
   b. The electricity went out during the sleepover party.
   c. There was an explosion in the basement after the sleepover party.
   d. The girls made a mess in the basement.

_____ 9. When it was Kei's turn to give her speech, her stomach did a flip, and her face felt as if it were on fire.
   a. Kei looked forward to giving her speech.
   b. Kei was experienced at giving speeches.
   c. Kei was nervous about giving her speech.
   d. Kei enjoyed giving speeches.

_____ 10. People filed out of the movie theater slowly and quietly; many of them wiped their eyes and noses with tissues as they walked to their cars.
   a. The movie was sad.
   b. The movie was funny.
   c. The theater was cold.
   d. The moviegoers were disappointed.

Figuring Out Implied Main Ideas

Implied main ideas, when they appear in paragraphs, are usually larger, more important ideas than the details. You might think of **implied ideas** as general ideas that are suggested by specifics.

What larger, more important idea do these details point to?

The wind was blowing at 35 mph.

The windchill was 5 degrees below zero.

Snow was falling at the rate of 3 inches per hour.

Together these three details suggests that a snowstorm or blizzard was occurring. You might visualize this as follows:

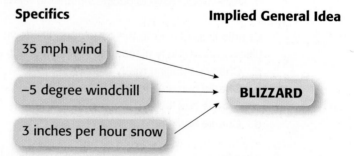

Now what idea does the following set of specifics suggest?

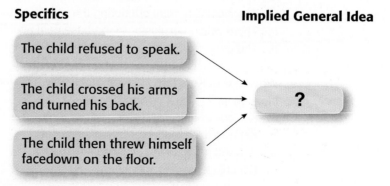

You probably determined that the child was angry or having a temper tantrum.

EXERCISE 6-11   ## Inferring General Ideas

Directions: Find a word from the list below that describes the larger idea or situation each set of specifics suggests. Each will require you to infer a general idea.

tonsillitis	closed	dying	flu	accident
power outage	accident	a burglary	going too fast	

1. The child has a headache.

   The child has a queasy stomach.

   The child has a mild fever.

   General Idea: The child has the ___flu___

2. The plant's leaves were withered.

   The blossoms had dropped.

   Its stem was drooping.

   General Idea: The plant was ___dying___

3. The windshield of the car was shattered.

   The door panel was dented.

   The bumper was crumpled.

   General Idea: The car had been in a(n) ___accident___

4. The lights went out.

   The television shut off.

   The refrigerator stopped running.

   General Idea: There was a ___power outage___

5. The supermarket door was locked.

   The parking lot was nearly empty.

   A few remaining customers were checking out.

   General Idea: The supermarket was ___closed___

Implied Ideas in Paragraphs

In paragraphs, writers sometimes leave their main idea unstated. The paragraph contains only details. It is up to you, the reader, to infer the writer's main point. You can visualize this type of paragraph as follows:

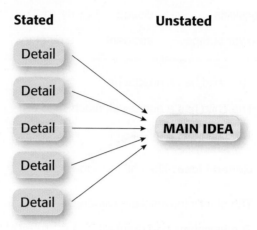

The details, when taken together, all point to a larger, more important idea. Think of the paragraph as a list of facts that you must add up or put together to determine the meaning of the paragraph as a whole. Use the following steps as a guide to find implied main ideas:

1. **Find the topic.** Ask yourself, "What is the one thing the author is discussing throughout the paragraph?"
2. **Decide what the writer wants you to know about that topic.** Look at each detail and decide what larger general idea each explains.
3. **Express this idea in your own words.** Make sure the main idea is a reasonable one. Ask yourself, "Does it apply to all the details in the paragraph?"

Read the following paragraph; then follow the three steps listed above.

> Some advertisers rely on star power. Commercials may use celebrities to encourage consumers to purchase a product. Other commercials may use an "everyone's buying it" approach that argues that thousands of consumers could not possibly be wrong in their choice, so the product must be worthwhile. Still other commercials may use visual appeal to catch the consumers' interest and persuade them to make purchases.

The topic of this paragraph is commercials. More specifically it is about devices advertisers use to build commercials. Three details are given: use of star power, an everyone's-buying-it approach, and visual appeal. Each of the three details is a different persuasive device. The main point the writer is trying to make, then, is that commercials use various persuasive devices to appeal to consumers. Notice that no single sentence states this idea clearly.

You can visualize this paragraph as follows:

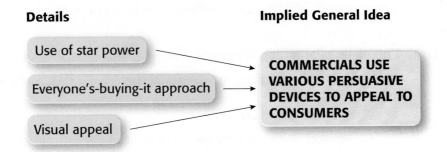

Details

Use of star power

Everyone's-buying-it approach

Visual appeal

Implied General Idea

COMMERCIALS USE VARIOUS PERSUASIVE DEVICES TO APPEAL TO CONSUMERS

Here is another paragraph. Read it and then fill in the diagram that follows:

Yellow is a bright, cheery color; it is often associated with spring and hopefulness. Green, since it is a color that appears frequently in nature (trees, grass, plants), has come to suggest growth and rebirth. Blue, the color of the sky, may suggest eternity or endless beauty. Red, the color of both blood and fire, is often connected with strong feelings such as courage, lust, and rage.

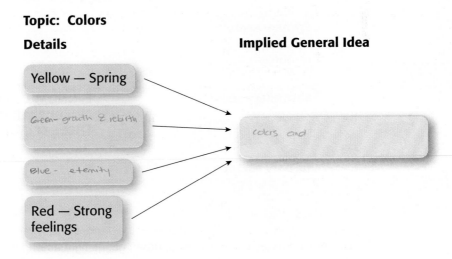

Topic: Colors

Details

Yellow — Spring

Green- growth & rebirth

Blue - eternity

Red — Strong feelings

Implied General Idea

colors and

How to Know if You Have Made a Reasonable Inference

There is a test you can perform to discover if you inferred a reasonable main idea. The idea you infer to be the main idea should be broad enough so that every sentence in the paragraph explains the idea you have chosen. Work through the paragraph, sentence by sentence. Check to see that each sentence explains or gives more information about the idea you have chosen. If some sentences do not explain your chosen idea, your main idea probably is not broad enough. Work on expanding your idea and making it more general.

EXERCISE 6-12 | **Completing Paragraph Diagrams**

Directions: Read each of the following paragraphs and complete the diagram that follows.

A.   Workers in the **primary sector** of an economy extract resources directly from the earth. Most workers in this sector are usually in agriculture, but the sector also includes fishing, forestry, and mining. Workers in the **secondary sector** transform raw materials produced by the primary sector into manufactured goods. Construction is included in this sector. All other jobs in an economy are within the **tertiary sector,** sometimes called the **service sector.** The tertiary sector includes a great range of occupations, from a store clerk to a surgeon, from a movie ticket seller to a nuclear physicist, from a dancer to a political leader.

—Bergman and Renwick, *Introduction to Geography,* p. 365

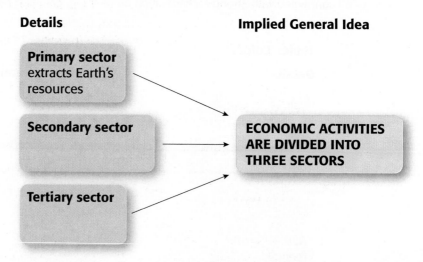

B.   Among many other activities, urban gangs fight among themselves and prey on the weak and vulnerable. They delight in demonstrating ownership and control of their "turf," and they sometimes turn neighborhoods into war zones in defense of it. Once gangs form, their graffiti soon adorn buildings and alleyways, and membership is displayed through hand signs, clothing, and special colors. As a newly formed gang grows in reputation and confidence, it soon finds itself attracting those who would like to be members in order to reap the benefits: safety, or girlfriends, or a reputation for toughness.

—Barlow, *Criminal Justice in America,* p. 271

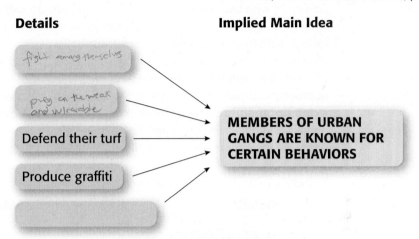

Details

fight among themselves

prey on the weak and vulnerable

Defend their turf

Produce graffiti

Implied Main Idea

MEMBERS OF URBAN GANGS ARE KNOWN FOR CERTAIN BEHAVIORS

C.   More than 30 percent of all foodborne illnesses result from unsafe handling of food at home. What can you do to prevent such illnesses? Among the most basic of precautions are to wash your hands and to wash all produce before eating it. Avoid cross-contamination in the kitchen by using separate cutting boards and utensils for meats and produce. Temperature control is also important; hot foods must be kept hot and cold foods kept cold in order to avoid unchecked bacterial growth. Leftovers need to be eaten within 3 days, and if you're unsure how long something has been sitting in the fridge, don't take chances. When in doubt, throw it out.

—adapted from Donatelle, *Health: The Basics*, p. 280

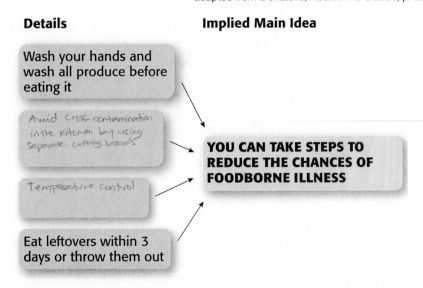

Details

Wash your hands and wash all produce before eating it

Avoid cross-contamination in the kitchen by using separate cutting boards

Temperature control

Eat leftovers within 3 days or throw them out

Implied Main Idea

YOU CAN TAKE STEPS TO REDUCE THE CHANCES OF FOODBORNE ILLNESS

D. How should you present your speech? Let's consider your options. An **impromptu speech** is delivered on the spur of the moment, without preparation. The ability to speak off the cuff is useful in an emergency, but impromptu speeches produce unpredictable outcomes. It's certainly not a good idea to rely on impromptu speaking in place of solid preparation. Another option is a **memorized speech.** Speakers who use memorized presentations are usually most effective when they write their speeches to sound like informal and conversational speech rather than formal, written essays. A **manuscript speech** is written out beforehand and then read from a manuscript or TelePrompTer. When extremely careful wording is required (for example, when the president addresses Congress), the manuscript speech is appropriate. However, most speeches that you'll deliver will be extemporaneous. An **extemporaneous speech** is one that is prepared in advance and presented from abbreviated notes. Extemporaneous speeches are nearly as polished as memorized ones, but they are more vigorous, flexible, and spontaneous.

—German et al., *Principles of Public Speaking,* pp. 190–91

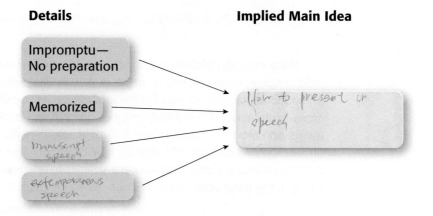

E. In order to measure social class standing, sociologists may use the *objective* method, which ranks individuals into classes on the basis of measures such as education, income, and occupational prestige. Sociologists may also use the *reputational* method, which places people into various social classes on the basis of reputation in the community. A third method, *self-identification,* allows people to place themselves in a social class. Although people can readily place themselves in a class, the results are often difficult to interpret. People might be hesitant to call themselves upper-class for fear of appearing snobbish, but at the same time they might be reluctant to call themselves lower-class for fear of being stigmatized. The net result is that the method of self-identification substantially overestimates the middle portion of the class system.

—Curry et al., *Sociology for the 21st Century,* p. 138

Details

Main Idea

objective

Reputational—Based on community reputation

Self-Identification— People place themselves in social class

Measure Standing / class

EXERCISE **6-13**   **Analyzing Paragraphs**

Directions: Read each of the following paragraphs and answer the questions that follow.

A. Thanks to the Internet, you can shop 24 hours a day without leaving home, you can read today's newspaper without getting drenched picking up a hard copy in a rainstorm, and you don't have to wait for the 6:00 news to find out what the weather will be like tomorrow—at home or around the globe. And, with the increasing use of handheld devices and wireless communications, you can get that same information—from stock quotes to the weather—even when you're away from your computer.

—Solomon and Stuart, *The Brave New World of E-Commerce*, p. 13

1. What is the topic? _The Internet_

2. What is the implied main idea? _____
    benefits

B. Research suggests that women who are considered attractive are more effective in changing attitudes than are women thought to be less attractive. In addition, more attractive individuals are often considered to be more credible than less attractive people. They are also perceived to be happier, more popular, more sociable, and more successful than are those rated as being less attractive. With respect to shape and body size, people with fat, round silhouettes are consistently rated as older, more old-fashioned, less good-looking, more talkative, and more good-natured. Athletic, muscular people are rated as more mature, better looking, taller, and more adventurous. Tall and thin people are rated as more ambitious, more suspicious of others, more tense and nervous, more pessimistic, and quieter.

—Beebe and Masterson, *Communicating in Small Groups*, p. 150

d Main Ideas

1. What is the
                       ied main idea? _peoples Co₂ &c ✓ @ 6_

2. What is
                  _r_

...keeper will tell you that the primate house is their most popular exhibit. A...e apes and monkeys. It is easy to see why—primates are curious, playful, ...In short, they are fun to watch. But something else drives our fascination ...onderful animals: We see ourselves reflected in them. The placement of ...their small noses appear humanlike. They have hands with fingernails ...with claws. Some can stand and walk on two legs for short periods. ...nipulate objects with their fingers and opposable thumbs. They ...tal care, and even their social relations are similar to ours— th...ss, and pout.

adapted from Belk and Maier, *Biology: Science for Life with Physiology*, p. 236

1. What is the topic? _____Primate_____

2. What is the implied main idea? _____

_____

> How do these photographs suggest the implied main idea?

D.   The Web has enabled people to work, "talk" to friends across town and across the ocean, and buy goods from online retailers without leaving their houses. It has also made some criminal enterprises and unethical behavior easier to accomplish and harder to trace—for example, people can scam others out of large sums of money, buy college term papers, and learn how to build a bomb.

—adapted from Divine et al., *America Past and Present*, p. 449

1. What is the topic? _____web_____

2. What is the implied main idea? _Positive & negative effects of web_ _advantages_ _dis-_

E.   Sleep conserves body energy so that we are rested and ready to perform during high-performance daylight hours. Sleep also restores the neurotransmitters that have been depleted during the waking hours. This process clears the brain of unimportant details as a means of preparing for a new day. Getting enough sleep to feel ready to meet daily challenges is a key factor in maintaining optimal physical and psychological status.

—Donatelle and Davis, *Access to Health*, p. 42

1. What is the topic? _____

2. What is the implied main idea? _functions of sleep_

EXERCISE 6-14   **Writing Implied Main Ideas**

Directions: None of the following paragraphs has a topic sentence. Read each paragraph and, in the space provided, write a sentence that expresses the main idea.

A.   When registering for online services under a screen name, it can be tempting to think your identity is a secret to other users. Many people will say or do things on the Internet that they would never do in real life because they believe that they are acting anonymously. However, most blogs, e-mail and instant messenger services, and social networking sites are tied to your real identity in some way. While your identity may be superficially concealed by a screen name, it often takes little more than a quick Google search to uncover your name, address, and other personal and possibly sensitive information.

—Ebert and Griffin, *Business Essentials*, p. 188

Implied Main Idea: _Personal Identity / information not safe on the internet_

B.   Governments in this country spend billions of dollars on schools, libraries, hospitals, and dozens of other public institutions. Some of these services, like highways and public parks, can be shared by everyone and cannot be denied to anyone. These kinds of services are called public goods. Other services, such as a college education or medical care, can be restricted to individuals who meet certain criteria and may be provided by the private sector as well. Governments typically provide these services to make them accessible to people who may not be able to afford privately available services.

—Edwards et al., *Government in America*, p. 9

Implied Main Idea: _Government services to the public wide range_

C.   Sociologists use the term **norms** to describe the rules of behavior that develop out of a group's values. The term **sanctions** refers to the reactions people receive for following or breaking norms. A positive sanction expresses approval for following a norm, and a negative sanction reflects disapproval for breaking a norm. Positive sanctions can be material, such as a prize, a trophy, or money, but in everyday life they usually consist of hugs, smiles, a pat on the back, or even handshakes and "high fives." Negative sanctions can also be material—being fined in court is one example—but negative sanctions, too, are more likely to be symbolic: harsh words, or gestures such as frowns, stares, clenched jaws, or raised fists.

—adapted from Henslin, *Sociology: A Down-to-Earth Approach*, p. 46

Implied Main Idea: _a group's values can lead to positive & nego sanctions_

D.   The amount of air forced past the vocal cords determines the volume of our speech, while muscles that control the length of the vocal cords help to determine the pitch of our speech. The shape or our mouths, lips, and tongue and the position of our teeth determine the actual sound that is produced. Sustained exposure to tobacco

Hw

Pg 202 ~ 216

smoke can cause parts of the larynx to become covered with scar tissue, often making long-time smokers sound quite hoarse.

—Belk and Maier, *Biology: Science for Life with Physiology*, p. 447

Implied Main Idea: _____

E.   Most sporting goods manufacturers have long sold products for women, but this often meant simply creating an inferior version of the male product and slapping a pink label on it. Then the companies discovered that many women were buying products intended for boys because they wanted better quality, so some of them figured out that they needed to take this market segment seriously. Burton Snowboard Company was one of the early learners. When the company started to offer high-quality clothing and gear made specifically for women, female boarders snapped them up. Burton also changed the way it promotes these products and redesigned its Web site after getting feedback from female riders.

—adapted from Solomon, *Consumer Behavior*, p. 189

Implied Main Idea: _____

_____

F.   If you've ever noticed that you feel better after a belly laugh or a good cry, you aren't alone. Old adages such as "laughter is the best medicine" and "smile and the world smiles with you" didn't just evolve out of the blue. Scientists have long recognized that smiling, laughing, singing, dancing, and other actions can elevate our moods, help us live longer, and help us improve our relationships. Crying can have similar positive physiological effects. Recent research has shown that laughter and joy can increase endorphin levels, increase oxygen levels in the blood, increase immune system functioning, decrease stress levels, relieve pain, enhance productivity, reduce risks of heart disease, and help fight cancer.

—Donatelle, *Health: The Basics*, p. 71

Implied Main Idea: _____

_____

G.   As the effects of caffeine begin to wear off, users may feel let down, mentally or physically depressed, exhausted, and weak. To counteract these effects, people commonly choose to drink another cup of coffee. But before you say yes to another cup of coffee, consider this. Although you would have to drink between 66 and 100 cups of coffee in a day to produce a fatal overdose of caffeine, you may experience sensory disturbances after consuming only 10 cups of coffee within a 24-hour period. These symptoms include tinnitus (ringing in the ears), spots before the eyes, numbness in arms and legs, poor circulation, and visual hallucinations. Because 10 cups of coffee is not an extraordinary amount for many people to drink within a 24-hour period, caffeine use is clearly something to think about.

—Donatelle and Davis, *Access to Health*, pp. 289–290

Implied Main Idea: _____

H. In 1946, the Levitt Company was finishing up Levittown. Practically overnight, what was formerly a Long Island potato field 25 miles east of Manhattan became one of America's newest suburbs, changing the way homes were built. The land was bulldozed and the trees removed, and then trucks dropped building materials at precise 60-foot intervals. Construction was divided into 26 distinct steps. At the peak of production, the company constructed 30 new single-family homes each day.

—Bergman and Renwick, *Introduction to Geography,* p. 422

Implied Main Idea: _____

_____

I. Children who exercise are more likely to continue exercising in adulthood than children who do not exercise. In a country where most adults do not get the recommended 30 to 60 minutes of exercise most days of the week, it makes sense to encourage everyone to become more athletic. When good exercise habits are carried into adulthood, there is a decreased risk of heart disease, obesity, diabetes, and many cancers. Additional benefits include lowered cholesterol, and studies suggest that exercise may decrease anxiety and depression.

—Belk and Maier, *Biology: Science for Life with Physiology*, p. 509

Implied Main Idea: _____

J. *Turn-requesting cues* tell the speaker that you, as a listener, would like to take a turn as speaker; you might transmit these cues by using some vocalized "er" or "um" that tells the speaker that you would now like to speak, by opening your eyes and mouth as if to say something, by beginning to gesture with a hand, or by leaning forward.

Through *turn-denying cues* you indicate your reluctance to assume the role of speaker by, for example, intoning a slurred "I don't know"; giving the speaker some brief grunt that signals you have nothing to say; avoiding eye contact with the speaker who wishes you now to take on the role of speaker; or engaging in some behavior that is incompatible with speaking—for example, coughing or blowing your nose.

Through *backchanneling cues* you communicate various meanings back to the speaker—but without assuming the role of the speaker. For example, you can indicate your *agreement* or *disagreement* with the speaker through smiles or frowns, nods of approval or disapproval; brief comments such as "right," "exactly," or "never"; or vocalizations such as "uh-huh" or "uh-uh."

—DeVito, *Messages*, pp. 224–25

Implied Main Idea: ___feedback_____

_____

EXERCISE 6-15 **Identifying Main Ideas**

Directions: Separate into groups. Using a reading selection from Part Seven of this book, work with your group to identify and underline the topic sentence of each paragraph. If any of the main ideas are unstated, write a sentence that states the main idea. When all the groups have completed the task, the class should compare the findings of the various groups.

SELF-TEST SUMMARY

OBJECTIVE 1 What are general and specific ideas?	A general idea is broad and can apply to many things. A specific idea is detailed and refers to a smaller group, or an individual item.
OBJECTIVE 2 How can you identify the topic of a paragraph?	Look for the one idea the author is discussing throughout the entire paragraph.
OBJECTIVE 3 How can you find the stated main idea of a paragraph?	Find the topic and then locate the one sentence in the paragraph that is the most general. Check to be sure that this one sentence relates to all the details in the paragraph.
OBJECTIVE 4 What is a topic sentence?	The topic sentence states the main idea of a paragraph. The topic sentence can be located anywhere in the paragraph. The most common positions are first or last, but the topic sentence can also appear in the middle, or first and last.
OBJECTIVE 5 How can one figure out implied main ideas?	Implied main ideas are suggested but not directly stated in a paragraph. To find implied main ideas: • find the topic • figure out what general idea the paragraph explains • express the idea in your own words

GOING ONLINE

1. What Is a Topic Sentence?

    http://cms.cerritos.edu/reading-center/topics-and-topic-sentences

    Review how to locate the topic sentence of a paragraph with these tips and exercises from Cerritos College.

2. Implied Main Idea Practice

    http://www.daltonstate.edu/faculty/mnielsen/implied_main_idea1.htm

    Practice identifying the main idea of a paragraph with this online tool. Evaluate your performance.

3. On Paragraphs

    http://owl.english.purdue.edu/owl/resource/606/01/

    Use this guide on paragraphs to analyze a newspaper or magazine article. Does the author follow standard paragraphing guidelines?

To check your progress in meeting chapter objectives, log in to **http://www.myreadinglab.com**, click on the Study Plan tab, and then click on the Reading Skills tab. Choose Main Idea from the list of subtopics. Read and view the information in the Review Materials section, and then complete the Practices and Tests in the Activities section. You can check your scores by clicking on the Gradebook tab.

MASTERY TEST 1 Paragraph Skills

Name _____ Section _____

Date _____ Number right _____ × 20 points = Score _____

Directions: Read each of the following paragraphs, and select the choice that correctly identifies the paragraph's main idea.

_____ 1.   Many "everyday" consumers have become entrepreneurs by participating in **virtual auctions.** Millions of consumers log on to eBay.com and other auction sites to bid on an enormous variety of new and used items offered by both businesses and individuals. From an economic standpoint, auctions offer savvy consumers the opportunity to buy overruns or excess inventories of new items at discounted prices much as they would in bricks-and-mortar discount stores. For many, however, the auctions also have become a form of entertainment. Players in the auction game spend hours a day on the auction sites, buying and selling collectibles or other items of (assumed?) value.

eBay Logo is a trademark of eBay Inc. Used with permission.

—Solomon and Stuart, *Brave New World of E-Commerce*, p. 16

a. Millions of consumers use eBay.com to buy and sell a wide variety of items.
b. Virtual auctions offer consumers the chance to buy and sell items and to be entertained.
c. Virtual auctions provide the same service as traditional discount stores.
d. Most consumers view virtual auctions as a form of entertainment.

_____ 2.   Pollutants have diverse sources. Some come from a *point source*—they enter a stream at a specific location, such as a wastewater discharge pipe. Others may come from a *nonpoint source*—they come from a large diffuse area, as happens when organic matter or fertilizer washes from a field during a storm. Point-source pollutants are usually smaller in quantity and much easier to control. Nonpoint sources usually pollute in greater quantities and are much harder to control.

—Bergman and Renwick, *Introduction to Geography*, p. 386

a. Point sources of pollution include wastewater discharge pipes.
b. Nonpoint sources of pollution are worse for the environment than point sources.
c. Nonpoint-source pollutants come from a widespread area, whereas point-source pollutants come from a specific location.
d. Pollutants can come from point or nonpoint sources.

_____ 3.   Much as feedback contains information about messages already sent, **feedforward** is information about messages before you send them. Opening comments such as "Wait until you hear this" or "Don't get me wrong, but . . ." are examples of feedforward. These messages tell the listener something about the messages to come or about the way you'd like the listener to respond. Nonverbally, feedforward is

How does the inclusion of this visual help you understand the main idea of the paragraph?

given by your facial expression, eye contact, and physical posture, for example; with these nonverbal messages you tell the other person something about the messages you'll be sending.

—DeVito, *Messages*, p. 140

a. Feedback is the opposite of feedforward.
b. Feedforward consists primarily of nonverbal messages.
c. Feedforward describes information that comes before a message is sent.
d. Feedback and feedforward are both necessary to communication.

_____ 4.   Support groups are an important part of stress management. Friends, family members, and co-workers can provide us with emotional and physical support. Although the ideal support group differs for each of us, you should have one or two close friends in whom you are able to confide and neighbors with whom you can trade favors. You should take the opportunity to participate in community activities at least once a week. A healthy, committed relationship can also provide vital support.

—Donatelle and Davis, *Access to Health*, p. 78

a. Support groups are important in managing stress.
b. Support groups consist of friends and family.
c. Participation in community activities is one way of managing stress.
d. The ideal support group is different for each person.

_____ 5.   In politics, as in many other aspects of life, the squeaky wheel gets the grease. The way citizens "squeak" in politics is to participate. Americans have many avenues of political participation open to them, and political scientists generally distinguish between two broad types: conventional and unconventional. Conventional participation includes many widely accepted modes of influencing government—voting, trying to persuade others, ringing doorbells for a petition, running for office, and so on. In contrast, unconventional participation includes activities that are often dramatic, such as protesting, civil disobedience, and even violence.

—adapted from Edwards et al., *Government in America*, pp. 205–206

a. Politics are like many other aspects of life.
b. Political participation can generally be classified as conventional or unconventional.
c. Influencing government primarily consists of voting and running for office.
d. Unconventional political participation may involve violent activities.

MASTERY TEST 2 Paragraph Skills

Name _____ Section _____

Date _____ Number right _____ × 10 points = Score _____

Directions: Read the following selection from a nutrition textbook, and select the choice that best completes each of the following statements.

Nutrition Myth or Fact?

IS BOTTLED WATER SAFER THAN TAP WATER?

1   Bottled water has become increasingly popular during the past 20 years. Many people prefer the taste of bottled water to that of tap water. They also feel that bottled water is safer than tap water. Is this true?

2   The water we drink in the United States generally comes from two sources: surface water and groundwater.

- *Surface water* comes from lakes, rivers, and reservoirs. Common contaminants of surface water include runoff from highways, pesticides, animal wastes, and industrial wastes. Many of the cities across the United States obtain their water from surface-water sources.
- *Groundwater* comes from spaces between underground rock formations called *aquifers*. People who live in rural areas generally pump groundwater from a well as their water source. Hazardous substances leaking from waste sites, dumps, landfills, and oil and gas pipelines can contaminate groundwater. Groundwater can also be contaminated by naturally occurring substances such as arsenic or high levels of iron.

3   The most common chemical used to treat and purify our water is *chlorine*. Chlorine is effective in killing many contaminants in our water supply. Ozone is also commonly used. Water treatment plants also routinely check our water supplies for hazardous chemicals, minerals, and other contaminants. Because of these efforts, the United States has one of the safest water systems in the world.

What idea does this photograph suggest?

4   The Environmental Protection Agency (EPA) sets and monitors the standards for our municipal water systems. The EPA does not monitor water from private wells, but it publishes recommendations for well owners to help them maintain a safe water supply. Local water regulatory agencies must provide

an annual report on specific water contaminants to all households served by that agency.

5   In contrast, the Food and Drug Administration (FDA) regulates bottled water. It does not require that bottled water meet higher quality standards than public water. As with tap water, bottled water is taken from either surface water or groundwater sources. Bottled water is often treated and filtered differently than tap water, which changes its taste and appearance.

6   Although bottled water may taste better than tap water, there is no evidence that it is safer to drink. Look closely at the label of your favorite bottled water. If the label states "From a public water source," it has come directly from the tap! Some types of bottled water may contain more minerals than tap water, but there are no other additional nutritional benefits of drinking bottled water.

—adapted from Thompson and Manore, *Nutrition for Life*, p. 240

_____ 1. The main point of this selection is to
   a. recommend the use of bottled water.
   b. discuss the safety of bottled water versus tap water.
   c. describe the effects of water pollution.
   d. promote stricter water regulations.

_____ 2. The main idea of paragraph 2 is expressed in the
   a. first sentence.
   b. second sentence.
   c. third sentence.
   d. last sentence.

_____ 3. The topic of paragraph 2 is
   a. bottled water.
   b. sources of water.
   c. water pollution.
   d. pesticides.

_____ 4. According to the selection, groundwater comes from
   a. lakes.
   b. rivers.
   c. reservoirs.
   d. aquifers.

_____ 5. The topic of paragraph 3 is
   a. chlorine treatment.
   b. ozone treatment.
   c. treatment of water supply.
   d. hazardous chemicals.

_____ 6. The main idea of paragraph 3 is that
   a. chlorine kills contaminants in our water.
   b. ozone is used to treat and purify water.
   c. water treatment plants routinely check our water supplies.
   d. our water system is one of the safest in the world.

_____ 7. The implied main idea of paragraph 4 is that
   a. the EPA does not monitor well water.
   b. water safety is regulated locally and by the EPA.
   c. local agencies report on water contaminants.
   d. many households are served by local agencies.

_____ 8. The topic of paragraph 5 is
   a. tap water.
   b. public water.
   c. bottled water.
   d. water standards.

_____ 9. The main idea of paragraph 6 is expressed in the
   a. first sentence.
   b. second sentence.
   c. third sentence.
   d. last sentence.

_____ 10. The conclusion reached in this selection is that
   a. tap water tastes better than bottled water.
   b. bottled water is much safer than tap water.
   c. bottled water is no safer than tap water.
   d. tap water has more nutritional value than bottled water.

MASTERY TEST 3 Reading Selection

Name _____ Section _____

Date _____ Number right* _____ × 10 points = Score _____

War Torn

Joshua Kors

This selection, which first appeared in a November 2008 issue of *Current Science* magazine, discusses the traumatic effects of war on veterans and their families.

> **Vocabulary Preview**
> **insurgents** (par. 1) armed rebels; guerillas

Veterans and their families are coping with the lingering trauma of Iraq and Afghanistan

1   Chuck Luther woke up in a cold sweat. Nightmares again. The former Army sergeant was home in Killeen, Texas. But in his dreams, he was still in Iraq, where he had led an elite unit that battled insurgents. Two years earlier, Luther had been stationed in a combat outpost north of Baghdad when a mortar blast exploded nearby and knocked him to the floor. Luther survived the attack. However, the jolt to his head damaged his hearing and left him with severe headaches.

2   Luther was also plagued by visions of the mortar attack and haunted by the blood and pain he had seen. The memories made functioning as a husband and father difficult when he returned home to Texas. He began experiencing panic attacks and uncharacteristic bursts of rage.

3   "Before Iraq, my wife and I never fought at all," says Luther. "But when I got back, I was so angry. We started fighting all the time. I'd tear up the house and break things. My kids became scared of me. It was awful."

4   Luther suffers from a psychological illness common among soldiers returning from war. During World War I, it was called shell shock; during World War II, battle fatigue. Today the condition is known as post-traumatic stress disorder (PTSD). The illness has become epidemic (widespread) in the United States. A recent RAND Corporation study found that 300,000 soldiers returning from Iraq and Afghanistan suffer from it.

*To calculate the number right, use items 1–10 under "Mastery Test Skills Check."

NEVER-ENDING CRISIS

5   During war, the demands on the human brain are <u>relentless</u>. Soldiers on the battlefield are in constant crisis. Staying <u>alert</u> and focused is more than a necessity; it's a matter of life and death.

6   The brain can become locked into that state of <u>hypervigilance</u> and remain that way, even when the threat of war is gone and the soldier has returned home. That's when PTSD can develop. Keith Armstrong is a professor of psychiatry at the University of California, San Francisco. He says that soldiers with PTSD are "always scanning the environment for threats. During battle, that <u>vigilance</u> might help save another soldier's life." Back home, however, that focus makes the soldiers overprotective of their children and more critical of their kids' mistakes. "Their reaction to everything becomes much more dramatic. That can strain relations in families," Armstrong says.

7   Many <u>veterans</u> try to cope with PTSD on their own, often in inappropriate ways, says Michelle Sherman, a psychologist who treats soldiers at a veterans hospital in Oklahoma City. They might refuse to leave the house. Or they might avoid everything that <u>triggers memories</u> of war—the screaming crowds at their daughters' basketball games or the loud bangs of a Fourth of July parade.

8   A large number of vets also try to <u>numb</u> themselves with drugs and alcohol, according to Sherman. "The thing is, when you <u>numb</u> the pain, you numb the pleasure," says Sherman. "My goal is to show soldiers that they don't need to emotionally withdraw or create a wall between themselves and their families. With help, they can learn to turn that page and move on to the next chapter of their lives."

PAGE TURNERS

9   There are many emerging ways to treat PTSD. Some vets get regular massages to ease the tension left over from war. Others enroll in group therapy, where they can discuss their situations in safe settings with other soldiers who have experienced the traumas of war. Armstrong has pioneered a family counseling program in which vets bring their wives and children and talk as families about the challenges they're facing. "When a soldier talks with family, his family has the ability to be supportive," says Armstrong. "Family can be part of the healing process."

10   Sherman is <u>coauthor</u> of *Finding My Way: A Teen's Guide to Living with a Parent Who Has Experienced Trauma*. In it, she speaks directly to young readers, offering them guidance about how to help their parents—and how to care for themselves.

11   She encourages soldiers' children to recognize that changes in parental behavior are due to struggles with PTSD. The changes have nothing to do with the kids or their parents' love for them. She asks readers to understand the new limitations on their mother's or father's abilities. A parent may not be able to attend band concerts because the bang of the drums is too loud, too much like the gunfire of war. "Teens need to ask themselves, Is there someone else who can come to my recital,

someone else I can turn to when I need a laugh or feel like crying?'" says Sherman.

12   Luther recently purchased Sherman's book for his 14-year-old daughter, Alexa. She and her siblings have struggled with the change in their father's temperament and tried their best to be patient and sympathetic. "Things are hard now; there's no denying that" says Luther. "But with time, I do believe things will get better for me and my family."

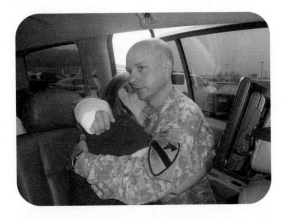

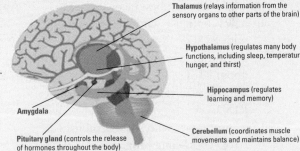

Under Fire

13   The human brain is organized into many regions, some of which are shown here. Each one has a separate function. Neurologists studying post-traumatic stress disorder (PTSD) have zeroed in on the amygdala, the part of the brain that processes emotions. A recent study found that soldiers with PTSD have a hyperactive amygdala; the neurons (nerve cells) in that region fire at a faster-than-normal rate. With the emotion center of the brain working overtime, soldiers who were even-tempered before war may be quicker to anger and more easily frightened when they return.

MASTERY TEST SKILLS CHECK

Directions: Select the choice that best completes each of the following statements.

Checking Your Comprehension

_____ 1. The purpose of this selection is to
   a. compare the experiences of soldiers in different wars.
   b. explore different causes of post-traumatic stress disorder (PTSD).
   c. describe how PTSD affects war veterans and their families.
   d. argue for better treatment programs for war veterans.

_____ 2. Chuck Luther can best be described as
   a. a psychologist who treats veterans with PTSD.
   b. an author who has written a book about PTSD.
   c. an Iraq war veteran suffering from PTSD.
   d. a professor who has established PTSD counseling programs.

_____ 3. All of the following statements about PTSD are true _except_
   a. A recent study found that 300,000 soldiers returning from Iraq and Afghanistan suffer from PTSD.
   b. In soldiers with PTSD, the nerve cells in the emotion center of the brain fire at a slower-than-normal rate.
   c. Many soldiers with PTSD are sensitive to loud noises that trigger memories of war and gunfire.
   d. Chuck Luther's PTSD symptoms included panic attacks and uncharacteristic bursts of rage.

_____ 4. Based on the box "Under Fire," the part of the brain that processes emotions and is hyperactive in soldiers with PTSD is the
   a. thalamus.
   b. amygdala.
   c. cerebellum.
   d. pituitary gland.

_____ 5. According to the selection, emerging treatments for PTSD include
   a. regular massages.
   b. group therapy.
   c. family counseling.
   d. all of the above.

Applying Your Skills

_____ 6. The implied main idea of paragraph 2 is that Chuck Luther's war injuries
   a. occurred while he was stationed in a combat post north of Baghdad.
   b. were caused when a mortar blast exploded nearby.
   c. damaged his hearing and left him with severe headaches.
   d. were both physically and emotionally traumatic.

_____ 7. The topic of paragraph 4 is the
   a. shell shock of World War I veterans.
   b. battle fatigue of World War II veterans.
   c. PTSD and Iraq and Afghanistan veterans.
   d. stress-related psychological illness among war veterans.

_____ 8. The implied main idea of paragraph 6
is that
   a. soldiers' brains become locked into
      a state of hypervigilance.
   b. soldiers with PTSD are always on
      the lookout for threats.
   c. being vigilant can help save another
      soldier's life.
   d. hypervigilance is essential in war but
      causes problems at home.

_____ 9. The topic sentence of paragraph 9 is the
   a. first sentence.
   b. second sentence.
   c. third sentence.
   d. last sentence.

_____ 10. The main idea of paragraph 11 is that
Michelle Sherman's book encourages
soldiers' children to
   a. ignore the signs of PTSD in their
      parents.
   b. take part in family counseling
      programs.
   c. cope with the effects of PTSD on
      their own.
   d. realize that changes in parental be-
      havior are due to PTSD.

Studying Words

_____ 11. The word _elite_ (par. 1) means
   a. large.
   b. top quality.
   c. typical.
   d. remote.

_____ 12. The word _plagued_ (par. 2) means
   a. disappointed.
   b. interested.
   c. tormented.
   d. wondered.

_____ 13. The synonym clue for the word
epidemic (par. 4) is
   a. fatigue.
   b. condition.
   c. shock.
   d. widespread.

_____ 14. The prefix in the word _hypervigilance_
(par. 6) means
   a. excessive.
   b. against.
   c. before.
   d. under.

_____ 15. The word _temperament_ (par. 12)
means
   a. anger.
   b. speech.
   c. personality.
   d. ability.

For more practice, ask
your instructor for an
opportunity to work
on the mastery
tests that appear in
the Test Bank.

Summarizing the Reading

Directions: Complete the following summary of the reading by filling in the blanks.

Chuck Luther is an _____ suffering from _PPST_____.
Referred to in previous wars as _____*shell shock*_____, the ___*l*_____
illness is common to ____*vent*_____. The extreme _____ that soldiers must
have _____ can create ____*prophles*_____. Veterans with _____
may try to _____ or try to _____.
Emerging ways to treat ____*PTSD*_____ include ____*massages*_____
_____. _____and author Michelle Sherman offers guidance to
_____ about how to _____. Children are
encouraged to recognize that _____*PTSD*_____.

Reading Visually

1. What do the photographs that accompany this article tell you about soldiers in general and Chuck Luther in particular? What details do you notice about the two close-ups of Luther?
2. How does the diagram contribute to your understanding of the concepts discussed in the article? What aspects of the illustration made it helpful?
3. Explain how the title of this selection reflects the subject matter. How do the headings add to the readability of this selection?

Thinking Critically about the Reading

WRITE IN YOUR
JOURNAL

1. Why did the author begin by telling Chuck Luther's story? Explain how his personal experience contributes to your overall understanding of PTSD.
2. How would you describe the author's attitude toward this subject? What feelings are you left with at the end of the article?
3. Connect the information in this article with what you already know about PTSD. What other traumatic events can bring about this condition?

Understanding Paragraphs: Supporting Details and Transitions

Looking at . . .
Supporting Details and Transitions

Parent Teacher Yellow Cake
2 cups of flour
2 teaspoons of double-acting baking powder
1/2 teaspoon of salt
1 stick of unsalted butter, room temperature
1 cup of sugar
3 egg yolks
1 cup milk
2 teaspoons of pure vanilla extract

Preheat oven to 375 degrees.
Mix all of your dry ingredients except sugar in a bowl. Put aside. With an electric mixer, cream your butter and sugar until light and fluffy, add the egg yolks and mix thoroughly. Add the dry ingredients to the butter mixture, alternating with milk until thoroughly blended. Stir in the vanilla.
Bake in 2 greased and floured 8-inch cake pans for 25 minutes.

LEARNING OBJECTIVES

This chapter will show you how to:

 Recognize supporting details

 Identify types of supporting details

 Use transitions to guide your reading

 Paraphrase paragraphs

In order to produce the cake shown in the photo above, the baker had to follow the recipe closely, paying attention to each detailed step. The baker also had to complete each step in the order presented. Reading a paragraph involves a similar process. The reader must pay attention to all the details that support the main idea. Also, the reader must pay attention to the order of details and their relationship to one another, often signaled by the use of connecting words called transitions.

Suppose you read the following sentence in a communication textbook. It appears as the opening sentence of a paragraph.

Men and women communicate differently in their nonverbal messages.

After reading this sentence you are probably wondering how nonverbal communication, also known as body language, differs between the sexes.

Only poor writers make statements without supporting them. So you expect, then, that in the remainder of the paragraph the author will support his statement about gender differences in nonverbal communication. Here is the full paragraph.

> Men and women communicate differently in their nonverbal messages. You may have observed some or all of these differences in your daily interactions. Women smile more than men. Women stand closer to each other than men do. When they speak, both men and women look at men more than at women. Women both touch and are touched more than men. Men extend their bodies, taking up greater areas of space than women.
>
> —DeVito, *Messages*, p. 150

In this paragraph, the author explained his statement by giving examples of gender differences. The first sentence expresses the main idea; the remaining sentences are supporting details. You will recall from Chapter 6 that a paragraph has four essential elements.

- **Topic**—the one thing the whole paragraph is about
- **Main idea**—the broad, general idea the whole paragraph is concerned with
- **Supporting details**—the ideas that explain or support the main idea
- **Transitions**—the words or phrases that link ideas together

This chapter will focus on how to recognize supporting details and how to use transitions to guide your reading. You will also learn how to paraphrase paragraphs and longer pieces of writing.

myreadinglab

To practice recognizing supporting details, go to
▼ STUDY PLAN
  ▼ READING SKILLS
    ▼ SUPPORTING DETAILS

RECOGNIZING SUPPORTING DETAILS

OBJECTIVE 1

Supporting details are those facts and ideas that prove or explain the main idea of a paragraph. While all the details in a paragraph support the main idea, not all details are equally important. As you read, try to identify and pay attention to the most important details. Pay less attention to details of lesser importance.

The **key details** directly explain the main idea. Other **minor details** may provide additional information, offer an example, or further explain one of the key details.

The diagram in Figure 7-1 shows how details relate to the main idea and how details range in degree of importance. In the diagram, less important details appear below the important details they explain.

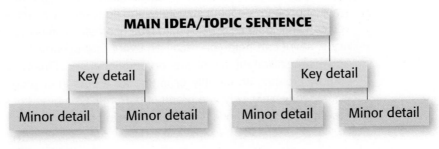

Figure 7-1

Read the following paragraph and study the diagram that follows.

The skin of the human body has several functions. First, it serves as a protective covering. In doing so, it accounts for 17 percent of the body weight. Skin also protects the organs within the body from damage or harm. The skin serves as a regulator of body functions. It controls body temperature and water loss. Finally, the skin serves as a receiver. It is sensitive to touch and temperature.

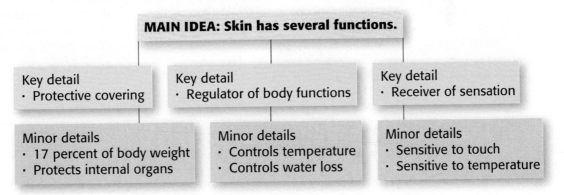

Figure 7-2

From the diagram in Figure 7-2 you can see that the details that state the three functions of skin are the key details. Other details, such as "protects internal organs," provide further information and are at a lower level of importance.

Read the following paragraph and try to pick out the more important details.

> Communication occurs with words and gestures but did you know it also oc-curs through the sense of smell? Odor can communicate at least four types of messages. First, odor can signal attraction. Animals give off scents to attract members of the opposite sex. Humans use fragrances to make themselves more appealing or attractive. Smell also communicates information about tastes. The smell of popcorn popping stimulates the appetite. If you smell a chicken roasting you can anticipate its taste. A third type of smell communication is through mem-ory. A smell can help you recall an event that occurred months or even years ago, especially if the event was an emotional one. Finally, smell can communi-cate by creating an identity or image for a person or product. For example, a woman may wear only one brand of perfume. Or a brand of shaving cream may have a distinct fragrance, which allows users to recognize it.
>
> —DeVito, *Messages*, p. 159

This paragraph could be diagrammed as follows:

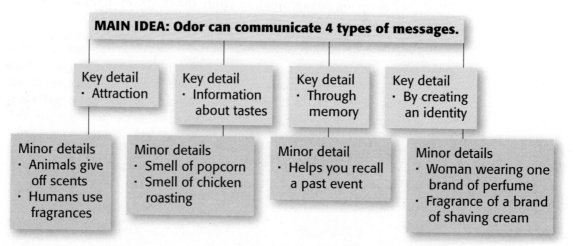

Figure 7-3

EXERCISE **7-1**   ## Identifying Key and Minor Details

Directions: Read each of the following paragraphs, and then answer the multiple-choice questions about the diagram that follows.

Paragraph 1

Don't be fooled by words that sound impressive but mean little. Doublespeak is language that fails to communicate; it comes in four basic forms. **Euphemisms** make the negative and unpleasant appear positive and appealing, for example, calling the firing of 200 workers "downsizing" or "reallocation of resources." **Jargon** is the specialized language of a professional class (for example, the computer language of the hacker); it becomes doublespeak when used to communicate with people who aren't members of the group and who don't know this specialized language. **Gobbledygook** is overly complex language that overwhelms the listener instead of communicating meaning. **Inflated language** makes the mundane seem extraordinary, the common exotic ("take the vacation of a lifetime; explore unsurpassed vistas"). All four forms can be useful in some situations, but, when spoken or listened to mindlessly, they may obscure meaning and distort perceptions.

—DeVito, *Messages*, p. 130

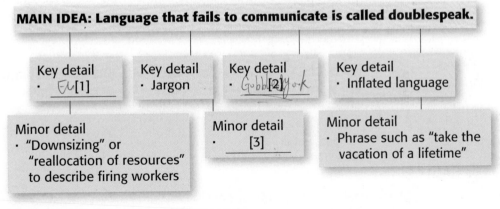

Figure 7-4

_____ 1. The correct word to fill in the blank labeled [1] is
  a. Doublespeak.
  b. Euphemisms.
  c. Negative.
  d. Positive.

___C___ 2. The correct word or phrase to fill in the blank labeled [2] is
    a. Complex language.
    b. Specialized language.
    c. Gobbledygook.
    d. Mundane.

___d___ 3. The correct phrase to fill in the blank labeled [3] is
    a. Obscure meanings.
    b. Distort perceptions.
    c. A professional class.
    d. The computer language of the hacker.

Paragraph 2

The risks associated with the consumption of alcohol are determined in part by how much an individual drinks. An **occasional drinker** is a person who drinks an alcoholic beverage once in a while. The occasional drinker seldom becomes intoxicated, and such drinking presents little or no threat to the health of the individual. A **social drinker** is someone who drinks regularly in social settings but seldom consumes enough alcohol to become intoxicated. Social drinking, like occasional drinking, does not necessarily increase health risks. **Binge drinking** is defined as having five drinks in a row for men or four in a row for women. Binge drinking can cause significant health and social problems. In comparison to nonbinge drinkers, binge drinkers are much more likely to have unprotected sex, to drive after drinking, and to fall behind in school.

—Pruitt and Stein, *Health Styles*, pp. 108, 110

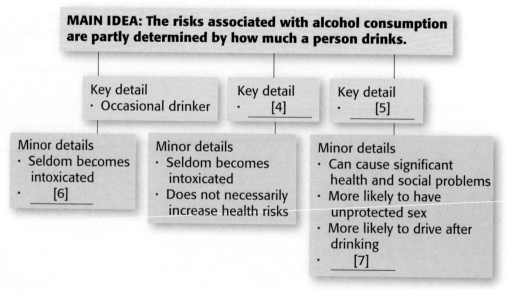

Figure 7-5

_d_ 4. The correct phrase to fill in the blank labeled [4] is
    a. Binge drinking.
    b. Alcohol consumption.
    c. Health risks.
    d. Social drinker.

_b_ 5. The correct phrase to fill in the blank labeled [5] is
    a. Social drinker.
    b. Binge drinking.
    c. Health problems.
    d. Social problems.

_c_ 6. The correct phrase to fill in the blank labeled [6] is
    a. Occasional drinker.
    b. Social drinker.
    c. Little or no health threat.
    d. Drinks regularly in social settings.

_a_ 7. The correct phrase to fill in the blank labeled [7] is
    a. More likely to fall behind in school.
    b. More likely to have health problems.
    c. Little or no health threat.
    d. Four or five drinks in a row.

Paragraph 3

There are four different dimensions of an arrest: legal, behavioral, subjective, and official. In **legal** terms, an arrest is made when someone lawfully deprives another person of liberty; in other words, that person is not free to go. The actual word *arrest* need not be uttered, but the other person must be brought under the control of the arresting individual. The **behavioral** element in arrests is often nothing more than the phrase "You're under arrest." However, that statement is usually backed up by a tight grip on the arm or collar, or the drawing of an officer's handgun, or the use of handcuffs. The **subjective** dimension of arrest refers to whenever people believe they are not free to leave; to all intents and purposes, they are under arrest. In any case, the arrest lasts only as long as the person is in custody, which might be a matter of a few minutes or many hours. Many people are briefly detained on the street and then released. **Official** arrests are those detentions that the police record in an administrative record. When a suspect is "booked" at the police station, a record is made of the arrest.

—Barlow, *Criminal Justice in America*, p. 238

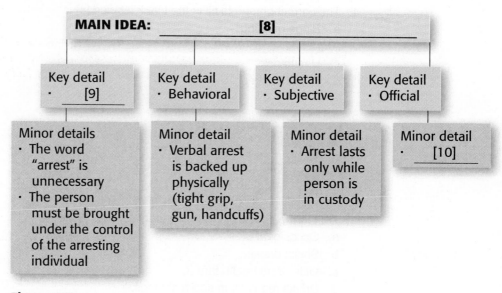

Figure 7-6

_b_   8. The correct sentence to fill in the blank labeled [8] is
a. When a person is lawfully deprived of freedom, it is not necessary to use the word *arrest.*
b. The four different dimensions of an arrest are legal, behavioral, subjective, and official.
c. People can be subjectively under arrest even when they are not officially under arrest.
d. The only official arrests are those that are recorded at the police station.

_d_   9. The correct word or phrase to fill in the blank labeled [9] is
a. Dimensions.
b. Liberty.
c. Not free to go.
d. Legal.

_a_   10. The correct word or phrase to fill in the blank labeled [10] is
a. Arrest is recorded at police station.
b. Detentions.
c. Briefly detained.
d. Booked.

EXERCISE **7-2** **Identifying Key Details**

Directions: Each of the following topic sentences states the main idea of a paragraph. After each topic sentence are sentences containing details that may or may not support the topic sentence. Read each sentence and write a *K* beside those that contain **key details** that support the topic sentence.

1. *Topic sentence:* Many dramatic physical changes occur during adolescence between the ages of 13 and 15.

   Details:

   _____ a. Voice changes in boys begin to occur at age 13 or 14.

   _____ b. Facial proportions may change during adolescence.

   _____ c. Adolescents, especially boys, gain several inches in height.

   _____ d. Many teenagers do not know how to react to these changes.

   _____ e. Primary sex characteristics begin to develop for both boys and girls.

2. *Topic sentence:* The development of speech in infants follows a definite sequence or pattern of development.

   Details:

   _____ a. By the time an infant is six months old, he or she can make 12 different speech sounds.

   _____ b. Mindy, who is only three months old, is unable to produce any recognizable syllables.

   _____ c. During the first year, the number of vowel sounds a child can produce is greater than the number of consonant sounds he or she can make.

   _____ d. Between 6 and 12 months, the number of consonant sounds a child can produce continues to increase.

   _____ e. Parents often reward the first recognizable word a child produces by smiling or speaking to the child.

3. *Topic sentence:* The main motives for attending a play are the desire for recreation, the need for relaxation, and the desire for intellectual stimulation.

   Details:

   _____ a. By becoming involved with the actors and their problems, members of the audience temporarily forget about their personal cares and concerns and are able to relax.

   _____ b. In America today, the success of a play is judged by its ability to attract a large audience.

   _____ c. Almost everyone who attends a play expects to be entertained.

_____ d. Even theater critics are often able to relax and enjoy a good play.

_____ e. There is a smaller audience that looks to theater for intellectual stimulation.

4. *Topic sentence:* Licorice is used in tobacco products because it has specific characteristics that cannot be found in any other single ingredient.

   Details:

   _____ a. McAdams & Co. is the largest importer and processor of licorice root.

   _____ b. Licorice blends with tobacco and provides added mildness.

   _____ c. Licorice provides a unique flavor and sweetens many types of tobacco.

   _____ d. The extract of licorice is present in relatively small amounts in most types of pipe tobacco.

   _____ e. Licorice helps tobacco retain the correct amount of moisture during storage.

5. *Topic sentence:* An oligopoly is a market structure in which only a few companies sell a certain product.

   Details:

   _____ a. The automobile industry is a good example of an oligopoly, even though it gives the appearance of being highly competitive.

   _____ b. The breakfast cereal, soap, and cigarette industries, although basic to our economy, operate as oligopolies.

   _____ c. Monopolies refer to market structures in which only one industry produces a particular product.

   _____ d. Monopolies are able to exert more control and price fixing than oligopolies.

   _____ e. In the oil industry there are only a few producers, so each producer has a fairly large share of the sales.

EXERCISE **7-3**   **Identifying Key Details**

Directions: Read each of the following paragraphs and write the numbers of the sentences that contain only the most important key details.

Paragraph 1

There are four main characteristics of a tourism product. [2]The first is service, which is intangible because it cannot be inspected physically. [3]For example, a tourist cannot sample a Caribbean cruise or a European tour before purchasing one. [4]The second characteristic is that the tourism product is largely psychological in its attraction. ⁵It is more than airline seats or car rentals; it is the temporary use of a different environment, its culture, heritage, and experiences. ⁶A third characteristic is that the product frequently varies in quality and standards. ⁷A tourist's hotel experience may be excellent one time and not so good at the next visit. ⁸A fourth characteristic of the tourism product is that the supply of the product is fixed. ⁹For example, more hotel rooms cannot be instantly created to meet increased demand.

—adapted from Walker and Walker, *Tourism: Concepts and Practices*, p. 11

Key Details: 2, 4, 6, 9   2 4 6 8

Paragraph 2

Political activists depend heavily on the media to get their ideas placed high on the governmental agenda. ²Their arsenal of weapons includes press releases, press conferences, and letter writing; convincing reporters and columnists to tell their side; trading on personal contacts; and, in cases of desperation, resorting to staging dramatic events. ³The media are not always monopolized by political elites; the poor and downtrodden have access to them too. ⁴Civil rights groups in the 1960s relied heavily on the media to tell their stories of unjust treatment. ⁵Many believe that the introduction of television helped to accelerate the movement by showing Americans just what the situation was. ⁶Protest groups have learned that if they can stage an interesting event that attracts the media's attention, at least their point of view will be heard. ⁷Radical activist Saul Alinsky once dramatized the plight of one neighborhood by having its residents collect rats and dump them on the mayor's front lawn. ⁸The story was one that local reporters could hardly resist.

—adapted from Edwards et al., *Government in America*, p. 239

Key Details: 2 4 6

These photographs depict examples of activism. Which example is more effective?

Paragraph 3

To be patented, an invention must be novel, useful, and nonobvious. [2]An invention is *novel* if it is new and has not been invented and used in the past. [3]If the invention has been used before, it is not novel and cannot be patented. [4]An invention is *useful* if it has some practical purpose. [5]For example, an inventor received a patent for "forkchops," which are a set of chopsticks with a spoon at one handle-end and a fork on the other handle-end. [6]This invention is useful. [7]If the invention is *nonobvious*, it qualifies for a patent; if the invention is obvious, then it does not qualify for a patent. [8]For example, inventors received a patent for a cardboard sleeve that can be placed over a paper coffee cup so that the cup will not be as hot as if there were no sleeve. [9]This invention is novel, useful, and nonobvious.

—adapted from Goldman and Cheeseman, *The Paralegal Professional*, pp. 736–737

Key Details: 2, 4, 7

Paragraph 4

People who exercise their mental abilities have been found to be far less likely to develop memory problems and even senile dementias such as Alzheimer's in old age. [2]"Use it or lose it" is the phrase to remember. [3]Working challenging crossword puzzles, for example, can be a major factor in maintaining a healthy level of cognitive functioning. [4]Reading, having an active social life, going to plays, taking classes, and staying physically active can all have a positive impact on the continued well-being of the brain.

—adapted from Ciccarelli and White, *Psychology: An Exploration*, p. 249

Key Details: 1, 3, 4

Paragraph 5

A general law practice is one that handles all types of cases. [2]This is what people usually think of as the small-town lawyer, the generalist to whom everyone in town comes for advice. [3]The reality is that the same generalists practice in cities as well as small towns throughout the country. [4]Their practices are as diverse as the law itself, handling everything from adoptions to zoning appeals. [5]As general practitioners, they serve the same function in the law as the general family practice doctor does in medicine. [6]Lawyers in this type of practice often work in several areas of law within the same day. [7]Their day may include attending a hearing in small-claims court in the morning, preparing a will before lunch, meeting with an opposing attorney to discuss settlement of an accident case, then helping someone who is forming a corporation, and finally appearing at a municipal government meeting in the evening to seek a zoning approval.

—adapted from Goldman and Cheeseman, *The Paralegal Professional*, p. 81

Key Details: 3, 4, 6

TYPES OF SUPPORTING DETAILS

There are many types of details that a writer can use to explain or support a main idea. As you read, be sure you know *how* or what types of detail a writer uses to support his or her main idea. As you will see in later chapters, the way a writer explains and supports an idea may influence how readily you accept or agree with it. The most common types of supporting details are (1) examples, (2) facts or statistics, (3) reasons, (4) descriptions, and (5) steps or procedures. Each will be briefly discussed here.

Examples

One way a writer may support an idea is by using examples. Examples make ideas and concepts real and understandable. In the following paragraph, an example is used to explain instantaneous speed.

> The speed that a body has at any one instant is called instantaneous speed. It is the speed registered by the speedometer of a car. When we say that the speed of a car at some particular instant is 60 kilometers per hour, we are specifying its instantaneous speed, and we mean that if the car continued moving as fast for an hour, it would travel 60 kilometers. So the instantaneous speed, or speed at a particular instant, is often quite different from average speed.
>
> —Hewitt, *Conceptual Physics*, p. 15

In this paragraph the author uses the speed of a car to explain instantaneous speed. As you read illustrations and examples, try to see the relationship between the examples and the concepts or ideas they illustrate.

Facts or Statistics

Another way a writer supports an idea is by including facts and/or statistics. The facts and statistics may provide evidence that the main idea is correct. Or the facts may further explain the main idea. For example, to prove that the divorce rate is high, the author may give statistics about the divorce rate and percentage of the population that is divorced. Notice how, in the following paragraph, the main idea stated in the first sentence is explained using statistics.

> The term **graying of America** refers to the increasing percentage of older people in the U.S. population. In 1900 only 4 percent of Americans were age 65 and older. Today almost 13 percent are. The average 65-year-old can expect to live another eighteen years. U.S. society has become so "gray" that the median age has doubled since 1850, and today there are seven million *more* elderly Americans than teenagers. Despite this change, on a global scale Americans rank fifteenth in life expectancy.
>
> —Henslin, *Sociology*, p. 383

In this paragraph, the main idea that the number of older Americans is increasing is supported using statistics.

Reasons

A writer may support an idea by giving reasons *why* a main idea is correct. A writer might explain *why* nuclear power is dangerous or give reasons *why* a new speed limit law should be passed by Congress. In the following paragraph, the author explains why warm air rises.

> We all know that warm air rises. From our study of buoyancy we can understand why this is so. Warm air expands and becomes less dense than the surrounding air and is buoyed upward like a balloon. The buoyancy is in an upward direction because the air pressure below a region of warmed air is greater than the air pressure above. And the warmed air rises because the buoyant force is greater than its weight.
>
> —Hewitt, *Conceptual Physics,* pp. 234–235

Descriptions

When the topic of a paragraph is a person, object, place, or process, the writer may develop the paragraph by describing the object. Descriptions are details that help you create a mental picture of the object. In the following paragraph, the author describes a sacred book of the Islamic religion by telling what it contains.

> The Koran is the sacred book of the Islamic religion. It was written during the lifetime of Mohammed (570–632) during the years in which he recorded divine revelations. The Koran includes rules for family relationships, including marriage and divorce. Rules for inheritance of wealth and property are specified. The status of women as subordinate to men is well defined.

Steps or Procedures

When a paragraph explains how to do something, the paragraph details are often lists of steps or procedures to be followed. For example, if the main idea of a paragraph is how to prepare an outline for a speech, then the details would list or explain the steps in preparing an outline. In the following paragraph the author explains how fog is produced.

> Warm breezes blow over the ocean. When the moist air moves from warmer to cooler waters or from warm water to cool land, it chills. As it chills, water vapor molecules begin coalescing rather than bouncing off one another upon glancing collisions. Condensation takes place, and we have fog.
>
> —Hewitt, *Conceptual Physics,* p. 259

EXERCISE 7-4   Identifying Types of Details

Directions: Each topic sentence is followed by a list of details that could be used to support it. Label each detail as example, fact or statistic, reason, description, or step or procedure.

1. *Topic sentence:* People make inferences about you by the way you dress.

   _____steps_____   First, they size you up from head to toe.

   _____E_____   College students assume casually dressed instructors are friendly and flexible.

   _____F_____   Robert Molloy wrote a book called *Dress for Success* in which he discusses appropriate business attire.

2. *Topic sentence:* Migration is the regular back-and-forth movement of animals between two geographic areas.

   _____R_____   Migration enables many species to access food sources throughout the year and to breed or winter in areas that favor survival.

   _____F_____   Researchers have found that migrating animals stay on course by using a variety of cues.

   _____E_____   One long-distance traveler is the gray whale, whose yearly round-trip of some 20,000 km is the longest made by any animal.

   —adapted from Campbell et al.,

   Biology: Concepts and Connections, p. 709

3. *Topic sentence:* Every April 15th, millions of Americans make their way to the post office to mail their income tax forms.

_____S____ ___F___   Corporate taxes account for about 10 cents of every federal revenue dollar, compared with 47 cents from individual income taxes.

_____E_____   This year, the Burnette family filed a return that entitles them to a substantial refund on their state income taxes.

_____S_____   In order to submit an income tax return, you must first obtain the proper forms.

—Edwards et al., *Government in America,* pp. 458–59

4. *Topic sentence:* Schizophrenia is one of the most difficult psychological disorders to understand.

_____R_____   Diagnosis is difficult due to the lack of physical tests for schizophrenia; researchers do not know if schizophrenia results from a single process or several processes.

_____F_____   Although the rate of schizophrenia is approximately equal in men and women, it strikes men earlier and with greater severity.

_____E_____   After spending time in mental hospitals and homeless shelters, Greg was finally diagnosed with schizophrenia; he has responded well to medication and now lives in a group home.

_____D & F_____   Schizophrenia involves a range of symptoms, including disturbances in perception, language, thinking, and emotional expression.

—Davis and Palladino, *Psychology,* pp. 563, 564, 566

5. *Topic sentence:* Many Americans are obsessed with losing weight.

_____R_____   Weight loss obsession is often triggered by major events looming in the near future, such as a high school reunion or a "milestone" birthday.

_____S & F_____   The two ways to lose weight are to lower caloric intake (through improved eating habits) and to increase exercise (expending more calories).

_____F_____   Studies show that on any given day in America, nearly 40 percent of women and 24 percent of men over the age of 20 are trying to lose weight.

_____E_____   Orlando, a college freshman from Raleigh, admits that he has been struggling with a weight problem since he reached puberty.

—Donatelle and Davis, *Access to Health,* pp. 358, 371

6. *Topic sentence:* In the 1920s, many young American writers and artists left their country behind and became expatriates.

_____ E _____	One of the most talented of the expatriates was Ernest Hemingway.
_____ R _____	The expatriates flocked to Rome, Berlin, and Paris, in order to live cheaply and escape what seemed to them the "conspiracy against the individual" in America.
_____ F & D _____	Some earned a living as journalists, translators, and editors, or made a few dollars by selling a poem to an American magazine or a painting to a tourist.

—Garraty and Carnes, *The American Nation,* p. 706

7. *Topic sentence:* Historical and cultural attractions can be found in a variety of shapes, sizes, and locations throughout the world.

_____ F _____	In Europe, for every museum that existed in 1950, there are now more than four.
_____ E _____	Living History Farms, located near Des Moines, Iowa, is an attraction that offers a "hands-on" experience for visitors.
_____ R _____	More and more communities and countries are taking action to preserve historical sites because they attract visitors and generate income for local residents.

—Cook, *Tourism,* p. 209

8. *Topic sentence:* Knitting has become a popular hobby for many young career women.

_____ S _____	Typically, aspiring knitters begin by visiting a yarn shop and then enrolling in a knitting class.
_____ R _____	Knitting is popular because it provides a relaxing outlet and an opportunity to create something beautiful as well as useful.
_____ E _____	Far from the image of the grandmotherly knitter, today's devoted knitters include a wide range of women, from Wall Street stockbrokers to movie stars like Julia Roberts.

9. *Topic sentence:* Using a search engine is an effective, though not perfect, method of searching the Internet.

_____ S _____	Each time you begin a Web search, start with a simple query to see how many responses, or hits, you get.
_____ F _____	In May 1997, the largest search engines reportedly indexed no more than 140 million documents, or less than 75 percent of those on the Web.

_____R_____ Used correctly, a search engine is efficient because it minimizes the time it takes to locate the information you're looking for.

—Lehnert, *Light on the Internet,* pp. 112, 131

10. *Topic sentence:* The Anasazi Indians are best known for their artistic, architectural, and technological achievements.

_____D/F_____ The Anasazi used all of the available materials to build their settlements; with wood, mud, and stone, they erected cliff dwellings and the equivalent of terraced apartment houses.

_____F/D_____ The Anasazi built one structure with 500 living units; it was the largest residential building in North America until the completion of an apartment house in New York in 1772.

_____E_____ One example of their technological genius was their use of irrigation: they constructed sand dunes at the base of hills to hold the runoff from the sometimes torrential rains.

_____E/D_____ The Anasazi produced pottery that could rank in beauty with any in the world.

—Brummet et al., *Civilization,* p. 348

EXERCISE 7-5   **Identifying Types of Details**

Directions: For each paragraph in Exercise 7-3 on pages 226–228, identify the type or types of details used to support the main idea. Write your answers below.

1. Type(s) of details: Step , example
2. Type(s) of details: example
3. Type(s) of details: example
4. Type(s) of details: ''
5. Type(s) of details: Description

EXERCISE 7-6   **Writing Supporting Details**

Directions: Write a topic sentence on one of following topics:

1. one value or danger of social networking
2. driving and the use of cell phones or texting
3. a currently popular movie

Working in groups of three, choose one topic sentence for each topic and generate a list of details that support the chosen topic sentence. Share results with the class. As a class, identify the types of supporting details used.

EXERCISE 7-7   **Identifying Topic Sentences and Supporting Details**

Working Together

Directions: Form small groups. Using a reading selection from Part Seven of this book, work with your group to identify and underline the topic sentence of each paragraph. Try to identify key supporting details and/or the type of supporting details. When all the groups have completed the task, the class should compare the findings of the various groups.

TRANSITIONS

OBJECTIVE 3

Transitions are linking words or phrases used to lead the reader from one idea to another. If you get in the habit of recognizing transitions, you will see that they often guide you through a paragraph, helping you to read it more easily.

In the following paragraph, notice how the circled transitions lead you from one important detail to the next.

> The principle of rhythm and line also contributes to the overall unity of the land-scape design. This principle is responsible for the sense of continuity between different areas of the landscape. (One) way in which this continuity can be developed is by extending planting beds from one area to another. (For example), shrub beds developed around the entrance to the house can be continued around the sides and into the backyard. Such an arrangement helps to tie the front and rear areas of the property together. (Another) means by which rhythm is given to a design is to repeat shapes, angles, or lines between various areas and elements of the design.
>
> —Reiley and Shry, *Introductory Horticulture*, p. 114

Not all paragraphs contain such obvious transitions, and not all transitions serve as such clear markers of major details. Transitions may be used to alert you to what will come next in the paragraph. If you see the phrase *for instance* at the beginning of a sentence, then you know that an example will follow. When you see the phrase *on the other hand*, you can predict that a different, opposing idea will follow. Table 7-1 (p. 236) lists some of the most common transitions used within a paragraph and indicates what they tell you.

TABLE 7-1 Common Transitions

Type of Transition	Example	What They Tell the Reader
Time/Sequence	first, later, next, finally	The author is arranging ideas in the order in which they happened.
Example	for example, for instance, to illustrate, such as	An example will follow.
Enumeration	first, second, third, last, one, another, next	The author is marking or identifying each major point (sometimes these may be used to suggest order of importance).
Continuation	also, in addition, and, further, another	The author is continuing with the same idea and is going to provide additional information.
Contrast	on the other hand, in contrast, however	The author is switching to a different, opposite, or contrasting idea from that previously discussed.
Comparison	like, likewise, similarly	The writer will show how the previous idea is similar to what follows.
Cause/Effect	because, thus, therefore, since, consequently	The writer will show a connection between two or more things, how one thing caused another, or how something happened as a result of something else.
Summation	to sum up, in conclusion	The writer will draw his or her ideas together.

EXERCISE 7-8 **Understanding Transitions**

Directions: Match each transition in Column A with a transition of similar meaning in Column B. Write the letter of your choice in the space provided.

	Column A		Column B
E	1. Because	a.	Therefore
G	2. In contrast	b.	Also
J	3. For instance	c.	Likewise
A	4. Thus	d.	After that
I	5. First	e.	Since
H	6. One way	f.	In conclusion
C	7. Similarly	g.	On the other hand
D	8. Next	h.	One approach
B	9. In addition	i.	In the beginning
F	10. To sum up	j.	For example

EXERCISE 7-9 | **Identifying Types of Transitions**

Directions: Use the list below to identify the type of transition that appears in each of the following sentences. Note that b (Example) and e (Contrast) are each used twice.

a. Time/sequence   e. Contrast (2)

b. Example (2)   f. Comparison

c. Enumeration   g. Cause/effect

d. Continuation   h. Summation

___C A___ 1. The first step in the listening process involves receiving, or hearing, the message.

___E___ 2. Some people consider computer games a purely passive activity. However, many games actually involve strategy, mathematical skills, and memorization.

___A___ 3. On election day, several television stations reported a clear winner in the presidential race. Later, those stations were forced to retract their statements and wait—along with the rest of the nation—for a final tally.

___H___ 4. In conclusion, proper soil preparation is essential to a successful garden.

___B___ 5. There are many kinds of service dogs. For instance, there are dogs that are trained specifically to assist blind or deaf people as well as therapy dogs that are part of physical rehabilitation programs.

___D___ 6. Always apply sunscreen before going out in the sun. In addition, a hat and protective clothing are recommended at high altitudes and near water.

___E___ 7. In contrast to carnivores, *herbivores* eat only plants.

___G___ 8. Vegetarians typically do not have to worry about elevated cholesterol because cholesterol is found only in animal products.

___f___ 9. Like Samuel Clemens, who became famous writing under the pen name Mark Twain, Mary Ann Evans found fame as the writer George Eliot.

___B___ 10. In some communities, judges sentence offenders to community service programs instead of jail time. For example, in one Chicago program, offenders trade a "day for a day"—every day they would have spent in jail equals a day spent doing community service work.

EXERCISE 7-10   **Choosing Transitional Words**

Directions: Read each of the following sentences. In each blank, write a transitional word or phrase from the list below that makes sense in the sentence.

next	however	for example	another	consequently
because	similarly	such as	to sum up	in addition

1. After a heart attack, the heart muscle is permanently weakened; ____consequently____ its ability to pump blood throughout the body may be reduced.

2. Some metals, ____such as____ gold and silver, are represented by symbols derived from their Latin names.

3. In order to sight-read music, you should begin by scanning it. ____next____, you should identify the key and tempo.

4. The *Oxford English Dictionary*, by giving all present and past definitions of words, shows how word definitions have changed with time. ____In addition____, it gives the date and written source where each word appears to have first been used.

5. Some scientists believe intelligence to be determined equally by heredity and environment. ____however____, other scientists believe heredity to account for about 60 percent of intelligence and environment for the other 40 percent.

6. Tigers tend to grow listless and unhappy in captivity. ____similarly____, pandas grow listless and have a difficult time reproducing in captivity.

7. ____To sum up____, the most important ways to prevent heat stress are to (1) allow yourself time to get used to the heat, (2) wear the proper clothing, and (3) drink plenty of water.

8. Many people who are dissatisfied with the public school system send their children to private schools. ____Another____ option that is gaining in popularity is homeschooling.

9. Studies have shown that it is important to "exercise" our brains as we age. ____For example____, crossword puzzles are a good way to keep mentally fit.

10. Buying smaller-sized clothing generally will not give an overweight person the incentive to lose weight. People with weight problems tend to eat when they are upset or disturbed, and ____because____ wearing smaller clothing is frustrating and upsetting, overweight people will generally gain weight by doing so.

EXERCISE **7-11**   **Making Predictions**

Directions: Each of the following beginnings of paragraphs uses a transitional word or phrase to tell the reader what will follow in the paragraph. Working in pairs, read each, paying particular attention to the underlined word or phrase. Then discuss what you would expect to find next in the paragraph. Summarize your findings in the space provided.

1. Price is not the only factor to consider in choosing a pharmacy. Many provide valuable services that should be considered. <u>For instance</u>, . . .

   suggestion

2. There are a number of things you can do to prevent a home burglary. <u>First</u>, . . .

   make sure every doors and windows are lock.   step

3. Most mail order businesses are reliable and honest. <u>However</u>, . . .

4. One advantage of a compact stereo system is that all the components are built into the unit. <u>Another</u> . . .

5. Taking medication can have an effect on your hormonal balance. <u>Therefore</u>, . . .

6. To select the presidential candidate you will vote for, you should examine his or her philosophy of government. <u>Next</u> …

7. Eating solely vegetables drastically reduces caloric and fat intake, two things on which most people overindulge. <u>On the other hand</u>, …

8. Asbestos, a common material found in many older buildings in which people have worked for decades, has been shown to cause cancer. <u>Consequently</u>, …

9. Cars and trucks are not designed randomly. They are designed individually for specific purposes. <u>For instance</u>, …

   Truck is design for carrying heavy loads, cars are design for lighter loads

10. Jupiter is a planet surrounded by several moons. <u>Likewise</u>, …

    the earth, mars, and other planets ..

EXERCISE 7-12 **Identifying Transitions**

Directions: Reread each paragraph in Exercise 7-3 on pages 226–228. Underline any transitions that you find.

PARAPHRASING PARAGRAPHS

OBJECTIVE 4

Paraphrasing paragraphs is a useful technique for both building and checking your comprehension. By taking a paragraph apart sentence by sentence, you are forced to understand the meaning of each sentence and see how ideas relate to one another. Paraphrasing paragraphs is similar to paraphrasing sentences. It involves the same two steps:

1. Substituting synonyms
2. Rearranging sentence parts

Here are some guidelines for paraphrasing paragraphs.

1. Concentrate on maintaining the author's focus and emphasis. Ideas that seem most important in the paragraph should appear as most important in your paraphrase.
2. Work sentence by sentence, paraphrasing the ideas in the order in which they appear in the paragraph.

Here are two sample paraphrases of a paragraph. One is a good paraphrase; the other is poor and unacceptable.

Paragraph

For the most part, the American media share one overriding goal: to make a profit. But they are also the main instruments for manipulating public opinion. Politicians want to win our hearts and minds, and businesses want to win our dollars. Both use the media to try to gain mass support by manipulating public opinion. In other words, they generate **propaganda**—communication tailored to influence opinion. Propaganda may be true or false. What sets it apart from other communications is the intent to change opinion.

—Thio, *Sociology,* p. 374

Good Paraphrase

American media (newspapers, TV, and radio) have one common purpose, which is to make money. Media are also vehicles for controlling how the public thinks. Politicians want us to like them; businesses want our money. Both use media to get support by controlling how people think. Both use propaganda. Propaganda is words and ideas that are used to affect how people think. Propaganda can be either true or false. It is different from other forms of communication because its purpose is to change how we think.

Poor and Unacceptable Paraphrase

In general, the media only wants to control people. But the media also manipulates public opinion. Both politicians and businesses want our money and they use the media to try to get it. To do that, they generate propaganda, which is communication tailored to influence opinion. What sets propaganda apart from other communications is whether it is true or false, and how well it changes people's opinions.

The above paraphrase is unacceptable because it is inaccurate and incomplete.

EXERCISE 7-13   **Writing a Paraphrase**

Directions: Write paraphrases of Paragraphs 1, 2, and 3 in Exercise 7-3 (pp. 226–228) on a separate sheet of paper.

SELF-TEST SUMMARY

OBJECTIVE 1 What are supporting details?	Supporting details explain or add support to a paragraph's main idea.
OBJECTIVE 2 What are the five types of details used to support the main idea?	The types of details are examples, facts or statistics, reasons, descriptions, and steps or procedures.
OBJECTIVE 3 What are transitions, and what information do they give the reader?	Transitions are linking words and phrases that lead the reader from one idea to another. They suggest time/sequence, example, enumeration, continuation, contrast, comparison, cause/effect, and summation.
OBJECTIVE 4 What two steps are involved in paraphrasing paragraphs?	Paraphrasing paragraphs involves: 1. substituting synonyms 2. rearranging sentence parts

GOING ONLINE

1. Building Paragraphs

   http://www.washburn.edu/services/zzcwwctr/paragraphs.txt

   Go through this site that reviews paragraph formation. Complete the exercises that are presented throughout the page.

2. Details in Paragraphs

   http://lrs.ed.uiuc.edu/students/fwalters/para.html#details

   Read about the importance of details in paragraphs at this site. After you have read and understood the information, follow the link to complete the exercise.

3. Supporting Sentences

   http://eolf.univ-fcomte.fr/uploads/ressources/academic/paragraph/tutorial_3/ support1.htm

   Practice identifying the supporting details in paragraphs using this online tutorial.

To check your progress in meeting chapter objectives, log in to **http://www.myreadinglab.com**, click on the Study Plan tab, and then click on the Reading Skills tab. Choose Supporting Details from the list of subtopics. Read and view the information in the Review Materials section, and then complete the Practices and Tests in the Activities section. You can check your scores by clicking on the Gradebook tab.

MASTERY TEST 1 **Paragraph Skills**

Name _____ Section _____

Date _____ Number right _____ × 20 points = Score _____

Directions: Read each of the following paragraphs; then select the choice that correctly identifies the type of details used in the paragraph.

_____ 1.   Many people do not know what to look for when considering the type of skin cancer called melanoma. A simple *ABCD* rule outlines the warning signals of melanoma: *A* is for asymmetry. One half of the mole does not match the other half. *B* is for border irregularity. The edges are ragged, notched, or blurred. *C* is for color. The pigmentation is not uniform. *D* is for diameter greater than 6 millimeters. Any or all of these symptoms should cause you to visit a physician.

—Donatelle and Davis, *Access to Health*, pp. 446–447

a. statistics
b. reasons
c. descriptions
d. procedures

_____ 2.   In the second week of May 1940, the German armies overran neutral Holland, Belgium, and Luxembourg. The next week they went into northern France and to the English Channel. Designated as an open city by the French in order to spare its destruction, Paris fell on June 14. As the German advance continued, the members of the French government who wanted to continue resistance were voted down. Marshall Philippe Pétain, a 74-year-old World War I hero, became premier.

He immediately asked Hitler for an armistice. On June 22, 1940, in the same dining car in which the French had imposed armistice terms on the Germans in 1917, the Nazis and French signed another peace agreement. The Germans had gained revenge for their shame in 1917.

—Brummet et al., *Civilization*, p. 919

a. facts
b. reasons
c. descriptions
d. examples

_____ 3.   Ethnic minority group members in the United States have a much higher dropout rate for psychotherapy than do white clients. Among the reasons ethnic clients terminate treatment so early are a lack of bilingual therapists and therapists' stereotypes about ethnic clients. The single most important reason may be that therapists do not provide culturally responsive forms of therapy. They may be unaware of values and customs within a culture that would help in understanding and treating certain behaviors. Therapy should be undertaken with an understanding of cultural values.

—Davis and Palladino, *Psychology*, p. 609

a. steps
b. procedures
c. facts
d. reasons

243

What type of celebration does this festival illustrate?

_____ 4.   Festivals celebrate a variety of special occasions and holidays. Some are derived from religious observances, such as New Orleans' or Rio de Janeiro's huge Mardi Gras festivals. Other festivals focus on activities as peaceful as ballooning (the Albuquerque Balloon Festival) or as terrifying as the running of the bulls in Pamplona, Spain. Often, festivals center on the cultural heritage of an area, such as the clan festivals that are prominent in the North Atlantic province of Nova Scotia. More recently, food has become the center of attention at locations such as the National Cherry Festival in Traverse City, Michigan, or the Garlic Festival in Gilroy, California.

—Cook, *Tourism*, p. 214

  a. statistics
  b. examples
  c. facts
  d. procedures

_____ 5.   The **dissolution** stage, in both friendship and romance, is the cutting of the bonds tying you together. At first it usually takes the form of *interpersonal separation*, in which you may not see each other anymore. If you live together, you move into separate apartments and begin to lead lives apart from each other. If this relationship is a marriage, you may seek a legal separation. If this separation period proves workable and if the original relationship is not repaired, you may enter the phase of *social* or *public separation*. If this is a marriage, this phase corresponds to divorce. Avoidance of each other and a return to being "single" are among the primary identifiable features of dissolution. In some cases, however, the former partners change the definition of their relationship; for example, ex-lovers become friends, or ex-friends become "just" business partners. This final, "goodbye," phase of dissolution is the point at which you become an ex-lover or ex-friend. In some cases this is a stage of relief and relaxation; finally it's over. In other cases this is a stage of anxiety and frustration, of guilt and regret, of resentment over time ill spent and now lost. In more materialistic terms, the goodbye phase is the stage when property is divided and when legal battles may ensue over who should get what.

—Devito, *Messages*, p. 284

  a. examples
  b. reasons
  c. descriptions
  d. steps

CHAPTER 7

MASTERY TEST 2 Paragraph Skills

HW P245-252
P96-99

Name _____ Section _____

Date _____ Number right _____ × 10 points = Score _____

Directions: Read the passage below, and select the choice that best completes each of the statements that follow.

1   A **punishment** is an unpleasant experience that occurs as a result of an undesirable behavior. Punishment is most effective if it has these three characteristics. First, punishment should be swift, occurring immediately after the undesired behavior. The old threat "Wait till you get home!" undermines the effectiveness of the punishment. Second, punishment must be consistent. The undesired behavior must be punished each and every time it occurs. Finally, the punishment should be sufficiently unpleasant without being overly unpleasant. For instance, if a child doesn't mind being alone in her room, then being sent there for pushing her brother won't be a very effective punishment.

2   Although punishment may decrease the frequency of a behavior, it doesn't eliminate the ability to perform that behavior. For example, your little sister may learn not to push you because your mother will punish her, but she may continue to push her classmates at school because the behavior has not been punished in that context. She may also figure out that if she hits you, but then apologizes, she will not get punished.

3   Furthermore, physical punishment, such as spanking, should be avoided. It may actually increase aggressive behavior in the person on the receiving end. In addition, the one being punished may come to live in fear of the one doing the punishing, even if the punishment is infrequent.

4   Overall, punishment alone hasn't been found to be an effective way of controlling behavior. This is because punishment doesn't convey information about what behavior should be exhibited in place of the undesired, punished behavior. That is, the person being punished knows what they should not do, but the person does not know what he or she should do.

—Kosslyn and Rosenberg,
Psychology, pp. 180–181

_____ 1. The primary purpose of the selection is to
    a. describe the concept of punishment.
    b. discourage the use of physical punishment.
    c. identify behaviors that require punishment.
    d. discuss alternative methods of discipline.

_____ 2. The main type of transition used in paragraph 1 is
    a. time/sequence.
    b. enumeration.
    c. continuation.
    d. summation.

_____ 3. The transition word or phrase in paragraph 1 that indicates an example will follow is
    a. first.
    b. second.
    c. finally.
    d. for instance.

245

_____ 4. The main idea of paragraph 1 is that
   a. punishment must be consistent.
   b. punishment must be unpleasant.
   c. punishment has three qualities.
   d. punishment is targeted toward undesired behavior.

_____ 5. The main idea of paragraph 2 is supported by
   a. examples.
   b. facts.
   c. reasons.
   d. description.

_____ 6. The main idea of paragraph 2 is that
   a. punishment decreases the frequency of a behavior.
   b. a behavior that is punished at home may not be punished elsewhere.
   c. punishment does not eliminate a person's ability to engage in a behavior.
   d. a child may learn to avoid punishment by apologizing for a behavior.

_____ 7. The transition words in paragraph 3 that indicate a continuation of the same idea are
   a. may actually.
   b. such as.
   c. even if.
   d. in addition.

_____ 8. A key detail in paragraph 3 that directly supports the main idea is
   a. spanking harms children.
   b. physical punishment may increase aggression in the person giving the punishment.

   c. physical punishment may increase aggression in the person receiving the punishment.
   d. physical punishment may become addictive.

_____ 9. The word or phrase that indicates a cause/effect transition in paragraph 4 is
   a. because.
   b. alone.
   c. overall.
   d. in place of.

_____ 10. The best paraphrase of paragraph 4 is
   a. Punishment alone is not an effective means of controlling behavior. Punishment does not convey information about what behavior should take the place of the undesired, punished behavior.
   b. Combining punishment and reinforcement is more effective than using punishment by itself. Punishment quickly lets people know what behaviors are not desirable.
   c. Punishment should never be used because it does not demonstrate desirable behavior.
   d. Punishment does not give information about what behavior should replace the undesired, punished behavior.

MASTERY TEST 3 Reading Selection

Name _____ Section _____

Date _____ Number right _____ × 10 points = Score _____

Sustainability on the Menu

Carl Pino

This selection first appeared in *E/The Environmental Magazine*. Read the article to find out how college cafeterias are playing an important role in the sustainability movement.

Tyler Ounham (left) and Misha Johnson dump food scraps into one of Connecticut College's commercial-size composting units.

Vocabulary Preview

composting (par. 1) collecting food waste and other decaying plant material in a pile or bin so that it can be used to fertilize soil

endowment (par. 1) funds donated to an institution as a source of income

1   Cafeterias are ground zero for "greening" a school, and the past year has seen great leaps in local and organic food purchasing: from cage-free eggs and fair-trade coffee to composting at schools nationwide. According to the Sustainable Endowments Institute's 2007 report card (which looks at environmental initiatives at the 200 colleges and universities with the largest endowment assets in the U.S. and Canada), 70 percent of schools "devote at least a portion of food budgets to buying from local farms and/or producers." Twenty-nine percent of schools on the institute's list earned an "A" in the "food and recycling" category.

2   Some schools clearly stand out. At Santa Clara University in California, 80 percent of the produce served in the dining halls comes from local farms. Carleton College in Minnesota purchases from 15 to 20 local farmers and producers, serves grass-fed meat and uses 100 percent organic flour in all baking. In Massachusetts, Smith College's dining services purchase organic produce, in addition to dairy and honey, from 18 local farms. The college has even removed bottled water from one to-go location and distributes polycarbonate bottles to be refilled and reused by students. Food scraps are brought to a local farm to be composted.

3   Bon Appètit Management Company provides food to 17 U.S. campuses, from American University in Washington, D.C. to Washington University in St. Louis.

---

*To calculate the number right, use items 1–10 under "Mastery Test Skills Check."

And the company purchases only sustainable seafood, cage-free eggs and hosts the Farm to Fork Program, bringing small, local farmers big business.

4   Chefs at Macalester College in Minneapolis buy cottage cheese direct from a local dairy, and bison meat from a local rancher. "The chefs are making commitments with local producers, and farmers can improve their business," says Haven Bourque of Bon Appétit.

IVY LEAGUE LESSONS

5   Yale University has provided healthy, sustainable eating options—organic and locally grown foods—for years. Daily menus announce the sustainable options, including all-sustainable Tuesday dinners. The Yale Sustainable Food Project shares its information through nutritional cards in dining halls. "Students start looking at their footprints," says Josh Viertel, one of the Food Project's directors. "It's about the ethics embedded in you through your education."

6   Viertel and fellow director Melina Shannon-DiPietro say that Yale's local purchasing program brings more local, organic, sustainable produce to campus cafeterias. "Food tied to tradition and tied to the environment around it helps students become more aware of their impacts," Viertel says.

7   Yale also has a student-run farm, three greenhouses that serve the community and a farmer's market in the spring and summer months. Says Anastasia Curley, coordinator at the Food Project, "We try to strike a balance between food and wellness and general information about agriculture and green events going on at Yale." On a brisk December afternoon, Curley showed off garden plots where carrots, cabbage, spinach and other cold-tolerant vegetables were growing in 30-degree weather. Students at Yale have even harvested carrots during blizzards.

8   But Robert Sullivan, assistant director of operations at Yale's dining services, says the majority of students have not fully embraced sustainability. "Some are focused on eating vegan, others on pizza," he says. "The balance is challenging." Yale's cafeterias offer grass-fed beef burgers, organic quiches and a whole assortment of locally grown produce. "We've been working with the distribution companies to ensure they buy from Connecticut and New Haven farmers," says Thomas Peterlik, executive chef at Yale.

9   A recent composting initiative at Yate was rejected after a trial period, but Sullivan says the impetus is still there. "We have a food salvage group that will contact the groups in the area to donate the food," he says.

10   Princeton University Dining Services has been working with the college's own "Greening Princeton" program. Student representative Kathryn Anderson says it started small. "The first thing we did was look at how to get organic cereal into the dining hall," she says. "We now have a large purchasing effort to make meats organic." All the chicken breast and ground beef the school serves is organic or local. Seafood purchased by dining services is raised and processed via sustainable means.

WASTE NOT

11   Princeton's excess food is packaged and distributed to local food shelters. And food wastes from the dining halls are collected into bins and sent to a local pig farm for feed.

12   Connecticut College's proposal for a composting system lost out on MTV and GE's "Ecoimagination Challenge," but an alumnus made a $25,000 contribution to fund the initiative. "By having a composting system on campus we can reduce the distance that the food scraps have to travel, and then we can use them to grow food locally, either on campus or in the local area," says Misha Johnson, a student who runs the campus' organic garden.

13   Pre- and post-consumer food waste generated by Connecticut College totals 8,000 and 9,000 pounds a week, but the compost initiative re-directs 500 pounds of waste daily. The college also sends food scraps to a local pig farm for feed. "By creating a community of consciousness around food producers and consumers, the environment can and will benefit," Johnson says. "We want students and the greater community to realize that food is more than just what one sits down to eat at a meal." That higher consciousness includes one all-vegetarian cafeteria on campus.

14   Campuses seeking sustainable waste disposal can go beyond compost piles and pig feed, too. Campus Kitchens Project allows volunteers to dispense unused foods to the elderly and homeless in local communities. Gonzaga College in Spokane, Washington, Northwestern University in Chicago, Augsburg College in Minnesota and Dillard University in New Orleans have all signed on to the program. Environmental concerns are tied to social ones, and initiatives like these serve not only the students, but the local population and the planet at large.

—*Carl Pino*

MASTERY TEST SKILLS CHECK

Directions: Select the choice that best completes each of the following statements.

Checking Your Comprehension

_____ 1. The purpose of this selection is to
   a. compare recycling programs in colleges across the country.
   b. encourage college students to adopt a vegetarian diet.
   c. describe sustainability programs in college cafeterias.
   d. discuss the environmental benefits of organic farming.

_____ 2. The sustainability initiatives in the article refer to programs that are designed primarily to
   a. save money through recycling.
   b. reduce negative effects on the environment.
   c. determine how carbon is emitted into the environment.
   d. support international hunger relief efforts.

_____ 3. Sustainability initiatives described in the article include all of the following *except*
   a. buying food from local farms and producers.
   b. providing disposable plastic water bottles with every meal.
   c. composting food scraps.
   d. donating excess food to local shelters.

_____ 4. The organization that examines and reports on environmental initiatives at 200 colleges and universities in the U.S. and Canada is the
   a. Sustainable Endowments Institute.
   b. Bon Appètit Management Company.
   c. Farm to Fork Program.
   d. North American Sustainable Food Project.

_____ 5. The main point of paragraph 2 is that
   a. Santa Clara University serves mostly locally grown produce.
   b. Carleton College uses food that is organically grown.
   c. Smith College brings food scraps to a local farm for composting.
   d. certain colleges are making exceptional efforts toward sustainability.

Applying Your Skills

_____ 6. The supporting details that the author uses in this selection include
   a. statistics.
   b. examples.
   c. facts.
   d. all of the above.

_____ 7. Which sentence states the main point of paragraph 7?
   a. Yale has a student-run farm, community greenhouses, and a farmer's market.
   b. Anastasia Curley is coordinator at the Yale Food Project.
   c. In garden plots, carrots, cabbage, spinach and other vegetables were growing in 30-degree weather.
   d. Yale students have harvested carrots during blizzards.

_____ 8. The author indicates a transition in paragraph 8 with the word
   a. But.   c. balance.
   b. majority.   d. offer.

_____ 9. The topic of paragraph 10 is
   a. Princeton University.
   b. organic cereal.
   c. sustainable dining.
   d. seafood.

_____ 10. In paragraph 13, the transition *also* indicates that the author is
   a. arranging ideas in order of importance.
   b. continuing with the same idea.
   c. switching to a contrasting idea.
   d. showing how one thing caused another.

Studying Words

_____ 11. The word "embedded" (paragraph 5) means
   a. prevented.   c. implanted.
   b. attempted.   d. removed.

_____ 12. From context, you can tell that the word "initiative" (paragraph 9) refers to
   a. a plan or program.
   b. a college course.
   c. an administrator.
   d. a news report.

_____ 13. The word "impetus" (paragraph 9) means
   a. indifference.
   b. motivation.
   c. requirement.
   d. decline.

_____ 14. The word "salvage" (paragraph 9) means
   a. reject.
   b. save.
   c. donate.
   d. contact.

_____ 15. The word "dispense" (paragraph 14) means
   a. allow.
   b. hold.
   c. distribute.
   d. destroy.

For more practice, ask your instructor for an opportunity to work on the mastery tests that appear in the Test Bank.

Summarizing the Reading

Directions: Complete the following summary of the reading by filling in the blanks.

Cafeterias at _____ nationwide support _____
by using _____. School that stand out in their efforts include

_____

_____ provides food to _____ and buys only

_____ in addition to supporting _____.

_____ has featured _____ for years and the

_____ uses _____ to share information in the
dining halls. Yale's other sustainability initiatives include _____
_____. Yale students have not _____
and recently rejected a _____ . Efforts at _____
include serving _____, donating _____
and sending _____. At _____ food waste
totals up to _____ but the college's _____ redirects
_____ daily. Food scraps are sent to _____ and the
campus has one _____. Several colleges have signed on to the
_____ which gives _____ to _____
_____ in the community.

Reading Visually

1. What is the purpose of the photo included with this article? Who are the people shown in the photo and what is their connection with the subject matter?
2. Consider some of the environmentally friendly programs described in the article. What other photographs or illustrations would you like to see with this article?
3. Explain how the title of this article relates to the subject. Can you think of another title that would also work for this selection?

Thinking Critically About the Reading

WRITE IN YOUR
JOURNAL

1. Consider what you already know about living "green." What kinds of sustainability programs are in place at your own school or in your town?
2. Why do you think students at Yale have not fully embraced sustainability in the dining halls? What would prevent you from embracing sustainability?
3. Which of the sustainability programs described in the article would you be most likely to participate in? Why?

Following the Author's Thought Patterns

Looking at …
Thought Patterns

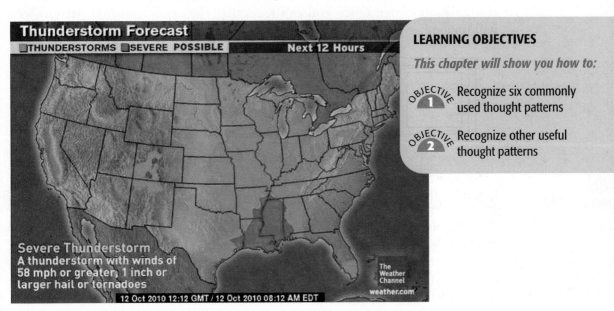

Thunderstorm Forecast

☐THUNDERSTORMS ☐SEVERE POSSIBLE   Next 12 Hours

Severe Thunderstorm
A thunderstorm with winds of
58 mph or greater, 1 inch or
larger hail or tornadoes

The
Weather
Channel
weather.com

12 Oct 2010 12:12 GMT / 12 Oct 2010 08:12 AM EDT

LEARNING OBJECTIVES

This chapter will show you how to:

OBJECTIVE **1**   Recognize six commonly used thought patterns

OBJECTIVE **2**   Recognize other useful thought patterns

This map shows a pattern of weather. You can see that while there is a significant chance of severe thunderstorms in most of Mississippi and Alabama and strong thunderstorms in a band reaching north to the Great Lakes, the majority of the mid-west and west coast will have calm weather. Just as weather map patterns are useful in helping you understand the weather that is coming your way, patterns in paragraphs are useful in helping you work your way through paragraphs. In this chapter you will see how writers organize their ideas using patterns.

-260

As a way to begin thinking about authors' thought patterns, complete each of the following steps:

1. Study each of the drawings below for a few seconds (count to ten as you look at each one).
2. Cover up the drawings and try to draw each from memory.
3. Check to see how many you had exactly correct.

Most likely you drew all but the fourth correctly. Why did you get that one wrong? How does it differ from the others?

Drawings 1, 2, 3, and 5 have patterns. Drawing 4, however, has no pattern; it is just a randomly jagged line.

From this experiment you can see that it is easier to remember drawings that have a pattern, some understandable form of organization. The same is true of written material. If you can see how a paragraph is organized, it will be easier to understand and remember. Writers often present their ideas in a recognizable order. Once you can recognize the organizational pattern, you will remember more of what you read.

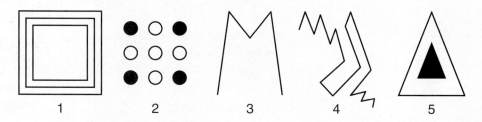

  1   2   3   4   5

SIX COMMON THOUGHT PATTERNS

OBJECTIVE 1

This chapter discusses six of the more common thought patterns that writers use and shows how to recognize them: (1) illustration/example, (2) definition, (3) comparison/contrast, (4) cause/effect, (5) classification, and (6) chronological order/process. A brief overview of other useful patterns is provided in the section that follows.

Illustration/Example

One of the clearest, most practical, and most obvious ways to explain something is to give an **example** to illustrate what you are saying. Suppose you had to explain what anthropology is. You might give examples of the topics you study. By using examples, such as the study of apes and early humans, and the development of modern humans, you would give a fairly good idea of what anthropology is all about. When a subject is unfamiliar, an example often makes it easier to understand.

  Usually a writer will state an idea first and then follow with examples. Several examples may be given in one paragraph, or a separate paragraph may be used for each example. It may help to visualize the illustration/example pattern this way:

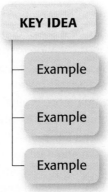

KEY IDEA
- Example
- Example
- Example

Notice how this thought pattern is developed in the following passage.

> Electricity is all around us. We see it in lightning. We receive electric shocks when we walk on a nylon rug on a dry day and then touch something (or someone). We can see sparks fly from a cat's fur when we pet it in the dark. We can rub a balloon on a sweater and make the balloon stick to the wall or the ceiling. Our clothes cling together when we take them from the dryer.
> These are all examples of *static electricity.* They happen because there is a buildup of one of the two kinds of electrical charge, either positive or negative. . . .
>
> —Newell, *Chemistry,* p. 11

In the preceding passage, the concept of static electricity was explained through the use of everyday examples. You could visualize the selection as follows:

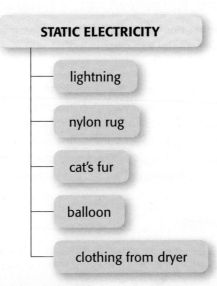

STATIC ELECTRICITY
- lightning
- nylon rug
- cat's fur
- balloon
- clothing from dryer

Here is another passage in which the main idea is explained through example:

> It is a common observation that all bodies do not fall with equal accelerations. A leaf, a feather, or a sheet of paper, for example, may flutter to the ground slowly. That the air is the factor responsible for these different accelerations can be shown very nicely with a closed glass tube containing a light and heavy object, a feather and a coin, for example. In the presence of air, the feather and coin fall with quite unequal accelerations. But if the air in the tube is evacuated by means of a vacuum pump, and the tube is quickly inverted, the feather and coin fall with the same acceleration. . . . Although air resistance appreciably alters the motion of falling feathers and the like, the motion of heavier objects like stones and baseballs is not appreciably affected by the air. The relationships $v = gt$ and $d = 1/2\ gt^2$ can be used to a very good approximation for most objects falling in air.
>
> —Hewitt, *Conceptual Physics*, p. 21

The author explains that objects do not fall at equal rates by using the examples of a leaf, a feather, and a sheet of paper.

Paragraphs and passages organized using illustration/example often use transitional words and phrases to connect ideas. Examples of such words and phrases include:

> *for example*　　　　　　*for instance*　　　　　　*to illustrate*

EXERCISE 8-1   Analyzing Illustration/Example Paragraphs

Directions: For each of the following paragraphs, underline the topic sentence and list the examples used to explain it.

1. Perception is the process of gathering information and giving it meaning. You see a movie and you give meaning to it: "It's one of the best I've seen." You come away from class after the third week and you give meaning to it: "It finally makes sense." We gather information from what our senses see, hear, touch, taste, and smell, and we give meaning to that information. Although the information may come to us in a variety of forms, it is all processed, or *perceived,* in the mind.

    —Weaver, *Understanding Interpersonal Communication*, p. 24

    Examples: _____

What does this photograph contribute to this passage?

2.   The action and reaction forces make up a *pair* of forces. Forces always occur in pairs. There is never a single force in any situation. For example, in walking across the floor, we push against the floor, and the floor in turn pushes against us. Likewise, the tires of a car push against the pavement, and the pavement pushes back on the tires. When we swim, we push the water backward, and the water pushes us forward. The reaction forces, those acting in the direction of our resulting accelerations, are what account for our motion in these cases. These forces depend on friction; a person or car on ice, for example, may not be able to exert the action force to produce the needed reaction force by the ice.

—Hewitt, *Conceptual Physics*, p. 56

Examples: _____

3.   Have you ever noticed that some foods remain hotter much longer than others? Boiled onions and squash on a hot dish, for example, are often too hot to eat when mashed potatoes may be eaten comfortably. The filling of hot apple pie can burn your tongue while the crust will not, even when the pie has just been taken out of the oven. And the aluminum covering on a frozen dinner can be peeled off with your bare fingers as soon as it is removed from the oven. A piece of toast may be comfortably eaten a few seconds after coming from the hot toaster, but we must wait several minutes before eating soup from a stove no hotter than the toaster. Evidently, different substances have different **capacities** for storing internal energy.

—Hewitt, *Conceptual Physics*, p. 224

Examples: _____

_____

EXERCISE 8-2   **Writing an Illustration/Example Paragraph**

Directions: Choose one of the following topics. On a separate sheet of paper, write a paragraph in which you use illustration/example to organize and express your ideas on the topic. Then draw a diagram showing the organization of your paragraph.

1. Parents or friends are helpful (or not helpful) in making decisions.

2. Attending college has (has not) made a major change in my life.

Definition

Another way to provide an explanation is to offer a definition. A **definition** should have two parts: (1) tell what general group or class an item belongs to and (2) explain how that item is different or distinguishable from other items in the group. Let us say that you see an opossum while driving in the country. You mention this to a friend. Since your friend does not know what an opossum is, you have to give a definition. Your definition should include the fact that an opossum is an animal (the general group it belongs to) and a description of the features of an opossum that would help someone tell the difference between it and other animals, such as dogs, raccoons, and squirrels. Thus, you could define an opossum as follows:

> An opossum is an animal with a ratlike tail that lives in trees. It carries its young in a pouch. It is active at night and pretends to be dead when trapped.

This definition can be diagrammed as follows:

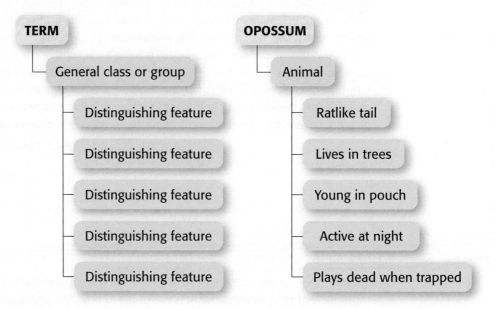

The following passage was written to define the term *ragtime music*.

> Ragtime music is a piano style that developed at the turn of the twentieth century. Ragtime music usually has four themes. The themes are divided into four musical sections of equal length. In playing ragtime music, the left hand plays chords and the right hand plays the melody. There is an uneven accenting between the two hands.

The thought pattern of this passage might be diagrammed as follows:

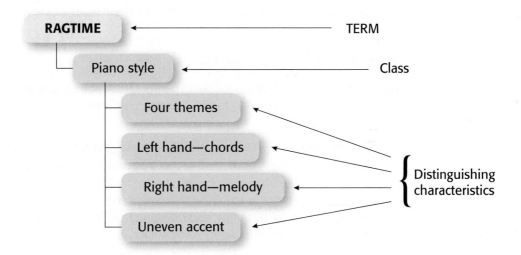

As you read passages that use the definition pattern, keep these questions in mind:

1. What is being defined?
2. What general group or class does it belong to?
3. What makes it different from others in the group?

Read the following passage and apply the above questions.

> Nez Perce Indians are a tribe that lives in north-central Idaho. The rich farmlands and forests in the area form the basis for the tribe's chief industries—agriculture and lumber.
>
> The name *Nez Perce* means *pierced nose,* but few of the Indians ever pierced their noses. In 1805, a French interpreter gave the name to the tribe after seeing some members wearing shells in their noses as decorations.
>
> The Nez Perce originally lived in the region where the borders of Idaho, Oregon, and Washington meet. Prospectors overran the Nez Perce reservation after discovering gold there in the 1860s.
>
> Part of the tribe resisted the efforts of the government to move them to a smaller reservation. In 1877, fighting broke out between the Nez Perce and U.S. troops. Joseph, a Nez Perce chief, tried to lead a band of the Indians into Canada. But he surrendered near the United States–Canadian border.
>
> —World Book Online Reference Center

This passage was written to define the Nez Perce. The general group or category is "Indian tribe." The distinguishing characteristics include the source of their name, their original location, and their fight against relocation.

EXERCISE 8-3   **Analyzing Definition Paragraphs**

Directions: Read each of the following paragraphs. Then identify the term being defined, its general class, and its distinguishing features.

1. The partnership, like the sole proprietorship, is a form of ownership used primarily in small business firms. Two or more owners comprise a partnership. The structure of a partnership may be established with an almost endless variation of features. The partners establish the conditions of the partnership, contribution of each partner to the business, and division of profits. They also decide on the amount of authority, duties, and liability each will have.

—Pickle and Abrahamson, *Introduction to Business*, p. 40

Term: _Partnership_____

General class: ___Proprietorship   small business_____

Distinguishing features: __establish the conditions of partnership, contribution__

of each partner to the business, division of profits, decide on the amount of

authority, duties, liability

2. A language is a complex system of symbols with conventional meanings, used by members of a society for communication. The term *language* is often thought to include only the spoken word, but in its broadest sense language contains verbal, nonverbal and written symbols. Whereas complex cultures employ all three kinds of symbols in communication, simple and preliterate cultures typically lack written symbols.

—Thompson and Hickey, *Society in Focus,* p. 70

Term: __language_____

General class: ___complex system of symbols_____

Distinguishing features: ___verbal, nonverbal, written symbols_____

_____

3. The Small Business Administration (SBA) is an independent agency of the federal government that was created by Congress when it passed the Small Business Act in 1853. Its administrator is appointed by and reports to the President. Purposes of the SBA are to assist people in getting into business, to help them stay in business,

to help small firms win federal procurement contracts, and to act as a strong advocate for small business.

—Pickle and Abrahamson, *Introduction to Business*, p. 119

Term: ___SBA_____

General class: _fedral government_____

Distinguishing features: _assist peop_____

_____

_____

_____

Paragraphs and passages that are organized using definition often use transitional words and phrases to connect ideas. Examples of theses transitional words and phrases include:

can be defined as	*consists of*	*involves*
is	*is called*	*is characterized by*
means	*refers to*	

EXERCISE 8-4   **Writing Definition Paragraphs**

Directions: Choose one of the topics listed below. On a separate sheet of paper, write a paragraph in which you define the topic. Be sure to include both the general group and what makes the item different from other items in the same group. Then draw a diagram showing the organization of your paragraph.

1. A type of music

2. Social networks

3. Junk food

Comparison/Contrast

Often a writer will explain something by using **comparison** or **contrast**—that is, by showing how it is similar to or different from a familiar object or idea. Comparison treats similarities, while contrast emphasizes differences. For example, an article comparing two car models might mention these common, overlapping features: radial tires, clock, radio, power steering, and power brakes. The cars may differ in gas mileage, body shape, engine power, braking distance, and so forth. When comparing the two models, the writer would focus on shared features. When contrasting the two cars the writer would focus on individual differences. Such an article might be diagrammed as follows:

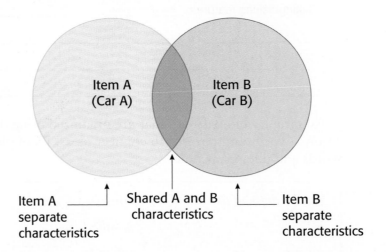

In this diagram, Items A and B are different except where they overlap and share the same characteristics.

In most articles that use the comparison/contrast method, you will find some passages that only compare, some that only contrast, and others that both compare and contrast. To read each type of passage effectively, you must follow the pattern of ideas. Passages that show comparison and/or contrast can be organized in a number of different ways. The organization depends on the author's purpose.

Comparison   If a writer is concerned only with similarities, he or she may identify the items to be compared and then list the ways in which they are alike. The following paragraph shows how chemistry and physics are similar.

Although physics and chemistry are considered separate fields of study, they have much in common. First, both are physical sciences and are concerned with studying and explaining physical occurrences. To study and record these occurrences, each field has developed a precise set of signs and symbols. These might be considered a specialized language. Finally, both fields are closely tied to the field of mathematics and use mathematics in predicting and explaining physical occurrences.

—Hewitt, *Conceptual Physics*, pp. 82–84

Such a pattern can be diagrammed as follows:

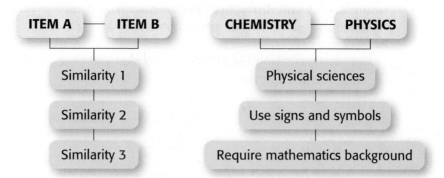

Contrast   A writer concerned only with the differences between sociology and psychology might write the following paragraph:

> Sociology and psychology, although both social sciences, are very different fields of study. Sociology is concerned with the structure, organization, and behavior of groups. Psychology, on the other hand, focuses on individual behavior. While a sociologist would study characteristics of groups of people, a psychologist would study the individual motivation and behavior of each group member. Psychology and sociology also differ in the manner in which research is conducted. Sociologists obtain data and information through observation and survey. Psychologists obtain data through carefully designed experimentation.

Such a pattern can be diagrammed as follows:

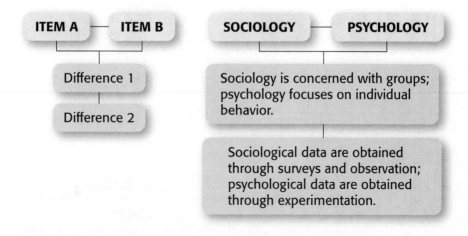

Comparison and Contrast   In many passages, writers discuss both similarities and differences. Suppose you wanted to write a paragraph discussing the similarities and differences between sociology and psychology. You could organize the paragraph in different ways.

1. You could list all the similarities and then all the differences, as shown in this diagram:

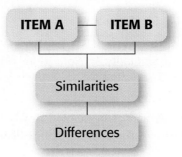

2. You could discuss Item A first, presenting both similarities and differences, and then do the same for Item B. Such a pattern would look like this:

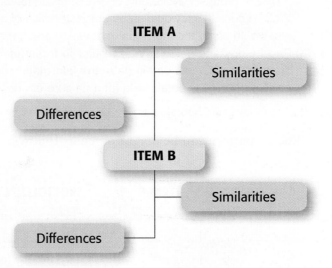

The following paragraph discusses amphibians and reptiles. As you read it, try to visualize its pattern.

Although reptiles evolved from amphibians, several things distinguish the two kinds of animals. Amphibians (such as frogs, salamanders, and newts) must live where it is moist. In contrast, reptiles (which include turtles, lizards and snakes, and crocodiles and alligators) can live away from the water. Amphibians employ external fertilization, as when the female frog lays her eggs on the water and the male spreads his sperm on top of them. By contrast, all reptiles employ internal fertilization—eggs are fertilized inside the female's body. Another difference between amphibians and reptiles is that reptiles have a tough, scaly skin that conserves water, as opposed to the thin amphibian skin that allows water to escape. Reptiles also have a stronger skeleton than amphibians, more efficient lungs, and a better-developed nervous system.

—adapted from Krogh, *Biology: A Guide to the Natural World*, pp. 466–467, 474

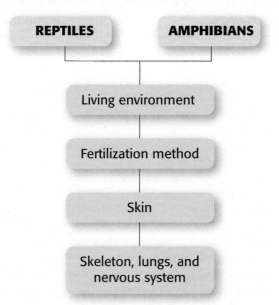

Now read the following passage and decide whether it discusses similarities, differences, or both.

Groups have two types of leaders. The first is easy to recognize. This person, called an **instrumental leader**, tries to keep the group moving toward its goals. These leaders try to keep group members from getting sidetracked, reminding them of what they are trying to accomplish. The **expressive leader**, in contrast, usually is not recognized as a leader, but he or she certainly is one. This person is likely to crack jokes, to offer sympathy or to do other things that help to lift the group's morale. Both types of leadership are essential: the one to keep the group on track, the other to increase harmony and minimize conflicts.

It is difficult for the same person to be both an instrumental and an expressive leader, for these roles tend to contradict one another. Because instrumental leaders are task oriented, they sometimes create friction as they prod the group to get on with the job. Their actions often cost them popularity. Expressive leaders, in contrast, who stimulate personal bonds and reduce friction, are usually more popular.

—adapted from Henslin, *Sociology: A Down-to-Earth Approach*, p. 164

This passage *contrasts* two types of group leaders, focusing on differences between the two types.

Paragraphs and passages that use comparison/contrast often contain transitional words and phrases that guide readers through the material. These include:

Comparison	Contrast
both, in comparison, in the same way, likewise, similarly, to compare	*as opposed to, differs from, however, in contrast, instead, on the other hand, unlike*

EXERCISE 8-5   Analyzing Comparison/Contrast Paragraphs

Directions: Read each of the following passages and identify the items being compared or contrasted. Then describe the author's approach to the items. Does the author compare, contrast, or both compare and contrast?

1.   Congress is bicameral, meaning that it is made up of two houses, the Senate and the House of Representatives. According to the Constitution, all members of Congress must be residents of the states that they have been elected to represent. The Constitution also specifies that representatives must be at least 25 years old and American citizens for 7 years, whereas senators must be at least 30 and American citizens for 9 years. The roles of majority and minority leaders are similar in both houses, and both use committees to review bills and to set their legislative agenda. Despite these similarities, there are many important differences between the two houses. First, the term of office is two years for representative but six years for senators. Further, each state is guaranteed two senators but its number of representatives is determined by the state's population; thus, the House of Representatives has 435 members and the Senate has 100. Another difference involves procedure: the House places limits on debate, whereas the Senate allows unlimited debate, which sometimes leads to a filibuster.

Items compared or contrasted: _____

Approach: _____

2.   African leopards have features that help them thrive alongside Africa's regal lion. Leopards tend to be nocturnal hunters, whereas lions hunt during the day. And leopards take a much larger variety of prey items than lions. With average weights of about 58 kilograms (128 pounds) for males and 38 kilograms (84 pounds) for females, African leopards are only about a third the size of a typical lion. But leopards

are slightly faster, with top running speeds of 64 kilometers (40 miles) per hour. And with superior jumping skills that propel leopards to 6 meters (20 feet) through the air horizontally and about 3 meters vertically, the cat is an exceptional climber. Powerful jaw, neck, and shoulder muscles give the leopard the ability to pounce and kill prey with a quick bite and the additional strength needed to haul prey upward, sometimes dragging a carcass as high as 15 meters into a tree.

—adapted from Campbell et al., *Biology: Concepts and Connections*, p. 1

Items compared or contrasted: _____

Approach: _____

3.   The first step in evaluating your computer system needs is determining whether you want a desktop or a laptop. The main distinction between desktops and laptops is portability. If you need to take your computer with you to work or school, or even want the flexibility to move from room to room in your house, a laptop is the best choice. If portability is not an absolute factor, you should consider a desktop. Desktop systems are invariably a better value than laptops in terms of computing power gained for your dollar. Because of the laptop's small size, you pay more for each component. In addition, a desktop system offers more expandability options. It's easier to add new ports and devices because of the amount of room available in the desktop computer's design. Desktop systems are also more reliable. Because of the amount of vibration that a laptop experiences and the added exposure to dust, water, and temperature fluctuations that portability provides, laptops do not last as long as desktop computers.

—adapted from Evans et al., *Technology in Action*, p. 271

Items compared or contrasted: _____

Approach: _____

EXERCISE 8-6   **Writing a Comparison/Contrast Paragraph**

Directions: Choose one of the topics listed below. On a separate sheet of paper, write a paragraph in which you compare and/or contrast the two items. Then draw a diagram showing the organization of your paragraph.

1. Two restaurants

2. Two friends

3. Two musical groups

Cause/Effect

The **cause/effect** pattern is used to describe an event or action that is caused by another event or action. A cause/effect passage explains why or how something happened. For example, a description of an automobile accident would probably follow a cause/effect pattern. You would tell what caused the accident and what happened as a result. Basically, this pattern describes four types of relationships:

1. Single cause/single effect

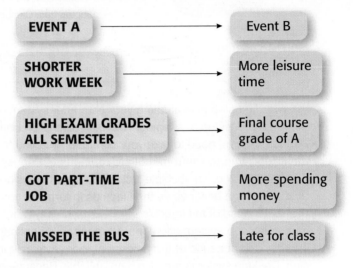

2. Single cause/multiple effects

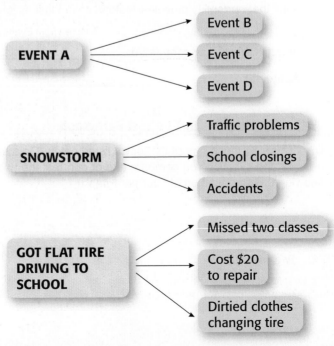

3. Multiple cause/single effect

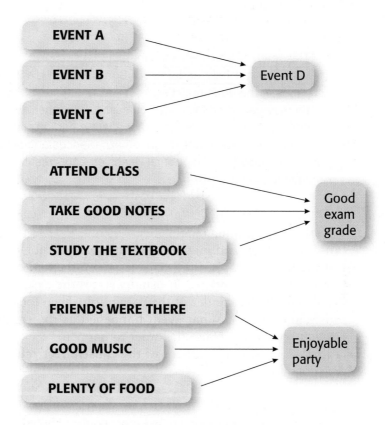

4. Multiple causes/multiple effects

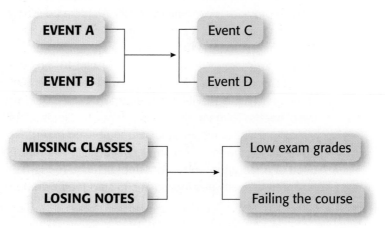

Read the following paragraph and determine which of the four relationships it describes.

Research has shown that mental illnesses have various causes, but the causes are not fully understood. Some mental disorders are due to physical changes in the brain resulting from illness or injury. Chemical imbalances in the brain may cause other mental illnesses. Still other disorders are mainly due to conditions in the environment that affect a person's mental state. These conditions include unpleasant childhood experiences and severe emotional stress. In addition, many cases of mental illness probably result from a combination of two or more of these causes.

In this paragraph a single effect (mental illness) is stated as having multiple causes (chemical and metabolic changes, psychological problems).

To read paragraphs that explain cause/effect relationships, pay close attention to the topic sentence. It usually states the cause/effect relationship that is detailed in the remainder of the paragraph. Then look for connections between causes and effects. What event happened as the result of a previous action? How did one event cause the other to happen?

Look for the development of the cause/effect relationship in the following paragraph about tourism.

Tourism offers several positive economic benefits. First, tourism can provide stability in an economy. Business travel remains relatively constant during changes in economic cycles; and even though people may cut back on the amount they spend on travel during harder economic times, citizens of most industrial nations have come to view vacationing as a necessity of life. Second, tourism provides economic diversity. A stable economy is one that provides jobs and revenues from a variety of industries; tourism can be added as another economic engine to the industry mix. Third, tourism often provides the economic incentive to improve infrastructure that can be enjoyed by residents as well as tourists. For example, state-of-the-art airports are built by communities primarily to increase accessibility, but the airport can also be used by locals to meet their travel needs. Tourism offers a fourth positive impact that you may find particularly appealing. Unlike most manufacturing-based enterprises, a tourism business can be started in the form of a small business. In this way, the tourism industry can be used to encourage entrepreneurial activity. Tourism provides plenty of chances for creative, motivated individuals to start their own businesses.

—adapted from Cook et al., *Tourism: The Business of Travel*, p. 282

This paragraph describes the positive effects of tourism. It can be diagrammed as follows:

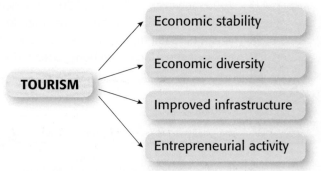

Paragraphs and passages that are organized using cause/effect often use transitional words and phrases to guide the reader. These include:

Cause	Effect
because, because of, for, since, stems from, one cause is, one reason is, for this reason, due to	*consequently, one result is, as a result, therefore, thus, hence, results in*

EXERCISE 8-7   **Analyzing Cause/Effect Paragraphs**

Directions: Read each of the following paragraphs and describe the cause/effect relationship in each.

1.   The effects of marijuana are relatively mild compared to the other hallucinogens. Most people do report a feeling of mild euphoria and relaxation, along with an altered time sense and mild visual distortions. Higher doses can lead to hallucinations, delusions, and the all-too-common paranoia. Most studies of marijuana's effects have concluded that while marijuana can create a powerful psychological dependency, it does not produce physical dependency or physical withdrawal symptoms. Newer studies, however, suggest that long-term marijuana use can produce signs of withdrawal such as irritability, memory difficulties, sleep difficulties, and increased aggression. A recent study of the long-term effects of marijuana use has also correlated smoking marijuana with an increased risk of psychotic behavior, with a greater risk for heavier users.

—adapted from Ciccarelli and White, *Psychology: An Exploration*, p. 280

Cause(s): _____

Effect(s): _____

_____

_____

2. Bees have suffered dramatic declines in recent years. Steady declines in wild and domesticated bee populations occurred from the 1970s through 2005; however, in 2006 and 2007, the declines reached crisis proportions. The exact causes of these dramatic declines are not known but are believed to result from an increased level of bee parasites, competition with the invading Africanized honeybees ("killer bees"), and habitat destruction.

—adapted from Belk and Maier, *Biology: Science for Life with Physiology*, p. 372

Cause(s): _____

Effect(s): 1970s through 2005, Steady declines in wild & domesticated
in 2006 & 2007 crisis proportions   bee pop.

What does this photo suggest about the importance of bees?

3. An important consequence of culture within us is ethnocentrism, a tendency to use our own group's ways of doing things as a yardstick for judging others. All of us learn that the ways of our own group are good, right, and even superior to other ways of life. Ethnocentrism has both positive and negative consequences. On the positive side, it creates in-group loyalties. On the negative side, ethnocentrism can lead to discrimination against people whose ways differ from ours.

—adapted from Henslin, *Sociology: A Down-to-Earth Approach*, p. 37

Cause(s): _____

Effect(s): _____

EXERCISE 8-8   Writing a Cause/Effect Paragraph

Directions: Choose one of the topics listed below. On a separate sheet of paper, write a paragraph using one of the four cause/effect patterns described above to explain the topic. Then draw a diagram showing the organization of your paragraph.

1. Why you are attending college

2. Why you chose the college you are attending

3. How a particularly frightening or tragic event happened

Classification

A common way to explain something is **classification**, dividing a topic into parts and explaining each part. For example, you might explain how a home computer works by describing what each major component does. You would explain the functions of the monitor (screen), the disc drives, and the central processing unit. Or you might explain the kinds of courses taken in college by dividing the courses into such categories as electives, required basic courses, courses required for a specific major, and so on, and then describing each category.

Textbook writers use the classification pattern to explain a topic that can easily be divided into parts. These parts are selected on the basis of common characteristics. For example, a psychology textbook writer might explain human needs by classifying them into two categories, primary and secondary. Or in a chemistry textbook, various compounds may be grouped or classified according to common characteristics, such as the presence of hydrogen or oxygen.

The following paragraph explains horticulture. As you read, try to identify the categories into which the topic of horticulture is divided.

> Horticulture, the study and cultivation of garden plants, is a large industry. Recently it has become a popular area of study. The horticulture field consists of four major divisions. First, there is pomology, the science and practice of growing and handling fruit trees. Then there is olericulture, which is concerned with growing and storing vegetables. A third field, floriculture, is the science of growing, storing, and designing flowering plants. The last category, ornamental and landscape horticulture, is concerned with using grasses, plants, and shrubs in landscaping.

This paragraph approaches the topic of horticulture by describing its four areas or fields of study. You could diagram the paragraph as follows:

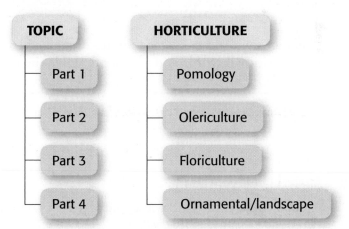

When reading textbook material that uses the classification pattern, be sure you understand *how* and *why* the topic was divided as it was. This technique will help you remember the most important parts of the topic.

Here is another example of the classification pattern:

> A newspaper is published primarily to present current news and information. For large city newspapers, more than 2,000 people may be involved in the distribution of this information. <u>The staff of large city papers, headed by a publisher, is organized into departments: editorial, business, and mechanical.</u> The editorial department, headed by an editor-in-chief, is responsible for the collection of news and preparation of written copy. The business department, headed by a business manager, handles circulation, sales, and advertising. The mechanical department is run by a production manager. This department deals with the actual production of the paper, including typesetting, layout, and printing.

You could diagram this paragraph as follows:

Paragraphs and passages that are organized using classification frequently use transitional words and phrases to guide the reader. These include:

another	*another kind*	*classified as*	*include*	*is composed of*	*one*	*types of*	

EXERCISE **8-9**   **Analyzing Classification Paragraphs**

Directions: Read each of the following passages. Then identify the topic and the parts into which each passage is divided.

1.   We can separate the members of the plant kingdom into a mere four types. These are the *bryophytes*, which include mosses; the *seedless vascular plants*, which include ferns; the *gymnosperms*, which include coniferous ("cone-bearing")

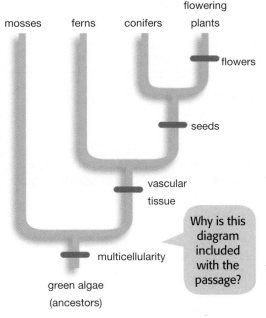

flowering plants

mosses   ferns   conifers   plants

flowers

seeds

vascular tissue

Why is this diagram included with the passage?

multicellularity

green algae (ancestors)

What needs does this photograph illustrate?

trees; and the *angiosperms*, a vast division of flowering plants—by far the most dominant on Earth today—that includes not only flowers such as orchids, but also oak trees, rice, and cactus.

—adapted from Krogh, *Biology: A Guide to the Natural World*, p. 429

Topic: _____

Parts: _bryophytes., the seedless vascular_
plants. the gymnosperms. the angiosperms

2.   People are born with a need for certain elements necessary to maintain life, such as food, water, air, and shelter. We also can be motivated to satisfy either utilitarian or hedonic needs. When we focus on a *utilitarian need* we emphasize the objective, tangible attributes of products, such as miles per gallon in a car; the amount of fat, calories, and protein in a cheeseburger; or the durability of a pair of blue jeans. *Hedonic needs* are subjective and experiential; here we might look to a product to meet our needs for excitement, self-confidence, or fantasy—perhaps to escape the mundane or routine aspects of life. Of course, we can also be motivated to purchase a product because it provides *both* types of benefits. For example, a woman (perhaps a politically incorrect one) might buy a mink coat because of the luxurious image it portrays and because it also happens to keep her warm through the long, cold winter.

—adapted from Solomon, *Consumer Behavior: Buying, Having, and Being*, pp. 132–133

Topic: _needs_____

Parts: _____

3.   The amount of space that people prefer varies from one culture to another. North Americans use four different "distance zones." *Intimate distance* extends to about 18 inches from our bodies. We reserve this space for comforting, protecting, hugging, intimate touching, and lovemaking. *Personal distance* extends from 18 inches to 4 feet. We reserve it for friends and acquaintances and ordinary conversations. *Social distance*, extending out from us about 4 to 12 feet, marks impersonal or formal relationships. We use this zone for such things as job interviews. *Public distance*, extending beyond 12 feet, marks even

more formal relationships. It is used to separate dignitaries and public speakers from the general public.

—adapted from Henslin, *Sociology: A Down-to-Earth Approach*, pp. 109, 111

Topic: _____ Space _____

Parts: _____

EXERCISE 8-10   Writing a Classification Paragraph

Directions: Choose one of the topics listed below. On a separate sheet of paper, write a paragraph explaining the topic, using the classification pattern. Then draw a diagram showing the organization of your paragraph.

1. Advertising

2. Colleges

3. Entertainment

Chronological Order/Process

myreadinglab

To practice recognizing chronological order and process patterns, go to
▼ STUDY PLAN
  ▼ READING SKILLS
    ▼ TIME ORDER

The terms **chronological order** and **process** both refer to the order in which something is done. Chronological order, also called sequence of events, is one of the most obvious patterns. In a paragraph organized by chronology, the details are presented in the order in which they occur. That is, the event that happened first, or earliest in time, appears first in the paragraph, and so on. Process refers to the steps or stages in which something is done. You might expect to read a description of the events in a World War II battle presented in the order in which they happened—in chronological order. Similarly, in a computer programming manual, the steps to follow to locate an error in a computer program would be described in the order in which you should do them.

Both chronological order and process patterns can be diagrammed as follows:

Read the following paragraph, paying particular attention to the order of the actions or steps.

> In the early 1830s, the newly established Federal Bureau of Narcotics took on a crucial role in the fight against marijuana. Under the directorship of Harry J. Anslinger, a rigorous campaign was waged against the drug and those using it. By 1837 many states had adopted a standard bill making marijuana illegal. In that same year, the federal government stepped in with the Marijuana Tax Act, a bill modeled after the Harrison "Narcotics" Act. Repressive legislation continued, and by the 1850s severe penalties were imposed on those convicted of possessing, buying, selling, or cultivating the drug.
>
> —Barlow, *Criminal Justice in America*, p. 332

This paragraph traces the history of actions taken to limit the use of marijuana. These actions are described in chronological order, beginning with the earliest event and concluding with the most recent.

When reading text material that uses the chronological order/process pattern, pay particular attention to the order of the information presented. Both chronological order and process are concerned with the sequence of events in time.

Paragraphs and passages that use chronological order/process to organize ideas often contain transitional words and phrases to guide the reader. They include:

after	*before*	*by the time*	*during*	*finally*	*first*	*later*
meanwhile	*on*	*second*	*then*	*until*	*when*	*while*

EXERCISE 8-11   Analyzing Chronological Order/Process Paragraphs

Directions: Read each of the following paragraphs. Identify the topic and write a list of the actions, steps, or events described in each paragraph.

1. Two important traditions are typically performed when new lodging properties are constructed. First, when the final floor is completed, an evergreen tree is placed on the top of the building. This act signifies that the building will rise no higher. It also symbolically ties the building safely to the ground through the "roots of the tree." The second important tradition is performed when the ceremonial ribbon is cut on opening day. At that time, the key to the front door is symbolically thrown onto the roof because it will

never be used again. This is a symbol signifying that the building is more than just a building. It has become a place that will always be open to those who are seeking a home for the night or more appropriately a "home away from home."

—adapted from Cook et al., *Tourism: The Business of Travel*, p. 170

Topic: _____traditions_____

Steps: _____

2.   In jury selection, the pool of potential jurors usually is selected from voter or automobile registration lists. Potential jurors are asked to fill out a questionnaire. Lawyers for each party and the judge can ask questions of prospective jurors to determine if they would be biased in their decision. Jurors can be "stricken for cause" if the court believes that the potential juror is too biased to render a fair verdict. Lawyers may also exclude a juror from sitting on a particular case without giving any reason for the dismissal. Once the appropriate number of jurors is selected (usually six to twelve jurors), they are impaneled to hear the case and are sworn in. The trial is ready to begin.

—adapted from Goldman and Cheeseman, *The Paralegal Professional*, p. 266

Topic: _____jury selection_____

Steps: _____

_____

3.   At 12:30 on the afternoon of May 1, 1915, the British steamship *Lusitania* set sail from New York to Liverpool. The passenger list of 1,257 was the largest since the outbreak of war in Europe in 1914. Six days later, the *Lusitania* reached the coast of Ireland. The passengers lounged on the deck. As if it were peacetime, the ship sailed straight ahead, with no zigzag maneuvers to throw off pursuit. But the submarine U-20 was there, and its commander, seeing a large ship, fired a single torpedo. Seconds after it hit, a boiler exploded and blew a hole in the *Lusitania's* side. The ship listed immediately, hindering the launching of lifeboats, and in eighteen minutes it sank. Nearly 1,200 people died, including 128 Americans. As the ship's bow lifted and went under, the U-20 commander for the first time read the name: *Lusitania*.

—adapted from Divine et al., *America Past and Present*, p. 596

Topic: _____Lusitania_____

Steps: _____

_____

EXERCISE 8-12   ## Writing a Process Paragraphs

Directions: On a separate sheet of paper, write a paragraph explaining how to do something that you do well or often, such as cross-country ski or change a tire, for example. Use the chronological order/process pattern. Then draw a diagram showing the organization of your paragraph.

EXERCISE 8-13   ## Identifying Thought Patterns

Directions: Working in pairs of groups of three, read each of the following passages and identify the thought pattern used. Write the name of the pattern in the space provided. Choose from among these patterns: *illustration/example*, *definition*, *comparison/contrast*, *cause/effect*, *classification*, and *chronological order/process*. Next, write a sentence explaining your choice. Identify any transitions. Then, on a separate sheet of paper, draw a diagram that shows the organization of each selection.

1.   **Optimists** are people who always tend to look for positive outcomes. For an optimist, a glass is half full, whereas for a pessimist, the glass is half empty. **Pessimists** seem to expect the worst to happen. Researchers have found that optimism is associated with longer life and increased immune system functioning. Mayo Clinic researchers conducted a study of optimists and pessimists over a period of 30 years. The results for pessimists were not good: They had a much higher death rate than did the optimists, and those that were still living in 1994 had more problems with physical and emotional health, more pain, less ability to take part in social activities, and less energy than optimists. The optimists had a 50 percent lower risk of premature death and were more calm, peaceful, and happy than the pessimists.

—adapted from Ciccarelli and White, *Psychology: An Exploration*, p. 321

Pattern: _CC_____

Reason: _____

2.   Along with polar ice, **tundra** is the biome of the far north, stretching in a vast, mostly frozen, ring around the northern rim of the world. So inaccessible is tundra that the average person may never have heard of it, yet it occupies about a fourth of Earth's land surface. The word *tundra* comes from a Finnish word that means "treeless plain," and the description is apt. Its flat terrain stretches out for mile after mile with little change in the vegetational pattern of low shrubs, mosses, lichens, grasses, and the grass-like sedge.

—adapted from Krogh, *Biology: A Guide to the Natural World*, p. 750

Pattern: _D_____

Reason: _____

3. In 1000 BC, the Cherokee Indians took up residence in the Smoky Mountains. They were virtually isolated until the Spanish conquistadors arrived in 1540, and, more than two hundred years later, other immigrants from the Old World began to settle, first in small groups, and then increasingly in overwhelming numbers. The two groups of people, indigenous and immigrants, lived side by side with only occasional quarreling. In 1838, however, more than 13,000 Cherokee were forced to leave their native lands. Only a few rebellious natives remained along with their Caucasian counterparts.

—adapted from Walker and Walker, *Tourism: Concepts and Practices*, pp. 53–54

Pattern: Chronological

Reason:

4. Several types of strikes have been held to be illegal and are not protected by federal labor laws. Illegal strikes take the form of violent strikes, sit-down strikes, and partial or intermittent strikes. In **violent strikes**, striking employees cause substantial damage to property of the employer or a third party. Courts usually tolerate a certain amount of isolated violence before finding that the entire strike is illegal. In **sit-down** strikes, striking employees continue to occupy the employer's premises. Such strikes are illegal because they deny the employer's statutory right to continue its operations during the strike. In **partial** or **intermittent strikes**, employees strike part of the day or workweek and work the other part. This type of strike is illegal because it interferes with the employer's right to operate its facilities at full operation.

—adapted from Goldman and Cheeseman, *The Paralegal Professional*, p. 641

Pattern: illustration Classifi

Reason:

5. The shallow rock pools of Sydney Harbor, Australia, offer a fascinating glimpse of diversity. The tentacles of colorful sea anemones sway lazily in the water. A pencil urchin, wedged into a crevice, waits out the daylight hours for feeding time to roll around. An elephant snail grazes briskly along the underside of a rock, its jet-black, sluglike body capped by an incongruously small white shell. A shrimp darts out from behind a rock but quickly retreats to its hiding place. The large blue sea star draped over a rock would be spotted easily by a casual observer, but it takes a sharp eye to see its tiny cousin, camouflaged against the background and surrounded by its even tinier offspring.

—adapted from Campbell et al., *Biology: Concepts and Connections*, p. 365

Pattern: classification illu

Reason:

6.   Behaviors, thoughts, and feelings always occur in a context, that is, in a situation. Situations can be divided into two components: the events that come before and those that come after. *Antecedents* are the setting events for a behavior; they stimulate a person to act in certain ways. Antecedents can be physical events, thoughts, emotions, or the actions of other people. *Consequences*—the results of behavior—affect whether a person will repeat that action. Consequences also can consist of physical events, thoughts, emotions, or the actions of other people.

—Donatelle, *Health: The Basics*, p. 20

Pattern: _____ Classification _____

Reason: _____

7.   Xylem is the plant tissue through which water moves *up*, from roots through leaves. The flowers we put in vases in our homes have lost their roots, of course, but they haven't lost their xylem, which continues to function long after the flower has been picked. Given this, many flowers can last a long time indoors if we follow a few simple rules. First, realize that the liquid in the xylem is under negative pressure—its natural tendency is to move up *into* the stem, not to flow out of it. As such, if the stems are cut when they are out of water, *air* gets sucked up into the cut ends, creating air bubbles that can then get trapped in the xylem and keep water from rising up through it. When this happens, flowers can wilt, even when their stems are submerged in clean water. Recutting the stem under water can remove this blockage.

—adapted from Krogh, *Biology: A Guide
to the Natural World*, p. 488

Pattern: _____ order process, cause & effect. _____

Reason: _____

Preserving beauty:
Following a few
simple rules can
prolong the life of
cut flowers.

8.   The risks of active smoking, in addition to lung and airway damage, include increased rates of throat, bladder, and pancreatic cancer; higher rates of heart attack, stroke, and high blood pressure; and premature aging of the skin. All of these effects occur because many of the components of tobacco smoke can cross into the bloodstream and move throughout the body.

—adapted from Belk and Maier, *Biology: Science
for Life with Physiology*, p. 451

Pattern: _____ cause & effect _____

Reason: _____

9.   Surveys or questionnaires can be broken down into several types. They may be based on opinion; interpretative; or based on facts. **Opinion surveys** ask respon-

dents questions regarding what they think about particular topics. Answers are based on personal opinion. Therefore, the answers are not necessarily right or wrong. An opinion survey may ask respondents to evaluate a certain topic or express their attitudes and beliefs. **Interpretative surveys** ask respondents to answer why they chose a particular course. For example, a hotel may ask its guests why they chose to stay at the hotel; an airline may ask why passengers chose to fly with them. **Factual surveys** can be thought of as being more concrete in the questions they ask. For example, they may ask travelers what recreational activities they participated in while they were traveling. The answers are based on fact alone, no interpretation or opinion is expressed.

—adapted from Walker and Walker, *Tourism: Concepts and Practices*, p. 241

Pattern: _____ (ᴄ Classification _____

Reason: _____

A soaring frigate bird, with a wingspan of 2 m.

10.   Nearly every part of the body of most birds reflects adaptations that enhance flight. Many features help reduce weight for flight: Present-day birds lack teeth; their tail is supported by only a few small vertebrae; their feathers have hollow shafts; and their bones have a honeycombed structure, making them strong but light. For example, the huge seagoing frigate bird has a wingspan of more than 2 m, but its whole skeleton weighs only about 113 g (4 oz). Flight feathers shape bird wings into airfoils, providing lift and maneuverability in the air. Providing power for flight are large breast (flight) muscles, which are anchored to a keel-like breastbone. Most of what we call white meat on a turkey or chicken is the flight muscles.

—adapted from Campbell et al., *Biology: Concepts and Connections*, p. 398

Pattern: _____ Illustration _____

Reason: _____

OTHER USEFUL PATTERNS OF ORGANIZATION

The patterns presented in the preceding section are the most common. Table 8-1 (page 283) presents a brief review of those patterns and their corresponding transitional words. However, writers do not limit themselves to these six patterns. Especially in academic writing, you may find one or more of the patterns listed in Table 8-2 (page 284), as well.

Statement and Clarification

Many writers make a statement of fact and then proceed to clarify or explain that statement. For instance, a writer may open a paragraph by stating that

TABLE 8-1   A Review of Patterns and Transitional Words

Pattern	Characteristics	Transitional Words
Illustration/ Example	Organizes examples that illustrate an idea or concept	*for example, for instance, such as, to illustrate*
Definition	Explains the meaning of a word or phrase	*are those that, can be defined as, consists of, corresponds to, entails, involves, is, is a term that, is called, is characterized by, is literally, means, occurs when, refers to*
Comparison/ Contrast	Discusses similarities and/or differences among ideas, theories, concepts, objects, or persons	Similarities: *also, as well as, both, correspondingly, in comparison, in the same way, like, likewise, resembles, share, similarly, to compare, too*
		Differences: *as opposed to, despite, differs from, however, in contrast, in spite of, instead, nevertheless, on the other hand, unlike, whereas*
Cause/Effect	Describes how one or more things cause or are related to another	Causes: *because, because of, cause is, due to, for, for this reason, one cause is, one reason is, since, stems from*
		Effects: *as a result, consequently, hence, one result is, results in, therefore, thus*
Classification	Divides a topic into parts based on shared characteristics	*another, another kind, classified as, comprises, different groups that, different stages of, finally, first, include, is composed of, last, one, second, types of, varieties of*
Chronological Order/Process	Describes events, processes, procedures	*after, as soon as, by the time, during, finally, first, following, in, last, later, meanwhile, next, on, second, then, until, when, while*

"The best education for you may not be the best education for someone else." The remainder of the paragraph would then discuss that statement and make its meaning clear by explaining how educational needs are individual and based on one's talents, skills, and goals. Here is another example:

> The Constitution of the United States of America is the *supreme law of the land*. This means that any law—federal, state, or local—that conflicts with the U.S. Constitution is unconstitutional and, therefore, unenforceable. The principles enumerated in the Constitution are extremely broad, because the founding fathers intended them to be applied to evolving social, technological, and economic conditions. The U.S. Constitution often is referred to as a "living document" because it is so adaptable. States also have their own constitutions, often patterned after the U.S. Constitution. Provisions of state constitutions are valid unless they conflict with the U.S. Constitution or any valid federal law.
>
> —adapted from Goldman and Cheeseman, *The Paralegal Professional*, p. 183

Transitional words associated with this pattern are listed in Table 8-2.

TABLE 8-2   A Review of Additional Patterns and Transitional Words

Pattern	Characteristics	Transitional Words
Statement and Clarification	Gives information explaining an idea or concept	*clearly, evidently, in fact, in other words, obviously*
Summary	Provides a condensed review of an idea or piece of writing	*in brief, in conclusion, in short, in summary, on the whole, to sum up, to summarize*
Addition	Provides additional information	*additionally, again, also, besides, further, furthermore, in addition, moreover*
Spatial Order	Describes physical location or position in space	*above, behind, below, beside, in front of, inside, nearby, next to, opposite, outside, within*

Summary

A summary is a condensed statement that recaps the key points of a larger idea or piece of writing. The summaries at the end of each chapter of this text provide a quick review of the chapter's contents. Often writers summarize what they have already said or what someone else has said. For example, in a psychology textbook you will find many summaries of research. Instead of asking you to read an entire research study, the textbook author will summarize the study's findings. Other times a writer may repeat in condensed form what he or she has already said as a means of emphasis or clarification. Here is a sample paragraph:

> To sum up, the minimax strategy is a general principle of human behavior that suggests that humans try to minimize costs and maximize rewards. The fewer costs and the more rewards we anticipate from something, the more likely we are to do it. If we believe that others will approve an act, the likelihood increases that we will do it. In short, whether people are playing cards with a few friends or are part of a mob, the principles of human behavior remain the same.
>
> —Henslin, *Sociology*, p. 637

Transitional words associated with this pattern are listed in Table 8-2.

Addition

Writers often introduce an idea or make a statement and then supply additional information about that idea or statement. For instance, an education textbook may introduce the concept of homeschooling and then provide in-depth information about its benefits. This pattern is often used to expand, elaborate, or discuss an idea in greater detail. Here is an example:

> Millions of people work at home on computers connected to an office, an arrangement known as **telecommuting**. Telecommuting eases the pressure on transport facilities, saves fuel, and reduces air pollution. Moreover, it has been shown to increase workers' productivity and reduce absenteeism. It also allows employers to accommodate employees who want flexible work arrangements, thus opening employment opportunity to more people, such as women who are still homemakers.
>
> —Bergman and Renwick, *Introduction to Geography*, p. 430

Transitional words associated with this pattern are listed in Table 8-2.

Spatial Order

Spatial order is concerned with the physical location or position in space. Spatial order is used in disciplines in which physical descriptions are important. A photography textbook may use spatial order to describe the parts of a camera. An automotive technology textbook may use spatial order to describe disk brake operation. Here is a sample paragraph:

> We can taste food because chemoreceptors in the mouth respond to certain chemicals in food. The chemoreceptors for taste are located in structures called **taste buds**, each of which contains 50–150 receptor cells and numerous support cells. At the top of each bud is a pore that allows receptor cells to be exposed to saliva and dissolved food molecules. Each person has over 10,000 taste buds, located primarily on the tongue and the roof of the mouth, but also located in the pharynx.
>
> —Germann and Stanfield, *Principles of Human Physiology*, pp. 303–304

Transitional words associated with this pattern are listed in Table 8-2.

EXERCISE 8-14   **Identifying Thought Patterns**

Directions: For each of the following statements, identify the pattern that is evident and indicate it in the space provided. Choose from among the following patterns:

    a. statement and clarification
    b. summary
    c. addition
    d. spatial order

_____D_____ 1. Short fibers, dendrites, branch out around the cell body and a single long fiber, the axon, extends from the cell body.

_____C_____ 2. Aspirin is not as harmless as people think. It may cause allergic reactions and stomach irritation. In addition, aspirin has been linked to an often fatal condition known as Reye's syndrome.

_____A_____ 3. If our criminal justice system works, the recidivism rate—the percentage of people released from prison who return—should decrease. In other words, in a successful system, there should be a decrease in the number of criminals who are released from prison and then become repeat offenders.

_____C_____ 4. Students who are informed about drugs tend to use them in greater moderation. Furthermore, they tend to help educate others.

_____B_____ 5. To sum up, a successful drug addiction treatment program would offer free or very cheap drugs to addicts.

_____B_____ 6. In conclusion, it is safe to say that crime by women is likely to increase as greater numbers of women assume roles traditionally held by men.

_____B_____ 7. The pollutants we have just discussed all involve chemicals; we can conclude that they threaten our environment and our well-being.

_____D_____ 8. A residual check valve that maintains slight pressure on the hydraulic system is located in the master cylinder at the outlet for the drum brakes.

_____A_____ 9. Sociologists study how we are socialized into sex roles—the attitudes expected of males and females. Sex roles, in fact, identify some activities and behaviors as clearly male and others as clearly female.

_____D_____ 10. The meninges are three membranes that lie just outside the organs of the central nervous system.

EXERCISE **8-15**   **Predicting**

Directions: Locate and mark five paragraphs in one of your textbooks or in Part Seven of this text that are clear examples of the thought patterns discussed in this chapter. Write the topic sentence of each paragraph on a separate index card. Once your instructor has formed small groups, choose a group "reader" who will collect all the cards and read each sentence aloud. Groups should discuss each and predict the pattern of the paragraph from which the sentence was taken. The "finder" of the topic sentence then confirms or rejects the choice, quoting sections of the paragraph if necessary.

Using Transitional Words

As you learned earlier in the chapter, transitional words can help you identify organizational patterns. These words are called **transitional words** because they help you make the transition or connection between ideas. They may also be called *clue words* or *directional words* because they provide readers with clues about what is to follow.

Transitional words are also helpful in discovering or clarifying relationships between and among ideas in any piece of writing. Specifically, transitional words help you grasp connections between and within sentences. Transitional words can help you predict what is to come next within a paragraph. For instance, if you are reading along and come upon the phrase *in conclusion,* you know that the writer will soon present a summary. If you encounter the word *furthermore,* you know that the writer is about to present additional information about the subject at hand. If you encounter the word *consequently* in the middle of a sentence (The law was repealed; consequently, . . .), you know that the writer is about to explain what happened as a result of the repeal. Tables 8-1 and 8-2 on pages 283 and 284 list the transitional words that correspond to the patterns discussed in this chapter.

EXERCISE **8-16**   **Predicting**

Directions: Each of the following beginnings of paragraphs uses a transitional word or phrase to tell the reader what will follow in the paragraph. Read each, paying particular attention to the underlined transitional word or phrase. Working with a partner, discuss what you expect to follow. Then, in the space provided, summarize your findings.

1. Many Web sites on the Internet are reliable and trustworthy. <u>However,</u> . . .

   _____

2. One advantage of using a computer to take notes is that you can rearrange information easily. <u>Another</u> . . .

   _____

3. There are a number of ways to avoid catching the cold virus. <u>First of all,</u> . . .

   _____

4. Some pet owners care for their animals responsibly. <u>However,</u> others . . .

   _____

5. When planning a speech, you should choose a topic that is familiar or that you are knowledgeable about. <u>Next,</u> . . .

   _____

6. Following a high protein diet may be rewarding because it often produces quick weight loss. <u>On the other hand,</u> . . .

   _____

7. The iris is a doughnut-shaped portion of the eyeball. <u>In the center</u> . . .

   _____

8. Price is not the only factor consumers consider when making a major purchase. They <u>also</u> . . .

   _____

9. Cholesterol, commonly found in many fast foods, is associated with heart disease. <u>Consequently,</u> . . .

   _____

10. Many Web sites provide valuable links to related sites. <u>To illustrate,</u> visit . . .

   _____

LEARNING STYLE TIPS

If you tend to be a ...	Then identify thought patterns by ...
Spatial learner	Drawing a diagram of the ideas in the passage
Verbal learner	Outlining the passage

SELF-TEST SUMMARY

What are the six common thought patterns?

A thought pattern is the way in which an author organizes ideas. The six common thought patterns are:

1. **Illustration/example**—An idea is explained by providing specific instances or experiences that illustrate it.

2. **Definition**—An object or idea is explained by describing the general class or group to which it belongs and how the item differs from others in the same group (distinguishing features).

3. **Comparison/contrast**—A new or unfamiliar idea is explained by showing how it is similar to or different from a more familiar idea.

4. **Cause/effect**—Connections between events are explained by showing what caused an event or what happened as a result of a particular event.

5. **Classification**—An object or idea is explained by dividing it into parts and describing or explaining each.

6. **Chronological order/process**—Events or procedures are described in the order in which they occur in time.

What other thought patterns are used in academic writing?

1. **Statement and clarification**—An explanation will follow.

2. **Summary**—A condensed view of the subject will be presented.

3. **Addition**—Additional information will follow.

4. **Spatial order**—Physical location or position will be described.

GOING ONLINE

1. Rhetorical Patterns for Organizing Documents

   http://www.ecf.utoronto.ca/~writing/handbook-rhetoric.html

   The University of Toronto presents this site that reviews the ways information is organized. Choose some objects and activities you experience in your daily life. Write about them according to the appropriate guidelines presented here.

2. Logic Patterns

   http://www.learner.org/teacherslab/math/patterns/logic.html#activities

   Try these online logic pattern activities from The Teachers' Lab, the Annenberg/ CPB Math and Science Project. Observe patterns in your daily life. When do you find yourself sorting and classifying?

3. Types of Writing

   http://ksdl.ksbe.edu/writingresource/typeswriting.html

   Try the exercises and use the handouts here for each of the types of essays.

 To check your progress in meeting chapter objectives, log in to **http://www.myreadinglab.com**, click on the Study Plan tab, and then click on the Reading Skills tab. Choose Patterns of Organization from the list of subtopics. Read and view the information in the Review Materials section, and then complete the Practices and Tests in the Activities section. You can check your scores by clicking on the Gradebook tab.

MASTERY TEST 1 Identifying Patterns

Name _____ Section _____

Date _____ Number right _____ × 20 points = Score _____

Directions: Read the passage below and then se-lect the choice that best completes each of the statements that follow.

1   "Marry afar" is advice given by the pygmy men of Africa, by which they mean, "marry a woman who lives far from your home." The pygmies point to the hunting rights a man acquires by marrying a woman from a remote region, but there is another benefit to this practice: It helps ensure ge-netic diversity. When pygmies from remote locations marry, it cuts down on the chances of *inbreeding*, meaning mating in which close relatives produce offspring. Inbreeding can have harmful effects not only on hu-mans, but in any species.

2   Consider what has happened in the United States with "purebred" dogs, which is to say dogs that over many generations have been bred solely with members of their own breed (cocker spaniels mating only with cocker spaniels, and so forth). In the mid-1990s it was estimated that up to one-fourth of all U.S. purebred dogs had some sort of se-rious genetic defect—ranging from improper joint formation, to heart defects, to deafness.

3   You might think that there are no uses for genetic similarity, but consider what humans have been doing for centuries with dog breed-ing. Cocker spaniels did not come about by accident. Dogs with cocker spaniel features were bred together for many generations, ulti-mately giving us today's dog. While the breed-ing done to produce American cocker spaniels has resulted in dogs with cute, floppy ears, the unintended effect of this practice is a breed

What concept does this photograph illustrate?

that is also prone to ear infections and a "rage syndrome" that can result in unprovoked ag-gression. Inbreeding produces a range of unique features, some desirable but others more aptly referred to as genetic defects.

—adapted from Krogh, *Biology: A Guide to the Natural World*, pp. 318–319

_____ 1. The purpose of this passage is to
    a. describe the pygmy men of Africa.
    b. compare and contrast marriage rituals.
    c. classify types of purebred dogs.
    d. discuss the effects of inbreeding.

_____ 2. The pattern that the author uses to or-ganize his ideas in the first paragraph is
    a. classification.
    b. comparison/contrast.
    c. chronological order.
    d. definition.

_____ 3. The pattern that the author uses to organize his ideas in the second paragraph is
  a. illustration/example.
  b. classification.
  c. chronological order.
  d. process.

_____ 4. The type of cause/effect relationship that the author describes throughout this passage is
  a. single cause/single effect.
  b. single cause/multiple effects.
  c. multiple causes/single effect.
  d. multiple causes/multiple effects.

_____ 5. The pattern that the author uses to organize his ideas in the third paragraph is
  a. comparison/contrast.
  b. definition.
  c. cause/effect.
  d. classification.

MASTERY TEST 2 Identifying patterns

Name _____ Section _____

Date _____ Number right _____ × 10 points = Score _____

Directions: Read each of the following paragraphs. In the blank provided, write the letter of the main thought pattern used.

a. definition
b. comparison/contrast
c. illustration/example
d. cause/effect
e. classification
f. chronological order/process

___f___ 1. You need to take a few steps to prepare to become a better note-taker. First, get organized. It's easiest to take useful notes if you have a system. A loose-leaf notebook works best because you can add, rearrange, or remove notes for review. If you use spiral or other permanently bound notebooks, use a separate notebook for each subject to avoid confusion and to allow for expansion. Second, set aside a few minutes each day to review the syllabus for your course, to scan the assigned readings, and to review your notes from the previous class period. If you do this just before each lecture, you'll be ready to take notes and practice critical thinking. Finally, prepare your pages by drawing a line down the left margin approximately two inches from the edge of the paper. Leave this margin blank while you take notes so that later you can use it to practice critical thinking.

—Gronbeck, *Principles of Speech Communication*, pp. 32–33

___A___ 2. Genetics is the scientific study of heredity, the transmission of characteristics from parents to offspring. Genetics explains why offspring resemble their parents and also why they are not identical to them. Genetics is a subject that has considerable economic, medical, and social significance, and is partly the basis for the modern theory of evolution. Because of its importance, genetics has been a topic of central interest in the study of life for centuries. Modern concepts in genetics are fundamentally different, however, from earlier ones.

—Mix et al., *Biology*, p. 262

___C___ 3. Colors surely influence our perceptions and our behaviors. People's acceptance of a product, for example, is largely determined by its package. The very same coffee taken from a yellow can was described as weak, from a dark brown can too strong, from a red can rich, and from a blue can mild. Even our acceptance of a person may depend on the colors worn. Consider, for example, the comments of one color expert: "If you have to pick the wardrobe for your defense lawyer in court and choose anything but blue, you deserve to lose the case. . . ." Black is so powerful it could work against a lawyer with the jury. Brown lacks sufficient authority. Green would probably elicit a negative response.

—DeVito, *The Interpersonal Communication Book*, pp. 219–220

___ 4. Hospice care is built around the idea that the people who are dying and their families should control the process of dying. Whereas hospitals are dedicated to prolonging life, hospice care is dedicated to providing dignity in death and making people comfortable during the living-dying interval. In the hospital, the focus is on the patient; in hospice care, the focus switches to both the dying person and his or her friends and family. In the hospital, the goal is to make the patient well; in hospice care, it is to relieve pain and suffering and make death easier to bear. In the hospital, the primary concern is the individual's physical welfare; in hospice care, although medical needs are met, the primary concern is the individual's social—and in some instances, spiritual—well-being.

—adapted from Henslin, *Sociology: A Down-to-Earth Approach*, pp. 389–390

___ 5. It was at the 1893 World's Columbian Exposition in Chicago that Milton Hershey first became fascinated with the art of chocolate. Hershey, a small-time candy manufacturer, decided he wanted to make chocolate to coat his caramels. He opened his new establishment in Lancaster, Pennsylvania, and named it Hershey Chocolate Company. In the 1900s, the company started to produce mass quantities of milk chocolate, which resulted in immediate success. Soon after, Hershey decided to increase his production facilities so he built a new factory on the farmland of south-central Pennsylvania. The following decades brought many product-line expansions and, in 1968, the company was renamed Hershey Foods Corporation. Today, the company is the leading manufacturer of chocolate, non-chocolate confectionery, and grocery products in North America.

—adapted from Walker, *Introduction to Hospitality Management*, p. 361

___ 6. Five environmental systems influence the family: microsystems, mesosystems, exosystems, macrosystems, and chronosystems. The **microsystem** is the child's immediate environment, including any immediate relationships or organizations that the child interacts with, such as family members or teachers at school. The **mesosystem** describes how different parts of the child's microsystem interact. For example, children whose parents play an active role in their education often do better in school than children with poorer home-school connections. The **exosystem** includes outside influences that the child may not interact with personally, but that have a large impact on the child, such as parents' workplaces or members of the extended family. The **macrosystem** describes the culture in which an individual lives, including the relative freedoms permitted by the national government, cultural values, and the economy—all of which may affect a child positively or negatively. Finally, **chronosystems** examine the impact of life transitions, which may include puberty, changing schools, marriage, and retirement as well as unexpected events within a family, such as death or divorce.

—adapted from Kunz, *Think Marriages and Families*, p. 16

Diego Rivera.
Detail from *Detroit Industry*.
1932–1933.
Fresco.
Detroit Institute of Arts, MI. Gift of Edsel B. Ford. Bridgeman Art Library.

> Why was this image included in the text?

___f___ 7.   True fresco, or *buon fresco*, is an ancient wallpainting technique in which finely ground pigments suspended in water are applied to a damp lime-plaster surface. Generally, a full-size drawing called a cartoon is completed first, then transferred to the freshly laid plaster wall before painting. Because the plaster dries quickly, only the portion of the wall that can be painted in one day is prepared. The painter works quickly in a rapid staining process similar to watercolor. The lime in the plaster becomes the binder, creating a smooth, extremely durable surface. Once the surface has dried, the painting is part of the wall.

—adapted from Frank, *Prebles' Artforms*, p. 127

___f___ 8.   Glaciers erode the land primarily in two ways—plucking and abrasion. First, as a glacier flows over a fractured bedrock surface, it loosens and lifts blocks of rock and incorporates them into the ice. This process, known as **plucking**, occurs when meltwater penetrates the cracks and joints of bedrock beneath a glacier and freezes. When water freezes it expands, exerting tremendous leverage that pries the rock loose. The second major erosional process is **abrasion**. As the ice and its load of rock fragments slide over bedrock, they function like sandpaper to smooth and polish the surface below. The pulverized rock is appropriately called *rock flour*. So much rock flour may be produced that meltwater streams flowing out of a glacier often have the grayish appearance of skim milk and offer visible evidence of the grinding power of ice.

—adapted from Lutgens et al., *Essentials of Geology*, pp. 252–253

___A\ G___ 9.   **Marsupials** are mammals in which the young develop within the mother to a limited extent, inside an egg that has a membranous shell. Marsupials are represented by several Australian animals, including the kangaroo, and by several animals in the Western Hemisphere, including the North American opossum. Early in development, the egg's membrane disappears, and in a few days time, a developmentally immature but active marsupial is delivered from the mother. In the case of a kangaroo, the tiny youngster has just enough capacity to climb up its mother's body, into her "pouch," and begin suckling there.

—adapted from Krogh, *Biology: A Guide to the Natural World*, p. 471

___C___ 10.   **Database marketing** involves tracking specific consumers' buying habits very closely and crafting products and messages tailored precisely to people's wants and needs based on this information. Wal-Mart stores massive amounts of information on the 100 million people who visit its stores each week, and the company uses these data to fine-tune its offerings. When the company analyzed how shoppers' buying patterns react when forecasters predict a major hurricane, for example, it discovered that people do a lot more than simply stock up on flashlights. Sales of strawberry Pop-Tarts increase by about 700 percent and the top-selling product of all is—beer. Based on these insights, Wal-Mart loads its trucks with toaster pastries and six-packs to stock local stores when a big storm approaches.

—adapted from Solomon, *Consumer Behavior: Buying, Having, and Being*, p. 13

MASTERY TEST 3 Reading Selection

Name _____ Section _____

Date _____ Number right* _____ × 10 points = Score _____

Right Place, Wrong Face
Alton Fitzgerald White

In this selection, the author describes what it was like to be treated as a criminal on the basis of nothing more than having the "wrong face."

> **Vocabulary Preview**
>
> **ovation (par. 3)** enthusiastic, prolonged applause
>
> **overt (par. 4)** not secret, obvious
>
> **splurged (par. 5)** indulged in a luxury
>
> **vestibule (par. 5)** a small entrance hall or passage into the interior of a building
>
> **residue (par. 9)** something that remains after a substance is taken away
>
> **violation (par. 14)** the condition of being treated unfairly or disrespectfully

1   As the youngest of five girls and two boys growing up in Cincinnati, I was raised to believe that if I worked hard, was a good person, and always told the truth, the world would be my oyster. I was raised to be a gentleman and learned that these qualities would bring me respect.

2   While one has to earn respect, consideration is something owed to every human being. On Friday, June 16, 1999, when I was wrongfully arrested at my Harlem apartment building, my perception of everything I had learned as a young man was forever changed—not only because I wasn't given even a second to use the manners my parents taught me, but mostly because the police, whom I'd always naively thought were supposed to serve and protect me, were actually hunting me.

3   I had planned a pleasant day. The night before was payday, plus I had received a standing ovation after portraying the starring role of Coalhouse Walker Jr. in the Broadway musical *Ragtime*. It is a role that requires not only talent but also an honest emotional investment of the morals and lessons I learned as a child.

4   Coalhouse Walker Jr. is a victim (an often misused word, but in this case true) of overt racism. His story is every black man's nightmare. He is hardworking, successful, talented, charismatic, friendly, and polite. Perfect prey for someone with authority and not even a fraction of those qualities. On that Friday afternoon, I became a real-life Coalhouse Walker. Nothing could have prepared me for it. Not even stories told to me by other black men who had suffered similar injustices.

---

*To calculate the number right, use items 1–10 under "Mastery Test Skills Check."

Alton Fitzgerald White

5   Friday for me usually means a trip to the bank, errands, the gym, dinner, and then off to the theater. On this particular day, I decided to break my pattern of getting up and running right out of the house. Instead, I took my time, slowed my pace, and splurged by making strawberry pancakes. Before I knew it, it was 2:45; my bank closes at 3:30, leaving me less than 45 minutes to get to midtown Manhattan on the train. I was pressed for time but in a relaxed, blessed state of mind. When I walked through the lobby of my building, I noticed two light-skinned Hispanic men I'd never seen before. Not thinking much of it, I continued on to the vestibule, which is separated from the lobby by a locked door.

6   As I approached the exit, I saw people in uniforms rushing toward the door. I sped up to open it for them. I thought they might be paramedics, since many of the building's occupants are elderly. It wasn't until I had opened the door and greeted them that I recognized that they were police officers. Within seconds, I was told to "hold it"' they had received a call about young Hispanics with guns. I was told to get against the wall. I was searched, stripped of my backpack, put on my knees, handcuffed, and told to be quiet when I tried to ask questions.

7   With me were three other innocent black men who had been on their way to their U-Haul. They were moving into the apartment beneath mine, and I had just bragged to them about how safe the building was. One of these gentlemen got off his knees, still handcuffed, and unlocked the door for the officers to get into the lobby where the two strangers were standing. Instead of thanking or even acknowledging us, they led us out the door past our neighbors, who were all but begging the police in our defense.

8   The four of us were put into cars with the two strangers and taken to the precinct station at 165th and Amsterdam. The police automatically linked us, with no questions and no regard for our character or our lives. No consideration was given to where we were going or why. Suppose an ailing relative was waiting upstairs, while I ran out for her medication? Or young children, who'd been told that Daddy was running to the corner store for milk and would be right back? My new neighbors weren't even allowed to lock their apartment or check on the U-Haul.

9   After we were lined up in the station, the younger of the two Hispanic men was identified as an experienced criminal, and drug residue was found in a pocket of the other. I now realize how naive I was to think that the police would then uncuff me, apologize for their mistake, and let me go. Instead, they continued to search my backpack, questioned me, and put me in jail with the criminals.

10   The rest of the nearly five-hour ordeal was like a horrible dream. I was handcuffed, strip-searched, taken in and out for questioning. The officers told me that they knew exactly who I was, knew I was in *Ragtime,* and that in fact they already had the men they wanted.

11   How then could they keep me there, or have brought me there in the first place? I was told it was standard procedure. As if the average law-abiding citizen knows what that is and can dispute it. From what I now know, "standard procedure" is something that every citizen, black and white, needs to learn, and fast.

12   I felt completely powerless. Why, do you think? Here I was, young, pleasant, and successful, in good physical shape, dressed in clean athletic attire. I was carrying a backpack containing a substantial paycheck and a deposit slip, on my way to the bank. Yet after hours and hours I was sitting at a desk with two officers who not only couldn't tell me why I was there but seemed determined to find something on me, to the point of making me miss my performance.

13   It was because I am a black man!

14   I sat in that cell crying silent tears of disappointment and injustice with the realization of how many innocent black men are convicted for no reason. When I was handcuffed, my first instinct had been to pull away out of pure insult and violation as a human being. Thank God I was calm enough to do what they said. When I was thrown in jail with the criminals and strip-searched, I somehow knew to put my pride aside, be quiet, and do exactly what I was told, hating it but coming to terms with the fact that in this situation I was a victim. They had guns!

15   Before I was finally let go, exhausted, humiliated, embarrassed, and still in shock, I was led to a room and given a pseudo-apology. I was told that I was at the wrong place at the wrong time. My reply? "I was where I live."

16   Everything I learned growing up in Cincinnati has been shattered. Life will never be the same.

MASTERY TEST SKILLS CHECK

Directions: Select the choice that best completes each of the following statements.

Checking Your Comprehension

_____ 1. The author's main purpose in this selection is to
   a. describe his recent experience with racism.
   b. discuss the effects of racism on young people.
   c. criticize the New York police department.
   d. contrast Cincinnati with New York.

_____ 2. Coalhouse Walker Jr. is the name of
   a. the author of the article.
   b. a black actor in New York.
   c. the main character in a Broadway play.
   d. a racist police officer.

_____ 3. The main idea of paragraph 5 is that the author
   a. had errands to take care of.
   b. was making strawberry pancakes.
   c. lives 45 minutes from midtown Manhattan.
   d. changed his routine and was enjoying a leisurely day.

_____ 4. The two strangers in the lobby of the building were
   a. friends of the author.
   b. new residents of the building.
   c. undercover police officers.
   d. suspected criminals.

_____ 5. After opening the door for the police, the author was
   a. thanked by the police and released to go.
   b. assaulted by criminals.
   c. handcuffed and taken away by the police.
   d. harassed by his neighbors.

_____ 6. "Life will never be the same" for the author because he
   a. can no longer trust in what he was raised to believe about manners and respect.
   b. was injured by the police.
   c. does not understand the criminal justice system.
   d. cannot face his neighbors.

Applying Your Skills

_____ 7. The main thought pattern used in this selection is
   a. definition.
   b. chronological order.
   c. enumeration.
   d. classification.

_____ 8. In paragraph 2, the transitional word or phrase that indicates the chronological order thought pattern is
   a. while.   c. because.
   b. On Friday.   d. but.

_____ 9. In paragraph 9, all of the following transitional words indicate the chronological order thought pattern _except_
   a. after.   c. instead.
   b. now.   d. then.

_____ 10. The main thought pattern used in paragraphs 12 and 13 is
   a. cause/effect.   c. enumeration.
   b. summary.   d. definition.

Studying Words

_____ 11. In paragraph 2, the word _naively_ means
   a. innocently.   c. purposely.
   b. negatively.   d. unfortunately.

_____ 12. What is the correct pronunciation of the word _charismatic_ (par. 4)?
   a. KARE iz mat ik
   b. kar IZ ma tick
   c. kar iz MAT ik
   d. kare IZ ma tick

_____ 13. The word _vestibule_ (par. 5) originated from which of the following languages?
   a. Latin   c. German
   b. French   d. Greek

_____ 14. What is the best definition of the word _dispute_ as it is used in paragraph 11?
   a. strive to win
   b. question the truth of
   c. quarrel angrily
   d. engage in discussion

_____ 15. The prefix of the word _pseudo-apology_ (par. 15) indicates that the apology was
   a. excessive.   c. written.
   b. false.   d. small.

For more practice, ask your instructor for an opportunity to work on the mastery tests that appear in the Test Bank.

Summarizing the Reading

Directions: Complete the following summary of the reading by filling in the blanks.

On _____, Alton Fitzgerald White was starring in _____

_____. On his way out that day, White saw _____

_____. Soon after, _____ arrived, responding

to _____. After White let the police in the building, he

was _____ along with _____

_____. Even though the police knew

_____ and had _____, White was _____,

where police _____. When he was finally

released, the police _____ and told him _____

_____. The experience was _____; he knew it

happened because _____.

Reading Visually

1. What does the photograph on page 298 contribute to this reading? What details do you notice about it that help you understand the author's story?
2. What does the title of this selection mean? What made the author's face "wrong"?
3. How is White's profession as an actor important to his story? (See p. 297.) Did being a well-known actor seem to help his situation with the police?

Thinking Critically about the Reading

WRITE IN YOUR
JOURNAL

1. Why was it significant that the strangers in the lobby were Hispanic?
2. How do you think you would react in a similar situation?
3. Have you ever been misjudged based on your outward appearance? What was your response? How was it similar to or different from the author's?

Troubleshooting Guide: Solutions to the Top Ten Reading and Study Problems

Becoming a successful college reader requires taking charge of your learning. Success also entails recognizing difficult situations when they arise and actively looking for solutions. You can use this troubleshooting guide when you find yourself facing challenges with your college reading assignments. Many of these problems are extremely common, so you're not alone.

1.   Focus, Motivation, and Concentration

1a.   Everything I read seems equally important.

1b.   My mind wanders as I read.

1c.   My reading assignments are too long, and I can't get through them.

2.   Understanding and Remembering What I Read

2a.   I have to reread frequently to understand.

2b.   I have difficulty translating "textbook" language into a language I can understand.

2c.   I get overwhelmed by details and have trouble seeing the "big picture."

2d.   I find it hard to express textbook ideas in my own words.

2e.   I can't remember what I have read.

2f.   I think I understand what I've read, but I'm not doing well on the exams.

3.   Background Knowledge and Vocabulary

3a.   The author assumes I know things I do not.

3b.   I skip over words whose meanings I don't know.

3c.   All the technical terms in my textbook seem pointless; I don't know why I have to memorize the meanings of all these new words.

4.   Reading and Understanding Graphics

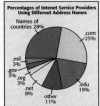

4a.   I'm not sure how visuals work with the textbook reading and how to connect them to the assignment.

4b.   I tend to ignore graphs and tables because I'm not a "numbers" person.

4c.   Sometimes I focus too much on the graphics and photographs at the expense of reading the text.

5. Exams and Assignments

      5a.   I get confused by multiple-choice questions.

      5b.   I have problems writing an effective essay exam.

6. Reading Speed

      6a.   I read everything too slowly, and this keeps me from making progress.

      6b.   I read too quickly and miss important points.

7. Critical Reading and Thinking (Inferences and Evaluation)

      7a.   My instructor keeps telling me to "read between the lines," but I don't know how.

      7b.   I tend to accept everything I read at face value without thinking more deeply about the material.

      7c.   I have trouble evaluating what I read.

8. Pulling Ideas Together (Synthesis)

      8a.   I don't see how ideas fit together.

      8b.   I have difficulty linking the textbook reading to the lectures.

      8c.   I wonder how what I'm reading is relevant to my life or my other college courses.

9. Working with Other Students (Collaboration)

      9a.   I don't see the value in doing collaborative activities.

      9b.   The group I'm working with isn't very effective and/or I'm not comfortable in it.

10. Course-Specific Concerns

      10a. I'm having difficulty in my college reading course.

      10b. I'm having difficulty in my college writing course.

      10c. I'm having difficulty in my mathematics course.

      10d. I'm having difficulty in another introductory course, such as sociology, psychology, or criminal justice.

1. Focus, Motivation, and Concentration

1a. Everything I read seems equally important. (See Chapters 6 and 7 of this book, "Understanding Paragraphs: Topics and Main Ideas" and "Understanding Paragraphs: Supporting Details and Transitions.")	• **Sort main ideas from supporting details.** To find the key point in a paragraph, find and highlight the topic sentence. Use textbook headings to guide you, and read chapter summaries. Headings announce what is important; summaries provide a review of main ideas. • **Understand that examples are usually not the main idea.** Instead, they are provided to help you understand the topic, main idea, or concept. Examples are usually less important than the concepts they are illustrating. • **After reading each textbook section, write out the main ideas in your own words.** This is also good practice for exams.
1b. My mind wanders as I read. (See Chapter 1 of this textbook, "Successful Attitudes Toward Reading and Learning," especially the section labeled "Build Your Concentration," pages 6–9.)	• **Improve your concentration skills.** • **Read not just with your eyes** but also with your hands. Highlight, make notes, or create outlines. • **Eliminate distractions.** Turn off the TV set, the radio, the iPod, and the cell phone. • **Find a quiet place to read in a location that is conducive to study,** such as the campus library. If you are having trouble reading at home, take your textbook to a local coffee shop (or other location) where you will not be interrupted.
1c. My reading assignments are too long, and I can't get through them.	• **Adjust your expectations.** College reading assignments are typically longer than what you may be accustomed to. Do not assume that you can rush through a 25-page chapter at the rate at which you would read a glossy magazine or surf the Internet. • **Break reading assignments up into chunks of manageable size.** Rather than reading a 25-page chapter in one sitting, plan to read eight pages per day over three days. • **Schedule your courses each term so that you have breaks between classes** that will allow you to go to the library to read. Don't take more classes than you can handle.

2. Understanding and Remembering What I Read

2a. I have to reread frequently to understand.	• **Rereading is a necessity in college.** Many students need to reread materials to completely understand them. • **The first time through a chapter, read for the "big ideas"** and make note of any areas in which you have difficulty. Go back and reread those sections, slowly and with a highlighter in hand. On your next full read-through, you'll be able to integrate the ideas better for a more complete understanding. • **Turn headings into questions and answer them as you read.** Make an outline on a separate sheet of notebook paper (which you can later use to review for exams).
2b. I have difficulty translating "textbook" language into a language I can understand.	• **Learning a new subject requires mastering its vocabulary.** Do not give in to the temptation to skip over words you don't know. • **Use marginal glossaries** that define key terms. • **Work with a classmate or friend to quiz each other on key terms and concepts.** Ask and answer questions out loud so that you can put the concepts into your own words. • **If your campus offers a tutoring service, make an appointment.** Tutors are often other students who may have experienced the same difficulties you are having.
2c. I get overwhelmed by details and have trouble seeing the "big picture." (Use Chapters 6 and 7 of this book, "Understanding Paragraphs: Topics and Main Ideas" and "Understanding Paragraphs: Supporting Details and Transitions.")	• **You need to actively differentiate between the main idea and supporting details.** Form a study group with classmates. Talk about the readings and the lectures, and work together to create a list of what the group sees as the most important points of the class. By working together, you can fill in the gaps in your knowledge and come up with a list that closely matches the instructor's intentions. • **Use textbook aids,** especially chapter goals and chapter summaries, to see the big picture. Preview the chapter headings to get a sense of a chapter's organization. Use SQ3R (see pages 155–160) to engage with the content before, during, and after reading.
2d. I find it hard to express textbook ideas in my own words.	• **Try writing rather than just mentally stating ideas.** • **Work sentence by sentence,** expressing each idea in your own words. When you finish each paragraph, express it in your own words.

2. Understanding and Remembering What I Read (Continued)

2e. I can't remember what I have read. (See "Building a System: SQ3R" in Chapter 5, page 155.)	• **Preview the chapter before you read it.** Use the SQ3R method to engage with the assignment before, during, and after reading. • **Practice, practice, practice.** Complete as many assignments, exercises, and/or problems from the textbook as possible. • **Use publisher- and instructor-provided materials for additional practice.** Most textbooks now have companion Web sites featuring a host of materials, such as quizzes and flash cards. • **Write as you read.** Writing out concepts, creating outlines, and sketching graphics helps you better remember the content. • **Quiz yourself as you go along.**
2f. I think I understand what I've read, but I'm not doing well on the exams.	• **Talk with students who have previously taken the class.** Ask them about the professor's tests and what you are expected to know. • **Analyze previous exams.** Think about the types of questions that are asked, and adapt your future study to those types of questions. • **Attend any pre-exam review sessions your instructor offers.** Very often instructors will focus on the material they plan to test on. • **Study returned exams for patterns of error.** What kinds of mistakes do you tend to make? For example, do you answer too quickly and miss key words? Have you not read the directions carefully enough? Are you answering with facts when the exam calls for analysis instead?

3. Background Knowledge and Vocabulary

3a. The author assumes I know things I do not.	• **Keep reading and finish the paragraph.** Ideas may become clearer as you acquire more information. • **Use reference sources** (dictionaries, encyclopedias, the Internet) to fill in information gaps. • **Purchase study aids,** such as study guides or Cliff Notes, in the college bookstore.

3b. I skip over words whose meanings I don't know. (See Chapters 3 and 4 for more help with vocabulary.)	• **Skipping over words is cheating yourself.** • **Use glossaries and key word lists.** Marginal glossaries, end-of-book glossaries, and key terms lists at the beginning or end of each chapter contain the terms your instructor will expect you to know for exams. Use online resources, such as the textbook's Web site, to quiz yourself on vocabulary.
3c. All the technical terms in my textbook seem pointless; I don't know why I have to memorize the meanings of all these new words.	• **Academic vocabulary exists because standard English words are not sufficient to describe complicated or detailed concepts.** Mastering academic vocabulary is your first step toward doing well in your college courses. Every profession and job has its own set of vocabulary terms, too. • **Create a vocabulary log** (either a notebook or a computer file); record terms you need to learn.

4. Reading and Understanding Graphics

4a. I'm not sure how visuals work with the textbook reading and how to connect them to the assignment. (See "An Introduction to Visual Learning" in Chapter 2, page 44.)	• **Most of the time the textbook will specifically refer to each visual** ("As Figure 1 shows . . ."). Read the sentence with the figure reference and immediately look at the figure. Go back and forth between the figure and the text as required. • **Pay attention to captions.** They often announce the topic and purpose of the graphic.
4b. I tend to ignore graphs and tables because I'm not a "numbers" person.	• **Graphs take long, boring sets of numbers and turn them into something much more visually appealing and easy to read.** Very often trends in the data become more apparent when the numbers are presented graphically. Graphics and tables are worth the effort required.
4c. Sometimes I focus too much on the graphics and photographs at the expense of reading the text.	• **Graphics often provide a good overview of a subject,** but the text is required to flesh out the details. You won't get the complete picture if you ignore either part. • **Think of graphics as aids to help you learn new material.**

5. Exams and Assignments
For further tips on how to take tests, see the online chapter.

| 5a. I get confused by multiple-choice questions. | Tips for answering multiple-choice questions.
• **Read the directions thoroughly.** The directions may contain crucial information you need to answer the questions correctly.
• **Leave nothing blank.** Even if you guess at the answer, you have nothing to lose.
• **In true/false or multiple-choice questions, watch for absolute words** such as *all*, *none*, *always*, and *never*. Absolute statements tend to be false or incorrect.
• **Read two-part statements carefully in true/false questions.** Unless both parts are correct, the answer must be "false."
• **Read all choices before choosing your answer,** even if you think you have found the correct one. In multiple-choice tests, remember that your job is to choose the *best* answer.
• **Avoid selecting answers that are unfamiliar** or that you do not understand.
• **When you have to guess at an answer, pick the one that seems complete and contains the most information.** Instructors are usually careful to make the best answer completely correct and recognizable. Such a choice often becomes long or detailed.
• **Play the odds.** In a multiple-choice test, if you can eliminate a couple of choices that are absolutely incorrect, you greatly increase your chances of getting the answer right. |
| 5b. I have problems writing an effective essay exam. | Tips for preparing for and taking essay exams.
• **Determine questions that are likely to be on the exam by reviewing your lecture notes,** thinking about the topics your instructor emphasized in class, or talking with your classmates about possible questions. Write up the possible questions and practice answering them.
• **Begin with a good topic sentence and provide adequate support.** Before you start writing, quickly outline your answer so that your essay has form and structure.
• **Bring a watch to class,** and plan how much time you will spend on each question.
• **Watch for questions that have multiple parts, and be sure to answer all parts of the questions.** For example, in the essay question "Discuss how the Equal Rights Amendment was developed and why it has aroused controversy," you must address two questions: *how* and *why*. |

6. Reading Speed

6a. I read everything too slowly, and this keeps me from making progress.	• **Reading too slowly is better than reading too fast.** • **Begin your assignments early;** don't wait until the night before they are due, or the night before the test. Break assignments into manageable chunks and read a little each day. • **Understand which materials you can read more quickly.** In general, chapter introductions and special-interest "boxes" in the chapter can be read more quickly because they rarely go into detail about new or essential concepts.
6b. I read too quickly and miss important points.	• **Do not read textbooks at the same pace as lighter materials such as magazines.** Slow down to understand key concepts. If you complete a chapter and find that you can't remember what you've read, that is a good signal that you have read too quickly. • **Slow down when you read a paragraph that includes a boldfaced term or a term in italics.** These are signals that a key concept is being introduced.

7. Critical Reading and Thinking (Inferences and Evaluation)
(For further information on critical reading and thinking, see Part Five of this text, "Critical Reading Skills.")

7a. My instructor keeps telling me to "read between the lines," but I don't know how.	• **"Reading between the lines" means going beyond surface meanings** to discover what the writer is really thinking. • **Pay close attention to the connotations of words**—that is, what the words suggest instead of just their literal meaning. • **Look for what an author suggests (implies) but does not directly state.** Look for clues about what the author would like to lead you to think or believe.
7b. I tend to accept everything I read at face value without thinking more deeply about the material.	• **Verify information and check sources.** • **Consult and compare several sources on a topic** instead of reading just one. • **Read personal narratives carefully.** In your liberal arts classes (English, history, art, and so on) you will most likely encounter personal narratives—people's stories about themselves or others. These are intended to give you insight into particular people or groups, but they also require close reading and careful thought because what applies to one individual or group may not apply to all of them. (For an example of a personal narrative, see page 297.)

7. Critical Reading and Thinking (Continued)

7c. I have trouble evaluating what I read. (For additional information, see Chapter 12 of this book, "Evaluating: Asking Critical Questions.")	• **Understand which materials require closer critical evaluation and which do not.** Textbooks are usually careful to present both sides of a story and to present factual material. In contrast, newspaper articles, editorials, magazines, and Web sites often have a specific agenda. When reading these materials, ask yourself: *Who* has written this, and *why*? *What* reaction is the writer trying to get out of me? Has the writer presented *all* the facts, or *just the facts that support* his or her case?

8. Pulling Ideas Together (Synthesis)

8a. I don't see how ideas fit together.	• **Use writing to learn.** Create maps, grids, outlines, paraphrases—anything that will help you connect ideas. • **Ask questions in class.** Your instructor will be delighted to answer questions that seek to link various ideas and concepts together.
8b. I have difficulty linking the textbook readings to the lectures.	• **Assess how closely your instructor follows the textbook in lectures** within the first few weeks of class. This will help you understand whether the textbook is intended as background reading or whether it forms the core of the course. • **Ask other students about their experiences with the instructor.** They may provide good tips on what the instructor looks for in papers and on exams, and how the instructor uses the textbook.
8c. I wonder how what I'm reading is relevant to my life or my other college courses.	• **Your most basic courses—reading, writing, and math—form the basis for learning in all other courses.** In every course you take, you will be expected to read and write. And most college disciplines do have a mathematical foundation, so you should get your math skills up to speed early in your college career. • **Look for applications to real life.** When you finish reading a section of each chapter, ask yourself, "How does this apply to me? Where have I seen this in the world around me?"

9. Working with Other Students (Collaboration)
(For more tips on collaboration, see "Learning from and with Other Students" in Chapter 2, pages 52–54.)

9a. I don't see the value in doing collaborative activities.	• **Think of group work as training for your career.** Almost every job requires you to work with others as part of a team. It is valuable to learn about the ins and outs of collaboration early in your college career. • **Members bring different strengths and experiences to the group.** An old saying goes, "two heads are better than one." Quite often a group member will be able to explain a topic in a way that will help you. As you help others understand concepts, they will become clearer to you, as well.
9b. The group I'm working with isn't very effective and/or I'm not comfortable in it.	• **Hold group members accountable.** If someone is not pulling his or her share of the weight, the other members should mention this politely. • **Stay focused.** If your study group is turning into a social hour, appoint one person in each study session to keep the group on track and to ensure that socializing occurs only after the required study has been done. • **Find an ally.** If you feel you don't fit into the study group, look for at least one person to become an ally or friend. This can help you manage the group dynamics. • **Establish ground rules.** Everyone must come prepared, and everyone must do his or her share of the work.

10. Course-Specific Concerns

10a. I'm having difficulty in my college reading course.	To succeed in your college reading course, try the following: • **Complete all your reading assignments.** The exercises and tests in each chapter will help you build your skills and track your progress. • **Work on developing your vocabulary skills.** Use Part Two of *Guide to College Reading* to practice recognizing context clues and word parts. • **Use the reading selections to explore areas of interest.** Keep track of which readings you like best. These may help point you in the direction of the best major for you. • **Get through the boring parts.** It would be unrealistic to expect to find every reading selection interesting. Do your best to keep an open mind. • **Make use of additional resources,** such as computer tutorials and textbook Web sites. For example, the textbook Web site that supports *Guide to College Reading* is My Reading Lab (http://www.myreadinglab.com).

10. Course-Specific Concerns (Continued)

10b. I'm having difficulty in my college writing course.	To help you make the most of your college writing course, try the following: • **Understand that writing skills are at the core of not only college success but also workplace success.** The writing skills you learn in college will be very useful on the job as well. • **Make use of electronic learning and editing aids,** such as grammar checkers and spell checkers. • **Write formal English, not informal English.** Abbreviations commonly used in e-mail and instant messages (for example, *u* instead of *you*) are not acceptable in college writing. • **Remember the key strategy of successful college writing:** Make a point, then support it with details and examples. • **Read and learn from the feedback** your instructor provides on your writing assignments. • **Write often.** The only way to learn how to write is to do it. • **Make use of the campus writing center and any tutoring support offered by your school.** Consider getting additional help if your first language is not English.
10c. I'm having difficulty in my mathematics course.	If you're having difficulty with your math course, try the following: • **Have a positive attitude.** Try to relax. Mathematics should not be feared. • **Math is sequential, so monitor your learning.** Make sure you understand everything as your course goes along. If you find yourself falling behind, seek assistance immediately, either from your instructor or the tutoring center. • **Recognize mathematical symbols** ($>, <, +, =, \sqrt{\ }$) and be able to translate them into English. • **Read slowly.** Reading in math is much slower than in other courses because so much "translation" work is required. • **Practice, practice, practice.** The only way to master mathematical concepts is to work problems.

10d. I'm having difficulty in another introductory course, such as sociology, psychology, or criminal justice. (See Chapter 5, p. 00 for more about the SQ3R method.)

At first new fields of study may seem confusing or intimidating. Use the following suggestions to help you make the transition.

- **Establish an overview of the field.** Spend time looking at the textbook's table of contents to get a sense of what you'll be learning. Use the SQ3R method for each chapter you read.
- **Purchase a study guide** to help you practice and master the textbook content.
- **Focus on key terms.** Fully understanding the specific vocabulary of a course is an important key to success.
- **Study the examples in the textbook.** Many students find that understanding examples is the single best way to understand a concept.
- **Make use of all the textbook aids,** including chapter summaries, chapter goals, and marginal glossaries. Use the visuals (graphs, tables, charts, and cartoons) to learn, study, memorize, and review key concepts.

CHAPTER
9

Reading Graphics and Electronic Sources

Looking at ...
Graphics and Electronic Sources

These signs are everyday visuals. They carry meaning with few or no words, yet they are easy to understand. In your textbooks you will also encounter a variety of visuals, including tables, graphs, charts, diagrams, maps, and photographs. This chapter focuses on reading and interpreting graphics. It also discusses evaluating another often highly visual type of information—online sources.

P314~23?

Students sometimes complain that reading graphics (tables, charts, diagrams, and photographs) is time-consuming. Others complain about assignments that require Internet research. These students do not realize that graphic aids are designed to make the chapter itself easier to read and that they summarize and condense information and actually save you time. In addition, Web sites and other electronic sources provide access to current, up-to-date information.

Try reading the following paragraph *without* looking at the diagram shown in Figure 9-1.

Skeletal muscle fibers, like most living cells, are soft and surprisingly fragile. Yet skeletal muscles can exert tremendous power—how so? The reason they are not ripped apart as they exert force is that thousands of their fibers are bundled together by connective tissue, which provides strength and support to the muscle as a whole. Each muscle fiber is enclosed in a delicate connective tissue called an **endomysium**. Several sheathed muscle fibers are then wrapped by a coarser fibrous membrane called a **perimysium** to form a bundle of fibers called a **fascicle**. Many fascicles are bound together by an even tougher "overcoat" of connective tissue called an **epimysium**, which covers the entire muscle. The epimysia blend into strong cordlike **tendons**, or sheetlike **aponeuroses**, which attach muscles indirectly to bones, cartilages, or connective tissue coverings of each other.

—Marieb, *Essentials of Human Anatomy & Physiology*, pp. 162, 164

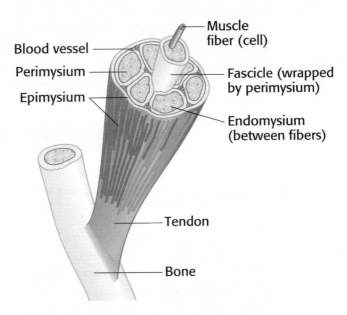

Figure 9-1 Diagram of connective tissue wrappings of skeletal muscles

—Marieb, *Essentials of Human Anatomy & Physiology*, p. 164

Did you find the paragraph difficult and confusing? Study Figure 9-1 and then reread the paragraph.

Now the paragraph should be easier to understand. So you can see that graphics are a valuable aid, not a hindrance. This chapter will describe the various types of graphics commonly included in college textbooks. You will learn how to approach and interpret each kind. You will also learn about various types of electronic learning aids.

TYPES OF GRAPHICS

myreadinglab

To practice interpreting graphics and visuals, go to

▼ STUDY PLAN

  ▼ READING SKILLS

    ▼ GRAPHICS AND VISUALS

This section will describe six types of graphics: *tables, graphs, charts, diagrams, maps,* and *photographs.*

Tables

A **table** is an organized arrangement of facts, usually numbers or statistics. A table condenses large amounts of data to allow you to read and interpret it easily. Use the steps listed below to read the table in Figure 9-2.

1. **Determine how the information is divided and arranged.** The table in Figure 9-2 is divided into three columns: date, estimated world population, and time required for population to double.

2. **Make comparisons and look for trends.** Do this by surveying rows and columns, noting how each compares with the others. Look for similarities, differences, or sudden or unexpected variations. Underline or highlight unusual or outstanding figures. For Figure 9-2, note that from 1650 on, dramatically less time has been required for each doubling of the world population—from 200 years in 1650 to only 40 years in 1990.

Doubling Times of the Human Population		
Date	**Estimated World Population**	**Time Required for Population to Double**
8000 B.C.	5 million	1,500 years
A.D. 1650	500 million	200 years
A.D. 1850	1,000 million (1 billion)	80 years
A.D. 1930	2,000 million (2 billion)	45 years
A.D. 1990	5,300 million (5.3 billion)	40 years
A.D. 2010	8,000 million (8 billion)	61 years

Figure 9-2 A sample table

—Wallace, *Biology*, p. 774

3. **Draw conclusions.** Decide what the numbers mean and what they suggest about the subject. This table appeared in a section of a biology textbook dealing with the growth of the human population. You can conclude that since the world population will have doubled in less than 40 more years, in 40 years we also will need to double our material goods just to maintain present living standards.

4. **Look for clues in corresponding text.** The textbook paragraph that corresponds to the table in Figure 9-2 is reprinted below.

Some countries have a much firmer grip on their population problems than others, as evidenced by their doubling times (see table). To go from five million people on earth (the present number in only three of New York City's five boroughs) in 8000 B.C. to 500 million in A.D. 1650 took six or seven doublings over a period of 9,000 to 10,000 years. During that time, the human population doubled on an average of about once every 1,500 years. A glance at the table will show that, all other things being equal, in only about 60 years, we will need two cars, two schools, two roads, two wells, two houses, and two cities throughout the world for every one that presently exists. And that will only maintain our status quo as far as material goods are concerned.

Notice the author explains and interprets the data presented in the table. He provides real-life examples (two cars, two schools, two wells) of what doubling the population means. Also, at the end of the paragraph, he interprets the data, questioning whether there are enough natural resources to support continued population growth.

EXERCISE 9-1   **Analyzing a Table**

Directions: Study the table in Figure 9-2 and answer the following questions.

1. How is the table arranged?

_____

2. Between what time periods did the world population increase most rapidly?

_____

3. What trend does this table reveal?

_____

Graphs

There are four types of graphs: *bar, multiple bar, stacked bar,* and *linear*. Each plots a set of points on a set of axes.

Bar Graphs A **bar graph** is often used to make comparisons between quantities or amounts, and is particularly useful in showing changes that occur with passing time. Bar graphs usually are constructed to emphasize differences. The graph shown in Figure 9-3 compares life expectancies in the early 1900s with those of today.

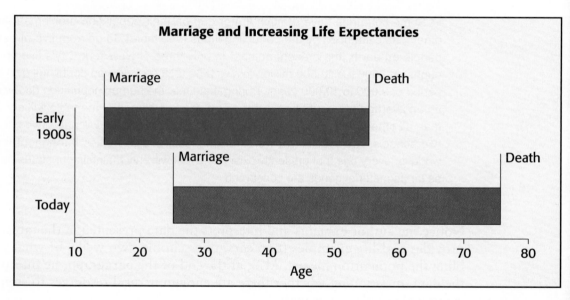

Figure 9-3 A sample bar graph

—Byer and Shainberg, *Living Well,* Fig. 65

EXERCISE **9-2** **Analyzing Bar Graphs**

Directions: Study the graph shown in Figure 9-3 and answer the following questions.

1. How is this graph organized?

   _____ year & ages _____

2. About how many years earlier did couples marry in the early 1900s than they do today?

   _____

3. Approximately how long were couples in the early 1900s married before they died? What about couples of today?

_____ 55 _____

4. About how much longer do married couples of today live compared to couples of the early 1900s?

_____

Multiple Bar Graphs   A **multiple bar graph** makes at least two or three comparisons simultaneously. As you read them, be sure to identify exactly what comparisons are being made. Figure 9-4 compares children's media usage according to age and type of media.

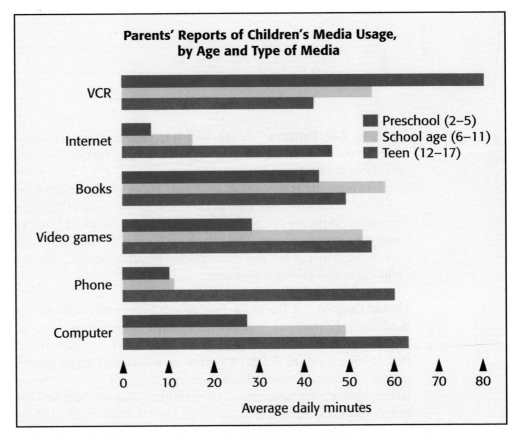

Figure 9-4   A sample multiple bar graph

—Fabes and Martin, *Exploring Child Development*, p. 281

EXERCISE 9-3   **Analyzing Multiple Bar Graphs**

Directions: Study the graph shown in Figure 9-4 and answer the following questions.

1. How is this graph organized?

   _____

   _____

2. For which type of media is there the greatest difference between preschool usage and teen usage?

   _____

3. What patterns are evident?

   _____

   _____

   _____

   _____

Stacked Bar Graphs   A **stacked bar graph** is an arrangement of data in which bars are placed one on top of another rather than side by side. This variation is often used to emphasize whole/part relationships. Stacked bar graphs show the relationship of a part to an entire group or class. The graph in Figure 9-5 shows day care arrangements by three ethnic groups: Caucasian American, African American, and Hispanic. Stacked bar graphs also allow numerous comparisons. The graph in Figure 9-5 compares five different day care arrangements for the three ethnic groups: parent, relative, nanny, family child care, and center-based care.

Linear Graphs   A **linear, or line, graph** plots and connects points along a vertical and a horizontal axis. A linear graph allows more data points than a bar graph. Consequently, it is used to present more detailed and/or larger quantities of information. A linear graph may compare two variables; if so, then it consists of a single line. Often, however, linear graphs are used to compare relationships among several sets of variables, and multiple lines are included. The graph shown in Figure 9-6 examines rate of technological change.

Linear graphs are usually used to display continuous data—data connected in time or events occurring in sequence. The data in Figure 9-6 are continuous, as they move from 2,000,000 B.C. to A.D. 2000.

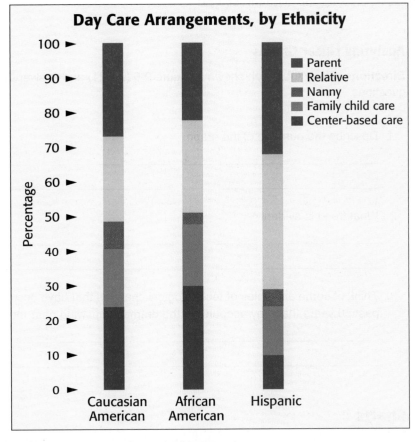

Figure 9-5   A sample stacked bar graph

—Fabes and Martin, *Exploring Child Development*, p. 196

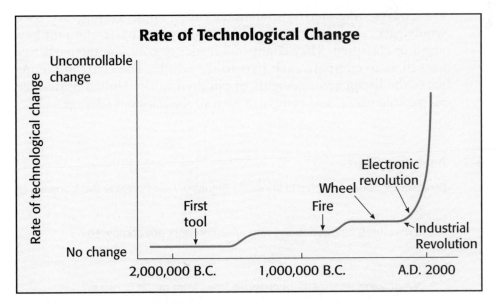

Figure 9-6   A sample linear graph

—Dunham and Pierce, *Management*, p. 721

Analyzing Linear Graphs

Directions: Study the graph shown in Figure 9-6 (p. 321) and answer the following questions.

1. Describe the purpose of the graph.

   _____

   _____

2. What trend is evident?

   _____

   _____

3. Think of some examples of technological changes that have occurred over the past 50 years that may account for the dramatic upswing near the year 2000.

   _____

   _____

Charts

Three types of charts are commonly used in college textbooks: *pie charts, organizational charts,* and *flowcharts.*

Pie Charts   **Pie charts,** sometimes called circle graphs, are used to show whole/part relationships or to depict how given parts of a unit have been divided or classified. They enable the reader to compare the parts to each other as well as to compare each part to the whole. The chart in Figure 9-7 compares the living arrangements of children in the United States according to race/ethnic origin and compares each to the national average.

Analyzing Charts

Directions: Study the charts shown in Figure 9-7 and answer the following questions.

1. What three categories of living arrangements are compared?

   _____

2. What living arrangement changes least from group to group?

   _____

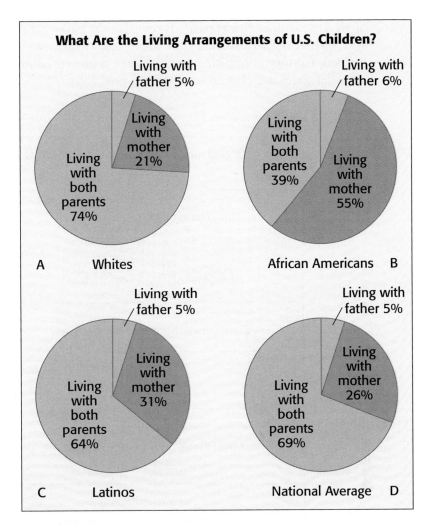

Figure 9-7 Sample pie charts

—Henslin, *Social Problems,* p. 368

3. What other patterns are evident?

_____

_____

_____

_____

Organizational Charts An **organizational chart** divides an organization, such as a corporation, a hospital, or a university, into its administrative parts, staff positions, or lines of authority. Figure 9-8 (p. 322) shows the organization of an American political party. It reveals that party members belong to precinct and ward organizations. From these organizations, county committees are formed. County committee members are represented on state committees, and state delegates are chosen for national positions.

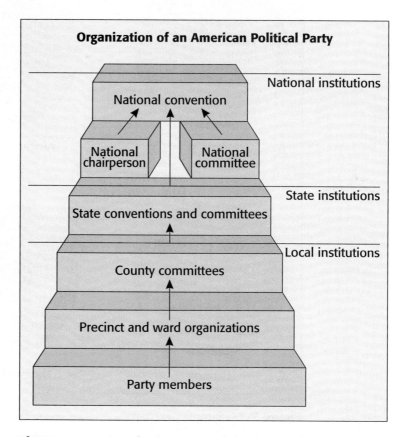

Figure 9-8 A sample organizational chart

—Lineberry and Edwards III, *Government in America,* p. 253

Flowcharts A **flowchart** is a specialized type of chart that shows how a process or procedure works. Lines or arrows are used to indicate the direction (route or routes) through the procedure. Various shapes (boxes, circles, rectangles) enclose what is done at each stage or step. You could draw, for example, a flowchart to describe how to apply for and obtain a student loan or how to locate a malfunction in your car's electrical system. Refer to the flowchart shown in Figure 9-9 (p. 325), taken from a business marketing textbook. It describes the steps in the development of an advertising campaign.

Steps to develop an advertising campaign

Developing an advertising campaign includes a series of steps that will ensure that the advertising meets communication objectives.

Figure 9-9   A sample flowchart

To read flowcharts effectively, use the following suggestions:

1. **Decide what process the flowchart shows.**
2. **Next, follow the chart, using the arrows and reading each step.** Start at the top or far left of the chart.
3. **When you have finished, summarize the process in your own words.** Try to draw the chart from memory without referring to the text. Compare your drawing with the chart and note discrepancies.

EXERCISE 9-6   Analyzing a Flowchart

Directions: Using the chart shown in Figure 9-9, complete the following tasks.

1. Summarize the chart's organization.

   _____

2. Explain the steps in the process in your own words.

   _____

   _____

Diagrams

Diagrams are often included in technical and scientific as well as many other college texts to explain processes. Diagrams are intended to help you visualize relationships between parts and understand sequences. They may also be used to illustrate ideas or concepts. Reading diagrams differs from reading other types of graphics in that diagrams often correspond to fairly large segments of text, requiring you to switch back and forth frequently between the text and the diagram to determine which part of the process each paragraph refers to. Figure 9-10, taken from a biology textbook, shows the structure of a nail. It accompanies the following text:

> A **nail** is a scalelike modification of the epidermis that corresponds to the hoof or claw of other animals. Each nail has a *free edge*, a *body*, (visible attached portion), and a *root* (embedded in the skin). The borders of the nail are overlapped by skin folds, called *nail folds*. The thick proximal nail is commonly called the *cuticle*. The stratus basale of the epidermis extends beneath the nail as the *nail bed*. Its thickened proximal area, called the *nail matrix*, is responsible for nail growth. The region over the thickened nail matrix that appears as a white crescent is called the *lunula*.
>
> —Marieb, *Essentials of Human Anatomy & Physiology*, p. 106

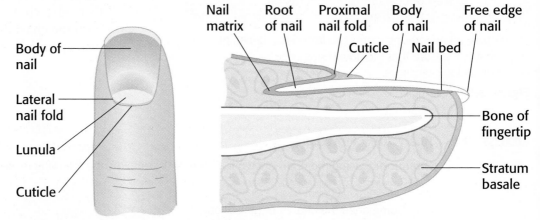

Structure of a nail. Surface view (left) and longitudinal section of the distal part of a finger (right), showing nail parts and the nail matrix that forms the nail.

Figure 9-10   Text and diagram showing the structure of the nail

—Marieb, *Essentials of Human Anatomy & Physiology*, p. 106

EXERCISE 9-7   Analyzing a Diagram

Directions: Study the diagram and text in Figure 9-10 and answer the following questions.

1. What is the purpose of the diagram?

2. Define the term *cuticle.*

_____

3. What part of the nail is responsible for nail growth?

_____

4. Could you accurately draw a diagram of the nail by referring only to the text, without referring to the diagram?

_____

Because diagrams of processes and their corresponding text are often difficult, complicated, or highly technical, plan on reading these sections more than once. Read first to grasp the overall process. In subsequent readings, focus on the details of the process, examining each step and understanding its progression.

One of the best ways to study a diagram is to redraw it in as much detail as possible without referring to the original. Or, test your understanding and recall of the process outlined in a diagram by explaining it, step by step in writing, using your own words.

Maps

Maps describe relationships and provide information about location and direction. They are commonly found in geography and history texts, and also appear in ecology, biology, and anthropology texts. While most of us think of maps as describing distances and locations, maps are also used to describe the placement of geographical and ecological features such as areas of pollution, areas of population concentration, or political data (voting districts).

When reading maps, use the following steps:

1. **Read the caption.** This identifies the subject of the map.
2. **Use the legend or key to identify the symbols or codes used.**
3. **Note distance scales.**
4. **Study the map, looking for trends or key points.** Often the text that accompanies the map states the key points the map illustrates.
5. **Try to visualize, or create a mental picture of, the map.**
6. **As a learning and study aid, write, in your own words, a statement of what the map shows.**

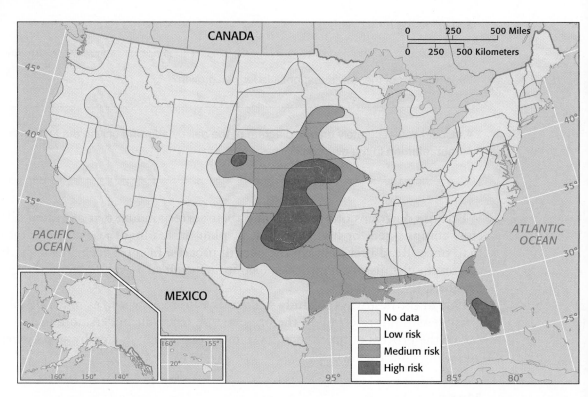

Tornado risk in the United States is greatest in the southern plains, the Southeast (especially central Florida), and the Midwest. (Alaska and Hawaii not to scale.)

Figure 9-11   A sample map

—Bergman and Renwick, *Introduction to Geography*, p. 69.

The map in Figure 9-11 shows the degree of risk for tornadoes in the United States.

Photographs

Although sometimes considered an art form instead of a graphic, **photographs** are used in place of words: their purpose is similar to other graphics—to replace verbal descriptions in presenting information. Photographs also are used to spark interest, and, often, to draw out an emotional response or feeling. Use these suggestions when studying a photograph:

1. **Read the caption.** It often provides a clue to the photographer's intended meaning.

2. **Ask: What is my first overall impression?** What details did I notice first? These questions will lead you to discover the purpose of the photograph.

EXERCISE 9-8   **Analyzing a Photograph**

Directions: Study the photograph in Figure 9-12, and answer the following questions.

1. Describe what may be happening in the picture.

   _____

2. What does this picture reveal that words alone cannot?

   _____

3. Why might this photograph be included in a section of a sociology textbook chapter titled "The Costs of War"?

   _____

Figure 9-12   A sample photograph

LEARNING STYLE TIPS

If you tend to be a . . .	Then study graphics by ...
Spatial learner	Examining the graphic so that you can visualize it
Verbal learner	Writing sentences that summarize what the graphic shows

EXERCISE **9-9**

Evaluating Graphics

Directions: Bring a copy of your local newspaper or *USA Today* to class. After your instructor forms groups, each group should select and tear out four or five graphics. For each graphic, the group should identify the type of graphic, analyze its purpose, and identify the trend or pattern it reveals. Groups should then discuss what other types of graphics could be used to accomplish the author's purpose. Each group should submit one graphic to the instructor along with a brief summary of the members' analysis.

EXERCISE **9-10**

Planning Graphics

Directions: Working in pairs, discuss what type(s) of graphic(s) would be most useful in presenting each of the following sets of information. Share and compare your findings with other teams.

1. Damage done to ancient carved figures by sulfur dioxide in the air
2. A comparison of the types of products the United States imports with those it exports
3. Changes in worker productivity each year from 1970 through 2010 in Japan, France, Germany, and the United States
4. The probabilities of being murdered, broken down by various racial and ethnic groups in the United States
5. Foreign revenue, total revenue, foreign operating profit, foreign assets, and total assets for the ten largest American multinational corporations
6. Living arrangements (one parent, two parents, neither parent) for white, black, and Hispanic-origin children under 18 years of age in 1960, 1970, 1980, 1990, and 2000
7. The basic components of a robot's manipulator arm
8. A description of how the AIDS virus affects the immune system
9. Sites of the earliest Neanderthal discoveries in Western Europe
10. Number of receipts of, and profits for, three types of businesses: sole proprietorships, partnerships, and corporations

EVALUATING INTERNET SOURCES

Although the Internet contains a great deal of valuable information and a great many resources, it also contains rumor, gossip, and misinformation. In other words, not all Internet sources are trustworthy. You must evaluate each source before accepting it.

P331~348

TABLE 9-1   Types of Web Sites

Type	Purpose	Description	URL Suffix
Informational	To present facts, information, and research data	May contain reports, statistical data, results of research studies, and reference materials	.edu or .gov
News	To provide current information on local, national, and international news	Often supplements print newspapers, periodicals, and television news programs	.com
Advocacy	To promote a particular cause or point of view	May be concerned with a controversial issue; often sponsored by nonprofit groups	.org
Personal	To provide information about an individual and his or her interests and accomplishments	May list publications or include the individual's résumé	URL will vary. May contain .com or .org or may contain a tilde (~)
Commercial	To promote goods or services	May provide news and information related to a company's products	.com

Discovering the Purpose of a Web Site

There are thousands of Web sites, and they vary widely in purpose. Table 9-1 summarizes five primary types of Web sites.

Evaluating the Content of a Web Site

When evaluating the content of a Web site, evaluate its appropriateness, its source, its level of technical detail, its presentation, its completeness, and its links.

Evaluate a Site's Appropriateness   To be worthwhile, a Web site should contain the information you need. It should answer one or more of your search questions. If the site only touches upon answers to your questions but does not address them in detail, check the links on the site to see if they will lead you to more detailed information. If they do not, search for a more useful site.

Evaluate the Source   Another important step in evaluating a Web site is to determine its source. Ask yourself, "Who is the sponsor?" and "Why was this site put up on the Web?" The sponsor of a Web site is the person or organization who paid for it to be created and placed on the Web. The sponsor will often suggest the purpose of a Web site. For example, a Web site sponsored by Nike is designed to promote its products, while a site sponsored by a university library is designed to help students learn to use its resources more effectively.

If you are not sure who sponsors a Web site, check its URL, its copyright, and the links it offers. The ending of the URL often suggests the type of sponsorship. The copyright indicates the owner of the site. Links may also reveal the sponsor. Some links may lead to commercial advertising, while others may lead to sites sponsored by nonprofit groups.

Evaluate the Level of Technical Detail   Some sites may provide information that is too sketchy for your search purposes; others assume a level of background knowledge or technical sophistication that you lack. For example, if you are writing a short, introductory-level paper on threats to the survival of marine animals, the Web site of the Scripps Institution of Oceanography (http://www.sio.ucsd.edu) may be too technical and contain more information than you need. Unless you have some previous knowledge in that field, you may want to search for a different Web site.

Evaluate the Presentation   Information on a Web site should be presented clearly and should be well written. If you find a site that is not clear and well written, you should be suspicious of it. If the author did not take time to present ideas clearly and correctly, he or she may not have taken time to collect accurate information either.

Evaluate the Completeness   Determine whether the site provides complete information on its topic. Does it address all aspects of the topic that you feel it should? For example, if a Web site on Important Twentieth-Century American Poets does not mention Robert Frost, then the site is incomplete. If you discover that a site is incomplete, search for sites that provide a more thorough treatment of the topic.

Evaluate the Links   Many reputable sites supply links to other related sites. Make sure that the links work and are current. Also check to see if the sites to which you were sent are reliable sources of information. If the links do not work or the sources appear unreliable, you should question the reliability of the site itself. Also determine whether the links provided are comprehensive or only present a representative sample. Either is acceptable, but the site should make clear the nature of the links it is providing.

EXERCISE **9-11**   **Evaluating the Content of Web Sites**

Directions: Evaluate the content of two of the following sites. Explain why you would either trust or distrust the content on each site.

1. **http://www.savethegreatbear.org/**

   _____

   _____

   _____

2. **http://www1.umn.edu/ohr/careerdev/resources/resume**

   _____

   _____

   _____

3. **http://www.hoosierherbalremedy.com**

   _____

   _____

Evaluating the Accuracy of a Web Site

When using information on a Web site for an academic paper, it is important to be sure that you have found accurate information. One way to determine the accuracy of a Web site is to compare it with print sources (periodicals and books) on the same topic. If you find a wide discrepancy between the Web site and the printed sources, do not trust the Web site. Another way to determine accuracy of the information on a site is to compare it with other Web sites that address the same topic. If discrepancies exist, further research is needed to determine which site is more accurate.

The site itself will also provide clues about the accuracy of its information. Ask yourself the following questions:

> ### Evaluating a Web Site's Accuracy
>
> 1. **Are the author's name and credentials provided?** A well-known writer with established credentials is likely to author only reliable, accurate information. If no author is given, you should question whether the information is accurate.

2. **Is contact information for the author included on the site?** Often, a site provides an e-mail address where the author may be contacted.

3. **Is the information complete, or in summary form?** If it is a summary, use the site to find the original source. Original information has less chance of containing errors and is usually preferred in academic papers.

4. **If opinions are offered, are they clearly presented as opinions?** Authors who disguise their opinions as facts are not trustworthy.

5. **Does the site provide a list of works cited?** As with any form of research, sources used to put information up on a Web site must be documented. If sources are not credited, you should question the accuracy of the Web site.

It may be helpful to determine if the information is available in print form. If it is, try to obtain the print version. Errors may occur when the article or essay is put up on the Web. Web sites move, change, and delete information, so it may be difficult for a reader of an academic paper to locate the Web site that you used in writing it. Also, page numbers are easier to cite in print sources than in electronic ones.

EXERCISE 9-12 **Evaluating the Accuracy of Web Sites**

Directions: Evaluate the accuracy of two of the following Web sites.

1. **http://gunscholar.com**

_____

_____

_____

2. **http://educate-yourself.org/**

_____

_____

_____

_____

3. **http://www.theonion.com/content/news/thousands_lose_jobs_as_michigan**

_____

_____

_____

Evaluating the Timeliness of a Web Site

Although the Web is well known for providing up-to-the-minute information, not all Web sites are current. Evaluate the timeliness by checking:

- the date on which the Web site was posted (put on the Web).
- the date when the document you are using was added.
- the date when the site was last revised.
- the date when the links were last checked.

This information is usually provided at the end of the site's home page or at the end of the document you are using.

EXERCISE 9-13 **Evaluate the Timeliness of Web Sites**

Directions: Evaluate the timeliness of two of the following Web sites, using the directions given for each site.

1. **http://www.state.gov/r/pa/ei/bgn**

   Choose a geographic region, and evaluate whether information is up-to-date.

   _____

2. **http://www.garynull.com/GNthisArticle.php?article=141**

   _____

   _____

3. **http://www.mountainbikepa.com/trails/trails.asp**

   Click on a county to find out about its bike trails. Evaluate the timeliness of the information and discuss why current information on this topic is crucial.

   _____

   _____

   _____

SELF-TEST SUMMARY

How many types of graphics are there, what are they, and how are they used?	There are six major types of graphics: 1. **Tables** are used to arrange and organize facts. 2. **Graphs**—including bar, multiple bar, stacked bar, and linear graphs—are used to make comparisons between or among sets of information. 3. **Charts**—including pie charts, organizational charts, and flowcharts—present visual displays of information. 4. **Diagrams** demonstrate physical relationships between parts and display sequences. 5. **Maps** describe information about location and direction. 6. **Photographs** are used to spark interest or to draw out an emotional response.
What factors should you consider when evaluating a Web site?	Consider the site's purpose to determine its type and usefulness. Evaluate the content: analyze the site's appropriateness, source, level of technical detail, presentation, completeness, and links. Judge the accuracy of a site by considering the author's credentials and contact information, completeness of information, opinionated content, and availability of works cited list. Check the timeliness of the site by checking the posting and revision dates.

GOING NLINE

1. Charts and Graphs
   http://mcckc.edu/longview/ctac/GRAPHS.HTM

   The Critical Thinking Across the Curriculum Project from Longview Community College invites you to analyze the way statistical information is represented visually. Look through some newspapers and magazines with a friend to locate charts and graphs. Analyze their reliability based on the information presented on this site. What is your perception of the media's use of statistics?

2. Web Site Evaluation Worksheet

    http://appserv.pace.edu/execute/page.cfm?doc_id=20964

    Print this worksheet from Pace University Library, and use it to evaluate a Web site that you use regularly. Notice that at the bottom of the site there are links to specialized criteria for specific types of Web pages. You might want to incorporate some of these into the worksheet you printed.

3. Smithsonian Images

    http://smithsonianimages.si.edu/

    Choose a photograph from the Smithsonian Images Collection. Describe the photo and explain the ways it could be used as part of an essay or article.

To check your progress in meeting chapter objectives, log in to **http://www.myreadinglab.com,** click on the Study Plan tab, and then click on the Reading Skills tab. Choose Graphics and Visuals from the list of subtopics. Read and view the information in the Review Materials section, and then complete the Practices and Tests in the Activities section. You can check your scores by clicking on the Gradebook tab.

MASTERY TEST 1 Graphic Skills

Name _____ Section _____

Date _____ Number right _____ × 20 points = Score _____

Directions: Use the text and table below to complete the statements that follow.

TABLE A What Cohabitation Means: Does It Make a Difference?

What Cohabitation Means	Percent of Couples	Split Up	Still Together	After 5 to 7 years Of Those Still Together	
				Married	Cohabitating
Substitute for Marriage	10%	35%	65%	37%	63%
Step toward Marriage	46%	31%	69%	73%	27%
Trial Marriage	15%	51%	49%	66%	34%
Coresidential Dating	29%	46%	54%	61%	39%

Source: Recomputed from Bianchi and Casper 2000.

From the outside, all cohabitation may look the same, but not to the people who are living together. As you can see from Table A, for about 10 percent of couples, cohabitation is a substitute for marriage. These couples consider themselves married but for some reason don't want a marriage certificate. Some object to marriage on philosophical grounds ("What difference does a piece of paper make?"); others do not yet have a legal divorce from a spouse. Almost half of cohabitants (46 percent) view cohabitation as a step on the path to marriage. For them, cohabitation is more than "going steady" but less than engagement. Another 15 percent of couples are simply "giving it a try." They want to see what marriage to one another might be like. For the least committed, about 29 percent, cohabitation is a form of dating. It provides a dependable source of sex and emotional support.

1. One purpose of the table is to compare
   a. marital success of those who cohabitate (live together) with those who marry.
   b. the meaning of cohabitation with the status of the relationship after 5 to 7 years.
   c. couples who cohabitate and couples who end up getting a divorce.

   d. characteristics of couples who split up with those of couples that stay together.

_____ 2. According to the table, the meaning of cohabitation that is most common is
   a. substitute for marriage.
   b. step toward marriage.
   c. trial marriage.
   d. coresidential dating.

_____ 3. After 5 to 7 years, which meaning of cohabitation shows the largest percentage of couples still cohabitating?
   a. substitute for marriage
   b. step toward marriage
   c. trial marriage
   d. coresidential dating

_____ 4. Couples in the coresidential dating category regard cohabitation as a source of
   a. sex and emotional support.
   b. a means of going steady.
   c. a way to give marriage a try without the legal issues.
   d. a step toward marriage.

_____ 5. Of the following facts, the only one that appears *both* in the text and in the graphic is
   a. 65 percent of couples who regard cohabitation as a substitute for marriage are still together five years later.
   b. of trial marriages, only 28 percent of the couples actually marry after five years.
   c. 15 percent of couples who cohabitate are doing so to give marriage a try.
   d. coresidential dating results in the second largest number of split-ups.

MASTERY TEST 2 **Graphic Skills**

Name _____ Section _____

Date _____ Number right _____ × 10 points = Score _____

Directions: Study the graph below from a sociology text and answer the questions that follow.

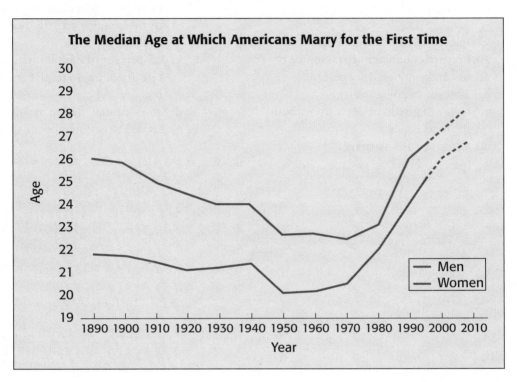

The Median Age at Which Americans Marry for the First Time

—Henslin, *Sociology*, p. 489.

_____ 1. What is the purpose of the graph?
  a. to compare the ages at which men and women marry from 1890 to 2010
  b. to show that the age at which Americans marry is decreasing
  c. to show that men and women marry at similar ages
  d. to compare how men and women have changed from 1890 to 2010

_____ 2. In which of the following years was there the largest difference in ages between men and women?
  a. 1990
  b. 1930
  c. 1970
  d. 1910

_____ 3. Which of the following statements describes the trend shown between 1890 and 1990?
  a. Women married at an older age than men.
  b. Men married at an older age than women.
  c. Men married older women.
  d. Women married younger men.

_____ 4. Which marriage trend does the graph show?
  a. The age gap between men and women has been gradually narrowing.
  b. Women's average age has been steadily decreasing throughout history.
  c. Men's average age has shown little change.
  d. Women's average age has shown a steady decline.

Directions: Study the pie chart below, and answer the questions that follow.

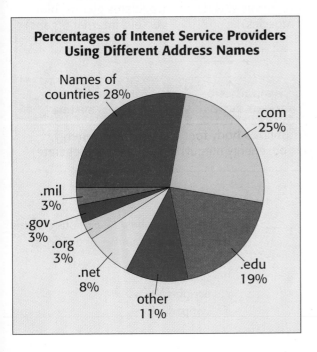

Percentages of Intenet Service Providers Using Different Address Names

_____ 5. Which of the following address names is used by the second largest percentage of Internet service providers?
  a. .edu
  b. other
  c. .com
  d. names of countries

_____ 6. Which of the following address names contain the same percentages of Internet service providers?
  a. .mil and .net
  b. .edu and .com
  c. .gov and .org
  d. .com and names of countries

_____ 7. What percentage of Internet service providers use the name of a country in their addresses?
  a. 25 percent
  b. 8 percent
  c. 10 percent
  d. 28 percent

Directions: Study the chart below, and answer the questions that follow.

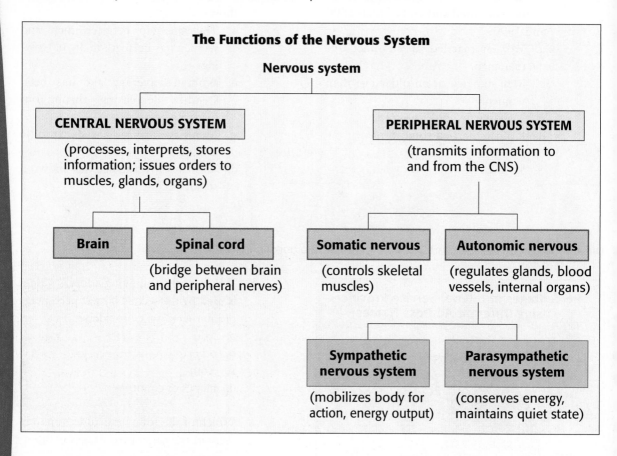

The Functions of the Nervous System

Nervous system

CENTRAL NERVOUS SYSTEM
(processes, interprets, stores information; issues orders to muscles, glands, organs)

PERIPHERAL NERVOUS SYSTEM
(transmits information to and from the CNS)

Brain

Spinal cord
(bridge between brain and peripheral nerves)

Somatic nervous
(controls skeletal muscles)

Autonomic nervous
(regulates glands, blood vessels, internal organs)

Sympathetic nervous system
(mobilizes body for action, energy output)

Parasympathetic nervous system
(conserves energy, maintains quiet state)

_____ 8. The brain is part of the
    a. spinal cord.
    b. autonomic nervous system.
    c. peripheral nervous system.
    d. central nervous system.

_____ 9. Which of the following nervous systems controls muscles?
    a. somatic nervous system
    b. autonomic nervous system
    c. brain
    d. central nervous system

_____ 10. Which of the following nervous systems has the greatest number of divisions?
    a. autonomic
    b. spinal cord
    c. peripheral
    d. sympathetic

MASTERY TEST 3 Reading Selection

Name _____ Section _____

Date _____ Number right _____ × 10 points = Score _____

Trends in Voter Turnout

Neal Tannahill

This selection, taken from an American government textbook, examines voter participation in the United States. Before reading, try to predict some trends based on your own observations and experience.

> **Vocabulary Preview**
>
> mobilization (par. 2) organizing and making ready for action
>
> electorate (par. 4) those qualified to vote

voting eligible population (VEP) the number of U.S. residents who are legally qualified to vote.

voting age population (VAP) the number of U.S. residents who are 18 years of age or older.

battleground states swing states in which the relative strength of the two major-party presidential candidates is close enough so that either candidate could conceivably carry the state.

1   Political scientists who study election participation measure voter turnout relative to the size of the **voting eligible population (VEP)**, the number of U.S. residents who are legally qualified to vote. The VEP differs from the **voting age population (VAP)**, which is the number of U.S. residents who are 18 years of age or older, because it excludes individuals who are ineligible to cast a ballot. In contrast to the VAP, the VEP does not include non-citizens, convicted criminals (depending on state law), and people who are mentally incapacitated.

2   The 2004 and 2008 presidential elections suggest that the United States is experiencing a voting revival. After years of declining or flat electoral participation rates, voter turnout has surged to a level not seen in nearly 40 years. The increase reflects the result of massive voter mobilization efforts coupled with high public interest in the election. The two major political parties, supported by their interest group allies, organized sophisticated get-out-the-vote (GOTV) campaigns in 2004 and 2008, focusing on the **battleground states,** which are swing states in which the relative strength of the two major party presidential candidates is close enough so that either candidate could conceivably carry the state. Campaign volunteers and paid organizers telephoned, mailed, e-mailed, or visited millions of potential voters, encouraging them to go to the polls. Exposure to intense campaign activity increases political engagement, especially among low-income voters, a group with typically low voter turnout rates. In the meantime, hot-button issues such as the war in Iraq,

think Should people with prior criminal convictions be permanently disqualified from voting?

---

*To calculate the number right, use items 1–10 under "Mastery Test Skills Check."

343

the war on terror, gay marriage, healthcare reform, taxes, high gas prices, and the economy energized citizens to go to the polls. According to the **ANES**, 40 percent of Americans said they were "very much interested" in the 2004 presidential campaign, the highest level of interest in the history of the poll and 14 percentage points higher than the level of interest expressed in 2000. Interest in the 2008 election may have been even higher.

ANES
American National Election Studies, a collaboration of Stanford University and the University of Michigan that produces data on voting, public opinion, and political participation

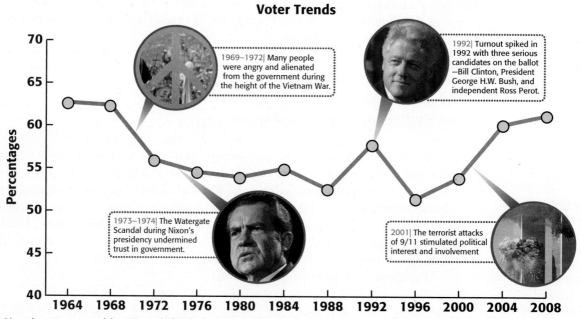

Voter Trends

1969–1972| Many people were angry and alienated from the government during the height of the Vietnam War.

1992| Turnout spiked in 1992 with three serious candidates on the ballot —Bill Clinton, President George H.W. Bush, and independent Ross Perot.

1973–1974| The Watergate Scandal during Nixon's presidency undermined trust in government.

2001| The terrorist attacks of 9/11 stimulated political interest and involvement

More than 62 percent of the VEP cast ballots in the 1964 presidential election, capping a steady 36-year rise in voter turnout. For the next 30 years, voter participation rates declined, reaching a 70-year low in 1996 at 51.7 percent. Election turnout subsequently rebounded to 54.2 percent in 2000, 60.3 percent in 2004, and 61.6 percent in 2008.

PARTICIPATION RATES IN COMPARATIVE PERSPECTIVE

3   Voting turnout in the United States is relatively low compared to other industrialized democracies. According to data collected by the International Institute for Democracy and Electoral Assistance, the United States lags behind most other countries in the world in electoral participation in national legislative elections.

4   More than a fourth of the potential electorate in the United States is not registered to vote. Political scientists identify three factors that result in the relatively lower American voter turnout rate. First, American election procedures are more cumbersome than they are in most other democracies. Before Americans can vote in most states, they must register, usually no later than 30 days before an election. In most other democracies, the government takes the initiative to register eligible voters. American elections

think

Does it really matter that many Americans do not vote?

traditionally take place on Tuesday, whereas other countries declare a national holiday so citizens can vote without missing work. The United States also holds more frequent elections and elects large numbers of public officials. Many Americans stay home, confused by the length and complexity of the ballot.

"I was just too busy."

The #1 reason Americans give for not voting is that they couldn't find the time.

5   Second, voter participation rates in the United States are lower because American political parties are weaker than those of other democracies. Strong political parties increase voter turnout by educating citizens about candidates and issues, stimulating interest in elections, and mobilizing citizens to vote. Political scientist G. Bingham Powell Jr. estimates that if American political parties were more centralized and had stronger ties to other social organizations, such as labor unions, religious bodies, and ethnic groups, then voter participation would rise by as much as 10 percent.

6   Finally, many American voters stay home because they do not perceive that elections have much impact on policy. Winning candidates may not be able to keep promises because of **separation of powers**, the division of political authority among the executive, legislative, and judicial branches of government. During the 2006 election campaign, for example, Democratic congressional candidates called for the withdrawal of American troops from Iraq. Even though the Democrats captured majorities in both the House and Senate, they could not keep this promise. Their majority was too slim to pass proposals to bring home the troops, or to override President George W. Bush's veto.

separation of powers
the division of political power among executive, legislative, and judicial branches of government

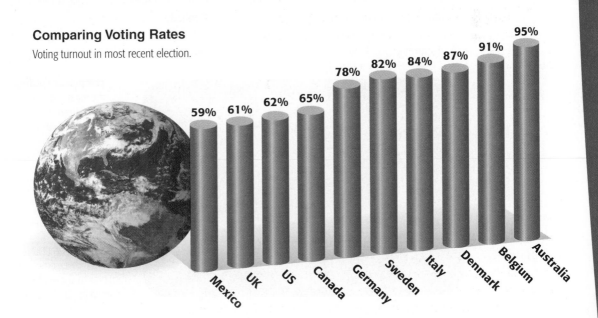

Comparing Voting Rates
Voting turnout in most recent election.

59% Mexico
61% UK
62% US
65% Canada
78% Germany
82% Sweden
84% Italy
87% Denmark
91% Belgium
95% Australia

Around The World

Compulsory in Australia

7   **Compulsory voting** is the legal requirement that citizens participate in national elections. It is a low-cost, efficient remedy to the problem of low turnout. Voter participation rates are almost 20 percent higher in nations with compulsory voting than they are in other democracies. Almost everyone votes in Australia, a nation that has had compulsory voting since 1924. For example, voter turnout was 94 percent in the 2004 national election.

8   The Australian Election Commission (AEC) enforces the nation's compulsory voting law. The AEC sends a "please explain" letter to people who fail to vote in a particular election. Election no-shows can either pay a fine or offer an explanation. If the AEC decides that the explanation is valid, it can waive the fine. The courts settle disputes between the AEC and individual non-voters over the validity of excuses. The proportion of Australians fined for failing to vote never exceeds 1 percent of the electorate.

9   Political scientists believe that compulsory voting strengthens political parties. Because parties do not have to devote resources to turning out the vote, they can focus on persuasion and conversion. Compulsory voting builds party loyalty. Survey research in Australia finds that most Australian voters express firm and longstanding commitments to a party. You have read that lower-income people are less likely to vote than middle-income citizens. So, compulsory voting also benefits political parties representing the working-class interests more than those representing middle- and upper-income voters because lower-income people are less likely to vote than middle-income citizens.

Question

1. Does the problem of non-voting need a legal remedy?
2. Do you think compulsory voting in the United States would increase turnout substantially?
3. Do you think that the United States will ever adopt compulsory voting? Why or why not?

compulsory voting
the legal requirment that citizens participate in national elections

Liberal Party leaders in Australia watch election results as their party loses power in the 2007 election.

MASTERY TEST SKILLS CHECK

Directions: Select the choice that best completes each of the following statements.

Checking Your Comprehension

1. The primary purpose of this selection is to
   a. describe the typical American voter.
   b. explain how the election process works in America.
   c. discuss voter participation in America and other democracies.
   d. explore issues that have an effect on voter participation.

2. In contrast to the voting age population (VAP), the voting eligible population (VEP) includes
   a. non-citizens.
   b. convicted criminals.
   c. people who are mentally incapacitated.
   d. only citizens who are legally qualified to vote.

3. According to the selection, the relatively low American voter turnout rate is a result of all of the following factors *except*
   a. complicated election procedures.
   b. weak political parties.
   c. ties between political parties and other social organizations.
   d. voters' belief that elections do not affect policy.

4. In comparison to the United States, other democracies
   a. hold more frequent elections.
   b. elect larger numbers of public officials.

c. require voters to register themselves.
   d. declare a national holiday so voters will not miss work.

5. Under Australia's compulsory voting system, people who fail to vote in an election are
   a. arrested and sent to jail for 30 days.
   b. allowed to pay a fine or offer an explanation.
   c. required to perform community service.
   d. disqualified from voting in future elections.

Applying Your Skills

6. According to the graph on p. 344, the two years with the lowest voter participation rates were
   a. 1964 and 1968.
   b. 1972 and 1976.
   c. 1988 and 1996.
   d. 2004 and 2008.

7. Based on the same graph on p. 344, voter participation in the year 2000 was
   a. over 60 percent.
   b. about 55 percent.
   c. exactly 50 percent.
   d. under 50 percent.

8. Of the following time periods, the graph on p. 344 indicates that voter participation dropped most dramatically during
   a. 1964–1968.
   b. 1972–1976.
   c. 1984–1988.
   d. 1992–1996.

_____ 9. The purpose of the [second] graph on p. 345 is to
   a. promote the idea of compulsory voting.
   b. compare voting rates around the world.
   c. identify reasons for low voter participation.
   d. show trends in voter participation around the world.

_____ 10. The graph on p. 345 indicates all of the following about the most recent national elections *except*
   a. Mexico had the lowest voter turnout.
   b. Australia had the highest voter turnout.
   c. the United States had a higher voter turnout than Canada.
   d. Belgium had a higher voter turnout than all countries except Australia.

Studying Words

_____ 11. The word *incapacitated* (par. 1) means
   a. qualified.
   b. unable to act.
   c. included.
   d. outnumbered.

_____ 12. The word *surged* (par. 2) means
   a. declined.
   b. poured.
   c. increased.
   d. faltered.

_____ 13. From context, you can tell that the phrase *hot-button* (par. 2) means
   a. dangerous.
   b. controversial or emotionally charged.
   c. not interesting.
   d. offensive.

_____ 14. The word *cumbersome* (par. 4) means
   a. difficult to use.
   b. clumsy.
   c. plain.
   d. fearsome.

_____ 15. The word *compulsory* (in the "Around the World" box) means
   a. optional.
   b. expensive.
   c. complicated.
   d. required.

For more practice, ask your instructor for an opportunity to work on the mastery tests that appear in the Test Bank.

Summarizing the Reading

Directions: Complete the following summary of the reading by filling in the blanks.

Election participation is measured by _____
_____. In the 2004 and 2008 elections, voter turnout _____
_____, reflecting _____. Parties focused
on battleground states, in which _____
_____. Voters were very interested in issues _____
_____.

Voter turnout in the United States _____
_____. Three factors that result in the low American voter turnout rate are

_____

_____.

Reading Visually

1. What is the purpose of the "Think" light bulb graphics that accompany the reading? How would you answer the questions that the author poses?
2. How do the graphs contribute to your understanding of the material? Why are graphs more effective in illustrating this material than a photograph would be?
3. Why did the author include the feature on Australia's compulsory voting system? What does the photograph add to this part of the reading?
4. Consider the questions posed at the end of the feature about Australia and form your own answer to each one.

Thinking Critically about the Reading

WRITE IN YOUR
JOURNAL

1. Did the trends identified in the selection surprise you? Why or why not?
2. If you were eligible to vote in the 2008 election, did you? Why or why not?
3. Consider the number one reason Americans give for not voting ("too busy"). Do you accept this reason as valid, or do you think there should be a penalty for people who can't find the time to vote?

Organizing and Remembering Information

Looking at …
Organizing and Remembering Information

The blueprint above, created by an architect, is used by the contractor to build the house to specifications. The blueprint organizes all the details about the house, such as the size of rooms and the location of windows, electrical outlets, and appliances. Can you imagine how difficult it would be to keep track of all the details involved in building a house without a blueprint? Textbook chapters are also filled with details, and you need a system to keep track of them all. This chapter shows you four ways to create a "blueprint" or learning guide of a textbook chapter.

Suppose you are planning a cross-country trip next summer. To get ready you begin to collect all kinds of information: maps, newspaper articles on various cities, places to visit, names of friends' friends, and so forth. After a while, you find that you have a great deal of information and that it is difficult to locate any one item. You begin to realize that the information you have collected will be of little or no use unless you organize it in some way. You decide to buy large envelopes and put different kinds of information into separate envelopes, such as information on individual states.

In this case, you found a practical, commonsensical solution to a problem. The rule or principle that you applied was this: When something gets confusing, organize it.

This rule also works well when applied to college textbooks. Each text contains thousands of pieces of information—facts, names, dates, theories, principles. This information quickly becomes confusing unless it is organized. Once you have organized it, you will be able to find and remember what you need more easily than if your text were still an unsorted heap of facts.

Organizing information requires sifting, sorting, and in some cases rearranging important facts and ideas. There are five common methods of organizing textbook materials:

- Highlighting
- Marking
- Outlining
- Mapping
- Summarizing

In this chapter you will learn techniques for doing each. You will also see how to study and review more effectively.

HIGHLIGHTING AND MARKING

Highlighting and marking important facts and ideas as you read are effective methods of identifying and organizing information. They are also the biggest time-savers known to college students. Suppose it took you four hours to read an assigned chapter in sociology. One month later you need to review that chapter to prepare for an exam. If you did not highlight or mark as you read the first time, then, in order to review the chapter once, you would have to spend another four hours rereading it. However, if you had highlighted and marked as you read, you could review the chapter in an hour or less—a savings of 300 percent. This means you can save many hours each semester. More important, the less time you spend identifying what to learn, the more thoroughly you can learn the necessary information. This strategy can help improve your grades.

Highlighting Effectively

Here are a few basic suggestions for highlighting effectively:

How to Highlight

1. **Read a paragraph or section first.** Then go back and highlight what is important.
2. **Highlight important portions of the topic sentence.** Also highlight any supporting details you want to remember (see Chapter 7).
3. **Be accurate.** Make sure your highlighting reflects the content of the passage. Incomplete or hasty highlighting can mislead you as you review the passage and may cause you to miss the main point.
4. **Use a system for highlighting.** There are several from which to choose: for instance, using two or more different colors of highlighters to distinguish between main ideas and details, or placing a bracket around the main idea and using highlighter to mark important details. No one system is more effective than another. Try to develop a system that works well for you.
5. **Highlight as few words as possible in a sentence.** Seldom should you highlight an entire sentence. Usually highlighting the key idea along with an additional phrase or two is sufficient. Read the following paragraph. Notice that you can understand its meaning from the highlighted parts alone.

   Police are primarily a reactive force. In the vast majority of cases, police are informed of an incident *after* it occurs by a complaining victim, a witness, or an alarm. (A study of police response time found that only about 6 percent of callers reported crimes while they were in progress.) In addition, the National Crime Victimization Survey (NCVS) reveals that only about a third of serious crime is reported to police. It is difficult to hold police responsible for increases in the crime rate when they are not called for most crimes or are called after the incident has ended. Several other factors may cause the crime rate to rise, such as an increase in the proportion of young people in the population, higher rates of long-term unemployment, and the criminalization of drug use. Police have no control over these conditions. Thus, the crime rate is really not a useful indictor of police effectiveness.

6. **Use headings to guide your highlighting.** Use the headings to form questions that you expect to be answered in the section (see Chapter 5). Then highlight the answer to each question.

Highlighting the Right Amount

If you highlight either too much or too little, you defeat the purpose. By highlighting too little, you miss valuable information, and your review and study of the material will be incomplete. On the other hand, if you highlight too much, you are not identifying the most important ideas and eliminating less important facts. The more you highlight, the more you will have to reread when studying and the less of a time-saver the procedure will prove to be. As a general rule of thumb, highlight no more than 20 to 30 percent of the material.

Here is a paragraph highlighted in three different ways. First read the paragraph that has not been highlighted; then look at each highlighted version. Try to decide which version would be most useful if you were rereading it for study purposes.

The Maglevs are coming. Not aliens from outer space, but superfast trains suspended in the air and propelled* by magnetic force. Maglevs can travel at speeds of more than 300 miles per hour, lifted off the ground on a cushion formed by magnetic forces and pulled forward by magnets. They run more quietly and smoothly and can climb steeper grades than conventional trains can. Maglevs are more energy efficient, have lower maintenance costs, and require fewer staff than does comparable transportation. However, given the high cost of construction, the concept may not prove viable.

—adapted from Walker, *Introduction to Hospitality Management*, p. 45

Example 1
The Maglevs are coming. Not aliens from outer space, but superfast trains suspended in the air and propelled by magnetic force. Maglevs can travel at speeds of more than 300 miles per hour, lifted off the ground on a cushion formed by magnetic forces and pulled forward by magnets. They run more quietly and smoothly and can climb steeper grades than conventional trains can. Maglevs are more energy efficient, have lower maintenance costs, and require fewer staff than does comparable transportation. However, given the high cost of construction, the concept may not prove viable.

Example 2
The Maglevs are coming. Not aliens from outer space, but superfast trains suspended in the air and propelled by magnetic force. Maglevs can travel at speeds of more than 300 miles per hour, lifted off the ground on a cushion formed by magnetic forces and pulled forward by magnets. They run more quietly and smoothly and can climb steeper grades than conventional trains can. Maglevs are more energy

efficient, have lower maintenance costs, and require fewer staff than does comparable transportation. However, given the high cost of construction, the concept may not prove viable.

Example 3

The Maglevs are coming. Not aliens from outer space, but superfast trains suspended in the air and propelled by magnetic force. Maglevs can travel at speeds of more than 300 miles per hour, lifted off the ground on a cushion formed by magnetic forces and pulled forward by magnets. They run more quietly and smoothly and can climb steeper grades than conventional trains can. Maglevs are more energy efficient, have lower maintenance costs, and require fewer staff than does comparable transportation. However, given the high cost of construction, the concept may not prove viable.

The last example is the best example of effective highlighting. Only the most important information has been highlighted. In the first example, too little of the important information has been highlighted, while what *has* been highlighted is either unnecessary or incomplete. The second example, on the other hand, has too much highlighting to be useful for review.

EXERCISE 10-1   **Practicing Highlighting**

Directions: Read and highlight the following passage using the guidelines presented in this section.

Generic Names

When filing for a trademark, if a word, name, or slogan is too generic, it cannot be registered as a trademark. If it is not generic, it can be trademarked. For example, the word "apple" cannot be trademarked because it is a generic name. However, the brand name "Apple Computer" is permitted to be trademarked because it is not a generic name. Similarly, the word "secret" cannot be trademarked because it is a generic name, but the brand name "Victoria's Secret" is permitted to be trademarked because it is not a generic name.

Once a company has been granted a trademark, the company usually uses the mark as a brand name to promote its goods or services. However, sometimes a company may be *too* successful in promoting a mark and at some point the public begins to use the brand name as a common name for the product or service being sold, rather than as the trademark of the individual seller. A trademark that becomes a common term for a product line or type of service is called a **generic name**. Once a trademark becomes a generic name, the term loses its protection under federal trademark law. To illustrate, sailboards are surfboards that have sails mounted on them and are used by one person to glide on oceans and lakes. There were many manufacturers and sellers of sailboards. The most successful brand was "Windsurfer." However, the word "windsurfing" was used so often by the public for all brands of sailboards that the trademarked name "Windsurfer" was found to be a generic name and its trademark was canceled.

—adapted from Goldman and Cheeseman, *The Paralegal Professional*, p. 745

EXERCISE 10-2 **Highlighting Chapter 5**

Directions: Read or reread and highlight Chapter 5 in this book. Follow the guidelines suggested in this chapter.

Testing Your Highlighting

As you highlight, check to be certain your highlighting is effective and will be helpful for review purposes. To test the effectiveness of your highlighting, take any passage and reread only the highlighted portions. Then ask yourself the following questions:

> ### Testing Your Highlighting
>
> • Does the highlighting tell what the passage is about?
> • Does it make sense?
> • Does it indicate the most important idea in the passage?

EXERCISE 10-3 **Evaluating Your Highlighting**

Directions: Test the effectiveness of your highlighting for the material you highlighted in Exercises 10-1 and 10-2. Make changes, if necessary.

Marking

Highlighting alone will not clearly identify and organize information in many types of textbooks. Also, highlighting does not allow you to react to or sort ideas. Try making notes in the margin in addition to highlighting. Notice how the marginal notes in the following passage organize the information in a way that highlighting cannot.

Seasonal Affective Disorder (SAD)

def. of SAD

Some people only get depressed at certain times of the year. In particular, depression seems to set in during the winter months and goes away with the coming of spring and summer. If this describes someone you know, it could be seasonal affective disorder (SAD). SAD is a mood disorder caused by the body's reaction to low levels of light present in the winter months.

Symptoms

SAD can cause feelings of tiredness, lack of energy, and daytime sleepiness that the mind interprets as depression. Other symptoms include excessive eating, a craving for sugary and starchy foods, excessive sleeping, and weight gain. The worst months for SAD are January and February, and true SAD disappears in the spring and summer.

treatment

Treatment of SAD can include antidepressant drugs, but one of the most effective treatments is **phototherapy**, or daily exposure to bright light. Lamps are used to create an "artificial daylight" for a certain number of hours during each day, and the person with SAD sits under that light. Milder symptoms can be controlled with more time spent outdoors when the sun is shining and increasing the amount of sunlight that comes into the workplace or home.

—adapted from Ciccarelli and White, *Psychology: An Exploration*, p. 454

Here are a few examples of useful types of marking:

1. **Circle words you do not know.**

   Sulfur is a yellow, solid substance that has several (allotropic) forms

2. **Mark definitions with an asterisk.**

   Chemical reactivity is the tendency of an element to participate in chemical reactions.

3. **Write summary words or phrases in the margin.**

   reaction w/air

   Some elements, such as aluminum (Al) or Copper (Cu), tarnish just from sitting around in the air. They react with oxygen (O_2) in the air.

4. **Number lists of ideas, causes, and reasons.**

   ① ② ③
   Metallic properties include conductivity, luster, and ductility.

5. **Place brackets around important passages.**

   In Group IVA, carbon (C) is a nonmetal, silicon (Si) and germanium (Ge) are metaloids, and tin (Sn) and lead (Pb) are metals.

6. **Draw arrows or diagrams to show relationships or to clarify information.**

graphite

> Graphite is made up of a lot of carbon layers stacked on top of one another, like sheets of paper. The layers slide over one another, which makes it a good lubricant.

7. **Make notes to yourself, such as "good test question," "reread," or "ask instructor."**

Test!

> Carbon is most important to us because it is a basic element in all plant and animal structures.

8. **Put question marks next to confusing passages or when you want more information.**

why?

> Sometimes an element reacts so violently with air, water, or other substances that an explosion occurs.

Try to develop your own code or set of abbreviations. Here are a few examples:

Types of Marking	Examples
ex	example
T	good test question
sum	good summary
def	important definition
RR	reread later

EXERCISE 10-4   Practicing Highlighting and Marking

Directions: Read each of the following passages and then highlight and mark each. Try various ways of highlighting and marking.

Passage A

National and Regional Presidential Primary Proposals

1   The idea of holding a **national primary** to select party nominees has been discussed virtually ever since state primaries were introduced. In 1913, President Woodrow Wilson proposed it in his first message to Congress. Since then, over 250

proposals for a national presidential primary have been introduced in Congress. These proposals do not lack public support; opinion polls have consistently shown that a substantial majority of Democrats, Republicans, and Independents alike favor such reform.

2   According to its proponents, a national primary would bring directness and simplicity to the process for the voters as well as the candidates. The length of the campaign would be shortened, and no longer would votes in one state have more political impact than votes in another. The concentration of media coverage on this one event, say its advocates, would increase not only political interest in the nomination decision but also public understanding of the issues involved.

3   A national primary would not be so simple, respond the critics. Because Americans would not want a candidate nominated with 25 percent of the vote from among a field of six candidates, in most primaries a runoff election between the top two finishers in each party would have to be held. So much for making the campaign simpler, national primary critics note. Each voter would have to vote three times for president—twice in the primaries and once in November.

4   Perhaps more feasible than a national primary is holding a series of **regional primaries** in which, say, states in the eastern time zone would vote one week, those in the central time zone the next, and so on. This would impose a more rational structure and cut down on candidate travel. A regional primary system would also put an end to the jockeying between states for an advantageous position in the primary season.

5   The major problem with the regional primary proposal, however, is the advantage gained by whichever region goes first. For example, if the Western states were the first to vote, any candidate from California would have a clear edge in building momentum. Although most of the proposed plans call for the order of the regions to be determined by lottery, this would not erase the fact that regional advantages would surely be created from year to year.

—adapted from Edwards et al., *Government in America*, p. 285

Passage B

Melting Point

1   The particles (atoms or molecules) of a solid are held together by attractive forces. . . . Heating up a solid, such as a piece of ice, gives its molecules more energy and makes them move. Pretty soon they are moving fast enough to overcome the attractive forces that were holding them rigidly together in the solid. The temperature at which this happens is the *melting point* of the solid. When a liquid, such as water, is cooled, the reverse process happens. We take energy away from the molecules, and pretty soon the molecules are moving slowly enough for their attractive forces to hold them rigidly together again and form a solid. The temperature at which this happens is the *freezing point* of the liquid. Melting point and freezing point are really the same thing, approached from opposite directions. To melt a substance, we supply heat; to freeze it, we remove heat.

2   While a solid is melting, its temperature stays constant at its melting point. Even though we keep heating a solid as it melts, we won't increase its temperature until all of the solid has changed to liquid. When a solid starts to melt, all of the heat that is put into it from then on goes into breaking up the attractive forces that hold the atoms or molecules together in the solid. When the solid is all melted, then the heat that is put in can once more go into increasing the temperature of the substance. The amount of heat that it takes to melt one gram of any substance at its melting point is called the *heat of fusion.* If we let the substance freeze, then it will give off heat in the amount of the heat of fusion. Freezing is a process that releases energy.

3   Every substance has a melting (or freezing) point except diamond, which no one has been able to melt yet. The stronger the attractive forces that hold atoms or molecules together in the solid, the higher its melting (or freezing) point will be. The forces holding a diamond together in the solid state are so strong that they can't be overcome by heating. Most elements are solids at "room temperature," a vague term meaning a range of about 20°C to 30°C. A substance that's a solid at room temperature has a melting point higher than room temperature. Some substances are borderline, and they can be either liquids or solids depending on the weather: we've all seen tar melt on a hot day. Olive oil will solidify (freeze) on a cold day. . . .

—Newell, *Chemistry*, pp. 47–48

EXERCISE 10-5   ## Comparing Highlighting and Marking

Working Together

Directions: Read, highlight, and mark a reading selection from Part Six assigned by your instructor. Then, working with a partner, review each other's highlighting, discuss similarities and differences, and settle upon an acceptable version.

myreadinglab

To practice outlining, go to
▼ STUDY PLAN
  ▼ READING SKILLS
    ▼ OUTLINING AND SUMMARIZING

OUTLINING

OBJECTIVE 2

Outlining is a good way to create a visual picture of what you have read. In making an **outline**, you record the writer's organization and show the relative importance of and connection between ideas.

Outlining has a number of advantages:

- It gives an overview of the topic and enables you to see how various subtopics relate to one another.
- Recording the information in your own words tests your understanding of what you read.
- It is an effective way to record needed information from reference books you do not own.

How to Outline

Generally, an outline follows a format like the one below.

> I. First major idea
>   A. First supporting detail
>   1. Detail
>   2. Detail
>   B. Second supporting detail
>   1. Detail
>   a. Minor detail or example
>   b. Minor detail or example
> II. Second major idea
>   A. First supporting idea

Notice that the most important ideas are closer to the left margin. Less important ideas are indented toward the middle of the page. A quick glance at an outline shows what is most important, what is less important, and how ideas support or explain one another.

Using the Outline Format

1. **Do not be overly concerned with following the outline format exactly.** As long as your outline shows an organization of ideas, it will work for you.
2. **Write words and phrases rather than complete sentences.**
3. **Use your own words.** Do not lift words from the text.
4. **Do not write too much.** If you need to record numerous facts and details, underlining rather than outlining might be more effective.
5. **Pay attention to headings.** Be sure that all the information you place underneath a heading explains or supports that heading. Every heading indented the same amount on the page should be of equal importance.

Now read the following passage on sleep apnea and then study the outline of it.

Sleep Apnea

Sleep apnea is a disorder in which breathing is briefly and repeatedly interrupted during sleep. *Apnea* refers to a breathing pause that lasts at least 10 seconds. During that time, the chest may rise and fall, but little or no air may be exchanged, or the person may actually not breathe until the brain triggers a gasping inhalation. Sleep apnea affects more than 18 million Americans, or 1 in every 15 people.

There are two major types of sleep apnea: central and obstructive. *Central sleep apnea* occurs when the brain fails to tell the respiratory muscles to initiate breathing. Consumption of alcohol, certain illegal drugs, and certain medications can contribute to this condition. *Obstructive sleep apnea (OSA)*, which is the more common form, occurs when air cannot move in and out of a person's nose or mouth, even though the body tries to breathe.

> What key point does this photograph illustrate?

From insomnia to sleepwalking to narcolepsy, sleep disorders are more common than you might think. There are more than 80 different clinical sleep disorders, and it is estimated that between 50 and 70 million Americans—children and adults—suffer from one. Many aren't even aware of their disorder, and many others never seek treatment.

Typically, OSA occurs when a person's throat muscles and tongue relax during sleep and block the airways. People who are overweight or obese often have more tissue that flaps or sags, which puts them at higher risk for sleep apnea. People with OSA are prone to heavy snoring, snorting, and gasping. These sounds occur because, as oxygen saturation levels in the blood fall, the body's autonomic nervous system is stimulated to trigger inhalation, often via a sudden gasp of breath. This response may wake the person, preventing deep sleep and causing the person to wake up in the morning feeling tired and unwell. More serious risks of OSA include chronic high blood pressure, irregular heartbeats, heart attack, and stroke. Apnea-associated sleeplessness may be a factor in an increased risk of type 2 diabetes, immune system deficiencies, and a host of other problems.

—Donatelle, *Health: The Basics*,
pp. 94 and 96

Sleep Apnea

I. Disorder with brief, repeated interruptions in breathing
    A. Pause in breathing for at least 10 seconds
    B. Over 18 million Americans (1 in 15) affected

II. Two major types
    A. Central sleep apnea
        1. Occurs when brain fails to initiate breathing
        2. Associated with alcohol, drugs, medications
    B. Obstructive sleep apnea (OSA)
        1. Occurs when air can't move in and out despite body's efforts
            a. Throat muscles and tongue relax in sleep and block airways
        2. Overweight or obese people at higher risk
        3. Low levels of oxygen trigger snoring, gasping
        4. Many health effects/risks
            a. Feeling tired, unwell from lack of deep sleep
            b. High blood pressure, irregular heartbeats, heart attack, stroke
            c. Increased risk of type 2 diabetes, immune system deficiencies

EXERCISE 10-6   **Completing an Outline**

Directions: Read the following passage and the incomplete outline that follows. Fill in the missing information in the outline.

Changing Makeup of Families and Households

The traditional definition of a typical U.S. household was one that contained a husband, a nonworking wife, and two or more children. That type of household accounts for only about nine percent of households today. In its place we see many single-parent households, households without children, households of one person, and other nontraditional households. A number of trends have combined to create these changes in families and households. Americans are staying single longer—more than one-half of the women and three-quarters of the men between 20 and 24 years old in the United States are still single. Divorce rates are at an all-time high. It is predicted that almost two-thirds of first marriages may end up in divorce. There is a widening gap between the life expectancy of males and females. Currently average life expectancy in the United States is 74 years for men and 78 years for women. Widows now make up more than one-third of one-person households in the United States. These trends have produced a declining average size of household.

The impact of all these changes is significant for marketers. Nontraditional households have different needs for goods and services than do traditional households. Smaller households often have more income per person than larger households, and require smaller houses, smaller cars, and smaller package sizes for food products. Households without children often spend more on personal entertainment and respond more to fads than do traditional households. More money may be spent on travel as well.

—Kinnear et al., *Principles of Marketing*, pp. 39–40

I. Typical U.S. household has changed

  A. Used to consist of

    1. husband

    2. nonworking wife

    3. two or more children

  B. _____

    1. _____

    2. _____

    3. _____

II. Trends that created this change

  A. _____

    1. _____

    2. _____

  B. Divorce rates higher

    1. maybe two-thirds of marriages

  C. _____

    1. _____

    2. _____

III. Impact of changes for marketers

  A. Different goods and services needed

  B. _____

  C. _____

  D. _____

  E. _____

MAPPING

Mapping is a visual method of organizing information. It involves drawing diagrams to show how ideas in an article or chapter are related. Some students prefer mapping to outlining because they feel it is freer and less tightly structured.

Maps can take numerous forms. You can draw them in any way that shows the relationships of ideas. Figure 10-1 shows two sample maps. Each was drawn to show the overall organization of Chapter 6 in this book. First refer back to Chapter 6 and then study each map.

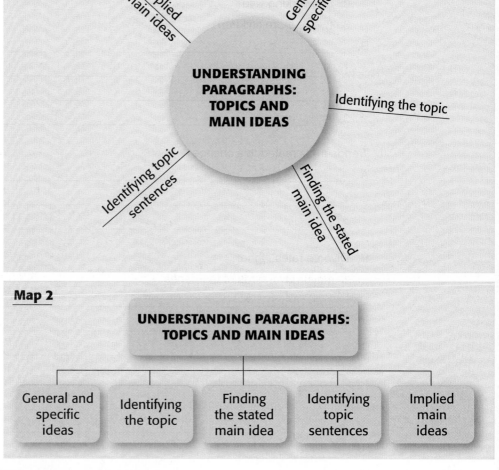

Figure 10-1   Sample maps

How to Draw Maps

Think of a map as a picture or diagram that shows how ideas are connected.

Drawing a Map

1. **Identify the overall topic or subject.** Write it in the center or at the top of the page.
2. **Identify major supporting information that relates to the topic.** Draw each piece of information on a line connected to the central topic.
3. **As you discover details that further explain an idea already mapped, draw a new line branching from the idea it explains.**

How you arrange your map will depend on the subject matter and how it is organized. Like an outline, it can be quite detailed or very brief, depending on your purpose. A portion of a more detailed map of Chapter 6 is shown in Figure 10-2.

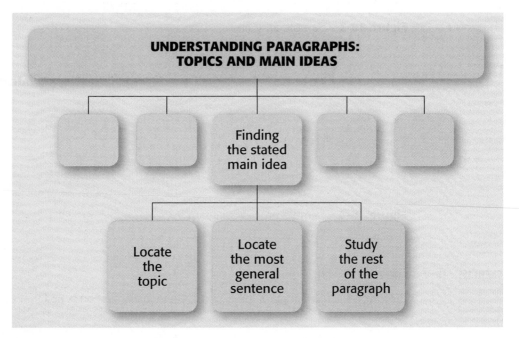

Figure 10-2   Map with greater detail

Once you are skilled at drawing maps, you can become more creative, drawing different types of maps to fit what you are reading. For example, you can draw a time line (see Figure 10-3) that shows historical events, or a process diagram to show processes and procedures (see Figure 10-4).

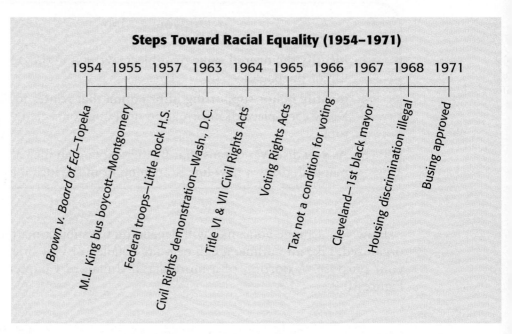

Figure 10-3   Sample time line

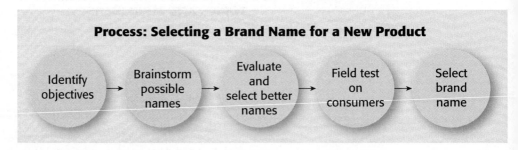

Figure 10-4   Sample process diagram

EXERCISE **10-7**   **Drawing a Map**

Directions: Draw a map of the excerpt "Generic Names" on p. 354.

EXERCISE 10-8   **Drawing a Map**

Directions: Draw a map of Chapter 7 of this book.

SUMMARIZING

A **summary** is a brief statement that reviews the major idea of something you have read. Its purpose is to make a record of the most important ideas in condensed form. A summary is much shorter than an outline and contains less detailed information.

    A summary goes one step beyond recording what the writer says. It pulls together the writer's ideas by condensing and grouping them.

How to Write a Summary

Before writing a summary, be sure you understand the material and have identified the writer's major points.

Steps in Writing a Summary

1. **Write a brief outline of the material or underline each major idea.**

2. **Write one sentence that states the writer's overall concern or most important idea.** To do this, ask yourself what one topic the material is about. Then ask what point the writer is trying to make about that topic. This sentence will be the topic sentence of your summary.

3. **Be sure to use your own words rather than those of the author.**

4. **Review the major supporting information that the author gives to explain the major ideas.** See Chapter 7 for further information.

5. **Decide on the level of detail you need.** The amount of detail you include, if any, will depend on your purpose for writing the summary.

6. **Normally, present ideas in the summary in the same order in which they appear in the original materials.**

7. **For other than textbook material, if the writer presents a clear opinion or expresses an attitude toward the subject matter, include it in your summary.**

8. **Do not concentrate on correctness when writing summaries for your own use.** Some students prefer to write summaries using words and phrases rather than complete sentences.

Read the following summary of "Changing Makeup of Families and Households," which appeared on p. 362.

Notice that this summary contains only the broadest, most important ideas. Details are not included. The first sentence shows how the typical household has changed, the second sentence lists the three trends that are causing this change, and the last sentence details the implications for marketers.

Sample Summary

> The typical U.S. household has changed from a husband, nonworking wife, and two or more children to a smaller-sized unit that might contain a single parent, no children, or even only one person. Three trends that have caused this change are: people are staying single longer, divorce rates are higher, and women are outliving men by more. Because of these changes, marketers have found that the current, smaller household needs different goods and services, has more income per person, tends to purchase smaller items, and spends more on entertainment, fads, and travel than the typical household of the past.

EXERCISE 10-9   **Writing a Summary**

Directions: Form teams of three or four students. Each team should choose and agree to watch a particular television show that airs before the next class. During the next class meeting, collaborate to write a summary of the show. Summaries may be presented to the class for discussion and evaluation.

EXERCISE 10-10   **Writing Summary**

Directions: On a separate sheet of paper, write a summary of one of the reading selections in Part Six of this text.

EXERCISE 10-11   **Writing a Summary**

Directions: Write a summary of the article "Sleep Apnea" on p. 361. When you have finished, compare it with the sample summary shown in Figure 10-5 on p. 369. Then answer the following questions.

1. How does your summary differ from the sample?

2. Did your summary begin with a topic sentence? How does it compare with the one in the sample?

3. Did your summary include ideas in the order in which they were given in the article?

> Sleep apnea is a disorder in which breathing is repeatedly interrupted during sleep, with pauses lasting at least 10 seconds. The two major types are central sleep apnea, in which the brain fails to initiate breathing, and obstructive sleep apnea (OSA), in which air is unable to move in and out of a person's nose or mouth, typically because airways are blocked. Falling oxygen saturation levels in the blood trigger sudden inhalation, which may prevent deep sleep. People with OSA may feel tired or unwell from sleep interruptions or they may face much more serious health problems.

Figure 10-5   Sample summary: "sleep apnea"

EXERCISE 10-12   ## Comparing Methods of Organization

Directions: Your instructor will choose a reading from Part Six and will then divide the class into three groups. Members of one group should outline the material, another group should draw maps, and the third should write summaries. When the groups have completed their tasks, the class members should review each other's work. Several students can read their summaries, draw maps, and write outlines on the chalkboard. Discuss which of the three methods seemed most effective for the material and how well prepared each group feels for (a) an essay exam, (b) a multiple-choice exam, and (c) a class discussion.

IMMEDIATE AND PERIODIC REVIEW

Once you have read and organized information, the last step is to learn it. Fortunately, this is not a difficult task if you have organized the information effectively. In fact, through underlining, outlining, and/or summarizing, you have already learned a large portion of the material. **Review**, then, is a way to fix, or store, information in your memory for later recall. There are two types of review, *immediate* and *periodic*.

How Immediate Review Works

Immediate review is done right after you have finished reading an assignment or writing an outline or summary. When you finish any of these, you may feel like breathing a sigh of relief and taking a break. However, it is worth the time and effort to spend another five minutes reviewing what you just read and refreshing your memory. The best way to do this is to go back through the chapter and reread the headings, graphic material, introduction, summary, and any underlining or marginal notes.

Immediate review works because it consolidates, or draws together, the material just read. It also gives a final, lasting impression of the content. Considerable research has been done on the effectiveness of immediate review. Results indicate that review done immediately rather than delayed until a later time makes a large difference in the amount remembered.

How Periodic Review Works

Although immediate review will increase your recall of information, it will not help you retain information for long periods of time. To remember information over time, periodically refresh your memory. This is known as **periodic review**. Go back over the material on a regular basis. Do this by looking again at those sections that carry the basic meaning and reviewing your underlining, outlining, and/or summaries. Below is an example of a schedule one student set up to periodically review assigned chapters in a psychology textbook. You can see that this student reviewed each chapter the week after reading it and again two weeks later. This schedule is only an example. You will need to make a schedule for each course that fits the course requirements. For math and science courses, for example, you may need to include a review of previous homework assignments and laboratory work. In other courses, less or more frequent review of previous material may be needed.

Week 1 Read ch. 1
Week 2 Review ch. 1
       Read ch. 2
Week 3 Review ch. 2
       Read ch. 3
Week 4 Review ch. 3
       Review ch. 1
       Read ch. 4
Week 5 Review ch. 4
       Review ch. 2
       Read ch. 5

EXERCISE 10-13   Planning a Review Schedule

Directions: Choose one of your courses that involves regular textbook reading assignments. Plan a reading and periodic review schedule for the next three weeks. Assume that new chapters will be assigned as frequently as in previous weeks and that you want to review whatever has been covered over the past three weeks.

LEARNING STYLE TIPS

If you tend to be a . . .	Strengthen your review strategies by . . .
Creative learner	Brainstorming before and after each assignment to discover new ways to tie the material together
Pragmatic learner	Creating, writing, and answering review questions; preparing and taking self-tests

SELF-TEST SUMMARY

OBJECTIVE 1 What is highlighting and marking and how are they used?	**Highlighting** is a way of sorting important information from less important information. It eliminates the need to reread entire textbook chapters in order to review their major content. It also has the advantage of helping you stay active and involved with what you are reading. **Marking** is a system that involves using signs, symbols, and marginal notes to react to, summarize, or comment on the material.
OBJECTIVE 2 What is outlining and how is it used?	**Outlining** is a method of recording the most important information and showing the organization and relative importance of ideas. It is particularly useful when you need to see how ideas relate to one another or when you want to get an overview of a subject.
OBJECTIVE 3 What is mapping and how is it used?	**Mapping** is a visual method of organizing information. It involves drawing diagrams to show how ideas in an article or chapter are related.
OBJECTIVE 4 What is summarizing and how is it used?	**Summarizing** is a way to pull together the most important ideas in condensed form. It provides a quick review of the material and forces you to explain the writer's ideas in your own words.
OBJECTIVE 5 Objective What are two types of review and how do they increase retention?	Immediate review is done right after finishing an assignment. It consolidates the material and makes it sticky in your memory. Periodic review is done regularly, at specified intervals. It keeps information fresh in your mind.

GOING ONLINE

1. Kinds of Concept Maps

    http://wik.ed.uiuc.edu/index.php/Concept_mapping#Kinds_of_Concept_Maps

    View these examples of the different types of concept maps. Using ideas, relationships, situations, and experiences from your own life, create a simple concept map of each type.

2. Textbook Marking

    http://ccc.byu.edu/textbook-marking

    Learn some strategies and see actual markings at this Brigham Young University site. Use them during your next textbook reading assignment. Write a paragraph about the advantages of highlighting and marking. Imagine you are trying to sway someone who thinks it is wrong to write in books.

3. Summarizing

    http://web.uvic.ca/wguide/Pages/SumEG.html

    Go through this exercise to practice summarizing information from a textbook. Then try it using one of your textbooks. Have a classmate read the summary and then the original. Ask for feedback on your summarizing skills.

 To check your progress in meeting chapter objectives, log in to **http://www.myreadinglab.com,** click on the Study Plan tab, and then click on the Reading Skills tab. Choose Note Taking and Highlighting from the list of subtopics. Read and view the information in the Review Materials section, and then complete the Practices and Tests in the Activities section. You can check your scores by clicking on the Gradebook tab.

MASTERY TEST 1 Mapping and Summarizing Skills

Name _____ Section _____

Date _____ Number right _____ × 20 points = Score _____

Directions: Read the passage below and then complete the map and the summary by answering the questions that follow each of them.

The first thing good listeners must do is figure out why they're listening. Researchers have identified five kinds of listening that reflect purposes you may have when communicating with others: appreciative, discriminative, empathic, comprehension, and critical.

Appreciative listening focuses on something other than the primary message. Some listeners enjoy seeing a famous speaker. Others relish a good speech, a classic movie, or a brilliant performance. On these occasions, you listen primarily to entertain yourself.

Discriminative listening requires listeners to draw conclusions from the way a message is presented rather than from what is said. In discriminative listening, people seek to understand the meaning behind the message. You're interested in what the speaker really thinks, believes, or feels. You're engaging in discriminative listening when you draw conclusions about how angry your parents are with you, based not on what they say but on how they say it. You draw inferences from the presentation of the message rather than from the message itself.

Empathic or therapeutic listening is intended to provide emotional support for the speaker. Although it is more typical of interpersonal than public communication, empathic listening does occur in public speaking situations, for example, when you hear an athlete apologize for unprofessional behavior or a classmate reveal a personal problem to illustrate a speech. In each case, your role is supportive.

Listening for comprehension occurs when you want to gain additional information or insights from the speaker. You are probably most familiar with this form of listening because you've relied heavily on it for your education. When you listen to a radio newscast, to a classroom lecture on marketing strategies, or to an elections official explaining new registration procedures, you're listening to understand—to comprehend information, ideas, and processes.

Critical listening is the most difficult kind of listening because it requires you to both interpret and evaluate the message. It demands that you go beyond understanding the message to interpreting it and evaluating its strengths and weaknesses. You'll practice this sort of listening in class. A careful consumer also uses critical listening to evaluate television commercials, political campaign speeches, or arguments offered by salespeople. When you are listening critically, you decide whether to accept or reject ideas and whether to act on the message.

—German and Gronbeck, *Principles of Public Speaking*, pp. 38–39

373

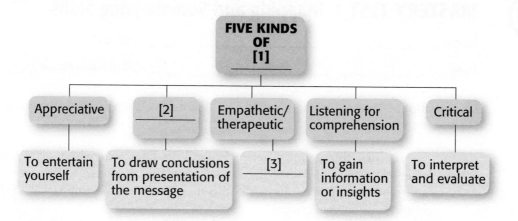

Refer to the map to answer questions 1–3.

_____ 1. The word that correctly fills in blank [1] is
a. purposes.
b. listening.
c. communicating.
d. responding.

_____ 2. The word that correctly fills in blank [2] is
a. conclusive.
b. emotional.
c. comprehensive.
d. discriminative.

_____ 3. The phrase that correctly fills in blank [3] is
a. to apologize for behavior.
b. to reveal a personal problem.
c. to illustrate a speech.
d. to provide emotional support.

Refer to the following summary of the passage to answer questions 4 and 5.

Summary: In communication, there are five types of listening. Appreciative listening is mainly for your own entertainment. Discriminative listening is when you have to figure out what the speaker means by _____ [4] _____. Empathic or therapeutic listening requires you to give emotional support to the speaker; it happens more in interpersonal communication than in public speaking situations. Listening for comprehension is when you are trying to learn information or gain understanding. Critical listening is the most difficult because you have to interpret and then _____ [5] _____ the message.

_____ 4. The phrase that correctly fills in blank [4] is
a. how the message is presented.
b. what the speaker says.
c. how you feel about the speaker.
d. what you want to hear.

_____ 5. The phrase that correctly fills in blank [5] is
a. understand.
b. repeat.
c. evaluate.
d. respond to.

MASTERY TEST 2 Outlining Skills

Name _____ Section _____

Date _____ Number right _____ × 10 points = Score _____

Directions: Read the following selection and answer the questions that follow.

PARTICIPATORY AND PASSIVE LISTENING

The general key to effective listening in interpersonal situations is active participation. Perhaps the best preparation for participatory listening is to act (physically and mentally) like a participant. For many people, this may be the most abused rule of effective listening. Recall, for example, how your body almost automatically reacts to important news: Almost immediately, you assume an upright posture, cock your head to the speaker, and remain relatively still and quiet. You do this almost reflexively because this is the way you listen most effectively. Even more important than this physical alertness is mental alertness. As a listener, participate in the communication interaction as an equal partner with the speaker, as one who is emotionally and intellectually ready to engage in the sharing of meaning.

Effective participatory listening is expressive. Let the listener know that you are participating in the communication interaction. Nonverbally, maintain eye contact, focus your concentration on the speaker rather than on others present, and express your feelings facially. Verbally, ask appropriate questions, signal understanding with "I see" or "yes," and express agreement or disagreement as appropriate.

Passive listening is, however, not without merit and some recognition of its value is warranted. Passive listening—listening without talking or directing the speaker in any obvious way—is a powerful means of communicating acceptance. This is the kind of listening that people ask for when they say, "Just listen to me." They are essentially asking you to suspend your judgment and "just listen." Passive listening allows the speaker to develop his or her thoughts and ideas in the presence of another person who accepts but does not evaluate, who supports but does not intrude. By listening passively, you provide a supportive and receptive environment. Once that has been established, you may wish to participate in a more active way, verbally and nonverbally.

—DeVito, *The Interpersonal Communication Book*, p. 141

_____ 1. Which of the following is the best out-line for paragraph 1?
    a. A. Actions of a participant
       1. physical
       2. interaction
    b. A. Actions of a participant
       1. sit straight
       2. be quiet
       3. head cocked
       4. be alert
    c. A. Physical actions
       1. sit straight
       2. be quiet
      B. mental actions
    d. A. Active participation in listening
       1. physical alertness
         a. sit straight
         b. quiet
         c. head cocked
       2. mental alertness

_____ 2. Which of the following is the best out-line for paragraph 2?
    a. B. Listening is expressive
       1. eye contact—maintain
       2. facial expressions verbally
       3. ask questions
    b. B. Communication interaction
       1. nonverbal
         a. agree / disagree
         b. signal understanding
       2. verbal
         a. eye contact
         b. facial expression
         c. ask questions
    c. B. Expressive participation
       1. nonverbal
         a. eye contact
         b. focus on speaker
         c. facial expressions
       2. verbal
         a. ask questions
         b. signal understanding
         c. agree / disagree

    d. B. Expressions of a participant
      C. Nonverbal expressions
      D. Verbal expressions

_____ 3. Which of the following is the best out-line for paragraph 3?
    a. C. Active listening
       1. definition
       2. reasons
    b. C. Reasons for passive listening
      D. Definition of passive listening
    c. C. Meaning of passive listening
       1. no talking or directing of speaker
       2. communicates acceptance
       3. suspend judgment and "just listen"
      D. Results of passive listening
       1. speaker can develop thoughts and ideas
       2. you provide supportive, receptive environment
    d. C. Passive listening
       1. judgmental
       2. supportive
       3. definition

_____ 4. Which group of words is best to highlight in the first sentence of the selection?
    a. key / effective listening / active participation
    b. general / interpersonal / participation
    c. general / key / situations / active
    d. key / interpersonal situations / is

_____ 5. Which of the following phrases from the first paragraph would be most important to highlight?
    a. cock your head
    b. for many people
    c. Recall, for example
    d. active participation

_____ 6. Which group of words is best to highlight in the last sentence of paragraph 2?

a. ask / questions / disagreement / as / appropriate

b. verbally / questions / signal / understanding / express / agreement / disagreement

c. ask / questions / signal / agreement / appropriate

d. verbally / I see / yes

_____ 7. Which of the following sentences from the last paragraph defines passive listening?

a. first   c. third

b. second   d. last

_____ 8. Which of the following marginal notations would be most useful for paragraph 1?

a. alert vs. engaged

b. still and quiet

c. physical actions / mental actions

d. physically alert

_____ 9. Which of the following marginal notations would be the best for paragraph 3?

a. passive listening = nonjudgmental & supportive

b. just listen = nonverbal

c. passive vs. active listening

d. listening vs. hearing

_____ 10. Which of the following maps best presents the ideas in the selection?

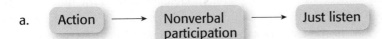

a. Action → Nonverbal participation → Just listen

b. Expressions → Actions → Supportive environment

c.
Actions
Passive   Active

d.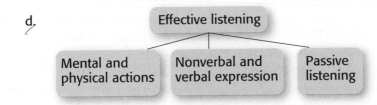
Effective listening
Mental and physical actions   Nonverbal and verbal expression   Passive listening

MASTERY TEST 3 Reading Selection

Name _____ Section _____

Date _____ Number right* _____ × 10 points = Score _____

Applying Psychology to Everyday Life: Are You Sleep Deprived?

Saundra K. Ciccarelli and J. Noland White

This selection, taken from a psychology textbook, explores the causes and hazards of sleep deprivation. Would you consider yourself sleep deprived?

> **Vocabulary Preview**
>
> **insomnia** (par. 4) the inability to fall asleep, stay asleep, or get enough sleep
>
> **narcolepsy** (par. 5) a disorder in which a person falls suddenly into a deep sleep

How serious is the problem of sleep deprivation?

1 Sleep deprivation has long been considered a fact of life for many people, especially college students. Dr. William Dement, one of the most renowned sleep experts in the field, believes that people are ignorant of the detrimental effects of sleep deprivation. Here are some of the facts he points out concerning the wide-spread nature of sleep deprivation:

- 55 percent of drowsy driving fatalities occur under the age of 25.
- 56 percent of the adult population reports that daytime drowsiness is a problem.
- In a study of 1,000 people who reported no daytime drowsiness, 34 percent were actually found to be dangerously sleepy.
- In samples of undergraduates, nurses, and medical students, 80 percent were dangerously sleep deprived.

2 Dr. Dement cautions that drowsiness should be considered a red alert. Contrary to many people's belief that drowsiness indicates the first step in failing asleep, he states that drowsiness is the last step—if you are drowsy, you are seconds away from sleep.

3 In an article published by CNN on its interactive Web site (**www.cnn.com/ HEALTH/9703/17/nfm/sleep.deprivation/index.html**), the National Commission on Sleep Disorders estimates that "sleep deprivation costs $150 billion a year in higher stress and reduced workplace productivity." Sleep deprivation was one of the factors indicated in such disasters as the explosion of the *Challenger*, the Exxon *Valdez* oil spill, and the Chernobyl disaster.

---

*To calculate the number right, use items 1–10 under "Mastery Test Skills Check."

The student in the background is unable to stay awake during his class, indicating that he is seriously sleep deprived. Has this happened to you?

More disturbing facts:

- 30 to 40 percent of all heavy truck accidents can be attributed to driver fatigue.
- Drivers who are awake for 17 to 19 hours were more dangerous than drivers with a blood alcohol level of .05.
- 16 to 60 percent of road accidents involve sleep deprivation (the wide variation is due to the inability to confirm the cause of accidents, as the drivers are often killed).
- Sleep deprivation is linked to higher levels of stress, anxiety, depression, and unnecessary risk taking.

4   Clearly, sleep deprivation is a serious and all-too-common problem. In today's 24-hour-a-day society, stores are always open, services such as banking and transporation are always available, and many professionals (such as nurses, doctors, and firefighters) must work varying shifts around the clock. As stated earlier, shift work can seriously disrupt the normal sleep–wake cycle, often causing insomnia.

CAUSES OF SLEEP DEPRIVATION

5   Many of the sleep disorders that were discussed in this chapter are themselves causes of sleep deprivation. Sleep apnea, narcolepsy, sleepwalking, night terrors, and a condition called "restless leg syndrome," in which a person constantly moves his or her legs that are tingly or have crawling sensations, are all causes. Yet these problems are not the sole, or most common, cause of sleep deprivation.

6   The most obvious cause is the refusal of many people to go to sleep at a reasonable time, so that they can get the 8 hours of sleep that most adults need in order to function well. People want to watch that last bit of news or get a little more work done or party into the wee hours. Another reason for sleep loss is worry. People live in stressful times, and many people worry about a variety of concerns: debts, the stock market, relationships, war, rising crime, and so on. Finally, some medications that people take, both prescription and over-the-counter drugs, interfere with the sleep–wake cycle. For example, decongestants that some people take to relieve sinus congestion may cause a racing heartbeat, preventing them from relaxing enough to sleep.

How Can You Tell If You Are Sleep Deprived?

7   You may be sleep deprived if you:

- actually need your alarm clock to wake up.
- find getting out of bed in the morning is a struggle.
- feel tired, irritable, or stressed out for much of the day.
- have trouble concentrating or remembering.
- fall asleep watching TV, in meetings, lectures, or warm rooms.
- fall asleep after heavy meals or after a low dose of alcohol.
- fall asleep within 5 minutes of getting into bed. (A well-rested person actually takes 15 to 20 minutes to fall asleep.)

8   If you are interested in learning more about sleep deprivation and sleep disorders that can cause it, try searching the Internet. There are some excellent sites about sleep and sleep disorders, including many with online tests that can help people decide whether or not they have a sleep disorder. Here are a few good sites:

- Sleepnet.com at **www.sleepnet.com** has detailed information about sleep disorders.
- The Sleep Mall at **www.sleepnet.com/sleeptest.html** has a sleep test that tests for many different kinds of sleep disorders.
- National Sleep Foundation at **www.sleepfoundation.org** has many links to sites with information about sleep, disorders, and sleep tips.

MASTERY TEST SKILLS CHECK

Directions: Select the choice that best completes each of the following statements.

Checking Your Comprehension

_____ 1. The focus of this selection is on
   a. the sleep-wake cycle.
   b. brain activity during sleep.
   c. sleep deprivation.
   d. common sleep disorders.

_____ 2. The main idea of paragraph 1 is that
   a. sleep deprivation is a fact of life for college students.
   b. sleep deprivation is widespread and harmful.
   c. Dr. William Dement is an authority on sleep deprivation.
   d. drowsiness is actually a sign of being dangerously sleepy.

_____ 3. Of the following signs, the only one that does *not* indicate you may be sleep deprived is
   a. you actually need your alarm clock to wake up.
   b. you fall asleep after heavy meals.
   c. it takes you 15 to 20 minutes to fall asleep after going to bed.
   d. it is a struggle to get out of bed in the morning.

_____ 4. According to the selection, the most obvious cause of sleep deprivation is
  a. restless leg syndrome.
  b. narcolepsy.
  c. sleep apnea.
  d. the failure to go to bed at a reasonable time.

_____ 5. The authors use all of the following types of supporting details in this selection *except*
  a. examples.   c. statistics.
  b. facts.   d. procedures.

Applying Your Skills

_____ 6. The most important words to highlight in the last sentence of paragraph 2 are
  a. drowsiness sleep.
  b. drowsiness last step from sleep.

  c. many people's belief drowsiness first step falling asleep last step drowsy away from sleep.
  d. Contrary many people's belief drowsiness indicates first step falling asleep drowsiness is last step you are drowsy seconds away from sleep.

_____ 7. The most important words to highlight in last sentence of paragraph 4 are
  a. shift work seriously normal.
  b. work can disrupt normal cycle often.
  c. shift work disrupt sleep–wake cycle insomnia.
  d. shift work seriously disrupt normal sleep–wake cycle often insomnia.

Use the following outline of paragraphs 5 and 6 to answer questions 8–10.

Causes of Sleep Deprivation

I. Sleep disorders

  A. Sleep apnea

  B. Narcolepsy

  C. _Sleep walking_

  D. Night terrors

  E. _rest less leg syndrome_

    1. Tingly/crawling sensations cause legs to move

II. Refusal to go to bed on time

III. Worry

IV. _Medications_

  A. Prescription and over-the-counter

  B. Interfere with sleep-wake cycle

_____ 8. The phrase that belongs next to [C] in the outline is
  a. Sleep deprivation.
  b. Sleepwalking.
  c. Sleep–wake cycle.
  d. Sleep disorder.

_____ 9. The phrase that belongs next to [E] in the outline is
  a. Shift work.
  b. Common cause.
  c. Restless leg syndrome.
  d. Sleepwalking.

_____ 10. The word or words that belong next to [IV] in the outline are
  a. Some medications.
  b. Illegal drugs.
  c. Decongestants.
  d. Racing heartbeat.

Studying Words

_____ 11. The word *renowned* (par. 1) means
  a. unpopular.
  b. famous.
  c. unfamiliar.
  d. local.

_____ 12. The word *detrimental* (par. 1) means
  a. harmful.
  b. emotional.
  c. pleasant.
  d. skillful.

_____ 13. The word *cautions* (par. 2) means
  a. reminds.
  b. guesses.
  c. warns.
  d. allows.

_____ 14. The prefix of the word *interactive* (par. 3) means
  a. away.
  b. between.
  c. over.
  d. without.

_____ 15. The word *disrupt* (par. 4) means
  a. assist.
  b. surround.
  c. maintain.
  d. disturb.

For more practice, ask your instructor for an opportunity to work on the mastery tests that appear in the Test Bank.

Summarizing the Reading

Directions: Complete the following summary of the reading by filling in the blanks.

Sleep deprivation is _____.

The National Commission on _____ estimates _____

_____. Sleep

deprivation was a factor _____ and is linked to _____

_____

_____. Sleep deprivation may be caused by _____

_____.

Reading Visually

1. What does the photograph contribute to the reading overall? What details do you notice about it that are relevant to the reading?
2. What is the purpose of the box included with the reading? How might the information in the box be helpful to the author's audience?
3. If you can, take the sleep test mentioned in paragraph 8. Did you identify a sleep problem?

Thinking Critically about the Reading

WRITE IN YOUR
JOURNAL

1. Do you consider yourself sleep deprived? Were you aware of any of the serious effects before you read this selection?
2. How does our "24-hour-a-day society" contribute to the problem of sleep deprivation?
3. If you knew someone suffering from sleep deprivation, what advice would you give him or her?

CHAPTER 11

Interpreting the Writer's Message and Purpose

Looking at …
Interpreting What You Read

Frank and Ernest

SOON WE'LL GIVE UP DOLLS AND HOPSCOTCH---BUT THEY'LL BE INTO FOOTBALL FOREVER.

12-10
THAVES

E-mail:BobThaves@aol.com
©2002 Thaves / Dist. by NEA, Inc.
www.frankandernest.com

LEARNING OBJECTIVES

This chapter will show you how to:

OBJECTIVE **1** 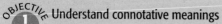 Understand connotative meanings

OBJECTIVE **2** 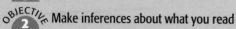 Make inferences about what you read

OBJECTIVE **3** 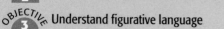 Understand figurative language

OBJECTIVE **4** 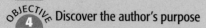 Discover the author's purpose

OBJECTIVE **5** 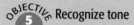 Recognize tone

OBJECTIVE **6** 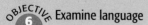 Examine language

What point or message does this cartoon convey? While the point is clear, it is not directly stated. You had to use the information in the cartoon to reason out its point. This chapter concentrates on the reasoning processes readers must use to figure out ideas that are not directly stated.

Up to this point, we have been primarily concerned with building vocabulary, understanding a writer's basic organizational patterns, acquiring factual information, and organizing that information for learning and recall. So far, each chapter has been concerned with understanding what the author *says*, with factual content. Now our focus must change. To read well, you must go beyond what the author says and also consider what he or she *means*.

Many writers directly state some ideas but only hint at others. It is left to the reader to pick up the clues or suggestions and use logic and reasoning skills to figure out the writer's unstated message as you did in the cartoon on the previous page. This chapter will explain several features of writing that suggest meaning. Once you are familiar with these, you will better understand the writer's unstated message. This chapter will also discuss how to discover the author's purpose and recognize tone.

CONNOTATIVE MEANINGS

OBJECTIVE 1

Which of the following would you like to be a part of: a *crowd, mob, gang, audience, congregation,* or *class*? Each of these words has the same basic meaning: "an assembled group of people." But each has a different *shade* of meaning. *Crowd* suggests a large, disorganized group. *Audience,* on the other hand, suggests a quiet, controlled group. Try to decide what meaning each of the other words in the list suggests.

This example shows that words have two levels of meaning—a literal meaning and an additional shade of meaning. These two levels of meaning are called denotative and connotative. A word's **denotative meaning** is the meaning stated in the dictionary—its literal meaning. A word's **connotative meaning** is the additional implied meanings, or nuances, that a word may take on. Often the connotative meaning carries either a positive or negative, favorable or unfavorable impression. The words *mob* and *gang* have a negative connotation because they imply a disorderly, disorganized group. *Congregation, audience,* and *class* have a positive connotation because they suggest an orderly, organized group.

Here are a few more examples. Would you prefer to be described as "slim" or "skinny"? As "intelligent" or "brainy"? As "heavy" or "fat"? As "particular" or "picky"? Notice that each pair of words has a similar literal meaning, but that each word within the pair has a different connotation.

Depending on the words they choose, writers can suggest favorable or unfavorable impressions of the person, object, or event they are describing. For example, through the writer's choice of words, the following two sentences create two entirely different impressions. As you read them, underline words that have a positive or negative connotation.

> The unruly crowd forced its way through the restraint barriers and ruthlessly attacked the rock star.
>
> The enthusiastic group of fans burst through the fence and rushed toward the rock star.

When reading any type of informative or persuasive material, pay attention to the writer's choice of words. Often a writer may communicate subtle or hidden messages, or he or she may encourage the reader to feel positive or negative toward the subject.

Read the following paragraph on athletes' nutrition and, as you read, underline words that have a strong positive or negative connotation.

> Athletes tend to eat either too much or too little protein, depending on their health consciousness, accuracy of nutrition education, or lifestyle. Some athletes fill up on too much meat. Others proclaim themselves vegetarian, yet they sometimes neglect to replace the beef with beans and are, in fact, only non-meat-eaters—and often protein deficient, at that. Although slabs of steak and huge hamburgers have no place in any athlete's diet—or anyone's diet—adequate amounts of protein are important for building muscles and repairing tissues.
>
> —Clark, *Nancy Clark's Sports Nutrition Guidebook*, pp. 21–22

EXERCISE **11-1** ## Examining Connotative Meanings

Directions: For each of the following pairs of words, underline the word with the more positive connotation.

1. request   demand

2. overlook   neglect

3. ridicule   tease

4. glance   stare

5. display   expose

6. garment   gown

7. gaudy   showy

8. clumsy   awkward

9. artificial   fake

10. token   keepsake

EXERCISE 11-2   **Writing Positive Connotations**

Directions: For each word listed below, write a word that has a similar denotative meaning but a negative connotation. Then write a word that has a positive connotation. Use your dictionary or thesaurus, if necessary.

	Negative	Positive
Example: eat	gobble	dine tuck in
1. take	steal. grab. pinch.	carry
2. ask	demand.	request
3. look at	star	inspect. observe
4. walk	stagger	wander.
5. dress	attire	clothes. garment
6. music		
7. car	beater.	
8. laugh	derisive	smile
9. large	fat.	massive. huge
10. woman	broad	lady.

IMPLIED MEANINGS

An **inference** is an educated guess or prediction about something unknown based on available facts and information. It is the logical connection that you draw between what you observe or know and what you do not know.

Suppose that you arrive ten minutes late for your sociology class. All the students have papers in front of them, and everyone is busily writing. Some students have worried or concerned looks on their faces. The instructor is seated and is reading a book. What is happening? From the known information you can make an inference about what you do not know. Did you figure out that the instructor had given the class a surprise quiz? If so, then you made a logical inference.

While the inference you made is probably correct, you cannot be sure until you speak with the instructor. Occasionally a logical inference can be wrong. Although it is unlikely, perhaps the instructor has laryngitis and has written notes on the board for the students to copy. Some students may look worried because they do not understand what the notes mean.

Here are more everyday situations. Make an inference for each.

- You are driving on an expressway and you notice a police car with flashing red lights behind you. You check your speedometer and notice that you are going ten miles an hour over the speed limit.

- A woman seated alone in a bar nervously glances at everyone who enters. Every few minutes she checks her watch.

In the first situation, a good inference might be that you are going to be stopped for speeding. However, it is possible that the officer only wants to pass you to get to an accident ahead or to stop someone driving faster than you. In the second situation, one inference is that the woman is waiting to meet someone who is late.

The following paragraphs are taken from a book by David Sedaris titled *Holidays on Ice*. First, read them for factual content.

A Christmas Elf

I was in a coffee shop looking through the want ads when I read, "Macy's Herald Square, the largest store in the world, has big opportunities for outgoing, fun-loving people of all shapes and sizes who want more than just a holiday job! Working as an elf in Macy's Santa Land means being at the center of the excitement. . . ."

I circled the ad and then I laughed out loud at the thought of it. The man seated next to me turned on his stool, checking to see if I was a lunatic. I continued to laugh, quietly. Yesterday I applied for a job at UPS. They are hiring drivers' helpers for the upcoming Christmas season and I went to their headquarters filled with hope. In line with three hundred other men and women my hope diminished. During the brief interview I was asked why I wanted to work for UPS and I answered that I wanted to work for UPS because I like the brown uniforms. What did they expect me to say?

"I'd like to work for UPS because, in my opinion, it's an opportunity to show-case my substantial leadership skills in one of the finest private delivery companies this country has seen since the Pony Express!"

I said I liked the uniforms and the UPS interviewer turned my application face-down on his desk and said, "Give me a break."

I came home this afternoon and checked the machine for a message from UPS but the only message I got was from the company that holds my student loan, Sallie Mae. Sallie Mae sounds like a naive and barefoot hillbilly girl but in fact they are a ruthless and aggressive conglomeration of bullies located in a tall brick build-ing somewhere in Kansas. I picture it to be the tallest building in that state and I have decided they hire their employees straight out of prison. It scares me.

The woman at Macy's asked, "Would you be interested in full-time elf or evening and weekend elf?"

I said, "Full-time elf."

I have an appointment next Wednesday at noon.

I am a thirty-three-year-old man applying for a job as an elf.

—Sedaris, *Holidays on Ice*, pp. 3–4

These paragraphs are primarily factual—they tell who did what, when, and where. However, some ideas are not directly stated and must be inferred from the information given. Here are a few examples. Some are fairly obvious in-ferences; others are less obvious.

- The author is unemployed.
- The author has attended college.
- The author dislikes Sallie Mae.
- The author did not expect to get the UPS job.
- The UPS interviewer was annoyed with the author.
- Macy's celebrates the Christmas holidays.
- The author is not proud to be applying for a job as an elf.
- The author distrusts Sallie Mae's employees.

Although none of the above ideas is directly stated, they can be inferred from clues provided in the passage. Some of the statements could be inferred from actions, others by adding facts together, and still others by the writer's choice of words.

Now read the following passage to find out what has happened to Katja's brother.

Due to her own hardship, Katja was not thrilled when her younger brother called her from Warsaw and said that he was going to join her in the U.K. Katja warned him that opportunities were scarce in London for a Polish immigrant. "Don't worry," he said in an effort to soothe her anxiety. "I already have a job in a factory."

An advertisement in a Warsaw paper had promised good pay for Polish workers in Birmingham. A broker's fee of $500 and airfare were required, so her brother borrowed the money from their mother. He made the trip with a dozen other young Polish men.

The "broker" picked the young men up at Heathrow and piled them in a van. They drove directly to Birmingham, and at nightfall the broker dropped the whole crew off at a ramshackle house inside the city. He ordered them to be ready to be picked up in the morning for their first day of work. A bit dazed by the pace, they stretched out on the floor to sleep.

Their rest was brief. In the wee hours of the night, the broker returned with a gang of 10 or so thugs armed with cricket bats. They beat the young Polish boys to a pulp and robbed them of all their valuables. Katja's brother took some heavy kicks to the ribs and head, then stumbled out of the house. Once outside, he saw two police cars parked across the street. The officers in the cars obviously chose to ignore the mayhem playing out in front of their eyes. Katja's brother knew better than try to convince them otherwise; the police in Poland would act no differently. Who knows, maybe they were part of the broker's scam. Or maybe they just didn't care about a bunch of poor Polish immigrants "invading" their town.

—Batstone, "Katja's Story," as appeared in *Sojourners Magazine*, June 2006

If you made the right inferences, you realized that Katja's brother became a victim of a scam. Let's look at the kinds of clues the writer gave that led to this inference.

1. **Description.** By the way the writer describes what happened to Katja's brother, you begin to understand the situation. He is promised a well-paying job, but is told that job opportunities are scarce for Polish immigrants. A broker's fee of $500 is charged. The house they are taken to on arrival is described as *ramshackle*. The young men slept on the floor.

2. **Conversation.** The brother sounded very confident, perhaps overconfident: "Don't worry. I already have a job in a factory."

3. **Action.** The actions make it clear what is happening. The brother is "piled" into a van with 12 other workers. They are robbed and brutally beaten after arriving at the house. The police do not respond.

4. **Writer's commentary/details.** As the writer describes the situation, he provides numerous clues. The trip was made with a dozen other men. The word *broker* is placed in quotation marks, suggesting the term is inaccurate or questionable. The men's rest was described as *brief*, suggesting that something is about to change. The broker returns with people the writer calls a "gang of . . . thugs." The police are described as having obviously chosen "to ignore the mayhem."

How to Make Inferences

Making an inference is a thinking process. As you read, you are following the author's thoughts. You are also alert for ideas that are suggested but not directly stated. Because inference is a logical thought process, there is no simple step-by-step procedure to follow. Each inference depends entirely on the situation, the facts provided, and the reader's knowledge and experience.

However, here are a few guidelines to keep in mind as you read. These will help you get in the habit of looking beyond the factual level to the inferential.

Making Inferences

1. **Be sure you understand the literal meaning.** You should have a clear grasp of the key idea and supporting details of each paragraph.

2. **Notice details.** Often a detail provides a clue that will help you make an inference. When you spot a striking or unusual detail, ask yourself: Why did the writer include this piece of information?

3. **Add up the facts.** Consider all the facts taken together. Ask yourself: What is the writer trying to suggest from this set of facts? What do all these facts and ideas point toward?

4. **Watch for clues.** The writer's choice of words and detail often suggest his or her attitude toward the subject. Notice, in particular, descriptive words, emotionally charged words, and words with strong positive or negative connotations.

5. **Be sure your inference is supportable.** An inference must be based on fact. Make sure there is sufficient evidence to justify any inference you make.

EXERCISE 11-3   ## Making Inferences

Directions: Read each of the following passages. Then answer the questions that follow. You will need to reason out, or infer, the answers.

Passage A

Schmoozing

If we want to be successful, we need to develop and enhance our conversational prowess in the face to face space. Schmooze or lose is the rule for both personal and professional success. Schmooze means relaxed, friendly, easygoing conversation. Period. End of story. There is no end result that is preplanned as a goal. Formal research from Harvard to Stanford and places in between indicates that the ability to converse and communicate is a key factor of successful leaders. Oral communication skills are consistently rated in the top three most important skill sets in surveys by universities and workplace specialists.

While we're able to communicate digitally, we must still be proficient in the face to face shared space as well as in cyberspace. As corporations continue to merge, jobs disappear and industries are offshored, we need conversation and communication more than ever before.

—Ane, *Face to Face*, pp. 2–3

1. What is the author's attitude toward digital communication?

   positive
   _____

2. Not everyone loves to schmooze. Why does the author think it is essential for success?

   _____

3. What information sources does the author trust?

   _____

4. What do you think the author considers success to be?

   _____

What does this photograph illustrate about surveillance?

Passage B

Government Surveillance

Governments have long relied on . . . spying. What is new about today's surveillance is the ease with which it can be conducted; over the past several decades, technological advances have vastly expanded the government's monitoring ability. Wiretapping and bugging have been joined by space-age eavesdropping and computer-hacking techniques that make interception of oral and written communications infinitely easier than in J. Edgar Hoover's day. Observation of physical activities, once reliant on naked eye observation and simple devices like binoculars, can now be carried out with night scopes and thermal imagers, sophisticated telescopic and magnification devices, tracking tools and "see-through" detection technology. Records of transactions with hospitals, banks, stores, schools, and other institutions, until the 1980s usually found only in file cabinets, are now much more readily obtained with the advent of computers and the Internet.

A second difference between the surveillance of yesteryear and today is the strength of the government's resolve to use it. Especially since September 11, 2001, the United States government has been obsessed, as perhaps it should be, with ferreting out national security threats, and modern surveillance techniques—ranging from data mining to global positioning systems—have played a major role in this pursuit. But the new surveillance has also increasingly been aimed at ordinary criminals, including those who represent only a trivial threat to public safety. And more than occasionally it has also visited significant intrusion on large numbers of law-abiding citizens—sometimes inadvertently, sometimes not.

Sophisticated surveillance technology and a powerful government eager to take advantage of it make a dangerous combination—a recipe for continuous mass surveillance. While surveillance can be a valuable law enforcement tool, it also poses a significant threat to our legitimate freedoms—to express what we believe, to do what we want to do, to be the type of person we really are. In short, it can diminish our privacy and autonomy.

—Slobogin, *Privacy at Risk*, pp. 3–4

1. What is the author's attitude toward the government?

2. Why should the government be more interested in monitoring the behavior of its citizens today?

3. How are surveillance techniques being misused?

4. Where do you think the author stands on the issue of right to privacy? (What rights to privacy do we or should we have?)

Passage C

George Washington

George Washington is remembered not for what he was but for what he should have been. It doesn't do any good to point out that he was an "inveterate landgrabber," and that as a young man he illegally had a surveyor stake out some prize territory west of the Alleghenies in an area decreed off limits to settlers. Washington is considered a saint, and nothing one says is likely to make him seem anything less. Though he was a wily businessman and accumulated a fortune speculating in frontier lands, he will always be remembered as a farmer—and a "simple farmer" at that.

Even his personal life is misremembered. While Washington admitted despising his mother and in her dying years saw her infrequently, others remembered his mother fondly and considered him a devoted son. While his own records show he was something of a dandy and paid close attention to the latest clothing designs, ordering "fashionable" hose, the "neatest shoes," and coats with "silver trimmings," practically no one thinks he was vain. Though he loved to drink and dance and encouraged others to join him, the first President is believed to have been something of a prude.

—Shenkman, *Legends, Lies, and Cherished Myths of American History,* pp. 37–38

1. Describe how Washington is usually remembered.

   _____

   _____

2. Describe the author's attitude toward Washington.

   _____

   _____

3. Does the author think attitudes toward Washington are likely to change?

   _____

   _____

4. Explain the term "inveterate landgrabber."

   _____

   _____

5. Why do you think there is such a discrepancy between what Washington did and how he is remembered?

   _____

   _____

Passage D

Personal Comfort Zone

It's an uncomfortable fact of life, but there are people in this world who simply can't live in peace with their fellow human beings. You try to cultivate a love your neighbor philosophy, and then some mutant wrecks it by killing you. Regrettably, one violent encounter can cut short a lifetime of altruism. So you must make a personal decision either to be wholly trusting (and vulnerable) or ever vigilant. Vigilance doesn't mean you have to walk around angry. Indeed, if you take the emotion out of it, vigilance merely becomes a relaxed, practical exercise for fully participating in life.

For example, establish a personal comfort zone that no stranger is allowed to enter. This is not paranoia, just good practical sense. You need a trigger that allows you to stay relaxed most of the time. At a minimum, the zone is about as far as you can extend your arm or leg.

—Perkins et al., *Attack Proof*, p. 7

1. What attitude would you predict the author would have toward his co-workers?

   wary

   _____

2. How realistic is it to keep a stranger-proof comfort zone the distance of our outstretched arm?

   _____

3. Does the author anticipate that not all readers will agree with his ideas? How do you know?

   _____

   _____

4. How would the author define the term *comfort zone*?

   _____

EXERCISE **11-4**   ## Making Inferences

Directions: Read each of the following passages and answer the questions that follow.

Passage A

Working Moms

Always a career woman, Sharon Allen panicked when she had her first child. "I thought, 'How can I have my career and a child?'" recalls the now-longtime law enforcement official. "The minute I held her, I knew she was the most important thing in my life."

Thus began Allen's personal and professional journey as a working mother and wife (she's been married to her husband for 28 years) that blended child care with police work. Whether she was a detective or now the assistant police chief, she had irregular hours and at one time worked a 4–10 shift giving her three days off—one day to take care of the house, one to be at the kids' school, and one for herself. During that time, she earned her BS and Masters Degree in Education at a local college, and even worked part-time as a security guard at a mall to make ends meet.

"I was doing well with my career even as a working mother before it was in style . . . and yes, sometimes I felt I had to work twice as hard. I made mistakes, too, such as when my son was in high school, and I badgered him to cut his long hair. 'Mother,' he said, 'I am a good person . . . I follow your rules and stay out of trouble . . . If I have long hair, it's not a big deal;' I learned to compromise. (He's now at West Point!)

"That 'S' on my chest can fade sometimes. I used to crash and burn and sleep on the weekends. People say I am so successful—I say if my children have grown up to be self-sufficient, good citizens, I've been a pretty good mom. Half the battle in life is choosing something you love to do. You need to have that sense of accomplishment in your heart and to serve people the way you would like to be served. That's key."

—Greenberg and Avigdor, *What Happy Working Mothers Know*, p. 97

1. What is Sharon Allen's attitude toward working mothers?

   _____

2. What does the "S" on her chest stand for?

   _____

3. Why do you think the author chose to profile Sharon Allen for a book about happy working mothers?

   _____

   _____

4. Why might Sharon have had to work twice as hard as others?

   _____

   _____

Passage B

Why Manners Matter

When we leave home, driven by the overwhelming need to earn a living or go to the January sales or eat good Italian food, our apprehension about what we might encounter in the world proves to be negatively reinforcing. We put on our dark glasses and avoid eye contact. Increasingly we plug in our iPods: less for tuning into the music than tuning out the people around us. We talk or text on our cell phones constantly, on the train or bus, in the shops and cinemas, on the street. It's as if we deprive ourselves of immediate sensory stimulation—shade our eyes, block our ears, stop our mouths—in order to experience the world through a protective mask.

Finally, when with reluctant resignation we do interact with a stranger—with say, a taxi driver or a coffee barista or a checkout person at the supermarket—we do it all with sign language and half sentences, often still talking on the phone to someone (anyone!) else as if to distract our attention away from the irritations inherent in any physical, material encounter with untested individuals. People we need, and upon whose goodwill we depend.

In our efforts to avoid all the latent rudeness and unpleasantness in the world, we, too, have become harder, and ruder, and less pleasant. Yet the more we distrust each other, the more we are confused and irritated by each other, the greater the risk that we abandon the task of finding a common language with which to peacefully interact.

In my block of units there's a different but connected problem. We share the same building, we see each other regularly, we pass close by each other in the foyer and on the stairs. But because we don't have manners, we have no formula for successfully relating to each other. Living in the noisy hubbub of the city, each one of us wants to protect our privacy, especially at home. Me, too. I consider myself something of an urban hermit. I don't want to be friends with people purely because we live in close proximity. On the other hand, it's rather strange to pretend you have no knowledge of someone who lives across the hall.

So when we cross paths we all shut our eyes or mumble Hi—but it's awkward. No one wants to cross that dreaded threshold into cozy familiarity or, God forbid, mutual obligation. Here is where manners would come in handy. In a more mannered world, we'd simply get the introductions over with, have a cup of tea and then return to pleasant but formal distance. Good morning Lovely day, isn't it? we would say. But instead we scuff and shuffle and we're not sure whether to smile or not and the whole process is uncomfortable. The fear of over familiarity with our neighbors has led to an inability to relate to each other in any way at all.

—Holdforth, *Why Manners Matter*, pp. 16–17

> What idea in the passage does this photograph illustrate?

1. What assumption does the author make about anyone who ventures out in public?

   _____

2. Why does the author think that people want to isolate themselves?

   _____

3. The author infers that people feel uncomfortable around close neighbors because they scuff and shuffle. Is this a reasonable inference?

   _____

4. How and why would manners be helpful?

   _____

5. The author states we talk on phones to avoid talking to people face-to-face. Do you agree with this assumption?

   _____

Making Inferences

Directions: Bring a magazine ad to class. Working in groups of three or four students, make as many inferences as possible about each ad. For example, answer questions such as "What is happening?" "How does each person feel?" and "How will this ad sell the product?" Group members who differ in their opinions should present evidence to support their own inferences. Each group should then state to the class, as clearly as possible, the purpose of each ad. Be specific; try to say more than "To sell the product."

FIGURATIVE LANGUAGE

Read each of the following statements:

> The cake tasted like a moist sponge.
> The wilted plants begged for water.
> Jean wore her heart on her sleeve.

You know that a cake cannot really have the same taste as a sponge, that plants do not actually request water, and that a person's heart cannot really be attached to her sleeve. However, you know what message the writer is communicating in each sentence. The cake was soggy and tasteless, the plants were extremely dry, and Jean revealed her feelings to everyone around her.

Each of these sentences is an example of figurative language. **Figurative language** is a way of describing something that makes sense on an imaginative level but not on a factual or literal level. Notice that while none of the above expressions is literally true, each is meaningful. In many figurative expressions, one thing is compared with another for some quality they have in common. Take, for example, the familiar expression in the following sentence:

> Sam eats like a horse.

The diagram below shows the comparison being made in this figurative expression:

> A horse eats large amounts of food.
>
> Sam eats large amounts of food.
>
> Sam eats like a horse.

You can see that two unlike things—Sam and a horse—are compared because they are alike in one particular way—the amount they eat.

The purpose of figurative language is to paint a word picture—to help you visualize how something looks, feels, or smells. Figurative language is a device writers use to express an idea or feeling and, at the same time, allow the reader the freedom of imagination. Since it is not factual, figurative language allows the writer to express attitudes and opinions without directly stating them. Depending on the figurative expression chosen, a writer can create a variety of impressions.

When reading an article that contains figurative language, be sure to pay close attention to the images and feelings created. Be sure you recognize that the writer is shaping your response to the topic or subject.

Figurative language is used in many types of articles and essays. It is also used in everyday speech and in slang expressions. Various types of literature, especially poetry, also use figurative language. Notice its use in the following excerpt from a play by William Shakespeare.

> All the world's a stage,
> And all the men and women merely players;
> They have their exits and entrances;
> And one man in his time plays many parts.
>
> —Shakespeare, *As You Like It*, II, vii,139

Here are a few more examples from other sources. Notice how each creates a visual image of the person, object, or quality being described.

> The red sun was pasted in the sky like a wafer.
>
> —Stephen Crane, *The Red Badge of Courage*

> In plucking the fruit of memory,
> one runs the risk of spoiling its bloom.
>
> —Joseph Conrad

> "I will speak daggers to her, but use none."
>
> —Shakespeare, *Hamlet*

> Life, like a dome of many-colored glass,
> Stains the white radiance of Eternity.
>
> —Shelley, "Adonais"

> Float like a butterfly, sting like a bee.
>
> —Muhammad Ali

EXERCISE **11-6**   **Analyzing Figurative Expressions**

Directions: Each of the following sentences includes a figurative expression. Read each sentence and explain in your own words what the expression means.

1. My psychology quiz was a piece of cake.

   _____simple_____

2. My life is a junkyard of broken dreams.

   _____

3. "Life is as tedious as a twice-told tale." (Shakespeare, *King John III*)

   _____

4. "A sleeping child gives me the impression of a traveler in a very far country." (Ralph Waldo Emerson)

   _____

5. "I refuse to accept the notion that nation after nation must spiral down a militaristic stairway into the hell of nuclear war." (Martin Luther King, Jr.)

   _____

EXERCISE **11-7**   **Analyzing Passages**

Directions: Read each of the following passages and answer the questions that follow.

Passage A

Love in the Afternoon—In a Crowded Prison Hall

1   Each time I visit my man in prison, I relive the joy of reunion—and the anguish of separation.

2   We meet at the big glass door at the entrance to the small visitors' hall at Lompoc Federal Correctional Institution. We look at each other silently, then turn and walk into a room jammed with hundreds of molded fiberglass chairs lined up side by side. Finding a place in the crowded hall, we sit down, appalled that we're actually in a prison. Even now, after four months of such clocked, supervised, regulated visits, we still can't get used to the frustrations.

3   Yet, as John presses me gently to his heart, I feel warm and tender, and tears well up inside me, as they do each weekend. I have seven hours to spend with the man I love—all too brief a time for sharing a lifetime of emotion: love and longing, sympathy and tenderness, resentment and anger.

What does this photograph reveal about the participants?

4   The guard's voice jars us: "Please keep the chairs in order!"

5   We can't keep from laughing, for we're struck by the absurdity of the scene: 60 couples, some with families, packed in a single room—each trying, somehow, to create an atmosphere of intimacy. And what's demanded by the single guard who's assigned to oversee us? *Chairs in a straight line.*

6   Nevertheless, John and I abide by the rules, holding each other as close as we can—without moving our chairs—and the loneliness of the past week gradually subsides.

7   We break our silent communion with small talk much like the kind we shared at home for the past three years. Like: *Should we have the van repaired, or sell it?*

8   Then we speak of our separate needs and fears. He feels defeated—by confinement, by prison life, by the 20 months left to serve on a two-year sentence for a drug-related charge that we think should never have come to trial. He feels deeply insecure, too, doubting my fidelity and hating himself for doubting me. He wants support and reassurance.

9   But what about me? *Doesn't he understand that this has been an ordeal for me, too?* My whole life fell apart when he went to prison. Our wedding plans were canceled; I had to quit school, sell everything, find a job, and move in with relatives.

10   Prison has become my second full-time occupation. Each weekend I spend 10 hours traveling. Always I must save money—money for my motel room in Lompoc, money for his collect phone calls to supplement the letters we write, money for his supplies at the prison commissary.

11   Worst of all, there's the almost unbearable burden of conducting my home life alone. At least in prison he has no decisions to make, no meals to worry about, no rent. So I, too, need reassurance and emotional support.

—King, *Los Angles Times*

1. Answer each of the following questions by making an inference.

   a. Who is visiting the man in prison?

   _____ wife _____

   b. Why is she there?

   _____ visit _____

   c. Does she go there often? How do you know?

   _____ Yes _____

   d. Why do they break the silence with small talk?

   _____

   e. Why does the guard insist that the chairs be kept in a straight line?

   _____

f. Why did the woman have to quit school?

_____

g. Does the writer feel sorry for herself? How do you know?

_____

2. List several words with negative connotations that suggest how the writer feels about the prison.

_____

3. List several words with positive connotations that suggest how the woman feels about the man she is visiting.

_____

4. What main point do you think the writer is trying to make?

_____

_____

Passage B

Stop Junk Mail Forever

Every American, on average, receives 677 sales pitches in his or her mailbox every year—thanks to low-cost, third-class postal rates. While the direct mailers who produce and distribute those 40 million tons of sales pitches take in over $200 billion annually, taxpayers bear the burden of some $320 million to cart their unsolicited promos, pleas, and promises to and from incinerators, garbage dumps (on land and sea), and recycling centers. Sixty-eight million trees and 28 billion gallons of water (and the animals who lived there) are used to produce each year's crop of catalogs and come-ons. Nearly half get trashed unopened.

Many of the environmental organizations that you'd expect to speak up for the trees, rivers, and wildlife are silent about junk mail. Why? Because they support themselves just like the other mailbox fishermen do . . . by casting an extremely wide net to catch a couple of fish. A "response rate" of 1% or 2%—that's 1 or 2 of every 100 pieces mailed—is considered typical, no matter if the mailer is a worthy charity . . . or the distributor of yet one more vegetable slicer.

There's another issue of great concern to us: Privacy. We think Americans should have the right to choose how personal information about them is marketed, if at all. What follows are some clear instructions on how to keep your name, business, address, and other personal information private—off of those thousands upon thousands of mailing lists that are regularly bought and sold, without our approval, for pennies a name.

—Eisenson, *Mother Earth News*, p. 18

P403~413

1. Underline three words in the passage that carry positive or negative connotative meanings.

   _____

2. What is the author's attitude toward environmental organizations?

   _____

3. What is the author's attitude toward vegetable slicers? Why does he or she use them as an example?

   _____

   _____

4. Explain why the phrase "mailbox fishermen" is an example of figurative language.

   _____

   _____

UNDERSTANDING THE AUTHOR'S PURPOSE

** myreadinglab**

practice identifying author's purpose, to

STUDY PLAN
▼ READING SKILLS
  ▼ PURPOSE
     AND TONE

Writers have many different reasons or purposes for writing. Read the statements below and try to decide why each was written:

1. About 14,000 ocean-going ships pass through the Panama Canal each year. This averages about three ships per day.

2. *New Unsalted Dry Roasted Almonds.* Finally, a snack with a natural flavor and without salt. We simply shell the nuts and dry-roast them until they're crispy and crunchy. Try a jar this week.

3. Man is the only animal that blushes or has a need to.

4. If a choking person has fallen down, first turn him or her faceup. Then knit together the fingers of both your hands and apply pressure with the heel of your bottom hand to the victim's abdomen.

5. If your boat capsizes, it is usually safer to cling to the boat than to try to swim ashore.

Statement 1 was written to give information, 2 to persuade you to buy almonds, 3 to amuse you and make a comment on human behavior, 4 to explain, and 5 to give advice.

In each of the examples, the writer's purpose was fairly clear, as it will be in most textbooks (to present information), newspaper articles (to communicate daily events), and reference books (to provide facts). However, in many other types of writing, authors have varied, sometimes less obvious, purposes. In these cases, an author's purpose must be inferred.

Often a writer's purpose is to express an opinion indirectly. Or the writer may want to encourage the reader to think about a particular issue or problem. Writers achieve their purposes by manipulating and controlling what they say and how they say it. This section will focus on techniques writers use and features of language that writers control to achieve the results they want.

Style and Intended Audience

Are you able to recognize a friend just by his or her voice? Can you identify family members by their footsteps? You are able to do so because each person's voice and footsteps are unique. Have you noticed that writers have unique characteristics as well? One author may use many examples; another may use few. One author may use relatively short sentences, another may use long, complicated ones. The characteristics that make a writer unique are known as **style**. By changing style, writers can create different effects.

Writers may vary their styles to suit their intended audiences. A writer may write for a general-interest audience (anyone who is interested in the subject but is not considered an expert). Most newspapers and periodicals, such as *Time* and *Newsweek,* appeal to a general-interest audience. On the other hand, a writer may have a particular interest group in mind. A writer may write for medical doctors in the *Journal of American Medicine,* for skiing enthusiasts in *Skiing Today,* or for antique collectors in *The World of Antiques.* A writer may also target his or her writing for an audience with particular political, moral, or religious attitudes. Articles in the *New Republic* often appeal to a particular political viewpoint, whereas the *Catholic Digest* appeals to a specific religious group.

Depending on the group of people for whom the author is writing, he or she will change the level of language, choice of words, and method of presentation. One step toward identifying an author's purpose, then, is to ask yourself the question: Who is the intended audience? Your response will be your first clue to determining why the author wrote the article.

EXERCISE **11-8** **Analyzing Intended Audience**

Directions: Read each of the following statements and decide for whom each was written. Write a sentence that describes the intended audience.

1. If you are worried about the state of your investments, meet with a broker to figure out how you can still reach your financial goals.

_____

_____

2. Think about all the places your drinking water has been before you drink another drop. Most likely it has been chemically treated to remove bacteria and chemical pollutants. Soon you may begin to feel the side effects of these treatments. Consider switching to filtered, distilled water today.

_____

_____

3. The new subwoofers from Gilberton put so much bass in your ride that they are guaranteed to keep your mother out of your car.

_____

4. Bright and White laundry detergent removes dirt and stains faster than any other brand.

_____

5. As a driver, you're ahead if you can learn to spot car trouble before it's too late. If you can learn the difference between drips and squeaks that occur under normal conditions and those that mean big trouble is just down the road, then you'll be ahead of expensive repair bills and won't find yourself stranded on a lonely road.

_____

_____

myreadinglab

practice identifying
ne, go to
STUDY PLAN
▼ READING SKILLS
▼ PURPOSE
AND TONE

TONE

The tone of a speaker's voice helps you interpret what he or she is saying. If the following sentence were read aloud, the speaker's voice would tell you how to interpret it: "Would you mind closing the door?" In print you cannot tell whether the speaker is polite, insistent, or angry. In speech you could tell by whether the speaker emphasized the word *would, door,* or *mind.*

Just as a speaker's tone of voice tells how the speaker feels, so does a writer convey a tone, or feeling, through his or her writing. Tone refers to the attitude or feeling a writer expresses about his or her subject. A writer may adopt a sentimental tone, an angry tone, a humorous tone, a sympathetic tone, an instructive tone, a persuasive tone, and so forth. Here are a few examples of different tones. How does each make you feel?

- Instructive

  When purchasing a piece of clothing, one must be concerned with quality as well as with price. Be certain to check for the following: double-stitched seams, matched patterns, and ample linings.

- Sympathetic

  > The forlorn, frightened-looking child wandered through the streets alone, searching for someone who would show an interest in helping her find her parents.

- Persuasive

  > Child abuse is a tragic occurrence in our society. Strong legislation is needed to control the abuse of innocent victims and to punish those who are insensitive to the rights and feelings of others.

- Humorous

  > "Those people who study animal behavior professionally must dread those times when their cover is blown at a dinner party. The unfortunate souls are sure to be seated next to someone with animal stories. The conversation will invariably be about some pet that did this or that, and nonsense is the polite word for it. The worst stories are about cats. The proud owners like to talk about their ingenuity, what they are thinking, and how they 'miss' them while they're at the party. Those cats would rub the leg of a burglar if he rattled the Friskies box."
  >
  > —Wallace, *Biology,* p. 659

- Nostalgic 怀旧

  > "Things change, times change, but when school starts, my little granddaughter will run up the same wooden stairs that creaked for all of the previous generations and I will still hate it when the summer ends."
  >
  > —Hastreiter, "Not Every Mother Is Glad Kids Are Back in School," *Buffalo Evening News.*

In the first example (p. 405), the writer offers advice in a straightforward, informative style. In the second, the writer wants you to feel sorry for the child. This is done through description. In the third example, the writer tries to convince the reader that action must be taken to prevent child abuse. The use of such words as *tragic, innocent,* and *insensitive* establish this tone.

The tone of an article directly affects how the reader interprets and responds to it. If, as in the fourth example, the writer's tone is humorous and you do not recognize this, you will miss the point of the entire selection. If the writer's tone is nostalgic, as in the fifth example, it is important to recognize this and the feelings it provokes in you the reader. From these examples, you can see, then, that you may not receive an objective, unbiased treatment of a subject.

The author's tone is intended to rub off on you, so to speak. If a writer's tone is humorous, the writer hopes you will be amused. If a writer's tone is persuasive, the writer hopes you will accept his or her viewpoint. You can see how tone can be important in determining an author's purpose. Therefore, a second question to ask when trying to determine an author's purpose is: What tone does the writer use? Or: How is the writer trying to make me feel about the subject?

EXERCISE 11-9 **Analyzing Tone**

Directions: Read each of the following statements, paying particular attention to the tone. Then write a sentence that describes the tone. Prove your point by listing some of the words that reveal the author's feelings.

1. No one says that nuclear power is risk free. There are risks involved in all methods of producing energy. However, the scientific evidence is clear and obvious. Nuclear power is at least as safe as any other means used to generate electricity.

   P _____

   _____

2. The condition of our city streets is outrageous. The sidewalks are littered with paper and other garbage—you could trip while walking to the store. The streets themselves are in even worse condition. Deep potholes and crumbling curbs make it unsafe to drive. Where are our city tax dollars going if not to correct these problems?

   P _____

   _____

3. I am a tired American. I am tired of watching criminals walk free while they wait for their day in court. I'm tired of hearing about victims getting as much as or more hassle than criminals. I'm tired of reading about courts of law that even accept a lawsuit in which a criminal sues his or her intended victim.

   Politic _____

   _____

4. Cross-country skis have heel plates of different shapes and materials. They may be made of metal, plastic, or rubber. Be sure that they are tacked on the ski right where the heel of your boot will fall. They will keep snow from collecting under your foot and offer some stability.

   Instructive _____

   _____

5. A parent often must reduce her work hours to take care of a sick or disabled child, to take the child to therapy or treatments, and to handle crisis situations. With a child with significant special needs, it can be very difficult, if not impossible, for the primary caregiver parent to maintain full-time employment and provide the care the child needs. The caregiver parent often must take part-time status at work to avoid being fired completely. When the parent becomes a part-time employee, she also usually loses her health insurance, retirement and other benefits. Often part-time employees are ineligible to participate in these benefits. These restrictions present a financial loss to this parent.

—Price, *The Special Needs Child and Divorce*, p. 4

6. My daughter, Lucy, was born with an underdeveloped brain. She was a beautiful little girl—at least to me and my husband—but her disabilities were severe. By the time she was two weeks old we knew that she would never walk, talk, feed herself, or even understand the concept of mother and father. It's impossible to describe the effect that her five-and-a-half-month life had on us; suffice it to say that she was the purest experience of love and pain that we will ever have, that she changed us forever, and that we will never cease to mourn her death, even though we know that for her it was a triumphant passing.

—Armstrong, *The Choices We Made*, p. 165

EXERCISE 11-10   Identifying Tone

Directions: Bring to class an advertisement, photograph, newspaper headline, or paragraph that clearly expresses tone. Working in groups, students should agree on the tone each piece expresses. Then groups should exchange materials and identify the tone of each new piece. Groups should compare findings.

LANGUAGE

One important feature that writers adjust to suit their purpose is the kind of language they use. There are two basic types of language: objective and subjective.

Objective and Subjective Language

Objective language is factual, whereas **subjective language** expresses attitudes and feelings.

Read each of the following descriptions of the death penalty. As you read, decide how they differ.

> The death penalty is one of the most ancient of all types of formal punishment for crime. In early criminal codes, death was the penalty for a wide range of offenses, such as kidnapping, certain types of theft, and witchcraft. Today, in the United States, the death penalty is reserved for only the most serious of crimes—murder, kidnapping, and treason.

> The death penalty is a prime example of man's inhumanity to man. The death penalty violates the Eighth Amendment to the Constitution, which prohibits cruel and unusual punishment.

You probably noticed that the first paragraph gave facts about the death penalty and that the second paragraph seemed to state a case against it. These two paragraphs are examples of two different types of writing.

The first paragraph is an example of objective language. The writer reports information without showing feelings. You cannot tell whether the writer favors or is opposed to the death penalty.

The second paragraph is an example of subjective language. Here, the writer expresses freely his or her own attitudes and feelings. You know exactly how the author feels about the death penalty. Through choice of words and selection of facts, a tone of moral disapproval is evident. Such words as *inhumanity, violates,* and *cruel* have negative connotations.

EXERCISE 11-11   Writing Using Objective and Subjective Language

Directions: Choose a topic that interests you, or use one of the topics listed below. On a separate sheet of paper, write two brief paragraphs. In the first, use only objective, factual information. In the second, try to show your feelings about the topic by using subjective language.

1. One of your college instructors

2. Managing your time

3. Current fashion fads

Descriptive Language

Descriptive language is a particular type of subjective language. It is the use of words that appeal to one or more of the reader's senses. Descriptive words help the reader create an imaginary picture of the object, person, or event being described. Here is a paragraph that contains numerous descriptive words and phrases. As you read, underline words and phrases that help you to imagine what the Oregon desert is like.

> You can camp in the Oregon desert for a week and see no one at all, no more than the glow of headlights hovering over a dirt road miles distant, disappearing soundlessly over the curve of the Earth. You can see, as you wander over those dry flats, that man has been there, that vast stretches of sagebrush have replaced the bunchgrass grazed off by his cattle and sheep. Against a hill you can find the dry-rotting foundation of a scuttled homestead. But the desert is not scarred by man's presence. It is still possible to be alone out there, to stare at your hands for an hour and have no one ask why. It is possible to feel the cracks in the earth, to sense the enormity of space, to roll, between the tips of your fingers, the dust of boulders gone to pieces.
>
> —Lopez, "Weekend," *Audubon*

Through descriptive language, a writer often makes you feel a certain way about the topic. In the preceding paragraph, the writer is trying to suggest that the desert is lonely, peaceful, and a good place to think or relax. Did you notice such words and phrases as *soundlessly, enormity of space, distant, wander, vast stretches?*

EXERCISE 11-12   Using Descriptive Language

Directions: Work with a partner to expand each of the following sentences to include as many descriptive details as possible.

1. The movie was enjoyable.

2. The restaurant serves terrible food.

3. The classmate was annoying.

EXERCISE 11-13   Analyzing Language, Tone, and Purpose

Directions: Read each of the following articles and answer the questions that follow.

Article 1

Americans and the Land

I have often wondered at the savagery and thoughtlessness with which our early settlers approached this rich continent. They came at it as though it were an enemy, which of course it was. They burned the forests and changed the rainfall; they swept the buffalo from the plains, blasted the streams, set fire to the grass, and ran a reckless scythe through the virgin and noble timber. Perhaps they felt that it was limitless and could never be exhausted and that a man could move on to new wonders endlessly. Certainly there are many examples to the contrary, but to a large extent the early people pillaged the country as though they hated it, as though they held it temporarily and might be driven off at any time.

—Steinbeck, *America and Indians,* pp. 127–128

1. Is this selection an objective or subjective account of the early settlement of America? Give examples to support your choice.

   _____

   _____

   _____

2. Describe the writer's tone. How does it make you feel?

   _____

   _____

3. Why do you think the author wrote this selection?

   _____

   _____

Article 2

Eat It Raw

Raw food is not just for hippies anymore. It is being embraced by hip-hop stars and New York restaurateurs.

The raw-food diet, once the exclusive domain of '70s food faddists, is making a comeback for the same reasons it flourished 30 years ago: health and politics. Many find it helpful in relieving a variety of maladies—including allergies, fibromyalgia, obesity, gum disease, and mood swings—while others see raw food as a way to resist the unhealthy products of an industrialized food system. No matter how you slice it, excitement about a diet of uncooked food is running high.

"Anecdotally, there's been a definite rise in interest in raw-foods diets," says nutritionist Suzanne Havala Hobbs, adjunct assistant professor at the University of North Carolina–Chapel Hill's School of Public Health. "There's been a lot of information out about celebrities that are eating raw foods, and naturally many younger people are interested in trying it out. There's also been a wave of raw-foods cookbooks and restaurants." Hobbs, who also serves as nutrition advisor to the Baltimore-based Vegetarian Resource Group, is currently conducting a research survey on the topic, called the Raw Foods Project.

A raw-food diet consists of foods that have not been processed or heated above 118 degrees Fahrenheit. These might include fresh fruits, vegetables, cold-pressed oils, sprouted grains, nuts, seeds, and even organic wine—but not meat or fish. According to June Butlin in *Positive Health* (Aug. 2001), a proper raw-food diet provides high levels of natural, essential nutrients such as fiber, essential oils, antimicrobials, plant hormones, bioflavonoids, vitamins, minerals, chlorophyll, digestive enzymes, and antioxidants. . . .

New York's raw foodists even have their own restaurant, Quintessence, a Manhattan bistro whose proprietors, Tolentin Chan and her husband, Dan Hoyt, understand the political and the personal power of the raw-food diet. "Major corporations are poisoning people with overprocessed, denatured food," says Hoyt. As for Chan, she suffered frequent colds and asthma attacks before trying a raw-food "cleanse"—the way most raw foodists get started—to see if she could get some relief. "My health improved tremendously," she says. "Now I'm 100 percent raw and my asthma is completely gone. I never get sick, and my energy is really high." Hoyt followed her lead and found relief from hay fever and food allergies. But both of them know how unappetizing raw food can seem at first.

"People think eating raw is gonna be like chewing on weeds," Hoyt says. But in the right hands, he says, it can be a refreshing culinary experience. "Raw food is very vibrant. We use lots of spices and sauces. The flavors are very strong and clean." Somebody out there must agree: Raw foods restaurants have sprung up across the United States, from Berkeley, Las Vegas, and Chicago to Minneapolis, Philadelphia, and Washington, D.C. It appears more are in the works.

—Olson, *Utne Reader,* pp. 20–22

1. What is the author's purpose?

   _____

2. For whom is this article written?

   _____

3. Explain the figurative expression "People think eating raw is gonna be like chewing on weeds."

_____

4. Describe the tone of the article.

    accessible _____

5. List several words or phrases that have a somewhat negative connotation.
   List several words or phrases with positive connotations.

_____

_____

6. This reading is an excerpt from a larger article. What do you expect the rest of the article to contain?

_____

LEARNING STYLE TIPS

If you tend to be a(n) . . .	Then build your interpretive reading skills by . . .
Applied learner	Asking the questions, How can I use this information? Of what value is this information?
Conceptual learner	Studying to see how the ideas fit together, looking for connections and relationships, as well as inconsistencies

SELF-TEST SUMMARY

OBJECTIVE **1** **What are connotative meanings?**	Connotative meanings are the shades of meaning a word may have in addition to its literal (denotative) meaning
OBJECTIVE **2** **What are implied meanings?**	Implied meanings are those suggested by facts and information given by the author, but not directly stated
OBJECTIVE **3** **What is figurative language?**	Figurative language is a way of describing things that make sense on an imaginative level but not on a factual level
OBJECTIVE **4** **How can you identify the author's purpose?**	Examine the writer's style: A writer will change his or her style (level of language, choice of words, and method of presentation) to suit the intended audience. Examine the intended audience: Analyzing the style and identifying the intended audience are the first steps toward identifying an author's purpose.
OBJECTIVE **5** **What is tone?**	A writer's tone (serious, humorous, angry, sympathetic) is a clue to how the writer wants you to feel about the topic.
OBJECTIVE **6** **What types of language provide clues about the author's purpose?**	A writer's language may be objective or subjective, depending on whether the writer is simply presenting facts or expressing an opinion or feelings. This language presents one or more clues to the writer's purpose.

GOING ONLINE

1. Writing as a Social Act

    http://writing.colostate.edu/guides/processes/writingsituations/graphic.cfm

    Explore this site about the ways in which authors and readers create and react to the written word. Then make your own graphic representation of the material using a concept map or other type of diagram.

2. Selling Yourself

    One of the most important arguments you will have to make is in your cover letter for job applications. Read over this information about selling yourself:

    http://owl.english.purdue.edu/handouts/pw/p_applettr.html

    Print out a sample cover letter and analyze it according to the site's tips.

3. Tone & Mood

    http://oak.cats.ohiou.edu/~dl314201/PDF/Tone&Mood.pdf

    Read about the differences between tone and mood in writing. Then complete the worksheet.

To check your progress in meeting chapter objectives, log in to **http://www.myreadinglab.com**, click on the Study Plan tab, and then click on the Reading Skills tab. Choose Critical Thinking, Inference, and Purpose and Tone from the list of subtopics. Read and view the information in the Review Materials section, and then complete the Practices and Tests in the Activities section. You can check your scores by clicking on the Gradebook tab.

P416~424

MASTERY TEST 1 Interpretive Skills

Name _____ Section _____

Date _____ Number right _____ × 20 points = Score _____

Directions: Read each of the following paragraphs and answer the questions that follow.

Paragraph 1

Over the past 20 years, psychologists have made a science of the joys and devastations of couples' relationships. They've come to understand, at least in part, why some relationships happily endure and what contributes to the hellhole interactions that claim over half of all first marriages, usually within the first seven years. Although these same psychologists note that most marriages start with great optimism and true love, they get into trouble for a very humbling reason: we just don't know how to handle the negative feelings that are a result of the differences between two people, the very differences that formed the basis for attraction in the first place.

—Donatelle and Davis,
Access to Health, p. 146

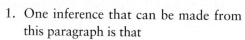
1. One inference that can be made from this paragraph is that
   a. the author disapproves of divorce.
   b. more than half of all first marriages end in divorce.
   c. the author is a marriage counselor.
   d. all divorces occur within the first seven years of marriage.

Paragraph 2

Alas, all is not perfect in the virtual world. E-commerce does have its limitations. Security is one important concern. We hear horror stories of consumers whose credit cards and other identity information have been stolen. While an individual's financial liability in most theft cases is limited to $50, the damage to one's credit rating can last for years. Some shady companies are making money by prying and then selling personal information to others. Pretty scary. Almost daily we hear of hackers getting into a business or even a government Web site and causing havoc. Businesses risk the loss of trade secrets and other proprietary information. Many must spend significant amounts to maintain security and conduct regular audits to ensure the integrity of their sites.

—Soloman and Stuart, *The Brave New World of E-Commerce*, p. 17

_____ 2. In this paragraph, an example of *objective* language is
   a. "horror stories."
   b. "individual liability."
   c. "shady companies."
   d. "Pretty scary."

Paragraph 3

If we want to create safe classrooms in which teachers and students have the right to question existing knowledge and produce new knowledge, we must prepare you, who are planning to teach, for the problems you will face. One of your most frustrating problems will revolve around your discovery that power can shape and even dominate your life and your school. Power is a basic reality of human existence, present in all human relationships, including those of lovers, business partners, basketball teams, teachers and students, college faculties, courts, government bodies and so on.

—Kincheloe, *Contextualizing Teaching*, pp. 90–91

_____ 3. For this paragraph, the author's intended audience is
   a. parents of school-age children.
   b. people who work in positions of power.
   c. college professors.
   d. people who are planning to become teachers.

Paragraph 4

Computer games are big business, but many of the best-sellers are filled with gore and violence that are not the best things for children to see. Is there an alternative? A company formed by five young people in Sweden thinks so, and they're succeeding by offering product alternatives that prove you don't need to be bloody to be the best. The company, called Daydream Software, got its start when one of the programmers gave a computer to his little sister for Christmas. He had a hard time finding appropriate games she could play, however. This frustrating discovery led to discussions with friends about finding methods to push players' thrill buttons other than endless blood and splatter. All of Daydream's founders have children, and they design games they would want their own kids to play. They want the player to come away with more than just the echo of machine guns and a sore trigger finger.

—Soloman and Stuart, _Marketing_, p. 59

_____ 4. One inference that can be made from this paragraph is that
   a. Daydream's computer games are nonviolent.
   b. Daydream's computer games are more expensive than other computer games.

   c. the people who produce violent computer games do not have children.
   d. violent computer games are always more exciting than nonviolent games.

Paragraph 5

Another shameful abandonment of human rights affected Native Americans. Between 1700 and 1763, thousands of white settlers poured into Indian lands west of the mountains. The result was bloody warfare, marked by barbarous atrocities on both sides. Looking to the British for protection, most of the tribes fought against Americans during the Revolution, only to have their territories put under control of their enemies in the peace of 1783. Protracted negotiations with the American government led to more surrenders and numerous treaties, all of which were broken as the flood of white land speculators and settlers moved westward. In desperation, the Indians attempted unification and a hopeless resistance. By 1800 enforced living on land set aside for Indians was already promoting the disintegration of Native American cultures.

—Brummett et al., _Civilization_, pp. 578–579

_____ 5. The authors' purpose in this paragraph is to
   a. explain the role of Native Americans in the settling of the west.
   b. describe the effect of westward expansion on Native Americans.
   c. criticize Native Americans for their treatment of whites in the 18th century.
   d. defend the actions of whites against Native Americans in the 18th century.

MASTERY TEST 2 Interpretive Skills

Name _____ Section _____

Date _____ Number right _____ × 10 points = Score _____

Directions: After reading the selection, select the choice that best completes each of the statements that follow.

Scar

The mark on my face made me who I am

1   Growing up, I had a scar on my face—a perfect arrow in the center of my cheek, pointing at my left eye. I got it when I was 3, long before I knew that scars were a bad thing, especially for a girl. I knew only that my scar brought me attention and tenderness and candy.

2   As I got older I began to take pride in my scar, in part to stop bullies from taunting me, but mainly to counter the assumption that I should feel embarrassed. It's true, I was embarrassed the first couple of times someone pointed at my cheek and asked "What's that?" or called me Scarface. But the more I heard how unfortunate my scar was, the more I found myself liking it.

3   When I turned 15, my parents—on the advice of a plastic surgeon—decided it was time to operate on what was now a thick, shiny red scar.

4   "But I don't mind the scar, really," I told my father as he drove me home from the local mall, explaining that I would have the surgery during my summer vacation. "I don't need surgery." It had been years since I'd been teased, and my friends, along with my boyfriend at the time, felt as I did—that my scar was unique and almost pretty in its own way. After so many years, it was part of me.

5   "You do need surgery," my father said, his eyes on the road, his lips tight.

6   "But I like it," I told him. "I don't want to get rid of it."

7   "You need surgery," he said again, and he lowered his voice. "It's a deformity."

8   I don't know what hurt more that day: hearing my father call my scar a deformity or realizing that it didn't matter to him how I felt about it.

9   I did have plastic surgery that summer. They cut out the left side of the arrow, leaving a thinner, zigzag scar that blended into the lines of my face when I smiled. The following summer they did the same to the right side of the arrow. Finally, when I was 18, the surgeon sanded my cheek smooth.

10   In my late 20s, I took a long look at my scar, something I hadn't done in years. It was still visible in the right light, but no one asked me about it anymore. I examined the small steplike pattern and the way it made my cheek dimple when I smiled. As I leaned in awkwardly toward the mirror, I felt a sudden sadness.

11   There was something powerful about my scar and the defiant, proud person I became because of it. I have never been quite so strong since they cut it out.

—Audet, "Scar," *The Sun*, Issue 325, p. 96

___a___ 1. The central thought of the reading is that
    a. the author's scar contributed to her self-identity and gave her power.
    (b.) parents should not make decisions for their children.
    c. people really do not notice deformities.
    d. beauty is in the eye of the beholder.

___b___ 2. The writer's primary purpose is to
    a. provide autobiographical information.
    b. explain how she feels about her scar.
    c. give a general overview of plastic surgery.
    d. criticize her father.

___c___ 3. What does the author mean when she says "scars were a bad thing, especially for a girl"?
    a. Faces reveal the inner person.
    b. Girls poke fun at other girls.
    c. Beauty is important for girls, and a scar is thought to detract.
    d. Boys do not care about how they look.

___c___ 4. The connotation of the word *deformity* (par. 7) is
    a. strong and forceful act.
    b. frequently recurring problem.
    c. unsightly, unpleasant disability.
    d. unfortunate accident.

_____ 5. This article seems written primarily for which of the following audiences?
    a. plastic surgery patients
    b. audiences interested in personal stories
    c. children with serious physical disabilities
    d. parents who make decisions for their children

___c___ 6. The meaning of the word *taunting* in paragraph 2 is
    a. complimenting.
    b. arguing with.
    c. insulting.
    d. accompanying.

___a___ 7. Which word best describes the author's attitude toward her scar?
    a. positive
    b. negative
    c. uncertain
    d. hateful

___d___ 8. Based on the reading, the author is likely to agree that
    a. plastic surgeons should be more sensitive to their patients' needs.
    b. parents seldom have their children's best interests in mind.
    c. disabled people should be pitied.
    d. disabilities can be a source of strength.

___a___ 9. The father probably wanted his daughter to have surgery because he
    a. thought she would look better without the scar.
    b. thought the scar disturbed her.
    c. blamed himself that she had a scar.
    d. knew she would be happier in the long run.

___c___ 10. The author helps readers make inferences about the father's attitude toward the scar by providing
    a. examples.
    b. opinions of others.
    c. dialogue.
    d. comparisons.

MASTERY TEST 3 Reading Selection

Name _____ Section _____

Date _____ Number right* _____ × 10 points = Score _____

The Mediocre Multitasker

Ruth Pennebaker

This selection first appeared online in 2009 in the *New York Times*. Read the article to learn what researchers have discovered about that modern phenomenon known as multitasking.

> **Vocabulary Preview**
>
> **irrelevancy** (par. 4) the quality or state of not being related or applicable to a subject
>
> **etiquette** (par. 9) proper manners

1   Read it and gloat. Last week, researchers at Stanford University published a study showing that the most persistent multitaskers perform badly in a variety of tasks. They don't focus as well as non-multitaskers. They're more distractible. They're weaker at

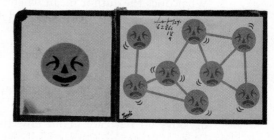

shifting from one task to another and at organizing information. They are, as a matter of fact, worse at multitasking than people who don't ordinarily multitask.

2   You know what this means. This means that the people around you—the husband who's tapping the computer keys during an important phone conversation with you, the S.U.V. driver with the grande latte and the cellphone, the dinner companion with the roving eye and twitching thumbs—are not only irritating, they are (let's not be fainthearted) incompetent.

3   But, wait. Should it be breaking news that a single person can't juggle knives and explain quantum physics while polishing off an artichoke? Breaking news and a shock to the researchers themselves, as it turns out. Originally, the team of researchers, whose findings are published in the Aug. 24 issue of the Proceedings of the National Academy of Sciences, were trying to find out what unusual cognitive gifts multitaskers possessed that made them so successful at multitasking. They're still looking.

*To calculate the number right, use items 1–10 under "Mastery Test Skills Check."

4   "Multitaskers were just lousy at everything," said Clifford I. Nass, a professor of communication at Stanford and one of the study's investigators. "It was a complete and total shock to me." Initially suspecting that multitaskers possessed some rare and enviable qualities that helped them process simultaneous channels of information, Professor Nass had been "in awe of them," he said, acknowledging that he himself is "dreadful" at multitasking. "I was sure they had some secret ability. But it turns out that high multitaskers are suckers for irrelevancy."

5   The study tested 100 college students rated high or low multitaskers. Experimenters monitored the students' focus, memory and distractibility with a series of electronic images of different-colored shapes, letters and numbers. Eyal Ophir, the study's lead investigator and a researcher at Stanford's Communication Between Humans and Interactive Media Lab, said: "We kept looking for multitaskers' advantages in this study. But we kept finding only disadvantages. We thought multitaskers were very much in control of information. It turns out, they were just getting it all confused."

6   The study's results were so strong and unexpected that the researchers are planning a series of follow-up experiments. "It keeps me up late at night," Professor Nass said. "I worry about both the short-term and long-term effects of multitasking. We're going to be testing the heck out of high and low multitaskers."

7   To the rest of the world, though, the people who trudge through life excited and unnerved by an occasional cellphone call while walking or watching the sun set (isn't that multitasking?), the study's findings aren't quite so shocking. A constant state of stress, deluges of ever-changing information, the frenzied, nanosecond-fast hustle and bustle—this is bad for you? It's surprising and it's news that it's bad for you? Before they lie down to take a well-deserved and uninterrupted nap, the trudgers of the world would like to say, "We told you so!"

8   Still, their sad sense of inferiority to the flash and dash of multitaskers lingers and may even interfere with a good sleep. "The core of the problem," Professor Nass said, is that the multitaskers "think they're great at what they do; and they've convinced everybody else they're good at it, too." Yes, they have. Take, for example, Robert Leleux, a New York writer and gentle soul who still struggles with a rotary phone. "My entire life, I've been so thoroughly cowed by multitaskers," said Mr. Leleux, author of *The Memoirs of a Beautiful Boy*. "I find it impossible to believe they're not superior to me. This study is like catnip! It validates my entire life."

9   As a child, Mr. Leleux recalls, his unitasking took a culinary turn. When eating, he could concentrate only on one food at a time. "Usually mashed potatoes first, and then maybe a vegetable," he said. "It drove my mother crazy. She kept threatening to send me to etiquette school if I didn't straighten out. I was scared to death till I turned 18 and realized going to etiquette school wouldn't be such a bad thing."

10   Today, Mr. Leleux finds himself in a mixed marriage with a fast-moving, multitasking husband whose professional life, Mr. Leleux said, resembles *His Girl Friday*.

"Michael can answer e-mails, talk on the phone, approve designs concepts and copy and artwork—all at the same time," he said. "As a person who can only eat mashed potatoes at one time, it's incredibly depressing there are people capable of working on 14 different things at a time." Even with scientific validation at his fingertips, Mr. Leleux frets that the Stanford study may have been done "by a bitter unitasker like me who wants to validate his own existence."

11   "Look at the tortoise and the hare. Even though the tortoise actually ends up winning the race, who would you rather be? A wrinkly, fat old tortoise or a lithe, quick-witted hare? I think the answer is clear."

MASTERY TEST SKILLS CHECK

Directions: Select the choice that best completes each of the following statements.

Checking Your Comprehension

_____ 1. The main question that the author answers in this selection is
   a. What makes multitaskers so efficient?
   b. Why do people try to multitask?
   c. How effective are multitaskers?
   d. When did multitasking become popular?

_____ 2. The Stanford University study indicates that multitaskers
   a. are persistent at completing tasks.
   b. are able to shift from one task to another.
   c. are not easily distracted.
   d. perform badly in a variety of tasks.

_____ 3. To the Stanford researchers, the study's results could best be described as
   a. irritating.   c. expected.
   b. shocking.   d. disappointing.

_____ 4. The study tested college students on all of the following traits *except*
   a. focus.   c. motor skills.
   b. memory.   d. distractibility.

_____ 5. The main point of paragraph 5 is that researchers
   a. found disadvantages rather than advantages for multitaskers.
   b. discovered that multitaskers were very much in control of information.
   c. were confused by the results of the study.
   d. worked at Stanford's Communications Between Humans and Interactive Media Lab.

Applying Your Skills

_____ 6. In paragraph 7, the author's tone can best be described as
   a. sympathetic and kind.
   b. humorous and sarcastic.
   c. disgusted and angry.
   d. shocked and upset.

_____ 7. One inference that can be made from the selection is that the author believes
   a. the researchers will discontinue their studies of multitasking.
   b. multitaskers are able to process simultaneous channels of information.
   c. many people share feelings of inferiority and irritation toward multitaskers.
   d. most people will give up multitasking after reading this article.

_____ 8. The author's intended audience is most likely
   a. research scientists.
   b. medical doctors.
   c. psychologists.
   d. a general-interest audience.

_____ 9. An example of *objective* language in this selection is
   a. "Should it be breaking news that a single person can't juggle knives and explain quantum physics while polishing off an artichoke?"
   b. "The researchers . . . were trying to find out what unusual cognitive gifts multitaskers possessed that made them so successful at multitasking."
   c. "Still, their sad sense of inferiority to the flash and dash of multitaskers lingers and may even interfere with a good sleep."
   d. "This study is like catnip!"

_____ 10. Robert Leleux's story is included in this selection because he
   a. participated in the Stanford study on multitasking.
   b. is the author of a book about multitasking.
   c. is a researcher who believes that multitasking is dangerous.
   d. is a unitasker married to a multitasker.

Studying Words

_____ 11. The root of the word *cognitive* (par. 3) means
   a. life.
   b. learn.
   c. take.
   d. hear.

_____ 12. The word *deluges* (par. 7) means
   a. floods.
   b. paths.
   c. mistakes.
   d. questions.

_____ 13. The prefix in the word *unitasking* (par. 9) means
   a. equal.
   b. one.
   c. ten.
   d. against.

_____ 14. From context, you can tell that the word *culinary* (par. 9) has something to do with
   a. work.
   b. art.
   c. food.
   d. money.

_____ 15. The word *lithe* (par. 11) means
   a. wrinkled.
   b. overweight.
   c. slow-moving.
   d. athletically slim.

For more practice, ask your instructor for an opportunity to work on the mastery tests that appear in the Test Bank.

Summarizing the Reading

Directions: Write a summary of the reading using the opening and closing below as your starting and ending points.

Researchers at Stanford University have published a study showing that _____

_____

_____

_____

_____

Despite the study's results, people who are not multitaskers still seem convinced that multitaskers are better at doing things.

Reading Visually

1. What concept is illustrated by the image that accompanies this article?
2. Think of a photograph that could be used to illustrate the term *multitasking*.
3. Explain how the title of this article relates to the subject. Why is the word *mediocre* appropriate? Think of another title that would also work for this selection.

Thinking Critically about the Reading

1. Would you consider yourself a multitasker, a unitasker, or something in between? Will the information in this article have an effect on your own task-related behavior? Why or why not?
2. Why do you think the author chose to approach her subject with humor? How might this material have been treated differently in a scientific journal?
3. Explain how Robert Leleux's story illustrates and enlivens the material that comes before it in the article.

CHAPTER 12

Evaluating: Asking Critical Questions

Looking at …
Evaluating What You Read

LEARNING OBJECTIVES

This chapter will show you how to:

OBJECTIVE 1 Evaluate sources

OBJECTIVE 2 Determine reliability of Internet sources

OBJECTIVE 3 Evaluate the authority of the author

OBJECTIVE 4 Examine assumptions

OBJECTIVE 5 Recognize bias

OBJECTIVE 6 Evaluate slanted writing

OBJECTIVE 7 Examine supporting ideas

OBJECTIVE 8 Distinguish between fact and opinion

OBJECTIVE 9 Identify value judgments

This excerpt from a movie review evaluates the movie *Alice in Wonderland*. Movie reviews examine the value and worth of a movie and may consider factors such as its historical accuracy, the effectiveness of the actors/actresses and the script, as well as how it is carried out—the cinematography, the music, and so forth. Written material needs to be similarly evaluated for worth, value, accuracy, and delivery technique. This chapter will show you how to read and evaluate persuasive material.

425

If you were thinking of purchasing a used car from a private owner, you would ask questions before deciding whether to buy it. You would ask about repairs, maintenance, gas mileage, and so forth. When it comes to buying something, most of us have learned the motto "Buyer beware." We have learned to be critical, sometimes suspicious, of a product and its seller. We realize that salespeople will often tell us only what will make us want to buy the item. They will not tell what is wrong with the item or whether it compares unfavorably with a competitor's product.

Although many of us have become wise consumers, few of us have become wise, critical readers. We need to adopt a new motto: *Reader beware.* You can think of some writers as sellers and their written material as the product to be sold. Just as you would ask questions about a car before buying it, so should you ask questions about what you read before you accept what is said. You should ask questions about who wrote the material and where it came from. You need to decide whether the writer is selling you a one-sided, biased viewpoint. You should evaluate whether the writer provides sufficient support for his or her ideas to allow you to accept them. This chapter will discuss these critical issues and show you how to apply them to articles and essays.

WHAT IS THE SOURCE OF THE MATERIAL?

Just as you might check the brand label on an item of clothing before you buy it, so should you check to see where an article or essay comes from before you read it. You will often be asked to read material that is not in its original form. Many textbooks, such as this one, include excerpts or entire selections borrowed from other authors. Instructors often photocopy articles or essays and distribute them or place them on reserve in the library for students to read.

A first question to ask before you even begin to read is: What is the source; from what book, magazine, or newspaper was this taken? Knowledge of the source will help you judge the accuracy and soundness of what you read. For example, in which of the following sources would you expect to find the most accurate and up-to-date information about computer software?

- An advertisement in *Time*
- An article in *Reader's Digest*
- An article in *Software Review*

The article in *Software Review* would be the best source. This is a magazine devoted to the subject of computers and computer software. *Reader's Digest,* on the other hand, does not specialize in any one topic and often reprints or condenses articles from other sources. *Time,* a weekly newsmagazine, does contain information, but a paid advertisement is likely to provide information on only one line of software.

Knowing the source of an article will give clues to the kind of information the article will contain. For instance, suppose you went to the library to locate information for a research paper on the interpretation of dreams. You found the following sources of information. What do you expect each to contain?

- An encyclopedia entry titled "Dreams"
- An article in *Psychological Review* titled "An Examination of Research on Dreams"
- An entry on a personal Web site titled "The Interpretation of Dreams"

You can predict that the encyclopedia entry will be a factual report. It will provide a general overview of the process of dreaming. The personal Web site will likely report personal experience and contain little or no research. The article from *Psychological Review,* a journal that reports research in psychology, will present a primarily factual, research-oriented discussion of dreams.

As part of evaluating a source or selecting an appropriate source, be sure to check the date of publication. For many topics, it is essential that you work with current, up-to-date information. For example, suppose you have found an article on the safety of over-the-counter (nonprescription) drugs. If the article was written four or five years ago, it is already outdated. New drugs have been approved and released; new regulations have been put into effect; packaging requirements have changed. The year a book was published can be found on the copyright page. If the book has been reprinted by another publisher or has been reissued in paperback, look to see when it was first published and check the year(s) in the copyright notice.

EXERCISE 12-1 | **Evaluating Sources**

Directions: For each set of sources listed below, choose the one that would be most useful for finding information on the stated topic. Then, in the space provided, give a reason for your choice.

_____ 1. **Topic:** gas mileage of American-made cars

Sources
a. A newspaper article titled "Gas-Eating American Cars"
b. The U.S. Department of Energy's fuel economy site: http://www .fueleconomy.gov/
c. A research report in *Car and Driver* magazine on American car performance

Reason: _____

_____ 2. **Topic:** viruses as a cause of cancer

Sources
  a. A textbook titled *Well-Being: An Introduction to Health*
  b. An article in *Scientific American* magazine on controlling viruses
  c. An issue of the *Journal of the American Medical Association* devoted to a review of current research findings on the causes of cancer

Reason: _____

_____ 3. **Topic:** the effects of aging on learning and memory

Sources
  a. An article from *Forbes* magazine titled "Fountain of Youth"
  b. A psychology textbook titled *A General Introduction to Psychology*
  c. A textbook titled *Adult Development and Aging*

Reason: _____

IS AN INTERNET SOURCE RELIABLE?

While the Internet contains a great deal of valuable information and resources, it also contains rumor, gossip, hoaxes, and misinformation. In other words, not all Internet sources are trustworthy. You must evaluate a source before accepting it. Unlike print sources, the Internet has no editors or publishers to verify the accuracy of the information presented. Any individual, company, or organization can put information on a Web site or in a newsgroup posting. Here are some guidelines to follow when evaluating Internet sources.

How to Evaluate Internet Sources

1. **Check the author.** For Web sites, look for professional credentials or affiliations. If no author is listed, you should be skeptical. For newsgroups or discussion groups, check to see if the author has given his or her name and a signature (a short biographical description included at the end of messages).

2. **Discover the purpose of the posting.** Many Web sites have an agenda such as to sell a product, promote a cause, advocate a position, and so forth. Look for bias in the reporting of information.

3. **Check the date of the posting.** Be sure you are obtaining current information. A Web site usually includes the date on which it was last updated.

4. **Check the sponsoring organization of the site.** If a site is sponsored or provided by a well-known organization, such as a reputable newspaper like the *New York Times*, the information is apt to be reliable.

5. **Check links (addresses of other sources suggested by the Web site).** If these links are no longer working, the Web site you are visiting may be outdated or not reputable.

6. **Cross-check your information.** Try to find the same information in, ideally, two other sources, especially if the information is vitally important (issues dealing with health, financial discussion, etc.) or if it is at odds with what seems logical or correct.

EXERCISE 12-2   Evaluating a Web Site

Directions: Visit a Web site and become familiar with its organization and content. Evaluate it using the suggested criteria. Then write a brief paragraph explaining why the Web site is or is not a reliable source.

WHAT IS THE AUTHORITY OF THE AUTHOR?

Another clue to the reliability of the information is the author's qualifications. If the author lacks expertise in or experience with a subject, the material may not be accurate or worthwhile reading.

In textbooks, the author's credentials may appear on the title page or in the preface. In nonfiction books and general market paperbacks, a summary of the author's life and credentials may be included on the book jacket or back cover. In many other cases, however, the author's credentials are not given. You are left to rely on the judgment of the editors or publishers about an author's authority.

If you are familiar with an author's work, then you can anticipate the type of material you will be reading and predict the writer's approach and attitude toward the subject. If, for example, you found an article on world banking written by former President Clinton, you could predict it will have a political point of view. If you were about to read an article on John Lennon written by Ringo Starr, one of the other Beatles, you could predict the article might possibly include details of their working relationship from Ringo's point of view.

EXERCISE 12-3 **Evaluating the Authority of the Author**

Directions: Read each statement and choose the individual who would seem to be the best authority on the subject.

_____ 1. Print newspapers are becoming obsolete.
   a. Michael Denton, a former *New York Times* print subscriber
   b. Todd Gitlin, professor, Columbia University School of Journalism
   c. Bill O'Reilly, television journalist

_____ 2. The president's recent news conference was a success.
   a. Katie Couric, a well-known news commentator
   b. David Axelrod, one of the president's advisors
   c. Howard Summers, a professor of economics

_____ 3. Amy Tan is one of the most important modern American novelists.
   a. Wayne Wang, director of the film adaptation of Tan's book, *The Joy Luck Club*
   b. Nancy Pearl, former librarian, author, and commentator on books
   c. David Gewanter, professor of modern literature at Georgetown University

DOES THE WRITER MAKE ASSUMPTIONS?

OBJECTIVE 4

An assumption is an idea, theory, or principle that the writer believes to be true. The writer then develops his or her ideas based on that assumption. Of course, if the assumption is not true or is one you disagree with, then the ideas that depend on that assumption are of questionable value. For instance, an author may believe that the death penalty is immoral and, beginning with that assumption, develop an argument for the best ways to prevent crime. However, if you believe that the death penalty *is* moral, then from your viewpoint, the writer's argument is invalid.

Read the following paragraph. Identify the assumption the writer makes, and write it in the space provided.

> Everyone suffers during an economic crisis. No one can come through unscathed, let alone better off. High unemployment and the unavailability of credit hurt all members of society as their negative effects trickle through the economic system. People who are not working cut back on their spending, which causes small businesses to close, which creates more unemployment. Closed businesses contribute to urban blight, which feeds crime and weakens our cities. Everyone across all levels suffers.

Assumption: _____

Here the assumption is stated in the first sentence—the writer assumes that an economic crisis negatively affects everyone. He makes no attempt to address how those who are independently wealthy or those who have not lost their jobs might not be suffering. He also fails to mention certain industries that thrive during troubled economic times, such as thrift stores.

EXERCISE 12-4 **Identifying Assumptions**

Directions: For each of the following paragraphs, identify the assumption that is made by the writer and write it in the space provided.

1. In high school, course selection is simple. Once all the mandatory courses are dropped into your schedule, you get to choose between art, drama or music. Then everything is put together automatically. In the university, things get a bit more complicated. You have some control over what day of the week each class is, or whether you take a course in three one-hour lectures a week or one three-hour lecture a week. You can even take into account who the instructor is. For incoming first-year students, choosing the right courses and putting together a schedule can seem like an impossible task.

   —Dobson-Mitchell, *Beat the Clock*, p. 114

   Assumption: _____

   _____

2. Our lifestyles are increasingly driven by technology. Phones, computers and the internet pervade our days. There is a constant, nagging need to check for texts and email, to update Facebook, MySpace and LinkedIn profiles, to acquire the latest notebook or 3G cellphone. Are we being served by these technological wonders or have we become enslaved by them? I study the psychology of technology, and it seems to me that we are sleepwalking into a world where technology is severely affecting our well-being. Technology can be hugely useful in the fast lane of modern living, but we need to stop it from taking over.

   —Amichai-Hamburger, *Depression Through Technology*, p. 28

   Assumption: _____

   _____

IS THE AUTHOR BIASED?

OBJECTIVE 5

As you evaluate any piece of writing, always try to decide whether the author is objective or one-sided (biased). Does the author present an objective view of the subject or is a particular viewpoint favored? An objective article presents all sides of an issue, while a biased one presents only one side.

You can decide whether a writer is biased by asking yourself these questions:

1. **Is the writer acting as a reporter—presenting facts—or as a salesperson—providing only favorable information?**

2. **Are there other views toward the subject that the writer does not discuss?**

Use these questions to determine whether the author of the following paragraph is biased:

> In order for children to become literate, they need to be exposed to good storytelling. Television is a great source of good storytelling. Because of the short time frame of many programs, television shows must deliver a structured, logical, interesting, visually captivating story in about 20 minutes. In fact, a study published in 2009 in the British Journal of Development Psychology showed that preschoolers from economically disadvantaged homes develop literacy skills from watching television. Since some minority children already suffer from literacy difficulties and sometimes do not have the opportunity to hear librarians or parents read to them, television can be an important tool in their education.

The subject of this passage is the development of children's literacy skills through television viewing. The passage makes a positive connection between literacy and television and reports evidence that suggests that some children should watch television as part of their education. The other side of the issue—the negative effects of television viewing—is not mentioned. There is no discussion of such negative effects as childhood obesity, the exposure to commercials and marketing to children, the emphasis on violence, and the hinderance of creative abilities. The author is biased and expresses only a positive attitude toward television.

IS THE WRITING SLANTED?

Slanting refers to the inclusion of details that suit the author's purpose and the omission of those that do not. Suppose you were asked to write a description of a person you know. If you wanted a reader to respond favorably to the person, you might write something like this:

> Alex is tall, muscular, and well-built. He is a friendly person and seldom becomes angry or upset. He enjoys sharing jokes and stories with his friends.

On the other hand, if you wanted to create a less positive image of Alex, you could omit the above information and emphasize these facts instead:

> Alex has a long nose and his teeth are crooked. He talks about himself a lot and doesn't seem to listen to what others are saying. Alex wears rumpled clothes that are too big for him.

While all of these facts about Alex may be true, the writer decides which to include, and which to omit.

Much of what you read is slanted. For instance, advertisers tell only what is good about a product, not what is wrong with it. In the newspaper advice column, Dear Abby gives her opinion on how to solve a reader's problem, but she does not discuss all the possible solutions.

As you read material that is slanted, keep these questions in mind:

1. **What types of facts has the author omitted?**
2. **How would the inclusion of these facts change your reaction or impression?**

EXERCISE 12-5 **Identifying Slanted Writing**

Directions: Below is a list of different types of writing. Working in pairs, decide whether each item has little slant (L), is moderately slanted (M), or is very slanted (V). Write L, M, or V in the space provided.

_____   1. Help-wanted ads

_____   2. An encyclopedia entry

_____   3. A newspaper editorial

_____   4. A biology textbook

_____   5. A letter inviting you to apply for a charge account

_____   6. A college admissions Web site

_____   7. An autobiography of a famous person

_____   8. An online use agreement.

_____   9. *Time* magazine

_____   10. *Catholic Digest* magazine

HOW DOES THE WRITER SUPPORT HIS OR HER IDEAS?

Suppose a friend said he thought you should quit your part-time job immediately. What would you do? Would you automatically accept his advice, or would you ask him why? No doubt you would not blindly accept the advice but would inquire why. Then, having heard his reasons, you would decide whether they made sense.

Similarly, when you read, you should not blindly accept a writer's ideas. Instead, you should ask why he or she believes them by checking to see how the writer supports or explains his or her ideas. Then, once you have examined the supporting information, decide whether you accept the idea.

Evaluating the supporting evidence a writer provides involves using your judgment. The evidence you accept as conclusive may be regarded by someone else as insufficient. The judgment you make depends on your purpose and background knowledge, among other things. In judging the quality of supporting information a writer provides, you should watch for the use of (1) generalizations, (2) personal experience, and (3) statistics as evidence.

Generalizations

What do the following statements have in common?

> Dogs are vicious and nasty.
> College students are more interested in having fun than in learning.
> Parents want their children to grow up to be just like them.

These sentences seem to have little in common. However, although the subjects are different, the sentences do have one thing in common: each is a generalization. Each makes a broad statement about a group—dogs, college students, parents. The first statement says that dogs are vicious and nasty. Yet the writer could not be certain that this statement is true unless he or she had seen *every* existing dog. No doubt the writer felt this statement was true based on his or her observation of and experience with dogs.

A generalization is a statement that is made about an entire group or class of individuals or items based on experience with some members of that group. It necessarily involves the writer's judgment.

The question that must be asked about all generalizations is whether they are accurate. How many dogs did the writer observe and how much research did he or she do to justify the generalization? Try to think of exceptions to the generalization, in this instance, a dog that is neither vicious nor nasty.

As you evaluate the supporting evidence a writer uses, be alert for generalizations that are presented as facts. A writer may, on occasion, support a statement by offering unsupported generalizations. When this occurs, treat the writer's ideas with a critical, questioning attitude.

EXERCISE 12-6 | **Identifying Generalizations**

Directions: Read each of the following statements and decide whether it is a generalization. Place a check mark next to the statements that are generalizations.

_____   1. My sister wants to attend the University of Chicago.

_____   2. Most engaged couples regard their wedding as one of the most important occasions in their lives.

_____   3. Senior citizens are a cynical and self-interested group.

_____   4. People do not use drugs unless they perceive them to be beneficial.

_____   5. Warning signals of a heart attack include pain or pressure in the left side of the chest.

EXERCISE 12-7 | **Identifying Generalizations**

Directions: Read the following passages and underline each generalization.

1. Child care workers are undereducated in relation to the importance of their jobs. A whole generation of children is being left day after day in the hands of women with little more than high-school-level education. These children will suffer in the future for our inattention to the child care employment pool.

2. For the past few years, drivers have been getting worse. Especially guilty of poor driving are the oldest and youngest drivers. There should be stricter tests and more classes for new drivers and yearly eye exams and road tests for drivers once they hit age 60. This is the only way to ensure the safety of our roads.

3. The things that attract men and women to each other have not changed a lot over the years. Throughout history and even to this day, men and women are valued for different qualities. Men are traditionally prized for their ability to hunt and gather (i.e., provide and achieve status in the group). Women, on the other hand, are valued for their youth and beauty, because this represents an ability to produce genetically desirable children.

—Papadopoulos, *What Men Say, What Women Hear*, p. 22

EXERCISE **12-8**   **Evaluating Generalizations**

Directions: Work in groups of three or four students. For each of the following generalizations, discuss what questions you would ask and what types of information you would need to evaluate the generalization.

1. Vegetarians are pacifists and they do not own guns.
2. Most crimes are committed by high school dropouts.
3. It always rains in Seattle.
4. Private school students get a better education than public school students.
5. Scientists don't believe in any kind of higher power.

Personal Experience

Writers often support their ideas by describing their own personal experiences. Although a writer's experiences may be interesting and reveal a perspective on an issue, do not accept them as proof. Suppose you are reading an article on drug use and the writer uses his or her personal experience with particular drugs to prove a point. There are several reasons why you should not accept the writer's conclusions about the drugs' effects as fact. First, the effects of a drug may vary from person to person. The drugs' effects on the writer may be unusual. Second, unless the writer kept careful records about times, dosages, surrounding circumstances, and so on, he or she is describing events from memory. Over time, the writer may have forgotten or exaggerated some of the effects. As you read, treat ideas supported only through personal experience as *one person's experience.* Do not make the error of generalizing the experience.

Statistics

People are often impressed by **statistics**—figures, percentages, averages, and so forth. They accept these as absolute proof. Actually, statistics can be misused, misinterpreted, or used selectively to give other than the most objective, accurate picture of a situation.

Here is an example of how statistics can be misused. Suppose you read that magazine *A* increased its readership by 50 percent, while magazine *B* had only a 10 percent increase. From this statistic, some readers might assume that magazine *A* has a wider readership than magazine *B*. The missing but crucial statistic is the total readership of each magazine prior to the increase. If magazine *A* had a readership of 20,000 and this increased by 50 percent, its readership would total 30,000. If magazine *B*'s readership was already 50,000, a 10 percent increase, bringing the new total to 55,000, would still give it the larger readership despite the smaller increase. Even statistics, then, must be read with a critical, questioning mind.

Here is another example:

> Americans in the workforce are better off than ever before. The average household income is $71,000.

At first the statement may seem convincing. However, a closer look reveals that the statistic given does not really support the statement. The term *average* is the key to how the statistic is misused. An average includes all salaries, both high and low. It is possible that some Americans earn $4,000 while others earn $250,000. Although the average salary may be $71,000, this does not mean that everyone earns $71,000.

EXERCISE **12-9** ## Evaluating the Use of Statistics

Directions: Read each of the following statements and decide how the statistic is misused. Write your explanation in the space provided.

1. Classrooms on our campus are not overcrowded. There are ten square feet of floor space for every student, faculty member, and staff member on campus.

   _____

   _____

   _____

2. More than 14,000 people bought a Prius last year, so it is a popular car.

   _____

   _____

   _____

3. The average water pollution by our local industries is well below the hazardous level established by the Environmental Protection Agency.

   _____

   _____

   _____

IS IT FACT OR OPINION?

Facts are statements that can be verified. They can be proven true or false. **Opinions** are statements that express a writer's feelings, attitudes, or beliefs. They are neither true nor false. Here are a few examples of each:

> **Facts**
>
> 1. My car insurance costs $1,500.
> 2. The theory of instinct was formulated by Konrad Lorenz.
> 3. Greenpeace is an organization dedicated to preserving the sea and its animals.

> **Opinions**
>
> 1. My car insurance is too expensive.
> 2. The slaughter of baby seals for their pelts should be outlawed.
> 3. Population growth should be regulated through mandatory birth control.

The ability to distinguish between fact and opinion is an essential part of evaluating an author's supporting information. Factual statements from reliable sources can usually be accepted as correct. Opinions, however, must be considered as one person's viewpoint that you are free to accept or reject.

EXERCISE 12-10   **Distinguishing Between Fact and Opinion**

Directions: Mark each of the following statements as either fact or opinion.

_____   1. Alligators provide no physical care for their young.

_____   2. Humans should be concerned about the use of pesticides that kill insects at the bottom of the food chain.

_____   3. There are 24 more humans living on the earth now than there were ten seconds ago.

_____   4. We must bear greater responsibility for the environment than our ancestors did.

_____   5. Nuclear power is the only viable solution to our dwindling natural resources.

6. Between 1850 and 1900 the death rate in Europe decreased due to industrial growth and advances in medicine.

_____

7. Dogs make the best pets because they can be trained to obey.

_____

8. Solar energy is available wherever sunlight reaches the earth.

_____

9. By the year 2020, many diseases, including cancer, will be preventable.

_____

10. Hormones are produced in one part of the body and carried by the blood to another part of the body where they influence some process or activity.

_____

Judgment Words

When a writer or speaker expresses an opinion he or she often uses words or phrases that can tip you off that a judgment or opinion is being offered. Here are a few examples.

> Professor Rodriguez is a *better* teacher than Professor Harrigan.
> My sister's behavior at the party was *disgusting*.

Here is a list of words that often suggests that the writer is interpreting, judging or evaluating, or expressing feelings.

bad	good	worthless	amazing	frightening
worse	better	worthwhile	wonderful	
worst	best	disgusting	lovely	

EXERCISE **12-11**   **Identifying Opinions**

Directions: For each of the following statements, underline the word or phrase that suggests the statement is an opinion.

1. Purchasing a brand new car is a terrible waste of money.

2. Many wonderful vegetarian cookbooks are available in bookstores.

3. Of all the film versions of Victor Hugo's novel *Les Miserables,* the 1935 version starring Charles Laughton is the best.

4. The introductory biology textbook comes with an amazing DVD.

5. Volunteers for Habitat for Humanity are engaged in a worthwhile activity.

Informed Opinion

The opinion of experts is known as **informed opinion.** For example, the Surgeon General is regarded as an authority on the health of Americans and his or her opinion on this subject is more trustworthy than that of casual observers or nonprofessionals.

Here are a few examples of expert opinions.

- Carol Dweck, Ph.D., Stanford University psychologist: *"One of the main jobs of parents is building and protecting their children's self-esteem."*

- Federal Reserve Chairman Ben S. Bernanke: *"Clearly, we still have much to learn about how best to make monetary policy and to meet threats to financial stability in this new era. Maintaining flexibility and an open mind will be essential for successful policymaking as we feel our way forward."*

- Jane Goodall, primate expert and ethologist: *"Chimps are in massive danger of extinction from dwindling habitats—forests are being cut down at an alarming rate."*

Textbook authors, too, often offer informed opinion. As experts in their fields, they may make observations and offer comments that are not strictly factual. Instead, they are based on years of study and research. Here is an example from an American government textbook:

> The United States is a place where the pursuit of private, particular, and narrow interests is honored. In our culture, following the teachings of Adam Smith, the pursuit of self-interest is not only permitted but actually celebrated as the basis of the good and prosperous society.
>
> —Greenberg and Page, *The Struggle for Democracy*, p. 186

The author of this statement has reviewed the available evidence and is providing his expert opinion on what the evidence indicates about American political culture. The reader, then, is free to disagree and offer evidence to support an opposing view.

Some authors are careful to signal the reader when they are presenting an opinion. Watch for words and phrases such as:

apparently	this suggests	in my view	one explanation is
presumably	possibly	it is likely that	according to
in my opinion	it is believed	seemingly	

Other authors do just the opposite; they try to make opinions sound like facts. In the following excerpt from a social problems textbook, notice how the author carefully distinguishes factual statements from opinion by using qualifying words and phrases (underlined here for easy identification).

> **Economic Change, Ideology, and Private Life**
>
> <u>It seems clear</u> that there has been a major change in attitudes and feelings about family relationships since the eighteenth century. <u>It is less clear</u> how and why the change came about. One question debated by researchers is: In what social class did the new family pattern originate—in the aristocracy, as Trumbach believes, or in the upper gentry, as Stone argued, or in the working class, as Shorter contended? Or was the rise of the new domesticity a cultural phenomenon that affected people in all social categories at roughly the same time? Carole Shammas <u>has found evidence</u> of such a widespread cultural change by looking at the kinds of things people had in their homes at various times in the past, as recorded in probate inventories. She found that in the middle of the eighteenth century all social classes experienced a change in living habits; even working-class households now contained expensive tools of domesticity, such as crockery, teapots, eating utensils, and so on. Thus, <u>according to Shammas</u>, the home was becoming an important center for social interaction, and family meals had come to occupy an important place in people's lives.
>
> —Skolnick, *The Intimate Environment*, p. 96

EXERCISE 12-12   ## Identifying Informed Opinion

Directions: Read each of the following statements. In each, underline the word or phrase that suggests that the author is offering an informed opinion.

1. It seems clear that parents who would bring a young child to an R-rated movie are putting their own interests ahead of what's best for the child.

2. Voters rejected the proposed rapid transit system connecting the southern and northern suburbs, possibly because of racial issues.

3. According to the city superintendent of schools, school uniforms lead to improved behavior and fewer disruptions in the classroom.

4. One explanation for low attendance at professional sporting events is the high price of tickets.

5. It is believed that most people practice some form of recycling in their daily lives.

EXERCISE 12-13 Distinguishing Between Fact and Opinion

Directions: Each of the following paragraphs contains both facts and opinions. Read each paragraph and label each sentence as fact or opinion.

Paragraph 1

¹Flowering plants that are native to the South include purple coneflower and rose verbena. ²In the view of many longtime gardeners, these two plants are an essential part of the Southern landscape. ³Trees that are native to the South include a variety of oaks, as well as flowering dogwoods and redbuds. ⁴Dogwoods are especially lovely, with their white, pink, or coral blossoms announcing the arrival of spring. ⁵For fall color, the deep red of Virginia willow makes a spectacular show in the native Southern garden.

Sentences

1. _____   4. _____

2. _____   5. _____

3. _____

Paragraph 2

¹Today, many companies provide child care assistance, either on- or off-site, for their employees. ²This suggests that employers are becoming aware that their workers' family concerns can affect the company's bottom line. ³The Eli Lilly pharmaceutical company, for example, has built two child-development centers with a total capacity of more than 400 children. ⁴In addition to assistance with daily child care, Bank of America reimburses employees for child-care expenses related to business travel. ⁵It seems clear that other, less progressive employers will have to follow these companies' leads in order to attract and retain the best employees.

Sentences

1. _____   4. _____

2. _____   5. _____

3. _____

Paragraph 3

¹Preparing a will is an important task that millions of people ignore, presumably because they prefer not to think about their own death. ²However, if you die without

What does the photo contribute to the passage?

a will, the courts will determine how your assets should be distributed, as directed by state law. ³Even more important than establishing a will, in my opinion, is expressing your willingness to be an organ donor upon your death. ⁴Each year, 25,000 new patients are added to the waiting list for organ transplants. ⁵The legacy of an organ donor is far more valuable than any material assets put in a will.

Sentences

1. _____

2. _____

3. _____

4. _____

5. _____

DOES THE WRITER MAKE VALUE JUDGMENTS?

OBJECTIVE 9

A writer who states that an idea or action is right or wrong, good or bad, desirable or undesirable is making a **value judgment.** That is, the writer is imposing his or her own judgment on the worth of an idea or action. Here are a few examples of value judgments:

> Divorces should be restricted to couples who can prove incompatibility.

> Hunting animals is wrong.

> Welfare applicants should be forced to apply for any job they are capable of performing.

> Social drinking is acceptable.

You will notice that each statement is controversial. Each involves some type of conflict or idea over which there is disagreement:

1. Restriction versus freedom
2. Right versus wrong
3. Force versus choice
4. Acceptability versus nonacceptability

You may know of some people who would agree and others who might disagree with each statement. A writer who takes a position or side on a conflict is making a value judgment.

As you read, be alert for value judgments. They represent one person's view *only* and there are most likely many other views on the same topic. When you identify a value judgment, try to determine whether the author offers any evidence in support of the position.

EXERCISE 12-14 Answering Critical Questions

Directions: Read the following passage and answer the questions that follow.

A Welfare Mother

I start my day here at five o'clock. I get up and prepare all the children's clothes. If there's shoes to shine, I do it in the morning. About seven o'clock I bathe the children. I leave the baby with the babysitter and I go to work at the settlement house. I work until twelve o'clock. Sometimes I'll work longer if I have to go to welfare and get a check for somebody. When I get back, I try to make hot food for the kids to eat. In the afternoon it's pretty well on my own. I scrub and clean and cook and do whatever I have to do.

Welfare makes you feel like you're nothing. Like you're laying back and not doing anything and it's falling in your lap. But you must understand, mothers, too, work. My house is clean. I've been scrubbing since this morning. You could check my clothes, all washed and ironed. I'm home and I'm working. I am a working mother.

A job that a woman in a house is doing is a tedious job—especially if you want to do it right. If you do it slipshod, then it's not so bad. I'm pretty much of a perfectionist. I tell my kids, hang a towel. I don't want it thrown away. That is very hard. It's a constant game of picking up this, picking up that. And putting this away, so the house'll be clean.

Some men work eight hours a day. There are mothers that work eleven, twelve hours a day. We get up at night, a baby vomits, you have to be calling the doctor, you have to be changing the baby. When do you get a break, really? You don't. This is an all-around job, day and night. Why do they say it's charity? We're working for our money. I am working for this check. It is not charity. We are giving some kind of home to these children.

I'm so busy all day I don't have time to daydream. I pray a lot. I pray to God to give me strength. If He should take a child away from me, to have the strength to accept it. It's His kid. He just borrowed him to me.

I used to get in and close the door. Now I speak up for my right. I walk with my head up. If I want to wear big earrings, I do. If I'm overweight, that's too bad. I've gotten completely over feeling where I'm little. I'm working now, I'm pulling my weight. I'm gonna get off welfare in time, that's my goal—get off.

It's living off welfare and feeling that you're taking something for nothing the way people have said. You get to think maybe you are. You get to think, Why am I so stupid? Why can't I work? Why do I have to live this way? It's not enough to live on anyway. You feel degraded.

The other day I was at the hospital and I went to pay my bill. This nurse came and gave me the green card. Green card is for welfare. She went right in front of me and gave it to the cashier. She said, "I wish I could stay home and let the money fall in my lap." I felt rotten. I was just burning inside. You hear this all the way around you. The doctor doesn't even look at you. People are ashamed to show that green card. Why can't a woman just get a check in the mail: Here, this check is for you. Forget welfare. You're a mother who works.

This nurse, to her way of thinking, she represents the working people. The ones with the green card, we represent the lazy no-goods. This is what she was saying. They're the good ones and we're the bad guys.

—Terkel, *Working*, pp. 303–304

1. What do you think is the source of this selection?

_____

_____

2. Do you consider this welfare mother to be an authority? Why or why not?

_____

_____

3. What assumptions does this welfare mother make? Do you agree or disagree? Why?

_____

_____

_____

4. Do you think this view of a welfare mother is biased? Why or why not?

_____

_____

5. Is the writing in this article slanted? If so, give some examples.

_____

_____

6. How does this welfare mother support her ideas?

_____

_____

7. Does this welfare mother make any value judgments? If so, what are they?

_____

_____

8. Does this welfare mother make any generalizations? If so, underline them.

_____

_____

EXERCISE 12-15 **Answering Critical Questions**

Directions: Read the following passage below and answer the questions that follow.

Consumer Privacy

1   To what extent should a consumer's personal information be available online? This is one of the most controversial ethical questions today. Scott McNealy, CEO of Sun Microsystems, said in 1999: "You already have zero privacy—get over it." Apparently many consumers don't agree: A study of 10,000 Web users found that 84 percent object to reselling of information about their online activity to other companies. One of the highest profile cases is that of DoubleClick Inc., a company that places "cookies" in your computer to let you receive targeted ads. The trouble began when DoubleClick bought Abacus Direct, a 90-million-name database, and began compiling profiles linking the two sets of data so clients would know who was receiving what kinds of ads.

2   DoubleClick's ability to track what you choose to buy and where you choose to surf is just one isolated example, though. Many companies can trace choices you make online and link them to other information about you. For example, when you register online for a product a Globally Unique Identity (GUID) is linked to your name and e-mail address. That means firms like RealJukebox, with 30 million registered users, can relay information to its parent company RealNetworks about the music each user downloads. Comet Systems, which creates customized cursors for companies featuring characters ranging from Pokemon to Energizer bunnies, reports each time a person visits any of the 60,000 Web sites that support its technology. Still other privacy violations are committed by consumers themselves: A site called disgruntledhousewife.com features a column to which women write to describe in excruciating detail the intimate secrets of former lovers. Be careful how you break off a relationship!

3   How can these thorny ethical issues be solved? One solution is an "infomediary;" an online broker who represents consumers and charges marketers for access to their data. As a Novell executive observed, "Slowly but surely consumers are going to realize that their profile is valuable. For loaning out their identity, they're going to expect something in return." Or, perhaps the solution is to hide your identity: Zero-Knowledge Systems of Montreal sells a software package called Freedom that includes five digital pseudonyms to assign to different identities.

4   All of these precautions may be irrelevant if regulations now being considered are ever implemented. One now being discussed is an "opt in" proposal that would forbid a Web site from collecting or selling personal data unless the user checked a box letting it do so. These efforts are being resisted by the online commerce lobby, which argues these safeguards would drastically reduce ad revenues.

—Solomon, *Consumer Behavior: Buying, Having, and Being*, p. 19

1. What is the main point of the passage?

   _____

2. What is the author's attitude toward women who use the digruntledhousewife site?

   _____

3. This passage appeared in a consumer behavior college text. Evaluate it as source for:

   a. a business marketing term paper

   b. computer users who want to learn more about privacy issues on the Internet.

   _____

   _____

4. Is the passage biased? Explain your answer.

   _____

   _____

5. What types of supporting evidence does the author provide? Mark several examples of each type in the passage.

   _____

6. What assumptions does the author make?

   _____

   _____

7. Describe the tone of the passage.

   _____

8. Identify the generalization that is contained in paragraph 1. How is it supported?

   _____

9. Identify a statement of opinion in paragraph 1.

_____

10. Identify a value judgment made in the passage.

_____

EXERCISE 12-16   ## Asking Critical Questions

Directions: Bring to class a brief (two- to three-paragraph) newspaper article, editorial, film review, etc. Working in groups of three or four students, each student should read his or her piece aloud. The group can then discuss and evaluate (1) assumptions, (2) bias, (3) slanted writing, (4) methods of support, and (5) value judgments for each article. Each group should choose one representative article and submit its findings to the class or instructor.

LEARNING STYLE TIPS

If you tend to be a . . .	Then build your critical reading skills by . . .
Creative learner	Asking "What if . . .?" and "So what?" questions to free new ideas and new ways of looking at the subject
Pragmatic learner	Writing marginal notes, recording your thoughts, reactions, and impressions

SELF-TEST SUMMARY

OBJECTIVE 1 How do you evaluate sources?	Source refers to the place the material was originally published. Be sure to use trustworthy and reliable sources and check to be sure they are current.
OBJECTIVE 2 How can you decide if an Internet source is reliable?	Check the author's credentials and affiliations, identify the site's purpose, check the date of posting, check the sponsor, check the links, and verify the information using other sources.

OBJECTIVE 3 How can you evaluate the authority of the author?	Evaluate the author's credentials and his or her qualifications to write about the topic. Evaluate his or her expertise with the subject matter as a further indication of the reliability of the information presented.
OBJECTIVE 4 What are assumptions, and how can you identify them?	Assumptions are ideas that the author believes to be true and upon which he or she bases further ideas. If an author makes no attempt to establish the accuracy or validity of a statement, it may be an assumption.
OBJECTIVE 5 What is bias, and how can you identify it?	Bias is a one-sided viewpoint; alternative viewpoints are not presented. To identify bias, look for statements that present only one side of an issue and do not present opposing or alternative ideas.
OBJECTIVE 6 What is slanted writing, and how can you identify it?	Slanted writing is the selection by the author of details that suit his or her purpose. To identify slanted writing, ask yourself what facts have been omitted and how might inclusion of these details change your response to the material.
OBJECTIVE 7 How does the writer support his or her ideas?	Writers may support their ideas using generalizations, statements about an entire group based on experience with some members of the group. Writers may also use personal experience, statistics, as well as facts and opinions.
OBJECTIVE 8 How can you distinguish between facts and opinions?	Facts are verifiable statements; opinions express beliefs, feelings and attitudes. To distinguish facts from opinions, look for information that can be checked as true; these are facts; also look judgment words that suggest that an author is expressing an opinion.
OBJECTIVE 9 What are value judgments, and how can you identify them?	Value judgments are statements that express the author's view of what is good or bad, or right or wrong. Look for statements on a controversial issue that indicate the author's moral or religious values.

GOING  NLINE

1. Fact or Opinion

 http://cuip.uchicago.edu/www4teach/97/jlyman/default/quiz/factopquiz.html
 http://dhp.com/~laflemm/RfT/Tut2.htm

 Try these online quizzes. Pay attention to what you hear during the day and try to keep track of the facts and opinions. When do you hear more of one than the other?

2. Evaluating Sources

 http://library.nyu.edu/research/tutorials/evaluate.html

 Read through the information in this tutorial from the New York University Libraries. Print the page and use it to evaluate a book or article that you are currently reading for school or pleasure.

3. Amy Tan Internet Comparison

 Look at the Web site for author Amy Tan: **http://www.amytan.net/**

 Read what she says about the accuracy of information about her on Wikipedia. Now read the Wikipedia article: **http://en.wikipedia.org/wiki/Amy_Tan**

 Which source are you more likely to trust and why?

 To check your progress in meeting chapter objectives, log in to **http://www.myreadinglab.com**, click on the Study Plan tab, and then click on the Reading Skills tab. Choose Critical Thinking from the list of subtopics. Read and view the information in the Review Materials section, and then complete the Practices and Tests in the Activities section. You can check your scores by clicking on the Gradebook tab.

P451-460

MASTERY TEST 1 Critical Reading Skills

Name _____ Section _____

Date _____ Number right _____ × 20 points = Score _____

Directions: Read each of the paragraphs below and select the choice that best completes each of the statements that follow.

Paragraph 1

Tuition vouchers have been proposed as a way to improve the quality of public schools. Under a tuition voucher program, the government gives parents of school-age children a set amount of money to pay for school tuition. Parents can use the money at either a public or private school. In order to attract students, public schools will have to improve their meager offerings dramatically; competition from more adaptive private schools will force public schools to wake up and pay better attention to the needs of students.

—Edwards III et al., *Government in America*, p. 685

_____ 1. The author's bias is revealed in the
   a. first sentence.
   b. second sentence.
   c. third sentence.
   d. last sentence.

Paragraph 2

Although the president's wife does not have an official government position, each First Lady of the past forty years has become known for her attention to a particular issue. For example, Lady Bird Johnson supported highway beautification, Rosalyn Carter was a mental health advocate, Barbara Bush promoted literacy, and Hillary Rodham Clinton was involved in health care reform during her husband's first term. During her husband's second term, however, Ms. Clinton took advantage of her position to launch her own political career as a U.S. senator. In doing so, Ms. Clinton became the first First Lady to run for political office.

_____ 2. The only sentence in this paragraph that contains an opinion is the
   a. first sentence.
   b. second sentence.
   c. third sentence.
   d. last sentence.

Paragraph 3

Traveling through Europe presents countless opportunities to meet people from other countries. Unfortunately, many of them don't speak English. Of course, that's part of the fun, as I discovered when I went to Europe as a senior in high school. My efforts to communicate with a Greek sailor, an Italian bus driver, and an Austrian bank teller at various times during that trip convinced me that with persistence, and a sense of humor, you can usually make yourself understood. It's not so important to be able to say the words correctly or to say them with the right accent, and it truly does not help to say the same words slowly and loudly. What works best, both abroad *and* at home, is to say them with a smile.

_____ 3. The author supports the ideas in this paragraph primarily with
   a. statistics.
   b. personal experience.
   c. generalizations.
   d. facts.

Paragraph 4

Welfare and related programs are expensive. Our country has amassed a large public debt, partially due to past spending on social services. Each year, welfare spending continues to increase. Despite the costs of welfare, it is unfair to blame welfare recipients for the past debt problems welfare programs created.

_____ 4. The statement in this paragraph that is a value judgment is the
   a. first sentence.
   b. second sentence.
   c. third sentence.
   d. last sentence.

Paragraph 5

Most of us believe that racism is a bad thing. However, when we are at a party or in another social setting where someone tells a racist joke, we often find it difficult to voice our objections. Why is that? Are we against racism only when it is convenient or easy? Our dilemma is that we see ourselves two ways: as polite people who would never purposely embarrass a friend or even an acquaintance, and as socially aware individuals who know racist comments are wrong. This moral inconsistency is even more troubling when we become parents and must serve as role models for our children. How do we explain the difference between "right" and "polite"—or is there really a difference?

_____ 5. One assumption that the author makes in this paragraph is that most people
   a. would rather not embarrass another person.
   b. believe children know right from wrong.
   c. want their children to behave properly at parties.
   d. enjoy racist jokes.

MASTERY TEST 2 Critical Reading Skills

Name _____ Section _____

Date _____ Number right _____ × 10 points = Score _____

Directions: Read each of the following paragraphs below and select the choice that best answers each of the questions that follow.

Paragraph 1

Having built four new elementary schools in the last five years, members of the Palmville School Board were convinced they had solved the problem with overcrowding that had plagued the public schools ever since the mid-1980s. As a result, they were disappointed when School Superintendent Marisa LaRoux made her mid-July Projected Enrollment Report. She pointed out that the town's population has expanded by several hundred more families than were projected because the good weather this year spurred home building and the low mortgage rates encouraged buyers. In addition, more families are deciding to have two or more children, bringing the average number of children per family to 1.9, much higher than the figure of 1.65 used in the past to calculate demands for school services. The superintendent also admitted that the decades-old policy of calculating a family of two as a family without children has proven to be a serious mistake because it ignored the many children growing up in single-parent families. Based on this information, the superintendent concluded that the overcrowding problem would continue this year and probably for many years in the future. Chairperson Clifton Washington summed up the school board's response this way: "The schools are overcrowded now and if more students are going to be coming to us

asking for instruction, then we'd better get back into the school-building business."

_____ 1. Which of the following types of evidence does the school superintendent use in her report?
   a. opinions
   b. personal experiences
   c. facts and statistics
   d. generalizations

_____ 2. Which of the following is a value judgment that the school board seems to have made?
   a. Public school boards should not study projected enrollments.
   b. Previous enrollment studies were always wrong.
   c. Overcrowding in schools helps education.
   d. Education and schools are important.

_____ 3. Which of the following sentences is *not* an assumption used by the school board when they studied school enrollment in the past?
   a. A household of two people does not have any children.
   b. The average number of children per family was 1.9.
   c. Low mortgage rates encourage home buying.
   d. Good weather increased new home building.

4. Which of the following, if added to the evidence, would *not* support the author's ideas?
   a. Reducing overcrowding is a good idea because students usually learn better in less crowded classrooms.
   b. The recent plant closing in the area has forced many people to move away from Palmville.
   c. All the teachers support building new schools over expanding the school year.
   d. If we build new schools, the best teachers will apply for the new jobs.

_____ 5. Which of the following is a conclusion reached by the school board?
   a. They need to build more schools.
   b. Schools will always be overcrowded.
   c. Four new elementary schools would solve overcrowding.
   d. Most families in the area have more than two children.

Paragraph 2

The latest state proposal to divert more water from agricultural to residential uses might be expected to gain support from rapidly urbanizing Palmville. Speaking through their Town Meeting, however, the citizens of the town argue that the state should not meddle with arrangements that have contributed so much to the economic and social health of the region. The report of the Town Meeting contained these arguments: (1) Farming in the Palmville area constitutes an important element in the state's food supply, which would be expensive to replace. (2) Farms and support industries provide a large proportion of the jobs of Palmville residents. (3) The farms are an important part of the social fabric of the town and the region, providing,

among other things, healthful summer employment for many of the town's youth. (4) Diverting water from the farms would cause many to be sold to real estate developers, thus increasing the population *and* the demand for water. (5) The town's zoning plan will limit growth over the next decade and should slow the increasing demand for water. Whether state officials will be persuaded by these arguments remains to be seen, but Palmville residents hope to prevent changes that might threaten the community they have built so carefully.

_____ 6. Which of the following types of evidence do the town citizens rely on in their arguments?
   a. statistics
   b. personal experiences
   c. facts
   d. generalizations

_____ 7. Which of the following value judgments seems to be the reason behind the arguments by the Palmville citizens?
   a. Residential areas are more important than farm areas.
   b. Proposals by the state should be supported.
   c. Changes will destroy the community.
   d. Water is not important to Palmville.

_____ 8. Which of the following sentences is an assumption (rather than an argument) made by the citizens?
   a. Farms are important to the town.
   b. The town's zoning plan will limit growth over the next decade.
   c. Farms and support industries provide jobs for Palmville residents.
   d. Farms provide summer employment for youths from Palmville.

_____ 9. Which of the following sentences would *not* provide evidence for the Palmville citizens' ideas?

a. The state proposals should not be supported because this is a local issue.

b. Fewer farms will probably increase unemployment in the area.

c. Because farms are beautiful, they are productive.

d. Diverting the water will cause taxes to rise.

_____ 10. Which of the following is supported by the evidence presented by the citizens of Palmville?

a. State officials will be persuaded by the citizens' arguments.

b. Change will occur even if Palmville residents fight it.

c. Farming around Palmville is an important part of the economy of the region.

d. The town's zoning plan is worse than the state's latest proposal.

MASTERY TEST 3 Reading Selection

Name _____ Section _____

Date _____ Number right* _____ × 10 points = Score _____

The Generation that Killed Rock 'n' Roll

Nathan Harden

This selection was written for the February 1, 2010, online issue of the *Huffington Post*. Read the article to learn what is happening to the music industry and why it should matter to music fans.

> **Vocabulary Preview**
>
> **optimization** (par. 8) making the best of something
>
> **longshoreman** (par. 8) a dock worker who loads and unloads ships

1   Ladies and gentlemen: you are witnessing the death of Rock 'n' Roll.

2   Consider this the obituary: from 2004 to 2008 album sales fell from 667 million to 428 million units, according to Neilsen SoundScan. That's a 35% decline in just four years. Last year the Virgin Megastore chain closed the last of its two Manhattan music stores. With this announcement, Virgin is following in the footsteps of the venerable Tower Records, which shuttered its stores and declared bankruptcy in 2006 after amassing $200 million in debt. The Virgin stores were the last big-box music retail shops left in New York.

3   And don't look for the iPod to save the music business. While digital downloads have been on the rise, they haven't come close to making up for the decline in CD sales. Even after digital downloads are accounted for, total music sales declined more than 20% in the U.S. over the last four years. In 2008, the world's four major recording companies: EMI, Sony, Universal, and Warner, posted record losses. Worst of all was EMI, which bled $1.2 billion.

4   The International Federation of the Phonographic Industry claims that 40 billion songs were downloaded illegally in 2008, and that 95% of all downloads were procured illegally, resulting

---

*To calculate the number right, use items 1–10 under "Mastery Test Skills Check."

in billions of losses. People haven't stopped listening to music; they've simply stopped paying for it. As a college student, I saw this firsthand. Surveys indicate that more than half the nation's college students frequently download music illegally.

5   My generation's attitude toward piracy is not likely to change. After all, anti-corporate rebellion is a time-honored Rock 'n' Roll tradition. It's relatively easy to steal music if you imagine that you are merely stealing from 'The Man'—some limo-riding fat cat, snorting coke off his Rolex, sipping Dom Pérignon.

6   By now, many people are familiar with the financial woes of the music industry. What isn't well understood, however, is how the economic misfortunes of the music business are transforming popular music itself, as we know it. In the past, record companies often spent years and, in some cases, millions of dollars to develop each new artist. It took Bruce Springsteen eight years and five albums to achieve his first top ten radio hit. Today, on the other hand, if a band's first album is not a hit, more often than not, that band is dropped from the label. No second chances. Most artists never turn a profit. According to Andy Karp, a top executive at Warner Music, "There are a lot of great classic bands that would have trouble getting a record deal now, like the Doors or others who didn't have their first hit record until their second or third album."

7   Labels are signing fewer artists overall. Mitch Bainwol, chairman of the Recording Industry Association of America estimates that the number of bands being signed to new labels has declined by a third. Who knows how many great artists have remained undiscovered as a result? The digital revolution was supposed to empower musicians. On my own MySpace page, I can upload my own band's music to the web in a matter of minutes, and sell it to anyone in the world with an internet connection. Theoretically, it has never been easier to be heard. Yet hundreds of thousands of other musicians are competing for attention online. Winning new fans and staying connected to them requires tremendous marketing sophistication.

8   Without support from a record label, musicians must master the intricacies of search engine optimization, social networking, email blasts, and twittering—not to mention traditional tasks like booking shows. Not surprisingly, many musicians lack such skills. Can you, even for a moment, imagine Janis Joplin poring over HTML manuals, or Jimi Hendrix spending hours each day spamming potential fans on MySpace? Not likely. Had those two tried to make it in today's marketplace, we may never have even heard of them. And what if internet piracy had existed in the 1960s? No Dylan? No Beatles? Would Bono be working today as a longshoreman?

9   National Academy of Recording Arts and Sciences President Neil Portnow made a plea last night during the Grammy Awards, essentially arguing that people should pay for music in order to support all the unknown artists out there who are trying to "make it." In other words, it may not hurt Beyoncé or AC/DC if you download their music. They are, after all, astonishingly wealthy. But it does hurt the record labels, which, in turn, cannot afford to sign, develop and promote as many new artists. Consequently, our music is becoming less diverse. In the long run, music lovers themselves are deprived.

10   Today, fewer artists are being offered record deals; and new artists are being set aside if they fail to achieve quick success. As a result, the music of an entire generation is being muffled. Many of today's would-be Dylans and Springsteens remain lost in obscurity. We will never hear their songs.

11   Fans of my generation are killing the very thing they love. Despite the self-promotional tools of the digital age, artists today rarely achieve large-scale success without the promotional power of a major label. Yet, increasingly, record labels are unable to develop and market deserving talent. And that is the real tragedy of the illegal downloading epidemic—we don't even know what we're missing.

MASTERY TEST SKILLS CHECK

Directions: Select the choice that best completes each of the following statements.

Checking Your Comprehension

_____ 1. The purpose of this selection is to
   a. call for stricter enforcement of Internet piracy laws.
   b. accuse established artists of not supporting new music.
   c. point out the causes and effects of a declining music industry.
   d. encourage record companies to adjust to a changing market.

_____ 2. The author blames the death of rock 'n' roll on
   a. the weak economy.
   b. a lack of new talent.
   c. illegal downloading.
   d. a lack of music fans.

_____ 3. The topic of paragraph 3 is
   a. the iPod.
   b. music sales.
   c. digital downloads.
   d. record companies.

_____ 4. As an example of an artist who achieved success only after a major investment of time and money by record companies, the author points to
   a. Beyoncé.
   b. Bono.
   c. Janis Joplin.
   d. Bruce Springsteen.

_____ 5. The main idea of paragraph 9 is that illegal downloading
   a. is prohibited by the National Academy of Recording Arts and Sciences.
   b. cuts into the profits of record labels.
   c. does not harm established artists.
   d. ultimately results in less diverse music.

Applying Your Skills

_____ 6. The author's tone throughout this selection can best be described as
   a. hopeful.
   b. objective.
   c. pessimistic.
   d. apologetic.

_____ 7. An example of *objective* language in this selection is
   a. "Ladies and gentlemen: you are witnessing the death of Rock 'n' Roll."

b. "Last year the Virgin Megastore chain closed the last of its two Manhattan music stores."

c. "Fans of my generation are killing the very thing they love."

d. "And that is the real tragedy of the illegal downloading epidemic."

_____ 8. An example of an *opinion* in this selection is

a. "My generation's attitude toward piracy is not likely to change."

b. "Total music sales declined more than 20% in the U.S. over the last four years."

c. "I can upload my own band's music to the web in a matter of minutes."

d. "National Academy of Recording Arts and Sciences President Neil Portnow made a plea last night during the Grammy Awards."

_____ 9. The author's intended audience is most likely

a. online marketers.

b. people interested in music.

c. classical musicians.

d. record label executives.

_____ 10. The types of evidence the author uses to support his ideas include

a. personal experience.

b. informed opinions.

c. statistics.

d. all of the above.

Studying Words

_____ 11. The word *venerable* (par. 2) means

a. related to religion.

b. worthy of respect due to age.

c. very old.

d. respectable.

_____ 12. The word *procured* (par. 4) means

a. obtained.

b. changed.

c. destroyed.

d. allowed.

_____ 13. The synonym clue for the word *woes* (par. 6) is

a. familiar.

b. industry.

c. misfortunes.

d. popular.

_____ 14. The word *intricacies* (par. 8) refers to

a. mistakes.

b. complex details.

c. performances.

d. connections.

_____ 15. The word *obscurity* as it is used in paragraph 10 means

a. the condition of being unknown.

b. an uncertain expression.

c. the absence of light.

d. a quality of being unclear.

For more practice, ask your instructor for an opportunity to work on the mastery tests that appear in the Test Bank.

Summarizing the Reading

Directions: Write a summary of the reading using the opening below as your starting point.

The music industry is in trouble. _____

_____

_____

_____

_____

Reading Visually

1. What illustrations or photographs do you think would enhance this selection?
2. Evaluate the effectiveness of the title and the first few lines of the article in capturing your interest. Why does the author call this article an obituary?
3. How might subheadings enhance the readability of this article? Try to come up with several subheadings that could be placed at different points in the reading.

Thinking Critically about the Reading

WRITE IN YOUR
JOURNAL

1. What types of facts has the author omitted in this article? How would these facts change your reaction or opinion?
2. What is your opinion of illegal downloading? If you feel strongly one way or the other, make a case in favor of your side.
3. In its online form, this article allows readers to make comments about the content, agreeing, disagreeing, or offering another viewpoint. Do you think this aspect of online writing is helpful? Why or why not?

PART VI

A Fiction Minireader

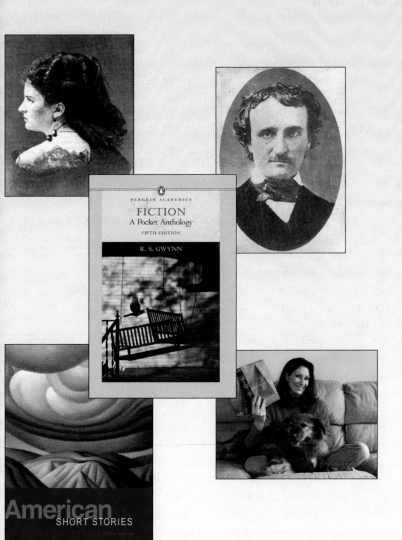

Reading and Interpreting Short Stories

The Story of an Hour
Kate Chopin

The Tell-Tale Heart
Edgar Allan Poe

Little Brother™
Bruce Holland Rogers

Reading and Interpreting Novels

Prologue from Water for Elephants
Sara Gruen

READING AND INTERPRETING SHORT STORIES

A short story is a creative or imaginative work describing a series of events for the purpose of entertainment and/or communicating a serious message. It has six basic elements. The next section describes each. But first, read the following short story, "The Story of an Hour," and then refer back to it as you read about each of the six elements.

The Story of an Hour

Kate Chopin

1   Knowing that Mrs. Mallard was afflicted with heart trouble, great care was taken to break to her as gently as possible the news of her husband's death.

2   It was her sister Josephine who told her, in broken sentences; veiled hints that revealed in half concealing. Her husband's friend Richards was there, too, near her. It was he who had been in the newspaper office when intelligence of the railroad disaster was received, with Brently Mallard's name leading the list of "killed." He had only taken the time to assure himself of its truth by a second telegram, and had hastened to forestall any less careful, less tender friend in bearing the sad message.

3   She did not hear the story as many women have heard the same, with a paralyzed inability to accept its significance. She wept at once, with sudden, wild abandonment, in her sister's arms. When the storm of grief had spent itself she went away to her room alone. She would have no one follow her.

4   There stood, facing the open window, a comfortable, roomy armchair. Into this she sank, pressed down by a physical exhaustion that haunted her body and seemed to reach into her soul.

5   She could see in the open square before her house the tops of trees that were all aquiver with the new spring life. The delicious breath of rain was in the air. In the street below a peddler was crying his wares. The notes of a distant song which someone was singing reached her faintly, and countless sparrows were twittering in the eaves.

6   There were patches of blue sky showing here and there through the clouds that had met and piled one above the other in the west facing her window.

7   She sat with her head thrown back upon the cushion of the chair, quite motionless, except when a sob came up into her throat and shook her, as a child who has cried itself to sleep continues to sob in its dreams.

8   She was young, with a fair, calm face, whose lines bespoke repression and even a certain strength. But now there was a dull stare in her eyes, whose gaze was fixed away off yonder on one of those patches of blue sky. It was not a glance of reflection, but rather indicated a suspension of intelligent thought.

9   There was something coming to her and she was waiting for it, fearfully. What was it? She did not know; it was too subtle and elusive to name. But she felt it, creeping out of the sky, reaching toward her through the sounds, the scents, the color that filled the air.

10   Now her bosom rose and fell tumultuously. She was beginning to recognize this thing that was approaching to possess her, and she was striving to beat it back with her will—as powerless as her two white slender hands would have been.

11   When she abandoned herself a little whispered word escaped her slightly parted lips. She said it over and over under her breath: "free, free, free!" The vacant stare and the look of terror that had followed it went from her eyes. They stayed keen and bright. Her pulses beat fast, and the coursing blood warmed and relaxed every inch of her body.

12   She did not stop to ask if it were or were not a monstrous joy that held her. A clear and exalted perception enabled her to dismiss the suggestion as trivial.

13   She knew that she would weep again when she saw the kind, tender hands folded in death; the face that had never looked save with love upon her, fixed and gray and dead. But she saw beyond that bitter moment a long procession of years to come that would belong to her absolutely. And she opened and spread her arms out to them in welcome.

14   There would be no one to live for her during those coming years; she would live for herself. There would be no powerful will bending hers in that blind persistence with which men and women believe they have a right to impose a private will upon a fellow-creature. A kind intention or a cruel intention made the act seem no less a crime as she looked upon it in that brief moment of illumination.

15   And yet she had loved him—sometimes. Often she had not. What did it matter! What could love, the unresolved mystery, count for in face of this possession of self-assertion which she suddenly recognized as the strongest impulse of her being!

16   "Free! Body and soul free!" she kept whispering.

17   Josephine was kneeling before the closed door with her lips to the keyhole, imploring for admission. "Louise, open the door! I beg; open the door—you will make yourself ill. What are you doing, Louise? For heaven's sake open the door."

18   "Go away. I am not making myself ill." No; she was drinking in a very elixir of life through that open window.

19   Her fancy was running riot along those days ahead of her. Spring days, and summer days, and all sorts of days that would be her own. She breathed a quick prayer that life might be long. It was only yesterday she had thought with a shudder that life might be long.

20   She arose at length and opened the door to her sister's importunities. There was a feverish triumph in her eyes, and she carried herself unwittingly like a goddess of Victory. She clasped her sister's waist, and together they descended the stairs. Richards stood waiting for them at the bottom.

21   Someone was opening the front door with a latchkey. It was Brently Mallard who entered, a little travel-stained, composedly carrying his grip-sack and umbrella. He had been far from the scene of the accident, and did not even know there had been one. He stood amazed at Josephine's piercing cry; at Richards' quick motion to screen him from the view of his wife.

22   But Richards was too late.

23   When the doctors came they said she had died of heart disease—of joy that kills.

Plot

The plot is the basic story line—the sequence of events as they occur in the work. The plot focuses on conflict and often follows a predictable structure. The plot frequently begins by setting the scene, introducing the main characters, and providing the background information needed to follow the story. Next, there is often a complication or problem that arises. Suspense builds as the problem or conflict unfolds. Near the end of the story, events reach a climax—the point at which the outcome (resolution) of the conflict will be decided. A conclusion quickly follows as the story ends.

The plot of "The Story of an Hour" involves a surprise ending: Mrs. Mallard learns that her husband has been killed in a railroad disaster. She ponders his death and relishes the freedom it will bring. At the end of the story, when Mrs. Mallard discovers that her husband is not dead after all, she suffers a heart attack and dies.

Setting

The setting is the time, place, and circumstances under which the action occurs. The setting provides the mood or atmosphere in which the characters interact. The setting of "The Story of an Hour" is the Mallards' home and takes place during the course of one hour.

Characterization

Characters are the actors in a narrative story. The characters reveal themselves by what they say—the dialogue—and by their actions, appearance, thoughts, and feelings. The narrator, or person who tells the story, may also comment on or reveal information about the characters. As you read, analyze the characters' traits and motives. Also analyze their personalities and watch for character changes. Study how the characters relate to one another.

In "The Story of an Hour" the main character is Mrs. Mallard; her thoughts and actions after learning of her husband's supposed death are the crux of the story.

Point of View

The point of view refers to the way the story is presented or the person from whose perspective the story is told. Often the story is not told from the narrator's perspective. The story may be told from the perspective of one of the characters, or that of an unknown narrator. In analyzing point of view, determine the role and function of the narrator. Is the narrator reliable and knowledgeable? Sometimes the narrator is able to enter the minds of some or all of the characters, knowing their thoughts and understanding their actions and motivations. In other stories, the narrator may not understand the actions or implications of the events in the story.

"The Story of an Hour" is told by a narrator not involved in the story. The story is told by a third-person narrator who is knowledgeable and understands the characters' actions and motives. In the story's last line, the narrator tells us that doctors assumed Mrs. Mallard died of "joy that kills."

Tone

The tone or mood of a story reflects the author's attitude. Like a person's tone of voice, tone suggests feelings. Many ingredients contribute to tone, including the author's choice of detail (characters, setting, etc.) and the language that is used. The tone of a story may be, for example, humorous, ironic, or tragic. The author's feelings are not necessarily those of the characters or the narrator. Instead, it is through the narrator's description of the characters and their actions that we infer tone. In "The Story of an Hour," the tone might be described as serious. Serious events occur that dramatically affect Mrs. Mallard's life. The story also has an element of surprise and irony. We are surprised to learn that Mr. Mallard is not dead after all, and it is ironic, or the opposite of what we expect, to learn that Mrs. Mallard dies "of joy that kills."

Theme

The theme of the story is its meaning or message. The theme of a work may also be considered its main idea or main point. Themes are often large, universal ideas dealing with life and death, human values, or existence. To establish the theme, ask yourself, "What is the author trying to say about life by telling the story?" Try to explain it in a single sentence. One theme of "The Story of an Hour" is freedom. Mrs. Mallard experiences a sense of freedom upon learning of her husband's supposed death. She sees "a long procession of years to come that would belong to her absolutely." There is also a theme of rebirth, suggested by references to springtime; her life without her husband was just beginning. The author also may be commenting on the restrictive or repressive nature of marriage during the time the story was written. After

Mr. Mallard's death, "There would be no powerful will bending hers. . . ." Mrs. Mallard, after all, dies not from losing her husband but from the thought of losing her newly found freedom.

If you are having difficulty stating the theme, try the following suggestions:

1. **Study the title.** Now that you have read the story, does it take on any new meanings?
2. **Analyze the main characters.** Do they change? If so, how and in reaction to what?
3. **Look for broad general statements.** What do the characters or the narrator say about life or the problems they face?
4. **Look for symbols, figurative expressions, meaningful names (example: Mrs. Goodheart), or objects that hint at larger ideas.**

The Tell-Tale Heart
Edgar Allan Poe

Edgar Allan Poe was born in Boston in 1809 and was orphaned at the age of two. He was raised by wealthy foster parents who provided him with a privileged upbringing, including education and travel. He embarked upon a successful literary career as both editor and contributor to several major journals. However, after his wife died in 1847, Poe's personal problems and heavy drinking became worse. This led to unemployment, poverty, and eventually to his death in Baltimore at the age of 40. Poe is most famous for his macabre poems and short stories, and he is considered by many to be the inventor of the modern detective story.

Vocabulary Preview

hearken (par. 1) listen, pay attention
dissimulation (par. 3) disguising one's true intentions
profound (par. 3) insightful
sagacity (par. 4) wisdom
suppositions (par. 7) assumptions or beliefs
crevice (par. 8) a narrow opening or crack
scantlings (par. 13) small pieces of lumber
suavity (par. 14) pleasantness; showing politeness and charm
deputed (par. 14) assigned or delegated
audacity (par. 15) boldness
gesticulations (par. 17) gestures or movements
derision (par. 17) ridicule or contempt

1   True!—nervous—very, very dreadfully nervous I had been and am; but why *will* you say that I am mad? The disease had sharpened my senses—not destroyed—not dulled them. Above all was the sense of hearing acute. I heard all things in the heaven and in the earth. I heard many things in hell. How, then, am I mad? Hearken! and observe how healthily—how calmly I can tell you the whole story.

2   It is impossible to say how first the idea entered my brain; but once conceived, it haunted me day and night. Object there was none. Passion there was none. I loved the old man. He had never wronged me. He had never given me insult. For his gold I had no desire. I think it was his eye! Yes, it was this! One of his eyes resembled that of a vulture—a pale blue eye, with a film over it. Whenever it fell upon me, my blood ran cold; and so by degrees—very gradually—I made up my mind to take the life of the old man, and thus rid myself of the eye for ever.

3   Now this is the point. You fancy me mad. Madmen know nothing. But you should have seen *me*. You should have seen how wisely I proceeded—with what caution—with what foresight—with what dissimulation I went to work! I was never kinder to the old man than during the whole week before I killed him. And every night, about midnight, I turned the latch of his door and opened it—oh, so gently! And then, when I had made an opening sufficient for my head, I put in a dark lantern, all closed, closed, so that no light shone out, and then I thrust in my head. Oh, you would have laughed to see how cunningly I thrust it in! I moved it slowly—very, very slowly, so that I might not disturb the old man's sleep. It took me an hour to place my whole head within the opening so far that I could see him as he lay upon his bed. Ha!—would a madman have been so wise as this? And then, when my head was well in the room, I undid the lantern cautiously—oh, so cautiously—cautiously (for the hinges creaked)—I undid it just so much that a single thin ray fell upon the vulture eye. And this I did for seven long nights—every night just at midnight—but I found the eye always closed; and so it was impossible to do the work; for it was not the old man who vexed me, but his Evil Eye. And every morning, when the day broke, I went boldly into the chamber, and spoke courageously to him, calling him by name in a hearty tone, and inquiring how he had passed the night. So you see he would have been a very profound old man, indeed, to suspect that every night, just at twelve, I looked in upon him while he slept.

4   Upon the eighth night I was more than usually cautious in opening the door. A watch's minute hand moves more quickly than did mine. Never before that night had I *felt* the extent of my own powers—of my sagacity. I could scarcely contain my feelings of triumph. To think that there I was, opening the door, little by little, and he not even to dream of my secret deeds or thoughts. I fairly chuckled at the idea; and perhaps he heard me; for he moved on the bed suddenly, as if startled. Now you may think that I drew back—but no. His room was as black as pitch with the thick darkness, (for the shutters were close fastened, through fear of robbers), and so I knew that he could not see the opening of the door, and I kept pushing it on steadily, steadily.

5   I had my head in, and was about to open the lantern, when my thumb slipped upon the tin fastening, and the old man sprang up in bed, crying out—"Who's there?"

6   I kept quite still and said nothing. For a whole hour I did not move a muscle, and in the meantime I did not hear him lie down. He was still sitting up in the bed, listening;—just as I have done, night after night, hearkening to the death watches* in the wall.

7   Presently I heard a slight groan, and I knew it was the groan of mortal terror. It was not a groan of pain or of grief—oh, no!—it was the low stifled sound that arises from the bottom of the soul when overcharged with awe. I knew the sound very well. Many a night, just at midnight, when all the world slept, it has welled up from my own bosom, deepening, with its dreadful echo, the terrors that distracted me. I say I knew it well. I knew what the old man felt, and pitied him, although I chuckled at heart. I knew that he had been lying awake ever since the first slight noise, when he had turned in the bed. His fears had been ever since growing upon him. He had been trying to fancy them causeless, but could not. He had been saying to himself—"It is nothing but the wind in the chimney—it is only a mouse crossing the floor," or "It is merely a cricket which has made a single chirp." Yes, he had been trying to comfort himself with these suppositions; but he had found all in vain. *All in vain;* because Death, in approaching him, had stalked with his black shadow before him, and enveloped the victim. And it was the mournful influence of the unperceived shadow that caused him to feel—although he neither saw nor heard—to *feel* the presence of my head within the room.

8   When I had waited a long time, very patiently, without hearing him lie down, I resolved to open a little—a very, very little crevice in the lantern. So I opened it—you cannot imagine how stealthily, stealthily—until, at length, a single dim ray, like the thread of the spider, shot from out the crevice and fell upon the vulture eye.

9   It was open—wide, wide open—and I grew furious as I gazed upon it. I saw it with perfect distinctness—all a dull blue, with a hideous veil over it that chilled the very marrow in my bones; but I could see nothing else of the old man's face or person: for I had directed the ray as if by instinct, precisely upon the damned spot.

10   And now have I not told you that what you mistake for madness is but overacuteness of the senses?—now, I say, there came to my ears a low, dull, quick sound, such as a watch makes when enveloped in cotton. I knew *that* sound well, too. It was the beating of the old man's heart. It increased my fury, as the beating of a drum stimulates the soldier into courage.

11   But even yet I refrained and kept still. I scarcely breathed. I held the lantern motionless. I tried how steadily I could maintain the ray upon the eye. Meantime the hellish tattoo of the heart increased. It grew quicker and quicker, and louder and louder every instant. The old man's terror *must* have been extreme! It grew louder, I say, louder every moment!—do you mark me well? I have told you that

---

death watches: beetles that infest timbers. Their clicking sound was thought to be an omen of death.

I am nervous: so I am. And now at the dead hour of the night, amid the dreadful silence of that old house, so strange a noise as this excited me to uncontrollable terror. Yet, for some minutes longer I refrained and stood still. But the beating grew louder, louder! I thought the heart must burst. And now a new anxiety seized me—the sound would be heard by a neighbor! The old man's hour had come! With a loud yell, I threw open the lantern and leaped into the room. He shrieked once—once only. In an instant I dragged him to the floor, and pulled the heavy bed over him. I then smiled gaily, to find the deed so far done. But, for many minutes, the heart beat on with a muffled sound. This, however, did not vex me; it would not be heard through the wall. At length it ceased. The old man was dead. I removed the bed and examined the corpse. Yes, he was stone, stone dead. I placed my hand upon the heart and held it there many minutes. There was no pulsation. He was stone dead. His eye would trouble me no more.

12   If still you think me mad, you will think so no longer when I describe the wise precautions I took for the concealment of the body. The night waned, and I worked hastily, but in silence. First of all I dismembered the corpse. I cut off the head and the arms and the legs.

13   I then took up three planks from the flooring of the chamber, and deposited all between the scantlings. I then replaced the boards so cleverly, so cunningly, that no human eye—not even *his*—could have detected anything wrong. There was nothing to wash out—no stain of any kind—no bloodspot whatever. I had been too wary for that. A tub had caught all—ha! ha!

14   When I had made an end of these labors, it was four o'clock—still dark as midnight. As the bell sounded the hour, there came a knocking at the street door. I went down to open it with a light heart,—for what had I *now* to fear? There entered three men, who introduced themselves, with perfect suavity, as officers of the police. A shriek had been heard by a neighbor during the night; suspicion of foul play had been aroused; information had been lodged at the police office, and they (the officers) had been deputed to search the premises.

15   I smiled,—for *what* had I to fear? I bade the gentlemen welcome. The shriek, I said, was my own in a dream. The old man, I mentioned, was absent in the country. I took my visitors all over the house. I bade them search—search *well*. I led them, at length, to *his* chamber. I showed them his treasures, secure, undisturbed. In the enthusiasm of my confidence, I brought chairs into the room, and desired them *here* to rest from their fatigues, while I myself, in the wild audacity of my perfect triumph, placed my own seat upon the very spot beneath which reposed the corpse of the victim.

16   The officers were satisfied. My *manner* had convinced them. I was singularly at ease. They sat, and while I answered cheerily, they chatted of familiar things, But, ere long, I felt myself getting pale and wished them gone. My head ached, and I fancied a ringing in my ears: but still they sat and still they chatted. The ringing became more distinct:—it continued and became more distinct: I talked more freely to get rid of the feeling: but it continued and gained definitiveness—until, at length, I found that the noise was *not* within my ears.

17   No doubt I now grew *very* pale—but I talked more fluently, and with a heightened voice. Yet the sound increased—and what could I do? It was *a low, dull, quick sound—much such a sound as a watch makes when enveloped in cotton.* I gasped for breath—and yet the officers heard it not. I talked more quickly—more vehemently; but the noise steadily increased. I arose and argued about trifles, in a high key and with violent gesticulations; but the noise steadily increased. Why *would* they not be gone? I paced the floor to and fro with heavy strides, as if excited to fury by the observations of the men—but the noise steadily increased. Oh God! what *could* I do? I foamed—I raved—I swore! I swung the chair upon which I had been sitting, and grated it upon the boards, but the noise arose over all and continually increased. It grew louder—louder—*louder!* And still the men chatted pleasantly and smiled. Was it possible they heard not? Almighty God!—no, no! They heard!—they suspected!—they *knew!*—they were making a mockery of my horror!—this I thought and this I think. But anything was better than this agony! Anything was more tolerable than this derision! I could bear those hypocritical smiles no longer! I felt that I must scream or die!—and now—again!—hark! louder! louder! louder! *louder!*—

18   "Villains!" I shrieked, "dissemble no more! I admit the deed!—tear up the planks!—here, here!—it is the beating of his hideous heart!"

Directions: Choose the best answer for each of the following questions.

Checking Your Comprehension

_____ 1. In this story, the main character describes how
      a. an old man tried to murder him.
      b. he prevented an old man's murder.
      c. he caught and arrested a murderer.
      d. he murdered an old man.

_____ 2. The character was inspired to kill the old man because
      a. he wanted the old man's gold.
      b. the old man had wronged him.
      c. the old man had insulted him.
      d. he was disturbed by one of the old man's eyes.

_____ 3. Once the character decided to kill the old man, he
      a. killed him later that day.
      b. waited until the next day to kill him.
      c. waited a whole week before killing him.
      d. waited almost a year and then changed his mind.

_____ 4. The reason the killer waited was that he
        a. wanted to find someone to help him kill the old man.
        b. could not kill the old man unless the old man's eye was open.
        c. needed to find a weapon.
        d. was afraid of being caught.

_____ 5. When the police came to the house, they
        a. immediately found the old man's body and arrested the killer.
        b. searched for clues but left without making an arrest.
        c. were suspicious of the man's story and took him in for questioning.
        d. were satisfied with the man's story.

The Elements of a Short Story

_____ 6. The tone of the story can best be described as
        a. suspenseful.
        b. humorous.
        c. ironic.
        d. sad.

_____ 7. The setting of the story is
        a. the old man's house.
        b. the police station.
        c. prison.
        d. an insane asylum.

_____ 8. This story is told from the perspective of
        a. the old man.
        b. the police.
        c. the killer.
        d. a neighbor.

_____ 9. The title is a reference to how the
        a. killer imagined the old man's heart beating so loudly that it gave him away.
        b. old man knew that he was going to be murdered.
        c. police officers found the old man's heart and knew he had been murdered.
        d. killer gave himself away by the loud beating of his own heart.

_____10. Which statement best expresses the theme of the story?
   a. Murder is immoral.
   b. Madness is a social disease.
   c. Law enforcement personnel deserve respect.
   d. Guilt is powerful and self-destructive.

Discussion Questions

1. How does Poe create feelings of suspense in this story?

2. How does Poe convince us that the narrator is mad?

3. What do you think is the relationship between the old man and his killer?

4. Why do you think Poe chose to tell this story from the killer's point of view?

Little Brother™

Bruce Holland Rogers

Bruce Holland Rogers is an American writer of award-winning fiction. This story appeared in *Strange Horizons*, a weekly online magazine that features science fiction and fantasy.

1   Peter had wanted a Little Brother™ for three Christmases in a row. His favorite TV commercials were the ones that showed just how much fun he would have teaching Little Brother™ to do all the things that he could already do himself. But every year, Mommy had said that Peter wasn't ready for a Little Brother™. Until this year.

2   This year when Peter ran into the living room, there sat Little Brother™ among all the wrapped presents, babbling baby talk, smiling his happy smile, and patting one of the packages with his fat little hand. Peter was so excited that he ran up and gave Little Brother™ a big hug around the neck. That was how he found out about the button. Peter's hand pushed against something cold on Little Brother™'s neck, and suddenly Little Brother™ wasn't babbling any more, or even sitting up. Suddenly, Little Brother™ was limp on the floor, as lifeless as any ordinary doll.

3   "Peter!" Mommy said.

4   "I didn't mean to!"

5   Mommy picked up Little Brother™, sat him in her lap, and pressed the black button at the back of his neck. Little Brother™'s face came alive, and it wrinkled up as if he were about to cry, but Mommy bounced him on her knee and told him what a good boy he was. He didn't cry after all.

6   "Little Brother™ isn't like your other toys, Peter," Mommy said. "You have to be extra careful with him, as if he were a real baby." She put Little Brother™

down on the floor, and he took tottering baby steps toward Peter. "Why don't you let him help open your other presents?"

7   So that's what Peter did. He showed Little Brother™ how to tear the paper and open the boxes. The other toys were a fire engine, some talking books, a wagon, and lots and lots of wooden blocks. The fire engine was the second-best present. It had lights, a siren, and hoses that blew green gas just like the real thing. There weren't as many presents as last year, Mommy explained, because Little Brother™ was expensive. That was okay. Little Brother™ was the best present ever!

8   Well, that's what Peter thought at first. At first, everything that Little Brother™ did was funny and wonderful. Peter put all the torn wrapping paper in the wagon, and Little Brother™ took it out again and threw it on the floor. Peter started to read a talking book, and Little Brother™ came and turned the pages too fast for the book to keep up.

9   But then, while Mommy went to the kitchen to cook breakfast, Peter tried to show Little Brother™ how to build a very tall tower out of blocks. Little Brother™ wasn't interested in seeing a really tall tower. Every time Peter had a few blocks stacked up, Little Brother™ swatted the tower with his hand and laughed. Peter laughed, too, for the first time, and the second. But then he said, "Now watch this time. I'm going to make it really big."

10   But Little Brother™ didn't watch. The tower was only a few blocks tall when he knocked it down.

11   "No!" Peter said. He grabbed hold of Little Brother™'s arm. "Don't!"

12   Little Brother™'s face wrinkled. He was getting ready to cry.

13   Peter looked toward the kitchen and let go. "Don't cry," he said. "Look, I'm building another one! Watch me build it!"

14   Little Brother™ watched. Then he knocked the tower down.

15   Peter had an idea.

16   When Mommy came into the living room again, Peter had built a tower that was taller than he was, the best tower he had ever made. "Look!" he said.

17   But Mommy didn't even look at the tower. "Peter!" She picked up Little Brother™, put him on her lap, and pressed the button to turn him back on. As soon as he was on, Little Brother™ started to scream. His face turned red.

18   "I didn't mean to!"

19   "Peter, I told you! He's not like your other toys. When you turn him off, he can't move but he can still see and hear. He can still feel. And it scares him."

20   "He was knocking down my blocks."

21   "Babies do things like that," Mommy said. "That's what it's like to have a baby brother."

22   Little Brother™ howled.

23   "He's mine," Peter said too quietly for Mommy to hear. But when Little Brother™ had calmed down, Mommy put him back on the floor and Peter let him toddle over and knock down the tower.

24   Mommy told Peter to clean up the wrapping paper, and she went back into the kitchen. Peter had already picked up the wrapping paper once, and she hadn't said thank you. She hadn't even noticed.

25   Peter wadded the paper into angry balls and threw them one at a time into the wagon until it was almost full. That's when Little Brother™ broke the fire engine. Peter turned just in time to see him lift the engine up over his head and let it drop.

26   "No!" Peter shouted. The windshield cracked and popped out as the fire engine hit the floor. Broken. Peter hadn't even played with it once, and his best Christmas present was broken.

27   Later, when Mommy came into the living room, she didn't thank Peter for picking up all the wrapping paper. Instead, she scooped up Little Brother™ and turned him on again. He trembled and screeched louder than ever.

28   "My God! How long has he been off?" Mommy demanded.

29   "I don't like him!"

30   "Peter, it scares him! Listen to him!"

31   "I hate him! Take him back!"

32   "You are not to turn him off again. Ever!"

33   "He's mine!" Peter shouted. "He's mine and I can do what I want with him! He broke my fire engine!"

34   "He's a baby!"

35   "He's stupid! I hate him! Take him back!"

36   "You are going to learn to be nice with him."

37   "I'll turn him off if you don't take him back. I'll turn him off and hide him someplace where you can't find him!"

38   "Peter!" Mommy said, and she was angry. She was angrier than he'd ever seen her before. She put Little Brother™ down and took a step toward Peter. She would punish him. Peter didn't care. He was angry, too.

39   "I'll do it!" he yelled. "I'll turn him off and hide him someplace dark!"

40   "You'll do no such thing!" Mommy said. She grabbed his arm and spun him around. The spanking would come next.

41   But it didn't. Instead he felt her fingers searching for something at the back of his neck.

Directions: Select the choice that best completes each of the following statements.

Checking Your Comprehension

_____ 1. Peter can best be described as
   a. the oldest of several children.
   b. the youngest of several children.
   c. an only child.
   d. a teenager.

_____ 2. Peter's initial reaction to Little Brother was
   a. excitement.
   b. disappointment.
   c. jealousy.
   d. fear.

_____ 3. When Peter hugged Little Brother, he discovered that Little Brother
   a. was able to talk.
   b. cried when he was held.
   c. was made of plastic.
   d. had a button on his neck.

_____ 4. Peter's mother became angry when
   a. Little Brother broke Peter's new fire engine.
   b. Peter did not pick up the wrapping paper as she had asked.
   c. Peter turned off Little Brother.
   d. Little Brother knocked down Peter's blocks.

_____ 5. At the end of the story, we find out that
   a. Peter's mother planned to take Little Brother back.
   b. Peter's father would be coming home soon.
   c. Little Brother was actually a real baby.
   d. Peter also had a button on his neck.

The Elements of a Short Story

_____ 6. The story is told from the perspective of
   a. Peter's mother.
   b. Little Brother.
   c. a knowledgeable narrator.
   d. Peter.

_____ 7. One possible theme of the story is
   a. Family is more valuable than material possessions.
   b. It is important to be patient with small children.
   c. Technology is replacing human relationships.
   d. Brothers should look out for each other.

_____ 8. The climax of the story occurs when
   a. Peter first hugs Little Brother.
   b. Peter's mother leaves the room to cook breakfast.
   c. Peter's mother reaches around to switch him off.
   d. Little Brother breaks the fire engine.

_____ 9. The setting of the story is
   a. a store at the mall.
   b. Peter's birthday party.
   c. Little Brother's birthday party.
   d. Christmas day at Peter's house.

_____ 10. The tone of this story can best be described as
   a. serious.
   b. comical.
   c. ironic.
   d. tragic.

Discussion Questions

1. Were you surprised by the ending of this story? Discuss what you think will happen next.

2. Why did the author include the trademark symbol (TM) in the title and throughout the story?

3. How would the story be different if it were told from the mother's point of view?

4. In addition to Little Brother, what other clues does the author give to reveal that the story is taking place in the future?

5. Evaluate the effectiveness of the story's title. Can you think of other titles that would work for this story?

READING AND INTERPRETING NOVELS

A **novel** is a full-length piece of fiction. In college, you will be expected to read novels in literature classes or for supplemental assignments in any of a wide variety of disciplines. In everyday life, you may choose to read them for fun and relaxation.

Why Read Novels?

Novels can be amusing, engaging, entertaining, and educational. But a novel is also an experience—an opportunity to get involved in a different world. Think of reading a novel as similar to watching a movie. (Many movies are actually based on novels. _The Girl with the Dragon Tattoo_ movies, for example, were novels before they became movies.) In a novel, you can become lost in the lives of the characters—you sympathize with them, you feel sadness for them, you share their emotions and life problems. The experience of reading a novel can be uplifting; it can be an escape from day-to-day life worries and stress; it can be educational. Through reading novels, you can learn a great deal about the ways other people live and have relationships, discover different cultures and ways of seeing and understanding the world, and "visit" different geographic places and historical periods.

How to Read a Novel

A novel is an extended story that can tell about several generations of a family, or an entire historical period, or can take place in the space of a day. Like a short story, it contains the following elements. Refer to pages 464–466 for a review of these elements.

- Plot
- Setting
- Characterization
- Point of view
- Tone
- Theme

Here are a few tips for reading a novel.

Before Reading

1. **Study the title.** Make some guesses about what the story might be about.
2. **Preview before reading.** Spend a few minutes reading the inside front cover flap and the back cover and studying the table of contents. Discover who the author is and what he or she typically writes about. Flip through the novel, and read the first paragraph. This will give you a sense of the setting and possibly of the main characters.

While Reading

3. **Reread the first paragraph.** Many opening paragraphs immediately engage you in an event or with a critical person or people.
4. **Watch the plot evolve.** Notice the development of events. Often the story leads up to a crisis or critical point that involves suspense, and its resolution leads to changes in the life of the main character and often of the people he or she is involved with.
5. **Determine the narrator's role.** Find out if the person telling the story is functioning as a reporter, reporting facts, or as a commentator, commenting and interpreting actions and events from their own point of view.

6. **Study the characters.** Pay attention to physical characteristics, as well as to dialogue and actions. Notice what other characters think of the main character(s) and what the narrator tells you about him- or herself.

7. **Highlight or make notes as you read.** When a character makes a meaningful statement or the narrator makes an insightful comment, highlight it. Also highlight important or significant actions, interesting descriptions, and unique uses of language. Make note of possible developing themes.

8. **Pay attention to language.** Writers often use figurative expressions (p. 398) and descriptive language to convey meaning.

9. **Watch for clues.** Writers often give you clues about what is going to happen next. (This is called foreshadowing.)

After Reading

10. **Reread the title.** Think about what it means now that you have read the book.

11. **Analyze the themes.** Determine the author's message; what is he or she trying to convey to the reader through telling the story? Reread your highlighting or notes for clues to why the author wrote the novel.

Reading and Analyzing the Prologue from *Water for Elephants*

Water for Elephants, by Sara Gruen, is a popular novel about a critical series of events that occurred when the main character dropped out of school and joined the Benzini Brothers circus. Below is the **prologue** (the introduction) to the novel. Read it now before continuing with this section.

Prologue

1   Only three people were left under the red and white awning of the grease joint: Grady, me, and the fry cook. Grady and I sat at a battered wooden table, each facing a burger on a dented tin plate. The cook was behind the counter, scraping his griddle with the edge of a spatula. He had turned off the fryer some time ago, but the odor of grease lingered.

2   The rest of the midway—so recently writhing with people—was empty but for a handful of employees and a small group of men waiting to be led to the cooch tent. They glanced nervously from side to side, with hats pulled low and hands thrust deep in their pockets. They wouldn't be disappointed: somewhere in the back Barbara and her ample charms awaited.

3   The other townsfolk—rubes, as Uncle Al called them—had already made their way through their menagerie tent and into the big top, which pulsed with frenetic music. The band was whipping through its repertoire at the usual

earsplitting volume. I knew the routine by heart—at this very moment, the tail end of the Grand Spectacle was exiting and Lottie, the aerialist, was ascending her rigging in the center ring.

4   I stared at Grady, trying to process what he was saying. He glanced around and leaned in closer.

5   "Besides," he said, locking eyes with me, "it seems to me you've got a lot to lose right now." He raised his eyebrows for emphasis. My heart skipped a beat.

6   Thunderous applause exploded from the big top, and the band slid seamlessly into the Gounod waltz. I turned instinctively toward the menagerie because this was the cue for the elephant act. Marlena was either preparing to mount or was already sitting on Rosie's head.

7   "I've got to go," I said.

8   "Sir," said Grady. "Eat. If you're thinking of clearing out, it may be a while before you see food again."

9   That moment, the music screeched to a halt. There was an ungodly collision of brass, reed, and percussion—trombones and piccolos skidded into cacophony, a tuba farted, and the hollow clang of a cymbal wavered out of the big top, over our heads and into oblivion.

10   Grady froze, crouched over his burger with his pinkies extended and lips spread wide.

11   I looked from side to side. No one moved a muscle—all eyes were directed at the big top. A few wisps of hay swirled lazily across the hard dirt.

12   "What is it? What's going on?" I said.

13   "*Shh*," Grady hissed.

14   The band started up again, playing "Stars and Stripes Forever."

15   "Oh Christ. Oh shit!" Grady tossed his food onto the table and leapt up, knocking over the bench.

16   "What? What is it?" I yelled, because he was already running away from me.

17   "The Disaster March!" he screamed over his shoulder.

18   I jerked around to the fry cook, who was ripping off his apron. "What the hell's he talking about?"

19   "The Disaster March," he said, wrestling the apron over his head. "Means something's gone bad—real bad."

20   "Like what?"

21   "Could be anything—fire in the big top, stampede, whatever. Aw sweet Jesus. The poor rubes probably don't even know it yet." He ducked under the hinged door and took off.

22   Chaos—candy butchers vaulting over counters, workmen staggering out from under tent flaps, roustabouts racing headlong across the lot. Anyone and everyone associated with the Benzini Brothers Most Spectacular Show on Earth barreled toward the big top.

23   Diamond Joe passed me at the human equivalent of a full gallop. "Jacob—it's the menagerie," he screamed. "The animals are loose. Go, go, *go!*"

24   He didn't need to tell me twice. Marlena was in that tent.

25   A rumble coursed through me as I approached, and it scared the hell out of me because it was on a register lower than noise. The ground was vibrating.

26   I staggered inside and met a wall of yak—a great expanse of curly-haired chest and churning hooves, of flared red nostrils and spinning eyes. It galloped past so close I leapt backward on tiptoe, flush with the canvas to avoid being impaled on one of its crooked horns. A terrified hyena clung to its shoulders.

27   The concession stand in the center of the tent had been flattened, and in its place was a roiling mass of spots and stripes—of haunches, heels, tails, and claws, all of it roaring, screeching, bellowing, or whinnying. A polar bear towered above it all, slashing blindly with skillet-sized paws. It made contact with a llama and knocked it flat—BOOM. The llama hit the ground, its neck and legs splayed like the five points of a star. Chimps screamed and chattered, swinging on ropes to stay above the cats. A wild-eyed zebra zigzagged too close to a crouching lion, who swiped, missed, and darted away, his belly close to the ground.

28   My eyes swept the tent, desperate to find Marlena. Instead I saw a cat slide through the connection leading to the big top—it was a panther, and as its lithe black body disappeared into the canvas tunnel I braced myself. If the rubes didn't know, they were about to find out. It took several seconds to come, but come it did—one prolonged shriek followed by another, and then another, and then the whole place exploded with the thunderous sound of bodies trying to shove past other bodies and off the stands. The band screeched to a halt for a second time, and this time stayed silent. I shut my eyes: *Please God let them leave by the back end. Please God don't let them try to come through here.*

29   I opened my eyes again and scanned the menagerie, frantic to find her. How hard can it be to find a girl and an elephant, for Christ's sake?

30   When I caught sight of her pink sequins. I nearly cried out in relief—maybe I did. I don't remember.

31   She was on the opposite side, standing against the sidewall, calm as a summer day. Her sequins flashed like liquid diamonds, a shimmering beacon between the multicolored hides. She saw me, too, and held my gaze for what seemed like forever. She was cool, languid. Smiling even. I started pushing my way toward her, but something about her expression stopped me cold.

32   That son of a bitch was standing with his back to her, red-faced and bellowing, flapping his arms and swinging his silver-tipped cane. His high-topped silk hat lay on the straw beside him.

33   She reached for something. A giraffe passed between us—its long neck bobbing gracefully even in panic—and when it was gone I saw that she'd picked up an iron stake. She held it loosely, resting its end on the hard dirt. She looked at me again, bemused. Then her gaze shifted to the back of his bare head.

34   "Oh Jesus," I said, suddenly understanding. I stumbled forward, screaming even though there was no hope of my voice reaching her. "Don't do it! *Don't do it!*"

35   She lifted the stake high in the air and brought it down, splitting his head like a watermelon. His pate opened, his eyes grew wide, and his mouth froze into an O. He fell to his knees and then toppled forward into the straw.

36   I was too stunned to move, even as a young orangutan flung its elastic arms around my legs.

37   So long ago. So long. But still it haunts me.

38   I DON'T TALK MUCH about those days. Never did. I don't know why—I worked on circuses for nearly seven years, and if that isn't fodder for conversation, I don't know what is.

39   Actually I do know why: I never trusted myself. I was afraid I'd let it slip. I knew how important it was to keep her secret, and keep it I did—for the rest of her life, and then beyond.

40   In seventy years, I've never told a blessed soul.

This prologue helps you get ready to read the novel and demonstrates many of the characteristics of a novel:

- **The setting is clearly established.** A place—the circus—is described in vivid detail.

- **The main characters are introduced.** Although he is not named, you meet the main character of the novel, the narrator. You are also introduced to the other principal characters: Marlena (the woman the narrator falls in love with), the evil ringmaster, "that son of a bitch," and the murderer.

- **Action immediately engages you.** You learn that the Disaster March is played because there is a crisis—the circus animals have escaped. You learn that someone has split someone's head open.

- **Suspense builds**. You are instantly dropped right into an action-packed story. While you learn much about the plot, there is much you do not know and you wonder about. You don't know how the animals escaped. You do not know who killed the man, who the man was, or why he was killed. You wonder what secret the narrator refers to in the last paragraph and why he has never told anyone.

- **The language is descriptive and engaging.** You can hear (the earsplitting band, the "thunderous applause" of the audience, and the screaming of the animals), smell (the odor of grease), and see (the terrified chimps, yak, polar bear, and lion) what is going on. Notice the use of figurative language—the polar bear has "skillet-sized paws," and the person's head was "split like a watermelon." Can you easily visualize the confusion and mayhem occurring as the animals escaped and the audience panicked and ran?

Based on the prologue, aren't you interested in reading the novel?

PART VII

A Contemporary Issues Minireader

Reading about Controversial Issues

P483~493 Ch 5.

READING ABOUT CONTROVERSIAL ISSUES

A controversial issue is one about which people disagree and hold different opinions. This section offers suggestions for how to read articles about controversial issues. But first, read "The High Cost of Having Fun," below, and then refer back to it as you read the guidelines that follow it.

The High Cost of Having Fun

A majority of Americans follow at least one professional sport. Unfortunately, rising costs are making it impossible for the average fan to watch his or her favorite athlete or team in person. According to *Team Marketing Report,* the average ticket price in the NFL is $58.95, and in the NBA it's $45.28. For professional baseball, the average ticket price is $22.21, while in hockey, it's $43.13. Some argue that the high prices are justified. After all, they say, in order to please fans, teams must win more games than they lose. The best way to win is to have the top players, but teams must spend large amounts of money to get these players. These costs are passed on to the fans through ticket prices and merchandising. However, instead of raising ticket prices, team owners should raise the fees paid by corporations who sponsor stadiums and put their logo on the TV next to the score or advertise in the arena, making use of the real money in the hands of big business. The love of sports cuts across socioeconomic lines; the ability to enjoy a game in person should too.

Guidelines for Reading about Controversial Issues

Use the following suggestions when reading about controversial issues:

1. **Plan on reading the article several times.** Read the article once to get a first impression. Read it another time to closely follow the author's line of reasoning. Read it again to analyze and evaluate it.

2. **Identify the issue.** The issue is the problem or controversy that the article discusses. In "The High Cost of Having Fun," the issue is the high cost of tickets to sporting events.

3. **Identify the author's position on the issue.** In many articles, the author takes one side of the issue. In the paragraph above, the author's position is that the cost of tickets is too high. A different author could take the opposite view—that tickets are reasonably priced for the level of entertainment provided. Or another article could examine and discuss both sides of the issue, explaining why some people feel the cost is too high and why others think it is reasonable.

4. **Examine the reasons and evidence.** As you read, look closely at the reasons and types of evidence the author provides in support of the position or positions presented in the article. In "The High Cost of Having Fun," the author presents statistics about the cost of tickets and recognizes that

running a professional sports team is expensive. The author argues that the costs are being unfairly passed on to the fans and suggests an alternate means of financing the teams—passing the costs on to sponsors. The author also argues that sports should not be only for wealthy people who can afford high ticket prices.

5. **Evaluate the evidence.** Once you have examined the evidence offered, decide whether it is of good quality and whether there is enough evidence to be convincing. In "The High Cost of Having Fun," the statistics about the cost of tickets is useful. However, the author does not present any information about how much cost sponsors already assume and how much additional costs they would need to assume in order to maintain or lower ticket prices.

6. **Opposing viewpoints.** If the writer presents only one viewpoint on the issue, be sure to consider the opposing viewpoints. Sometimes the author will recognize opposing viewpoints, and sometimes even refute (present arguments against) them. In "The High Cost of Having Fun," the writer does recognize that some feel the high ticket prices are justified in order to get and keep top players.

Issue 1: Genetic Testing

The Genetic Crystal Ball: Do We Really Want to Look?

John J. Macionis

In this selection taken from a sociology textbook, the author examines the social implications of genetic knowledge. As you read, identify the writer's position on the issue and evaluate the evidence offered in support of this position.

Vocabulary Preview

spiraling (par. 1) in the shape of a coil

genome (par. 3) the full DNA sequence of an organism

abnormalities (par. 4) deviations from what is normal

manipulate (par. 4) move around or change

inevitable (par. 6) unavoidable

prompt (photo caption) cause to happen

prospective (par. 7) likely, expected

dilemmas (par. 7) difficult or perplexing problems

Prereading

1. Do you expect this selection to be based on fact or opinion?

   _____

2. What do you think are the pros and cons of genetic testing?

   _____

> FELISHA: Before I get married, I want my partner to have a genetic screening. It's like buying a house or a car–you should check it out before you sign on the line.
>
> EVA: Do you expect to get a warranty, too?

1   The liquid in the laboratory test tube seems ordinary enough, like a syrupy form of water. But this liquid is one of the greatest medical breakthroughs of all time; it may even hold the key to life itself. The liquid is deoxyribonucleic acid, or DNA, the spiraling molecule found in cells of the human body that contains the blueprint for making each one of us human as well as different from every other person.

2   The human body is composed of some 100 million cells, most of which contain a nucleus of twenty-three pairs of chromosomes (one of each pair comes from each parent). Each chromosome is packed with DNA, in segments called genes. Genes guide the production of protein, the building block of the human body.

3   If genetics sounds complicated (and it is), the social implications of genetic knowledge are even more complex. Scientists discovered the structure of the DNA molecule in 1952, and in recent years they have made great gains in "mapping" the human genome. Charting the genetic landscape may lead to understanding how each bit of DNA shapes our being.

4   But do we really want to turn the key to unlock the secrets of life itself? And what do we do with this knowledge once we have it? Research has already identified genetic abnormalities that cause sickle-cell anemia, muscular dystrophy, Huntington's disease, cystic fibrosis, some forms of cancer, and other crippling and deadly afflictions. Genetic screening—gazing into a person's genetic "crystal ball"—could let people know their medical destiny and allow doctors to manipulate segments of DNA to prevent diseases before they appear.

5   But many people urge caution in such research, warning that genetic information can easily be abused. At its worst, genetic mapping opens the door to Nazi-like efforts to breed a

Scientists are learning more and more about the genetic factors that prompt the eventual development of serious diseases. If offered the opportunity, would you want to undergo a genetic screening that would predict the long-term future of your own health?

"super-race." In 1994, the People's Republic of China began to use genetic information to regulate marriage and childbirth with the purpose of avoiding "new births of inferior quality."

6   It seems inevitable that some parents will want to use genetic testing to evaluate the health (or even the eye color) of their future children. What if they want to abort a fetus because it falls short of their standards? Should parents be allowed to use genetic manipulation to create "designer children"?

7   Then there is the issue of "genetic privacy." Can a prospective spouse request a genetic evaluation of her fiancé before agreeing to marry? Can a life insurance company demand genetic testing before issuing a policy? Can an employer screen job applicants to weed out those whose future illnesses might drain the company's health care funds? Clearly, what is scientifically possible is not always morally desirable. Society is already struggling with questions about the proper use of our expanding knowledge of human genetics. Such ethical dilemmas will multiply as genetic research moves forward in the years to come.

What Do You Think?

1. Traditional wedding vows join couples "in sickness and in health." Do you think individuals have a right to know the future health of their potential partner before tying the knot? Why or why not?

2. Do you think parents should be able to genetically "design" their children? Why or why not?

3. Is it right that private companies doing genetic research are able to patent their discoveries so that they can profit from the results, or should this information be made available to everyone? Explain your answer.

Sources: D. Thompson (1999) and Golden & Lemonick (2000).

Checking Your Comprehension

1. What is the main point of this reading?

_____

_____

2. What is the substance that contains the blueprint for each individual's genetic characteristics?

_____

3. When did scientists discover the structure of the DNA molecule?

_____

4. Name four diseases caused by abnormalities identified through genetic research.

_____

_____

5. Why did the author mention China's use of genetic information?

_____

6. What does the term "designer children" mean?

_____

7. Describe three situations in which the issue of "genetic privacy" may lead to ethical dilemmas.

_____

_____

Critical Reading and Thinking

1. What is the author's purpose for writing this selection?

_____

_____

2. What kinds of evidence does the author present?

_____

3. What is the tone of the reading?

_____

4. Is the author biased or objective?

_____

5. What is the purpose of the opening dialogue between Felisha and Eva?

_____

_____

Words in Context

Directions: Locate each word in the paragraph indicated and reread that paragraph. Then, based on the way the word is used, write a synonym or brief definition. You may use a dictionary, if necessary.

1. blueprint (par. 1)

_____

2. implications (par. 3)

_____

3. afflictions (par. 4)

_____

4. evaluate (par. 6)

_____

Vocabulary Review

Directions: Match each word in Column A with its meaning in Column B.

	Column A	**Column B**
_____	1. spiraling	a. move around or change
_____	2. genome	b. likely, expected
_____	3. abnormalities	c. cause to happen
_____	4. manipulate	d. the full DNA sequence of an organism
_____	5. inevitable	e. in the shape of a coil
_____	6. prompt	f. difficult or perplexing problems
_____	7. prospective	g. unavoidable
_____	8. dilemmas	h. deviations from what is normal

Summarizing the Reading Selection

Directions: Write a summary of the reading "The Genetic Crystal Ball" on a separate sheet of paper.

Writing Exercises

1. How would you respond if your partner wanted you to have a genetic screening before marriage? Write a paragraph describing what you would do and why.

2. Write a paragraph answering this question from the photo caption: "If offered the opportunity, would you want to undergo a genetic screening that would predict the long-term future of your own health?"

3. Reread the questions in the box at the end of this selection. Choose one and write an essay explaining your answer.

4. What do you think is the best way to regulate how genetic information is used? Write a paragraph explaining your answer.

Issue 2: Cyberbullying

The New Bullying Technology: Gone Are the Days When Coming Home from School Was a Refuge for Kids

Linda T. Sanchez

This article, which first appeared in the *St. Louis Post-Dispatch*, was written by a congresswoman who has introduced legislation regarding bullying that occurs through the use of technology. As you read, identify the writer's position on the issue and evaluate the evidence offered in support of this position.

Vocabulary Preview
refuge (par. 1) a safe place
pernicious (par. 2) extremely harmful
immersed (par. 3) deeply involved
prohibiting (par. 4) forbidding
craze (par. 5) fad or trend
demeaning (par. 5) humiliating
coerce (par. 5) use pressure or threats
vigilant (par. 6) alertly watchful

Prereading

1. What position do you expect the author to take on the issue of cyberbullying?

   _____

2. What have you read or heard about instances of bullying via the Internet or cell phones?

   _____

1   There are new words that didn't exist just a couple of years ago: "sexting," "textual harassment" and "cyberbullying" are just a few words that describe the new kinds of bullying in which kids—and adults—are using technology to hurt and humiliate each other. If adolescence wasn't already hard enough, cyberbullying is the latest way that teens can showcase their mean streak. This faceless form of bullying uses e-mail, Web pages and cell phones to harass or harm others. Because of the use of electronic devices, cyberbullying can occur anywhere or any time—far beyond the schoolyard. Gone are the days when coming home from school was a refuge for kids.

2   Given the combination of anonymity and deception that the Internet enables, this form of bullying is particularly pernicious, yet there is no federal statute against cyberbullying, and most states have no laws against it. Cyberbullies are getting away with destructive behavior that should be labeled a crime, and it is time to put this to a stop.

3   Cyberbullying can have serious consequences and inflict lasting wounds on young people. Studies have found that bullying can have a negative impact on the academic performance, self-esteem and mental and physical health of children. Children who are the victims of bullying are more likely to commit suicide, and bullies are more likely to become criminals as adults. Youth experts say that because many teens are immersed in a new-technology culture, they are uniquely vulnerable to this growing problem.

How does this photograph illustrate the consequences of cyberbullying?

Tina and Ron Meir with a photograph of their daughter.

4   In 2006, when 13-year old Megan Meier of Dardenne Prairie used a MySpace account to make new friends, she wasn't expecting to befriend a phony boy named "Josh" who would later tell her that the world would be better off without her. After numerous personal insults and public online humiliation, Megan hanged herself. She would not survive to learn that "Josh" never existed and was the cruel creation of a 47-year-old neighbor, Lori Drew, the mother of Megan's former friend. Public anger over Megan's death was swift and strong. But the facts of the case did not constitute a crime under Missouri state law, so local prosecutors were unable to bring criminal charges against Drew. Because the federal government and most states do not have laws prohibiting cyberbullying, federal prosecutors were able to charge Drew only with fraud. If a cyberbullying law had been in place, it would have been simple to prosecute and convict Drew. Unfortunately, prosecutors in Megan's case and similar others are left with their hands tied.

5   Sadly, Megan's isn't the only case of extreme cyberbullying. In Palo Alto, Calif., this year, kids used this latest craze to start a group on Facebook called "I Hate . . ." to target a fellow middle-school student. Comments on the site were demeaning and insulting and even threatened violence. In 2003, 13-year-old Ryan Halligan of Vermont hanged himself as a result of cyberbullying. In 2005, 15-year-old Jeff Johnston of Florida, similarly harassed, followed suit. Tragedies that arise as a result of cyberbullying could turn into a national epidemic in a nanosecond if we do not act now to make the law clear and protect our youth. Last week, I reintroduced the "Megan Meier Cyberbullying Prevention Act" in Congress. This bill would give federal prosecutors the ability to punish those individuals who use electronic means to engage in bullying. Cyberbullying would be defined in law as any electronic communications with the intent to coerce, intimidate, harass or cause substantial emotional distress that are repeated, hostile and severe.

6   We need to make new laws in response to these new crimes. Sexting and textual harassment are only a couple of new tactics used by bullies who don't think they'll get caught because there are no bystanders in cyberspace. What they need to know is that cyberbullying is a serious crime, and is no less harmful than in-person threats, stalking and harassment. A lack of awareness exists not just among bullies, but among teachers, parents and, in some cases, even the police. If federal law recognizes this new form of bullying, police and prosecutors would be better equipped and educated to deal with this problem. More important, prosecutors would have the ability to punish this behavior in court. With the rapid rise of technology, the Internet has become like the Wild West with a bunch of unnamed outlaws running around and no sheriff in town. It is time that we bring in new laws and a new sheriff to become vigilant about cleaning up this place.

Checking Your Comprehension

1. What is the main point of this reading?

   _____

   _____

2. List three terms the author uses to describe new ways in which technology is used to bully others.

   _____

3. In addition to Web pages, what are two other tools used by cyberbullies to harass or harm others?

   _____

4. List at least four effects of bullying as described in the article.

   _____

   _____

   _____

5. Who was Megan Meier?

   _____

6. Who was the bully in Megan Meier's case and what charge was brought against her?

   _____

   _____

7. If the Megan Meier Cyberbullying Prevention Act becomes law, how would cyberbullying be legally defined?

_____

_____

8. According to the author, what has the Internet become like?

_____

Critical Reading and Thinking

1. What is the author's purpose for writing this article?

_____

2. What kinds of evidence does the author present?

_____

3. What is the tone of the reading?

_____

4. Does the author recognize or refute opposing viewpoints?

_____

5. What function does the final paragraph serve?

_____

6. What is the purpose of the photo that accompanies the article?

_____

_____

Words in Context

Directions: Locate each word in the paragraph indicated and reread that paragraph. Then, based on the way the word is used, write a synonym or brief definition. You may use a dictionary, if necessary.

1. anonymity (par. 2)

_____

2. inflict (par. 3)

_____

3. constitute (par. 4)

_____

4. nanosecond (par. 5)

_____

5. equipped (par. 6)

_____

Vocabulary Review

Directions: Match each word in Column A with its meaning in Column B.

Column A	Column B
_____ 1. refuge	a. deeply involved
_____ 2. pernicious	b. fad or trend
_____ 3. immersed	c. use pressure or threats
_____ 4. prohibiting	d. a safe place
_____ 5. craze	e. alertly watchful
_____ 6. demeaning	f. extremely harmful
_____ 7. coerce	g. humiliating
_____ 8. vigilant	h. forbidding

Summarizing the Reading Selection

Directions: Write a summary of the reading "The New Bullying Technology" on a separate sheet of paper.

Writing Exercises

1. Do you think antibullying laws will make a difference? Why or why not? Write a paragraph explaining your answer.
2. Have you ever experienced or observed bullying in any form, including cyberbullying? Describe your experience and your response to it.
3. In addition to the proposed legislation, what other tactics do you think should be used to address the problem of cyberbullying? Write a paragraph explaining your answer.
4. What evidence about this issue did you find most compelling? Write a paragraph explaining your answer.

Issue 3: Texting and Its Adverse Effects
Txting Away Ur Education
Patrick Welsh

This article, which originally appeared in *USA Today*, was written by a teacher who feels strongly about text messaging by students during the school day. As you read, identify the writer's position on the issue and evaluate the evidence offered in support of this position.

> **Vocabulary Preview**
> **presumptuous** (par. 2) overly bold
> **inconsistently** (par. 5) not regularly
> **subterfuge** (par. 7) deceptive strategy
> **hyperbole** (par. 8) exaggeration
> **punctured** (par. 11) damaged or ruined
> **facilitate** (par. 12) make easier
> **terse** (par. 12) brief and to the point
> **disable** (par. 16) put out of action

Prereading

1. Do you predict that this article will be based on fact or opinion?

_____

2. Do you think iPods and cell phones should be banned from classrooms?

_____

1   When students graduate from T.C. Williams High School in Alexandria, Va., on Thursday, school officials will do what they should have done back in September: Take possession of all the iPods and cellphones. As students go into the graduation ceremony, they will be searched and their electronic toys will be taken away. At a meeting of some 560 seniors a few weeks ago, the principal told them that they "could live without their cellphones for two hours."

2   He might have been a bit presumptuous. The iPods are bad enough. Every day, students—between and often during class—are plugged into their iPods, seemingly off in another world.

3   But it's cellphone text messaging that both parents and schools need to declare war on. Texting has become an obsession with teenagers

around the country. According to the Nielsen Co., in the last quarter of 2008, teens were averaging at least 80 texts a day, a figure double what it was the year before.

4   T.C. Williams' handbook for parents boldly declares, "The operation of electronic devices including cellphones and iPods is not permitted in the school building. These items will be confiscated for a minimum of 24 hours on the first offense."

5   Reality, though, is something else. The rules are so inconsistently enforced that kids consider them more an inconvenience than a real threat. Even parents send text messages to their kids during class time.

6   And the problem is getting worse, as students become more adept at disguising their texting. One student admitted to often sending 10 texts during my class. Others admitted to sending and receiving more than 200 texts over the course of a day. Most kids are such pros that they can text while the phone is in their pocket, a purse or under the desk, while maintaining eye contact with the teacher.

7   For the most part, all this subterfuge might seem like innocent adolescent behavior, but evidence suggests that texting is undermining students' ability to focus and to learn—and creating anxiety to boot.

8   Many students have come to feel that they cannot live without texting. Says senior Laura Killalea, with a hint of hyperbole: "Most of my friends would die if they had to go to school without their cellphones." Another student, Yasir Hussein, admits that when he doesn't have his phone he gets anxious. "I feel like I am in the dark, secluded, isolated." Cellphones have taken such control over teens that virtually all the students I talked to said they often feel as if their phones are vibrating when they don't even have them.

9   MIT professor Sherry Turkle told me that texting is "an always-on/always-on-you technology." She says cellphones cause not only "the anxiety of disconnection," but also "the anxiety of connection which comes from the expectation that you will respond immediately to a message you get."

10   Despite all the technological advances that were intended to increase communication and efficiency, adolescents as well as adults are living in what Maggie Jackson, author of *Distracted: The Erosion of Attention and the Coming Dark Age*, calls "an institutionalized culture of interruption, where our time and attention is being fragmented by a never-ending stream of phone calls, e-mails, instant messages, text messages and tweets."

11   For students, these "advancements" only add to the difficulties an already distracted generation has had maintaining focus to do serious school work. "Attention is at the heart of any in-depth intellectual activity. When your times of focus and reflection are always being punctured by a cellphone buzzing, it's hard to go deeply into thinking and problem solving. You cannot be creative," says Jackson. "Texting is undermining

kids' opportunities to learn. . . . They will shy away from challenging material."

12   One of the great ironies of the high-tech revolution is that devices meant to facilitate communication are actually helping to destroy it. For my students, rethinking what they wrote and hammering out second or third drafts is beyond all but a handful. In fact, texting has a language all its own, with its own abbreviations and terse messages, all of which hardly translates into good writing.

13   Math and science teachers at my school see the same, with kids wanting the quick answers instead of going through the struggle that will help them understand what is behind the mathematical or scientific principles involved.

14   Even so, there is hope.

15   "We have fallen into bad habits with all the new technology," Jackson says, "but we can push back on the distractions, control those habits. We need to look at it all with fresh eyes, tally up the cost that distraction is costing us and our children and make changes."

16   The summer break is upon us, but administrators and parents need to consider two changes before students return in the fall:

- Parents should disable the text messaging function of their kids' cellphones.
- Those students who curse teachers out and refuse to hand over their phones—as has happened often at T.C. Williams—will have to be punished. A crackdown the first day of school in September will set the get-tough tone for the rest of the year.

17   At the very least, administrators and parents can agree that the school day should be the one time when kids can do without their cellphones. Or maybe I'm just being presumptuous.

Checking Your Comprehension

1. What is the main point of this reading?

   _____

2. What will happen to students' cell phones and iPods at T.C. Williams High School graduation?

   _____

3. According to the Nielsen Co., how many text messages a day were teens averaging in the last quarter of 2008?

   _____

4. In the T.C. Williams parent handbook, what is the consequence for operating electronic devices in the school building?

_____

5. According to the article, what are the negative effects of texting?

_____

6. Who is Maggie Jackson and why is she included in the article?

_____

_____

_____

7. What does the author consider "one of the great ironies of the high-tech revolution"?

_____

8. List the two changes the author recommends for parents and administrators to consider before students return to school in the fall.

_____

_____

Critical Reading and Thinking

1. What is the author's purpose for writing this article?

_____

2. What kinds of evidence does the author present to support his position?

_____

3. What is the tone of the reading?

_____

4. Does the author recognize or refute opposing viewpoints?

_____

5. Is the author biased or objective?

_____

Words in Context

Directions: Locate each word in the paragraph indicated and reread that paragraph. Then, based on the way the word is used, write a synonym or brief definition. You may use a dictionary, if necessary.

1. obsession (par. 3)

   _____

2. confiscated (par. 4)

   _____

3. adept (par. 6)

   _____

4. undermining (par. 7)

   _____

5. fragmented (par. 10)

   _____

Vocabulary Review

Directions: Match each word in Column A with its meaning in Column B.

	Column A	Column B
_____	1. presumptuous	a. exaggeration
_____	2. inconsistently	b. put out of action
_____	3. subterfuge	c. damaged or ruined
_____	4. hyperbole	d. brief and to the point
_____	5. punctured	e. deceptive strategy
_____	6. facilitate	f. not regularly
_____	7. terse	g. overly bold
_____	8. disable	h. make easier

Summarizing the Reading Selection

Directions: Write a summary of the reading "Txting Away Ur Education" on a separate sheet of paper.

Writing Exercises

1. Why do you think the author feels so strongly about this issue? Write a paragraph explaining your answer.
2. What kinds of restrictions (if any) do you think schools should place on the use of electronic devices? Write a paragraph explaining your answer.

3. Write an essay disagreeing with the author's position and explaining the value or benefits of text messaging.

4. Do you agree with the author's statement that electronic devices are actually helping destroy communication? Write a paragraph explaining your answer.

Issue 4: Smokers' Rights
Should People Be Allowed to Smoke at Home?
Daniel B. Wood

Originally published in the *Christian Science Monitor* in February 2007, this article examines one aspect of smokers' rights—the right to smoke in one's own home. As you read, identify the writer's position on the issue and evaluate the evidence offered in support of this position.

Vocabulary Preview

scenarios (par. 2) possible situations

mandate (par. 2) to require or order

communal (par. 3) shared; used by all members of a group

susceptible (par. 3) easily influenced or affected

intrusion (par. 4) an unwelcome presence or disturbance

precedent (par. 4) an action or decision that can later be used as an example to justify a similar action/decision

statistics (par. 9) a collection of numerical data

ire (par. 9) anger

proliferate (par. 9) to increase greatly in number

intervening (par. 10) taking action in order to change or prevent something

Prereading

1. Do you think the article will be based primarily on research or personal experience?

_____

2. Do you know anyone who is bothered by secondhand smoke? Why do you think secondhand smoke bothers some people more than others?

_____

1   After retiree Judy Wilson moved from Georgia back to her hometown of Sault Ste. Marie, Mich., in 1997, life was sweet: fresh air, beautiful scenery, quiet neighbors. A year later, a heavy smoker moved in across the hall at Ms. Wilson's second-floor apartment in Arlington Town Apartments. Wilson says her life changed. "I started having all kinds of breathing problems and eye irritations," says Wilson, a retired assembly-line worker. After maintenance personnel tried and failed to stop the smoke in several ways, including ventilation changes, air filters, and intake fans, she was moved to an apartment down the hall. Everything was fine—until more smokers moved in across the hall. "My doctor told me . . . that I'd better move away from it or else," says Wilson.

2   As similar scenarios play out in apartment and condominium complexes across the country, they are resulting in a new frontier in antismoking policies: private dwellings. Not only are some condos and apartment houses banning smoking inside private units, but there is talk in Belmont, Calif., of a city law next month that would mandate that all complexes keep a portion of their units smoke-free. The war against smoking first ramped up in the 1980s when some of America's public buildings became smoke-free. Then, in the 1990s, a slew of restaurants and bars in U.S. cities banned smoking.

3   Now, seniors are leading the way in the new battle in part because many live in communal environments and they feel they are susceptible to the health and safety hazards of smoking. "The primary drive for smoke-free housing in America is coming from the elderly," says Jim Bergman, director of the Smoke-Free Environments Law Project in Ann Arbor, Mich.

4   Smoke-free policies in private dwellings are also taking hold because state and federal laws do not protect smokers in the same way that they protect people from discrimination based on race, ethnicity, and national origin, say experts. But banning a legal behavior in someone's own home is an intrusion of privacy that could set a dangerous precedent that, taken to extremes, could allow government to regulate too much in private life, opponents say.

5   Smoking can also be safety issue, particularly in close quarters, some say. "There is a great deal of growing interest in the senior housing community about senior smokers because seniors become forgetful and careless about smoking," says Serena Chen, policy director for the American Lung Association of California. Although cigarettes cause 10 percent of apartment fires, 40 percent of apartment fire deaths are attributed to smoking. Such fires cause death because they occur while more people are asleep.

6   Giving more teeth to the push is a finding in the U.S. Surgeon General report last June that there are no safe levels of secondhand smoke. Last year, the California Air Resources Board declared secondhand smoke to be a toxic air contaminant on par with other industrial pollutants.

7   For their part, condo and apartment owners are beginning to realize the additional costs of getting units ready for new tenants after smokers have lived there. Across the state of Michigan, 12 of 132 housing commissions have banned

smoking in multiunit apartments and condos in the past two years, Mr. Bergman says. Two-and-a-half years ago, no one could find a smoke-free apartment listing anywhere in the state; now there are more than 5,000, he says. About two or three public housing commissions in Michigan are adopting smoke-free policies each month; elsewhere in the U.S., Bergman says, perhaps another one commission per month is doing the same. So far, that means that the public buildings owned and run by such commissions—such as Arlington Courts in Sault Ste. Marie—are taking such actions voluntarily.

8   But that could change next month in California. In Belmont, the city attorney and city council are expected to break new ground by passing a law that affects all public and private apartment and condominium owners in the city, requiring them to adopt smoke-free policies for a certain percentage of their units. "Belmont will be watched nationally to see how far it goes in requiring apartment owners to have smoke-free policies," says Bergman. "Since no other city has passed a law requiring private apartment owners or condo associations to have a percentage of their units be smoke-free, this will be unique in the nation and other cities will seriously consider taking the step as well."

9   If Belmont's and Michigan's measures are being fueled in part by statistics showing that 80 percent of Americans don't smoke, they are also drawing ire from many among the 20 percent who do. Smokers wonder where they'll be allowed to smoke if new laws proliferate. Even top proponents of smoke-free policies question whether scientific evidence overstates the dangers of being exposed to secondhand smoke, and chases smokers into an ever-shrinking portion of the great outdoors.

10   "There really is no evidence that even a fleeting whiff of cigarette smoke will give you lung cancer, but that's how proponents of these policies seem to be advancing their cause," says Jacob Sullum, senior editor at *Reason Magazine*, who authored a book about the antismoking movement. If smokers are banned from apartments and condos, parks, and other public spaces, the only space left for them to smoke will be single-family homes, a place where children reside. "The next angle we are going to see on this is how to protect children from respiratory problems in the home, and that is not the kind of place where I think the government ought to be intervening," says Mr. Sullum.

Checking Your Comprehension

1. According to Judy Wilson, why did she start experiencing health problems?

_____

2. When did the trend toward smoke-free public buildings begin in the United States?

_____

3. What law is being considered in Belmont, California?

_____

_____

4. Give two reasons that seniors are leading the movement for smoke-free housing.

_____

_____

_____

5. Why do opponents of antismoking laws for private dwellings think that such laws are a bad idea?

_____

_____

6. According to the article, smokers are responsible for what percentage of apartment fire deaths?

_____

7. What is the U.S. Surgeon General's position on the safety of secondhand smoke?

_____

8. What is one reason that apartment and condominium owners might support antismoking policies in their complexes?

_____

_____

Critical Reading and Thinking

1. What is the author's main purpose in writing this article?

_____

_____

2. What types of information are used to support the main points of the article?

_____

3. How do the first two paragraphs relate to the rest of the article?

_____

_____

4. What is the tone of the reading?

_____

Words in Context

Directions: Locate each word in the paragraph indicated and reread that paragraph. Then, based on the way the word is used, write a synonym or brief definition. You may use a dictionary, if necessary.

1. slew (par. 2)

   _____

2. drive (par. 3)

   _____

3. regulate (par. 4)

   _____

4. advancing (par. 10)

   _____

5. angle (par. 10)

   _____

Vocabulary Review

Directions: Match each word in Column A with its meaning in Column B.

	Column A	Column B
_____	1. scenarios	a. anger
_____	2. mandate	b. an unwelcome presence or disturbance
_____	3. communal	c. shared; used by all members of a group
_____	4. susceptible	d. to require or order
_____	5. intrusion	e. a collection of numerical data
_____	6. precedent	f. easily influenced or affected
_____	7. statistics	g. taking action in order to change or prevent something
_____	8. ire	h. an action or decision that can later be used as an example to justify a similar action/decision
_____	9. proliferate	i. to increase greatly in number
_____	10. intervening	j. possible situations

Summarizing the Reading Selection

Directions: Write a summary of the reading "Should People Be Allowed to Smoke at Home?" on a separate sheet of paper.

Writing Exercises

1. Many seniors are concerned about secondhand smoke in communal environments such as apartment and condominium complexes. Do you think that the seniors' concerns are justified? Write a paragraph explaining your point of view.

2. Do you think that U.S. citizens who smoke are victims of discrimination? Write a paragraph explaining why or why not.

3. Would you support a law requiring all apartment and condominium complexes in your community to make some of their units smoke free? Write an essay explaining your position on this issue.

4. Do you think that the government has a responsibility to protect children from secondhand smoke in single-family homes? Write an essay explaining your point of view.

Issue 5: Cell Phones and Driving Safety
Driving While on Cell Phone Worse than Driving While Drunk
HealthDay

Published by HealthDay, this article examines the use of cell phones while driving. As you read, identify the writer's position on the issue and evaluate the evidence offered in support of this position.

Vocabulary Preview

tolerating (par. 2) putting up with

simulator (par. 3) a device used for testing or training that models actual operational conditions

impairments (par. 3) weakened physical functions

inebriated (par. 4) intoxicated; drunk

rear-ending (par. 4) crashing into another vehicle from behind

aggressive (par. 5) acting in an assertive/hostile manner

compensating (par. 8) making up for

multi-task (par. 10) to perform two or more activities at the same time

Prereading

1. Do you expect this article to be based primarily on fact or opinion?

   _____

2. Have you ever used a cell phone while driving or observed another driver using a cell phone? Do you feel that use of the phone was distracting or potentially unsafe?

   _____

1   Thursday, June 29 (HealthDay News)—Maneuvering through traffic while talking on the phone increases the likelihood of an accident fivefold and is actually more dangerous than driving drunk, U.S. researchers report. That finding held true whether the driver was holding a cell phone or using a hands-free device, the researchers noted.

2   "As a society, we have agreed on not tolerating the risk associated with drunk driving," said researcher Frank Drews, an assistant professor of psychology at the University of Utah. "This study shows us that somebody who is conversing on a cell phone is exposing him or herself and others to a similar risk—cell phones actually are a higher risk," he said. His team's report appears in the summer issue of the journal _Human Factors_.

3   In the study, 40 people followed a pace car along a prescribed course, using a driving simulator. Some people drove while talking on a cell phone, others navigated while drunk (meaning their blood-alcohol limit matched the legal limit of 0.08 percent), and others drove with no such distractions or impairments. "We found an increased accident rate when people were conversing on the cell phone," Drews said. Drivers on cell phones were 5.36 times more likely to get in an accident than non-distracted drivers, the researchers found.

4   The phone users fared even worse than the inebriated, the Utah team found. There were three accidents among those talking on cell phones—all of them involving a rear-ending of the pace car. In contrast, there were no accidents recorded among participants who were drunk, or the sober, cell-phone-free group. The bottom line: Cell-phone use was linked to "a significant increase in the accident rate," Drews said.

5   He said there was a difference between the behaviors of drunk drivers and those who were talking on the phone. Drunk drivers tended to be aggressive, while those talking on the phone were more sluggish, Drews said. In addition, the researchers found talking on the cell phone reduced reaction time by 9 percent in terms of braking and 19 percent in terms of picking up speed after braking. "This is significant, because it has an impact on traffic as a system," Drews said. "If we have drivers who are taking a lot of time in accelerating once having slowed down, the overall flow of traffic is dramatically reduced," he said.

6   In response to safety concerns, some states have outlawed the use of hand-held cell phones while driving. But that type of legislation may not be effective, because the Utah researchers found no difference in driver performance whether the driver was holding the phone or talking on a hands-free model. "We have seen again and again that there is no difference between hands-free and hand-held devices," Drews said. "The problem is the conversation," he added.

7   According to Drews, drivers talking on the phone are paying attention to the conversation—not their driving. "Drivers are not perceiving the driving environment," he said. "We found 50 percent of the visual information wasn't processed at all—this could be a red light. This increases the risk of getting into an accident dramatically," he said.

8   The reason that there aren't more accidents linked to cell phone use is probably due to the reactions of other—more alert—drivers, Drews said, "Currently, our system seems to be able to handle 8 percent of cell-phone drivers, because other drivers *are* paying attention," he said. "They are compensating for the errors these drivers are causing," he speculated.

9   This is a growing public health problem, Drews said. As more people are talking and driving, the accident rate will go up, he said. One expert agreed that driving and cell phone use can be a deadly mix. "We don't believe talking on a cell phone while driving is safe," said Rae Tyson, a spokesman for the U.S. National Highway Traffic Safety Administration (NHTSA). "It is a level of distraction that can affect your driving performance," he said. NHTSA has just completed a study that showed that 75 percent of all traffic accidents were preceded by some type of driver distraction, Tyson said. Tyson pointed out that talking on the phone is very different than talking to the person in the passenger seat. "If you are engaged in a conversation with a passenger, the passenger has some situational awareness, whereas a person on the phone has no idea what you are dealing with on the road," he said.

10   "Our recommendation is that you should not talk on the phone while driving, whether it's a hand-held or hand-free device," Tyson said. "We realize that a lot of people believe that they can multi-task, and in a lot of situations they probably can, but it's that moment when you need your full attention, and it's not there because you are busy talking, that you increase the likelihood that you are going to be involved in a crash," he said.

11   Tyson also sees this as a growing public health issue. "Every time we do a survey, there are more people using cell phones while driving," he said. "And the popularity of hand-held devices like Palm Pilots or Blackberries, and people using them in the car, is another problem," he added.

12   An industry spokesman said cell phones don't cause accidents, people do. "If cell phones were truly the culprit some studies make them out to be, it's only logical that we'd see a huge spike in the number of accidents [since their introduction]," said John Walls, a vice president at the industry group, the Cellular Telecommunications & Internet Association-The Wireless Association. "To the

contrary, we've experienced a decline in accidents, and an even more impressive decline in the accident rate per million miles driven," he said. "We believe educating drivers on how to best handle all of the possible distractions when you're behind the wheel is the most effective means to make better drivers, and that legislation focusing on a specific behavior falls short of that well-intended goal and creates a false sense of security," Walls said.

Checking Your Comprehension

1. What is the main point of this article?

   _____

   _____

2. In the Utah study led by Frank Drews, how much did use of a cell phone while driving increase the risk of an accident?

   _____

   _____

3. In the Utah study, what kinds of accidents did drivers using cell phones experience?

   _____

4. According to the Utah study, how were the reactions of drunk drivers different from the reactions of drivers using cell phones?

   _____

   _____

5. According to Frank Drews, why is the use of a hands-free cell phone while driving just as dangerous as the use of a handheld cell phone?

   _____

   _____

   _____

6. How does Frank Drews explain the fact that the number of traffic accidents has not increased since people began using cell phones while driving?

   _____

   _____

7. According to the NHTSA study, what proportion of all traffic accidents were preceded by some type of driver distraction?

   _____

8. According to Rae Tyson, why are driver conversations with passengers less distracting than cell phone conversations?

_____

_____

Critical Reading and Thinking

1. What kind of evidence does the author present?

_____

2. How does the author organize the article?

_____

_____

_____

3. Does the author recognize or refute opposing viewpoints?

_____

4. What kind of information is not included in this selection that might help readers evaluate the issue?

_____

_____

5. What is the tone of the reading?

_____

Words in Context

Directions: Locate each word or phrase in the paragraph indicated and reread that paragraph. Then, based on the way the word is used, write a synonym or brief definition. You may use a dictionary, if necessary.

1. prescribed (par. 3)

_____

2. situational awareness (par. 9)

_____

3. culprit (par. 12)

_____

4. spike (par. 12)

_____

Vocabulary Review

Directions: Match each word in Column A with its meaning in Column B.

        Column A   Column B

_____ 1. tolerating   a. crashing into another vehicle from behind

_____ 2. simulator   b. intoxicated; drunk

_____ 3. impairments   c. acting in an assertive/hostile manner

_____ 4. inebriated   d. to perform two or more activities at the
same time

_____ 5. rear-ending   e. a device used for testing or training that models
actual operational conditions

_____ 6. aggressive   f. making up for

_____ 7. compensating g. weakened physical functions

_____ 8. multi-task   h. putting up with

Summarizing the Reading Selection

Directions: Write a summary of the reading "Driving While on Cell Phone Worse than Driving While Drunk" on a separate sheet of paper.

Writing Exercises

1. After reading this article, what advice would you give someone who routinely talks on a cell phone while driving? Write your advice in paragraph form.

2. Do you think there should be a law against using cell phones while driving? Write an essay explaining your answer.

Issue 6: Global Warming
Global Warming
Holli Riebeek

Published by NASA for the "earth observatory" Web site, this article examines global warming. As you read, identify the writer's position on the issue and evaluate the evidence offered in support of this position.

Vocabulary Preview

intergovernmental (par. 1) involving representatives of more than one government

unequivocal (par. 1) certain

greenhouse gases (par. 2) certain gases that trap solar radiation and warm the earth's atmosphere

virtually (par. 3) almost

infectious (par. 4) contagious

infestation (par. 8) invasion by insects

malaria (par. 9) a disease spread by infected mosquitoes

ozone (par. 9) a form of oxygen that pollutes the earth's lower atmosphere

emissions (par. 10) substances that are released into the air

Prereading

1. Does this article appear to be primarily fact or opinion?

_____

> How does this photo and caption contribute to the reading?

2. Why is global warming important?

_____

Cars, factories, and power plants pump billions of tons of carbon dioxide into the atmosphere every year. . . .

1   Over the last five years, 600 scientists from the Intergovernmental Panel on Climate Change [IPCC] sifted through thousands of studies about global warming published in forums ranging from scientific journals to industry publications and distilled the world accumulated knowledge into this conclusion: "Warming of the climate system is unequivocal."

2   Far from being some future fear, global warming is happening now, and scientists have evidence that humans are to blame. For decades, cars and factories have spewed billions of tons of greenhouse gases into the atmosphere, and these gases caused temperatures to rise between 0.6°C and 0.9°C (1.08°F to 1.62°F) over the past century. The rate of warming in the last 50 years was double the rate observed over the last 100 years. Temperatures are certain to go up further.

3   But why should we worry about a seemingly small increase in temperature? . . . Even the temperature change of a degree or two that has occurred over the last century is capable of producing significant changes in our environment and way of life. In the future, it is very likely that rising temperatures will lead to more frequent heat waves, and virtually

certain that the seas will rise, which could leave low-lying nations awash in sea-water. Warmer temperatures will alter weather patterns, making it likely that there will be more intense droughts and more intense rain events. Moreover, global warming will last thousands of years. To gain an understanding of how global warming might impact humanity, it is necessary to understand what global warming is, how scientists measure it, and how forecasts for the future are made.

POTENTIAL EFFECTS OF GLOBAL WARMING

4   The most obvious impact of global warming will be changes in both average and extreme temperature and precipitation, but warming will also enhance coastal erosion, lengthen the growing season, melt ice caps and glaciers, and alter the range of some infectious diseases, among other things.

CLIMATE CHANGES

5   For most places, global warming will result in more hot days and fewer cool days, with the greatest warming happening over land. Longer, more intense heat waves will become more frequent. High latitudes and generally wet places will tend to receive more rainfall, while tropical regions and generally dry places will probably receive less rain. Increases in rainfall will come in the form of bigger, wetter storms, rather than in the form of more rainy days. In between those larger storms will be longer periods of light or no rain, so the frequency of drought will increase. Hurricanes will likely increase in intensity due to warmer ocean surface temperatures.

6   It is impossible to pin any one unusual weather event on global warming, but evidence is emerging that suggests that global warming is already influencing the weather. The IPCC reports that both heat waves and intense rain events have increased in frequency during the last 50 years, and human-induced global warming more likely than not contributed to the trend. Satellite-based rainfall measurements show tropical areas got more rain in the form of large storms or light rainfall instead of moderate storms between 1979 and 2003. Since the 1970s, the area affected by drought and the number of intense tropical cyclones also have increased, trends that IPCC scientists say were more likely than not influenced by human activities, though in the case of cyclones, the record is too sparse to draw any certain conclusions.

RISING SEA LEVEL

7   The weather isn't the only thing global warming will impact: rising sea level will erode coasts and cause more frequent coastal flooding. The problem is serious because as much as 10 percent of the world's population lives in coastal areas

less than 10 meters (about 30 feet) above sea level. The IPCC estimates that sea levels will rise between 0.18 and 0.59 meters (0.59 to 1.9 feet) by 2099 because of expanding sea water and melting mountain glaciers. . . .

ECOSYSTEM EFFECTS

8   Global warming is also putting pressure on ecosystems, the plants and animals that co-exist in a particular climate. Warmer temperatures have already shifted the growing season in many parts of the globe. Spring is coming earlier, and that means that migrating animals have to start earlier to follow food sources. And since the growing season is longer, plants need more water to keep growing or they will dry out, increasing the risk of fires. Shorter, milder winters fail to kill insects, increasing the risk that an infestation will destroy an ecosystem. As the growing season progresses, maximum daily temperatures increase, sometimes beyond the tolerance of the plant or animal. To survive the climbing temperatures, both marine and land-based plants and animals have started to migrate towards the poles. Those species that cannot migrate or adapt face extinction. The IPCC estimates that 20–30 percent of plant and animal species will be at risk of extinction if temperatures climb more than 1.5° to 2.5°C.

9   The people who will be hardest hit will be residents of poorer countries who do not have the resources to fend off changes in climate. As tropical temperature zones expand, the reach of some infectious diseases like malaria will change. More intense rains and hurricanes, rising sea levels, and fast-melting mountain glaciers will lead to more severe flooding. Hotter summers and more frequent fires will lead to more cases of heat stroke and deaths, and to higher levels of near-surface ozone and smoke, which would cause more 'code red' air quality days. Intense droughts could lead to an increase in malnutrition. On a longer time scale, fresh water will become scarcer during the summer as mountain glaciers disappear, particularly in Asia and parts of North America. On the flip side, warmer winters will lead to fewer cold-related deaths, and the longer growing season could increase food production in some temperate areas.

10   Ultimately, global warming will impact life on Earth in many ways, but the extent of the change is up to us. Scientists have shown that human emissions of greenhouse gases are pushing global temperatures up, and many aspects of climate are responding to the warming in the way that scientists predicted they would. Ecosystems across the globe are already affected and surprising changes have already taken place. Polar ice caps are melting, plants and animals are migrating, tropical rain is shifting, and droughts are becoming more widespread

and frequent. Since greenhouse gases are long-lived, the planet will continue to warm and changes will continue to happen, but the degree to which global warming changes life on Earth depends on our decisions.

Checking Your Comprehension

1. What is the main point of this article?

_____

_____

2. According to the article, how large an increase in global temperature is required to produce significant changes in the environment?

_____

3. Why are coastal communities especially at risk as global warming progresses?

_____

_____

4. Why does global warming increase the risk of insect infestation?

_____

5. What changes are some plants and animals making in response to global warming?

_____

6. What are two health problems that global warming will likely cause?

_____

_____

7. According to the article, what are two positive changes that could result from global warming?

_____

_____

8. According to the article, what are two examples of environmental changes that already have occurred as a result of global warming?

_____

_____

Critical Reading and Thinking

1. How does the first paragraph relate to the rest of the selection?

   _____

   _____

   _____

2. What kinds of evidence does the author present?

   _____

3. How do the photograph and its caption support the author's purpose?

   _____

   _____

   _____

4. What function does the final paragraph serve?

   _____

   _____

Words in Context

Directions: Locate each word in the paragraph indicated and reread that paragraph. Then, based on the way the word is used, write a synonym or brief definition. You may use a dictionary, if necessary.

1. sifted (par. 1)

   _____

2. distilled (par. 1)

   _____

3. enhance (par. 4)

   _____

4. range (par. 4)

   _____

5. ecosystems (par. 8)

   _____

6. tolerance (par. 8)

   _____

Vocabulary Review

Directions: Match each word or phrase in Column A with its meaning in Column B.

Column A   Column B

_____ 1. intergovernmental   a. certain gases that trap solar radiation and warm the earth's atmosphere

_____ 2. unequivocal   b. a disease spread by infected mosquitoes

_____ 3. greenhouse gases   c. contagious

_____ 4. virtually   d. involving representatives of more than one government

_____ 5. infectious   e. substances that are released into the air

_____ 6. infestation   f. certain

_____ 7. malaria   g. a form of oxygen that pollutes the earth's lower atmosphere

_____ 8. ozone   h. an invasion by insects

_____ 9. emissions   i. almost

Summarizing the Reading Selection

Directions: Write a summary of the reading "Global Warming" on a separate sheet of paper.

Writing Exercises

1. What evidence about the consequences of global warming did you find most compelling? Write a paragraph explaining your answer.

2. What are some obstacles that individuals and governments face in preparing for possible effects of global warming or in trying to reduce its effects? Write an essay explaining your answer.

3. Write an essay describing actions that you could take to help address problems associated with global warming.

Progress Charts

Directions: As you complete each mastery test, record its chapter number, the date, and your percentage score.

Mastery Test 1

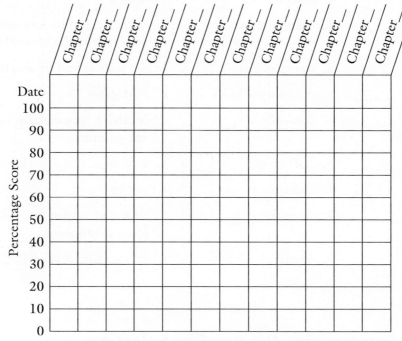

Mastery Test 2

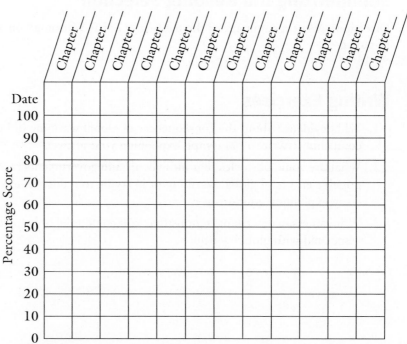

Mastery Test 3

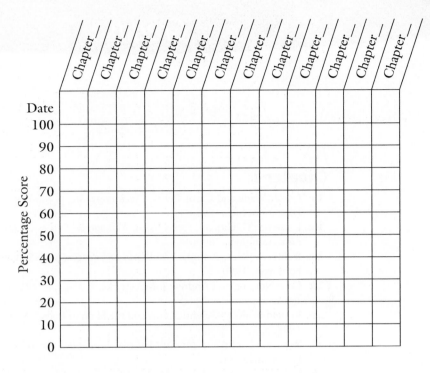

Date

Percentage Score

100
90
80
70
60
50
40
30
20
10
0

Chapter___ Chapter___ Chapter___ Chapter___ Chapter___ Chapter___ Chapter___ Chapter___ Chapter___ Chapter___ Chapter___ Chapter___

Credits

TEXT CREDITS

Chapter 1

18: Carole Wade and Carol Tavris, *Psychology*, 3/e, p. 82. Upper Saddle River, NJ: Pearson Education, Inc., 1993.

18: Lawrence G. Gitman, *Principles of Managerial Finance*, 12/e. Boston: Pearson Education, Inc., 2009.

20: Robert Wallace, *Biology: The World of Life*, 5/e, p. 185. Glenview, IL: Scott Foresman, 1990.

22: Knut Norstog and Andrew J. Meyerricks, *Biology*, p. 193. Toronto: Charles E. Merrill, 1985.

22: Ronald White, "Weightlessness and the Human Body," *Scientific American Online*, September 1998, p. 2.

23: Roger Chisholm and Marilu McCarty, *Principles of Economics*, p. 443. Glenview, IL: Scott Foresman, 1981.

26: Scott Keyes, "Stop Asking Me My Major," *The Chronicle of Higher Education*, January 10, 2010. Reprinted by permission of the author.

Chapter 2

30: Neil A. Campbell et al., *Biology: Concepts and Connections, Media Update*, 5/e, p. 70. © 2008. Reproduced by permission of Pearson Education, Inc., Upper Saddle River, NJ.

42: James M. Henslin, *Sociology: A Down-to-Earth Approach*, 10/e, p. G4. © 2010 James M. Henslin. Reproduced by permission of Pearson Education, Inc.

43: Kathleen McWhorter and Jane Aaron, *The Successful Writer's Handbook*, p. 572. New York: Longman, 2009.

48: Richard Fabes and Carol Lynn Martin, *Exploring Child Development*, 2/e, p. 454. Copyright © 2003 by Pearson Education. Reprinted by permission.

50: Michael C. Mix et al., *Biology: The Network of Life*, 1/e, p. 165, Table 10.1. ©1992. Reproduced by permission of Pearson Education, Inc., Upper Saddle River, NJ.

51: Michael R. Solomon, *Consumer Behavior*, 8/e, p. 325, Fig. 9.1. © 2009. Reproduced by permission of Pearson Education, Inc., Upper Saddle River, NJ.

57: Patrick Frank, *Prebles' Artforms: An Introduction to the Visual Arts*, 9/e, p. 100. Upper Saddle River, NJ: Pearson Education, Inc., 2009.

58: Stephen Kosslyn and Robin Rosenberg, *Fundamentals of Psychology*, 3/e, pp. 368–369. Boston: Pearson Education, Inc., 2007.

62: John Vivian, *The Media of Mass Communication*, 9/e, pp. 336–338. Boston: Pearson Education, Inc., 2009.

66: Shelley Lane, *Interpersonal Communication: Competence and Contexts*, 2/e, pp. 199–201. © 2010 by Pearson Education, Inc. Reproduced by permission of Pearson Education, Inc.

Chapter 3

83: James M. Henslin, *Sociology: A Down-to-Earth Approach*, 10/e, p. 386. © 2010 James M. Henslin. Reproduced by permission of Pearson Education, Inc.

84: Michael R. Solomon, *Consumer Behavior*, 8/e, p. 19. © 2009. Reproduced by permission of Pearson Education, Inc., Upper Saddle River, NJ.

84: Rebecca J. Donatelle, *Health: The Basics, Green Edition*, 9/e, p. 57. © 2011. Reproduced by permission of Pearson Education, Inc., Upper Saddle River, NJ.

89: James M. Henslin, *Sociology: A Down-to-Earth Approach*, 10/e, p. 83. © 2010 James M. Henslin. Reproduced by permission of Pearson Education, Inc.

90: Rebecca J. Donatelle, *Access to Health, Green Edition*, 11/e, pp. 355–356. © 2010. Reproduced by permission of Pearson Education, Inc., Upper Saddle River, NJ.

Chapter 4

115: James M. Henslin, *Sociology: A Down-to-Earth Approach*, 10/e, p. 52. © 2010 James M. Henslin. Reproduced by permission of Pearson Education, Inc.

115: Michael R. Solomon, *Consumer Behavior*, 8/e, pp. 62–63. © 2009. Reproduced by permission of Pearson Education, Inc., Upper Saddle River, NJ.

116: Rebecca J. Donatelle, *Health: The Basics, Green Edition*, 9/e, p. 34. © 2011. Reproduced by permission of Pearson Education, Inc., Upper Saddle River, NJ.

117: Neil A. Campbell et al., *Biology: Concepts and Connections with MyBiology*, 6/e, p. 680. © 2009. Reproduced by permission of Pearson Education, Inc., Upper Saddle River, NJ.

119: By permission. From *Merriam-Webster's Online Dictionary*, © 2010 by Merriam-Webster, Incorporated. (www.Merriam-Webster.com)

120: Entry "drink." Copyright © 2010 by Houghton Mifflin Harcourt Publishing Company. Reproduced by permission from *The American Heritage Dictionary of the English Language, Fourth Edition*.

123: Entry "oblique." Copyright © 2010 by Houghton Mifflin Harcourt Publishing Company. Reproduced by permission from *The American Heritage Dictionary of the English Language, Fourth Edition*.

133: Jenifer Kunz, *Think Marriages and Families*, 1/e, text excerpt beginning "In the U.S. legal system . . ." pp. 278–279. © 2011 Pearson Education, Inc. Reproduced by permission of Pearson Education, Inc.

133: Jenifer Kunz, *Think Marriages and Families*, 1/e, Graph Data "Percentages of Americans Approving of Marriage Between African Americans and Whites," p. 278. © 2011 Pearson Education, Inc. Reproduced by permission of Pearson Education, Inc.

134: Entry "panoply." Copyright © 2010 by Houghton Mifflin Harcourt Publishing Company. Reproduced by permission from *The American Heritage Dictionary of the English Language, Fourth Edition*.

134: Entry "ventilate" Copyright © 2010 by Houghton Mifflin Harcourt Publishing Company. Reproduced by permission from *The American Heritage Dictionary of the English Language, Fourth Edition*.

134: Entry "manifest." Copyright © 2010 by Houghton Mifflin Harcourt Publishing Company. Reproduced by permission from *The American Heritage Dictionary of the English Language, Fourth Edition*.

135: Entry "besiege." Copyright © 2010 by Houghton Mifflin Harcourt Publishing Company. Reproduced by permission from *The American Heritage Dictionary of the English Language, Fourth Edition*.

135: Entry "facile." Copyright © 2010 by Houghton Mifflin Harcourt Publishing Company. Reproduced by permission from *The American Heritage Dictionary of the English Language,* Fourth Edition.

137: Andy Greenberg, "A Step Beyond Human" from *Forbes,* December 14, 2009. Reprinted by permission of Forbes Media LLC, © 2010.

Chapter 5

146: Joseph A. DeVito, *Messages: Building Interpersonal Communication Skills,* 4/e, pp. 145–146. © 1999. Reproduced by permission of Pearson Education, Inc.

157: Janice Thompson and Melinda Manore, *Nutrition for Life,* 1/e, pp. 109–111. © 2007. Reproduced by Pearson Education, Inc., Upper Saddle River, NJ.

163: Rebecca J. Donatelle and Lorraine G. Davis, *Access to Heath (with Interactive Companion CD-ROM),* 6/e, pp. 560–561. © 2000. Reproduced by permission of Pearson Education, Inc., Upper Saddle River, NJ.

165: Rebecca J. Donatelle, *Health: The Basics, Green Edition,* 9/e, p. 66. © 2011. Reproduced by permission of Pearson Education, Inc., Upper Saddle River, NJ.

168: Rebecca J. Donatelle and Lorraine G. Davis, *Access to Health,* 7/e, pp. 470–471. © 2002. Reproduced by permission of Pearson Education, Inc., Upper Saddle River, NJ.

Chapter 6

178: Rebecca J. Donatelle, *Health: The Basics, Green Edition,* 9/e, p. 424. ©2011. Reproduced by permission of Pearson Education, Inc., Upper Saddle River, NJ.

179: Frederick K. Lutgens et al., *Essentials of Geology,* 10/e, p. 62. Upper Saddle River, NJ: Pearson Education, Inc., 2009.

179: Michael R. Solomon, *Consumer Behavior,* 8/e, p. 35. © 2009. Reproduced by permission of Pearson Education, Inc., Upper Saddle River, NJ.

179: Colleen Belk and Virginia Borden Maier, *Biology: Science for Life with Physiology,* 3/e, p. 438. © 2010. Reproduced by permission of Pearson Education, Inc., Upper Saddle River, NJ.

180: James M. Henslin, *Sociology: A Down-to-Earth Approach,* 10/e, p. 148. © 2010 James M. Henslin. Reproduced by permission of Pearson Education, Inc.

180: Michael R. Solomon, *Consumer Behavior,* 8/e, pp. 392–393. © 2009. Reproduced by permission of Pearson Education, Inc., Upper Saddle River, NJ.

181: Rebecca J. Donatelle, *Health: The Basics, Green Edition,* 9/e, p. 282. © 2011. Reproduced by permission of Pearson Education, Inc., Upper Saddle River, NJ.

181: Ronald J. Ebert and Ricky W. Griffin, *Business Essentials,* 7/e, p. 12. Upper Saddle River, NJ: Pearson Education, Inc., 2009.

181: John D. Carl, *Think Sociology,* p. 51. Upper Saddle River, NJ: Pearson Education, Inc., 2010.

181: Roy A. Cook et al., *Tourism: The Business of Travel,* 4/e, p. 347. © 2010. Reproduced by permission of Pearson Education, Inc., Upper Saddle River, NJ.

182: Peter Facione, *Think Critically,* p. 90. Upper Saddle River, NJ: Pearson Education, Inc., 2011.

182: Roy A. Cook et al., *Tourism: The Business of Travel,* 4/e, p. 52. © 2010. Reproduced by permission of Pearson Education, Inc., Upper Saddle River, NJ.

184: Richard Campbell, *Media and Culture,* p. 196. New York: St. Martin's Press, 1997.

184: Patrick Frank, *Prebles' Artforms: An Introduction to the Visual Arts,* 9/e, p. 5. Upper Saddle River, NJ: Pearson Education, Inc., 2009.

185: John D. Carl, *Think Sociology,* p. 128. Upper Saddle River, NJ: Pearson Education, Inc., 2010.

185: Rebecca J. Donatelle, *Health: The Basics, Green Edition,* 9/e, p. 18. © 2011. Reproduced by permission of Pearson Education, Inc., Upper Saddle River, NJ.

186: John D. Carl, *Think Sociology*, p. 122. Upper Saddle River, NJ: Pearson Education, Inc., 2010.

186: Ronald J. Ebert and Ricky W. Griffin, *Business Essentials*, 7/e, p. 161. Upper Saddle River, NJ: Pearson Education, Inc., 2009.

186: George C. Edwards III et al., *Government in America: People, Politics, and Policy*, 14/e, p. 306. © 2009. Reproduced by permission of Pearson Education, Inc.

186: Neil A. Campbell et al., *Biology: Concepts and Connections with MyBiology*, 6/e, p. 712. © 2009. Reproduced by permission of Pearson Education, Inc., Upper Saddle River, NJ.

187: James M. Henslin, *Sociology: A Down-to-Earth Approach*, 10/e, p. 6. © 2010 James M. Henslin. Reproduced by permission of Pearson Education, Inc.

187: Colleen Belk and Virginia Borden Maier, *Biology: Science for Life with Physiology*, 3/e, p. 305. © 2010. Reproduced by permission of Pearson Education, Inc., Upper Saddle River, NJ.

187: Michael R. Solomon, *Consumer Behavior*, 8/e, p. 21. © 2009. Reproduced by permission of Pearson Education, Inc., Upper Saddle River, NJ.

187: Neil A. Campbell et al., *Biology: Concepts and Connections with MyBiology*, 6/e, p. 73. © 2009. Reproduced by permission of Pearson Education, Inc., Upper Saddle River, NJ.

188: James M. Henslin, *Sociology: A Down-to-Earth Approach*, 10/e, p. 85. © 2010 James M. Henslin. Reproduced by permission of Pearson Education, Inc.

188: Frederick K. Lutgens et al., *Essentials of Geography*, 10/e, p. 144. Upper Saddle River, NJ: Pearson Education, Inc., 2009.

196: Edward Bergman and William Renwick, *Introduction to Geography*, 2/e, p. 365. Upper Saddle River, NJ: Pearson Education, Inc., 2002.

196: Hugh D. Barlow, *Criminal Justice in America*, p. 271. Upper Saddle River, NJ: Pearson Education, Inc., 2000.

197: Rebecca J. Donatelle, *Health: The Basics, Green Edition*, 9/e, p. 280. © 2011. Reproduced by permission of Pearson Education, Inc., Upper Saddle River, NJ.

198: Kathleen German and Bruce Gronbeck, *Principles of Public Speaking*, 14/e, pp. 190–191. New York: Longman, 2001.

198: Tim Curry et al., *Sociology for the 21st Century*, 3/e, p. 138. Upper Saddle River, NJ: Prentice-Hall, 2001.

199: Michael Solomon and Elnora Stuart, *The Brave New World of E-Commerce (Supplement to Marketing: Real People, Real Choices)*, p. 13. Upper Saddle River, NJ: Prentice-Hall, 2001.

199: Steven A. Beebe and John T. Masterson, *Communicating in Small Groups: Principles and Practices*, 6/e, p. 150. New York: Longman, 2001.

201: Ronald J. Ebert and Ricky W. Griffin, *Business Essentials*, 7/e, p. 188. Upper Saddle River, NJ: Pearson Education, Inc., 2009.

200: Colleen Belk and Virginia Borden Maier, *Biology: Science for Life with Physiology*, 3/e, p. 236. © 2010. Reproduced by permission of Pearson Education, Inc., Upper Saddle River, NJ.

200: Robert A. Divine, et al., *America: Past and Present*, Combined Volume, 9/e, p. 449. Upper Saddle River, NJ: Pearson Education, Inc., 2011.

200: Rebecca J. Donatelle and Lorraine G. Davis, *Access to Heath (with Interactive Companion CD-ROM)*, 6/e, p. 42. © 2000. Reproduced by permission of Pearson Education, Inc., Upper Saddle River, NJ.

201: Ronald J. Ebert and Ricky W. Griffin, *Business Essentials*, 7/e, p. 188. Upper Saddle River, NJ: Pearson Education, Inc., 2009.

201: George C. Edwards III et al., *Government in America: People, Politics, and Policy*, 14/e, p. 9. © 2009. Reproduced by permission of Pearson Education, Inc.

201: James M. Henslin, *Sociology: A Down-to-Earth Approach*, 10/e, p. 46. © 2010 James M. Henslin. Reproduced by permission of Pearson Education, Inc.

201: Colleen Belk and Virginia Borden Maier, *Biology: Science for Life with Physiology*, 3/e, p. 447. © 2010. Reproduced by permission of Pearson Education, Inc., Upper Saddle River, NJ.

202: Michael R. Solomon, *Consumer Behavior*, 8/e, p. 189. © 2009. Reproduced by permission of Pearson Education, Inc., Upper Saddle River, NJ.

202: Rebecca J. Donatelle, *Health: The Basics, Green Edition*, 9/e, p. 71. © 2011. Reproduced by permission of Pearson Education, Inc., Upper Saddle River, NJ.

202: Rebecca J. Donatelle and Lorraine G. Davis, *Access to Heath (with Interactive Companion CD-ROM)*, 6/e, pp. 289–290. © 2000. Reproduced by permission of Pearson Education, Inc., Upper Saddle River, NJ.

203: Edward F. Bergman and William H. Renwick, *Introduction to Geography: People, Places, and Environment*, 3/e, p. 422. © 2005. Reproduced by permission of Pearson Education, Inc., Upper Saddle River, NJ.

203: Colleen Belk and Virginia Borden Maier, *Biology: Science for Life with Physiology*, 3/e, p. 509. © 2010. Reproduced by permission of Pearson Education, Inc., Upper Saddle River, NJ.

203: Joseph A. DeVito, *Messages: Building Interpersonal Communication Skills*, 5/e, pp. 224–225. © 2002. Reproduced by permission of Pearson Education, Inc.

206: eBay™ is a trademark of eBay Inc. Used with permission.

206: Michael Solomon and Elnora Stuart, *The Brave New World of E-Commerce (Supplement to Marketing: Real People, Real Choices)*, p. 16. Upper Saddle River, NJ: Prentice-Hall, 2001.

206: Edward F. Bergman and William H. Renwick, *Introduction to Geography: People, Places, and Environment*, 3/e, p. 386. © 2005. Reproduced by permission of Pearson Education, Inc., Upper Saddle River, NJ.

206: Joseph A. DeVito, *Messages: Building Interpersonal Communication Skills*, 4/e, p. 140. © 1999. Reproduced by permission of Pearson Education, Inc.

207: Rebecca J. Donatelle and Lorraine G. Davis, *Access to Heath (with Interactive Companion CD-ROM)*, 6/e, p. 78. © 2000. Reproduced by permission of Pearson Education, Inc., Upper Saddle River, NJ.

207: George C. Edwards III et al., *Government in America: People, Politics, and Policy*, 14/e, pp. 206–207. © 2009. Reproduced by permission of Pearson Education, Inc.

208: Janice Thompson and Melinda Manore, *Nutrition for Life*, 2/e, p. 240. © 2010. Reproduced by permission of Pearson Education, Inc., Upper Saddle River, NJ.

211: Joshua Kors, "War Torn," *Current Science*, November 28, 2008. Special permission granted by Weekly Reader, published and copyrighted by Weekly Reader Corporation. All rights reserved.

213: KRT/Newscom graphic "Under Fire." © McClatchy-Tribune Information Services. All rights reserved. Reprinted with permission.

Chapter 7

217: Amy Sedaris, from *I Like You*. Copyright © 2006 by Amy Sedaris. By permission of Grand Central Publishing. All rights reserved.

218: Joseph A. DeVito, *Messages: Building Interpersonal Communication Skills*, 4/e, pp. 150. © 1999. Reproduced by permission of Pearson Education, Inc.

220: Joseph A. DeVito, *Messages: Building Interpersonal Communication Skills*, 4/e, pp. 159–161. © 1999. Reproduced by permission of Pearson Education, Inc.

221: Joseph A. DeVito, *Messages: Building Interpersonal Communication Skills*, 4/e, p. 130. © 1999. Reproduced by permission of Pearson Education, Inc.

222: B.E. Pruitt and Jane J. Stein, *Healthstyles: Decisions for Living Well*, 2/e, pp. 108, 110. Boston: Allyn and Bacon, 1999.

223: Hugh D. Barlow, *Criminal Justice in America*, p. 238. Upper Saddle River, NJ: Pearson Education, Inc., 2000.

226: John R. Walker and Josielyn T. Walker, *Tourism: Concepts and Practices*, p. 11. Upper Saddle River, NJ: Pearson Education, Inc., 2011.

227: George C. Edwards III et al., *Government in America: People, Politics, and Policy*, 14/e, p. 239. © 2009. Reproduced by permission of Pearson Education, Inc.

228: Thomas F. Goldman and Henry R. Cheeseman, *The Paralegal Professional*, 3/e, pp. 736–737. © 2011. Reproduced by permission of Pearson Education, Inc., Upper Saddle River, NJ.

228: Saundra Ciccarelli and J. Noland White, *Psychology: An Exploration*, 1/e, p. 249. © 2010. Reproduced by permission of Pearson Education, Inc., Upper Saddle River, NJ.

228: Thomas F. Goldman and Henry R. Cheeseman, *The Paralegal Professional*, 3/e, p. 81. © 2011. Reproduced by permission of Pearson Education, Inc., Upper Saddle River, NJ.

229: Paul G. Hewitt, *Conceptual Physics*, 5/e, p. 15. © 1985. Reproduced by permission of Pearson Education, Inc., Upper Saddle River, NJ.

230: James M. Henslin, *Sociology: A Down-to-Earth Approach*, 6/e, p. 383. © 2003 James M. Henslin. Reproduced by permission of Pearson Education, Inc.

230: Paul G. Hewitt, *Conceptual Physics*, 5/e, pp. 234–235. © 1985. Reproduced by permission of Pearson Education, Inc., Upper Saddle River, NJ.

231: Paul G. Hewitt, *Conceptual Physics*, 5/e, p. 259. © 1985. Reproduced by permission of Pearson Education, Inc., Upper Saddle River, NJ.

231: Neil A. Campbell et al., *Biology: Concepts and Connections with MyBiology*, 6/e, p. 709. © 2009. Reproduced by permission of Pearson Education, Inc., Upper Saddle River, NJ.

232: George C. Edwards III et al., *Government in America: People, Politics, and Policy*, 9/e, pp. 458–459. © 2000. Reproduced by permission of Pearson Education, Inc.

232: Stephen F. Davis and Joseph J. Palladino, *Psychology*, 3/e, pp. 563, 564, 566. Upper Saddle River, NJ: Pearson Education, Inc., 2000.

232: Rebecca J. Donatelle and Lorraine G. Davis, *Access to Heath (with Interactive Companion CD-ROM)*, 6/e, pp. 358, 371. © 2000. Reproduced by permission of Pearson Education, Inc., Upper Saddle River, NJ.

233: John A. Garraty and Mark C. Carnes, *The American Nation*, 10/e, p. 706. New York: Longman, 2000.

233: Roy A. Cook et al., *Tourism: The Business of Travel*, 4/e, p. 209. © 2010. Reproduced by permission of Pearson Education, Inc., Upper Saddle River, NJ.

233: Wendy G. Lehnert, *Light on the Internet: Essentials of the Internet and the World Wide Web*, pp. 112, 131. Reading, MA: Addison Wesley Longman, 1999.

234: Palmira Brummett et al., *Civilization: Past and Present*, 9/e, p. 348. New York: Longman, 2000.

235: Edward H. Reiley and Carroll L. Shry, *Introductory Horticulture*, p. 114. Albany, NY: Delmar Publishers, 1979.

240: Alex Thio, *Sociology*, p. 374. New York: HarperCollins College Publishers, 1994.

243: Rebecca J. Donatelle and Lorraine G. Davis, *Access to Heath (with Interactive Companion CD-ROM)*, 6/e, pp. 446–447. © 2000. Reproduced by permission of Pearson Education, Inc., Upper Saddle River, NJ.

243: Palmira Brummett et al., *Civilization: Past and Present*, 9/e, p. 919. New York: Longman, 2000.

243: Stephen F. Davis and Joseph J. Palladino, *Psychology*, 3/e, p. 609. Upper Saddle River, NJ: Pearson Education, Inc., 2000.

244: Roy A. Cook et al., *Tourism: The Business of Travel*, 4/e, p. 214. © 2010. Reproduced by permission of Pearson Education, Inc., Upper Saddle River, NJ.

244: Joseph A. DeVito, *Messages: Building Interpersonal Communication Skills*, 5/e, p. 284. © 2002. Reproduced by permission of Pearson Education, Inc.

245: Stephen Kosslyn and Robin Rosenberg, *Psychology: The Brain, The Person, The World*, pp. 180–181. Boston: Allyn and Bacon, 2001.

247: Carl Pino, "Sustainability on the Menu: College Cafeterias Are Buying Local and Going Organic" from *E Magazine*, March/April 2008, Vol. 19, No. 2, pp. 30–31. Used by permission.

Chapter 8

253: National Doppler Radar image from The Weather Channel, www.weather.com. Used by permission of The Weather Channel Interactive, Inc.

255: Sydney B. Newell, *Chemistry: An Introduction*, p. 11. Boston: Little, Brown, 1980.

256: Paul G. Hewitt, *Conceptual Physics*, 5/e, p. 21. © 1985. Reproduced by permission of Pearson Education, Inc., Upper Saddle River, NJ.

256: Richard L. Weaver, *Understanding Interpersonal Communication*, p. 24. Boston: Allyn and Bacon, 1996.

257: Paul G. Hewitt, *Conceptual Physics*, 5/e, p. 56. © 1985. Reproduced by permission of Pearson Education, Inc., Upper Saddle River, NJ.

257: Paul G. Hewitt, *Conceptual Physics*, 5/e, p. 224. © 1985. Reproduced by permission of Pearson Education, Inc., Upper Saddle River, NJ.

259: From "Nez Perce Indians." Excerpted from *The World Book Online Reference Center*, © 2010. www.worldbookonline.com. By permission of the publisher. All rights reserved. This content may not be reproduced in whole or in part in any form without prior written permission from the publisher.

260: Hal B. Pickle and Royce L. Abrahamson, *Introduction to Business*, p. 40. Upper Saddle River, NJ: Prentice-Hall, 1987.

260: Walter Thompson and Joseph V. Hickey, *Society in Focus*, 4/e, p. 70. Boston: Allyn and Bacon, 1994.

260: Hal B. Pickle and Royce L. Abrahamson, *Introduction to Business*, p. 119. Upper Saddle River, NJ: Prentice-Hall, 1987.

262: Paul G. Hewitt, *Conceptual Physics*, 5/e, pp. 82–84. © 1985. Reproduced by permission of Pearson Education, Inc., Upper Saddle River, NJ.

264: David Krough, *Biology: A Guide to the Natural World with MyBiology*, 4/e, pp. 474, 466–477. © 2009. Reproduced by permission of Pearson Education, Inc., Upper Saddle River, NJ.

265: James M. Henslin, *Sociology: A Down-to-Earth Approach*, 10/e, p. 164. © 2010 James M. Henslin. Reproduced by permission of Pearson Education, Inc.

266: Neil A. Campbell et al., *Biology: Concepts and Connections with MyBiology*, 6/e, p. 1. © 2009. Reproduced by permission of Pearson Education, Inc., Upper Saddle River, NJ.

267: Alan Evans et al., *Introductory Technology in Action*, 7/e, p. 271. Upper Saddle River, NJ: Pearson Education, Inc., 2011.

270: Roy A. Cook et al., *Tourism: The Business of Travel*, 4/e, p. 282. © 2010. Reproduced by permission of Pearson Education, Inc., Upper Saddle River, NJ.

271: Saundra Ciccarelli and J. Noland White, *Psychology: An Exploration*, 1/e, p. 280. © 2010. Reproduced by permission of Pearson Education, Inc., Upper Saddle River, NJ.

272: Colleen Belk and Virginia Borden Maier, *Biology: Science for Life with Physiology*, 3/e, p. 372. © 2010. Reproduced by permission of Pearson Education, Inc., Upper Saddle River, NJ.

272: James M. Henslin, *Sociology: A Down-to-Earth Approach*, 10/e, p. 37. © 2010 James M. Henslin. Reproduced by permission of Pearson Education, Inc.

274: David Krough, *Biology: A Guide to the Natural World with MyBiology*, 4/e, p. 429. © 2009. Reproduced by permission of Pearson Education, Inc., Upper Saddle River, NJ.

275: Michael R. Solomon, *Consumer Behavior*, 8/e, pp. 132–133. © 2009. Reproduced by permission of Pearson Education, Inc., Upper Saddle River, NJ.

275: James M. Henslin, *Sociology: A Down-to-Earth Approach*, 10/e, pp. 109, 111. © 2010 James M. Henslin. Reproduced by permission of Pearson Education, Inc.

277: Hugh D. Barlow, *Criminal Justice in America*, p. 332. Upper Saddle River, NJ: Pearson Education, Inc., 2000.

277: Roy A. Cook et al., *Tourism: The Business of Travel*, 4/e, p. 170. © 2010. Reproduced by permission of Pearson Education, Inc., Upper Saddle River, NJ.

278: Thomas F. Goldman and Henry R. Cheeseman, *The Paralegal Professional*, 3/e, p. 266. © 2011. Reproduced by permission of Pearson Education, Inc., Upper Saddle River, NJ.

272: Robert A. Divine, et al., *America: Past and Present*, Combined Volume, 9/e, p. 596. Upper Saddle River, NJ: Pearson Education, Inc., 2011.

279: Saundra Ciccarelli and J. Noland White, *Psychology: An Exploration*, 1/e, p. 321. © 2010. Reproduced by permission of Pearson Education, Inc., Upper Saddle River, NJ.

279: David Krough, *Biology: A Guide to the Natural World with MyBiology*, 4/e, p. 750. © 2009. Reproduced by permission of Pearson Education, Inc., Upper Saddle River, NJ.

280: John R. Walker and Josielyn T. Walker, *Tourism: Concepts and Practices*, pp. 53–54. Upper Saddle River, NJ: Pearson Education, Inc., 2011.

280: Thomas F. Goldman and Henry R. Cheeseman, *The Paralegal Professional*, 3/e, p. 641. © 2011. Reproduced by permission of Pearson Education, Inc., Upper Saddle River, NJ.

280: Neil A. Campbell et al., *Biology: Concepts and Connections with MyBiology*, 6/e, p. 365. © 2009. Reproduced by permission of Pearson Education, Inc., Upper Saddle River, NJ.

281: Rebecca J. Donatelle, *Health: The Basics, Green Edition*, 9/e, p. 20. © 2011. Reproduced by permission of Pearson Education, Inc., Upper Saddle River, NJ.

281: David Krough, *Biology: A Guide to the Natural World with MyBiology*, 4/e, p. 488. © 2009. Reproduced by permission of Pearson Education, Inc., Upper Saddle River, NJ.

281: Colleen Belk and Virginia Borden Maier, *Biology: Science for Life with Physiology*, 3/e, p. 451. © 2010. Reproduced by permission of Pearson Education, Inc., Upper Saddle River, NJ.

281: John R. Walker and Josielyn T. Walker, *Tourism: Concepts and Practices*, p. 241. Upper Saddle River, NJ: Pearson Education, Inc., 2011.

282: Neil A. Campbell et al., *Biology: Concepts and Connections with MyBiology*, 6/e, p. 398. © 2009. Reproduced by permission of Pearson Education, Inc., Upper Saddle River, NJ.

283: Thomas F. Goldman and Henry R. Cheeseman, *The Paralegal Professional*, 3/e, p. 183. © 2011. Reproduced by permission of Pearson Education, Inc., Upper Saddle River, NJ.

284: James M. Henslin, *Sociology: A Down-to-Earth Approach*, 6/e, p. 637. © 2003 James M. Henslin. Reproduced by permission of Pearson Education, Inc.

285: Edward F. Bergman and William H. Renwick, *Introduction to Geography: People, Places, and Environment*, 3/e, p. 430. © 2005. Reproduced by permission of Pearson Education, Inc., Upper Saddle River, NJ.

285: William Germann and Cindy Stanfield, *Principles of Human Physiology*, pp. 303–304. San Francisco: Benjamin Cummings, 2002.

291: David Krough, *Biology: A Guide to the Natural World with MyBiology*, 4/e, p. 318–319. © 2009. Reproduced by permission of Pearson Education, Inc., Upper Saddle River, NJ.

293: Bruce E. Gronbeck et al., *Principles of Speech Communication*, 13th brief ed, pp. 32–33. New York: Longman, 1998.

293: Michael C. Mix et al., *Biology: The Network of Life*, 2/e, p. 262. ©1996. Reproduced by permission of Pearson Education, Inc., Upper Saddle River, NJ.

293: Joseph A. DeVito, *The Interpersonal Communication Book*, 9/e, pp. 219–220. Boston: Allyn and Bacon, 2001.

294: James M. Henslin, *Sociology: A Down-to-Earth Approach*, 10/e, p. 389–390. © 2010 James M. Henslin. Reproduced by permission of Pearson Education, Inc.

294: John R. Walker, *Introduction to Hospitality Management*, 3/e, p. 361. Upper Saddle River, NJ: Pearson Education, Inc., 2010.

294: Jenifer Kunz, *Think Marriages and Families*, 1/e, text excerpt beginning "Five environmental systems . . ." p. 16. © 2011 Pearson Education, Inc. Reproduced by permission of Pearson Education, Inc.

295: Patrick Frank, *Prebles' Artforms: An Introduction to the Visual Arts*, 9/e, p. 127. Upper Saddle River, NJ: Pearson Education, Inc., 2009.

295: Frederick K. Lutgens et al., *Essentials of Geology*, 10/e, pp. 252–253. Upper Saddle River, NJ: Pearson Education, Inc., 2009.

295: David Krough, *Biology: A Guide to the Natural World with MyBiology*, 4/e, p. 471. © 2009. Reproduced by permission of Pearson Education, Inc., Upper Saddle River, NJ.

296: Michael R. Solomon, *Consumer Behavior*, 8/e, p. 13. © 2009. Reproduced by permission of Pearson Education, Inc., Upper Saddle River, NJ.

297: Alton Fitzgerald White, "Right Place, Wrong Face," originally published as "Ragtime, My Time." Reprinted with permission from the October 11, 1999 issue of *The Nation*. For subscription information, call 1-800-333-8536. Portions of each week's Nation magazine can be accessed at http://www.thenation.com.

Chapter 9

315: Elaine Marieb, *Essentials of Human Anatomy and Physiology*, 7/e, pp. 162, 164. © 2003. Reproduced by permission of Pearson Education, Inc.

315: Elaine Marieb, *Essentials of Human Anatomy and Physiology*, 7/e, pp. 164, Fig 6.1. © 2003. Reproduced by permission of Pearson Education, Inc.

316: Robert Wallace, *Biology: The World of Life*, 6/e, p. 774. © 1992. Reproduced by permission of Pearson Education, Inc., Upper Saddle River, NJ.

317: Robert Wallace, *Biology: The World of Life*, 6/e, p. 774. © 1992. Reproduced by permission of Pearson Education, Inc., Upper Saddle River, NJ.

318: Curtis Byer and Louis Shainberg, *Living Well: Health in Your Hands*, 2/e, Fig G5. © 2005 Jones and Bartlett Learning, Sudbury, MA. www.jblearning.com. Reprinted with permission.

319: Richard Fabes and Carol Lynn Martin, *Exploring Child Development*, 2/e, p. 281. Copyright © 2003 by Pearson Education. Reprinted by permission.

321: Richard Fabes and Carol Lynn Martin, *Exploring Child Development*, 2/e, p. 196. Copyright © 2003 by Pearson Education. Reprinted by permission.

321: Randall B. Dunham and Jon L. Pierce, *Management*, p. 721. © 1989. Reproduced by permission of Pearson Education, Inc. (Electronic rights: Reproduced by permission of Randall B. Dunham).

323: James M. Henslin, *Social Problems*, 6/e, p. 368, Fig. 11.5. © 2003 James M. Henslin. Reproduced by permission of Pearson Education, Inc.

324: George C. Edwards III et al., *Government in America: People, Politics, and Policy*, 4/e, p. 253. © 1989. Reproduced by permission of Pearson Education, Inc.

325: Michael R. Solomon et al, *Marketing: Real People, Real Choices*, 6/e, p. 406. © 2009. Reproduced by permission of Pearson Education, Inc., Upper Saddle River, NJ.

326: Elaine Marieb, *Essentials of Human Anatomy and Physiology*, 7/e, p. 106 and Fig 4.9. © 2003. Reproduced by permission of Pearson Education, Inc.

328: Edward F. Bergman and William H. Renwick, *Introduction to Geography: People, Places, and Environment*, 3/e, p. 69. © 2005. Reproduced by permission of Pearson Education, Inc., Upper Saddle River, NJ.

338: James M. Henslin, *Sociology: A Down-to-Earth Approach*, 10/e, p. 483. © 2010 James M. Henslin. Reproduced by permission of Pearson Education, Inc.

340: James M. Henslin, *Sociology: A Down-to-Earth Approach*, 6/e, p. 489. © 2003 James M. Henslin. Reproduced by permission of Pearson Education, Inc.

343: Neal Tannahill, *Think American Government*, 1/e, pp. 106–109. © 2010. Reproduced by permission of Pearson Education, Inc.

Chapter 10

353: John R. Walker, *Introduction to Hospitality Management*, 3/e, p. 45. Upper Saddle River, NJ: Pearson Education, Inc., 2010.

354: Thomas F. Goldman and Henry R. Cheeseman, *The Paralegal Professional*, 3/e, p. 745. © 2011. Reproduced by permission of Pearson Education, Inc., Upper Saddle River, NJ.

356: Saundra Ciccarelli and J. Noland White, *Psychology: An Exploration*, 1/e, p. 454. © 2010. Reproduced by permission of Pearson Education, Inc., Upper Saddle River, NJ.

357: George C. Edwards III et al., *Government in America: People, Politics, and Policy*, 14/e, p. 285. © 2009. Reproduced by permission of Pearson Education, Inc.

358: Sydney B. Newell, *Chemistry: An Introduction*, p. 47–48. Boston: Little, Brown, 1980.

361: Rebecca J. Donatelle, *Health: The Basics, Green Edition*, 9/e, pp. 94, 96. © 2011. Reproduced by permission of Pearson Education, Inc., Upper Saddle River, NJ.

362: Thomas Kinnear et al., *Principles of Marketing*, 4/e, pp. 39–40. Upper Saddle River, NJ: Prentice-Hall, 1995.

373: Kathleen German and Bruce Gronbeck, *Principles of Public Speaking*, 14/e, pp. 38–39. New York: Longman, 2001.

375: Joseph A. DeVito, *The Interpersonal Communication Book*, 8/e, p. 141. New York: Longman, 1998.

378: Saundra Ciccarelli and J. Noland White, *Psychology*, 2/e, pp. 169–171. © 2009. Reproduced by permission of Pearson Education, Inc., Upper Saddle River, NJ.

Chapter 11

386: Nancy Clark, *Nancy Clark's Sports Nutrition Guidebook*, pp. 21–22. Champaign, IL: Human Kinetics, 2008.

388: David Sedaris, from *Holidays on Ice*. Copyright © 1997 by David Sedaris. By permission of Little, Brown and Company. All rights reserved. (Electronic rights: Copyright © 1994 by David Sedaris. Reprinted by permission of Don Congdon Associates, Inc.).

390: David Batstone, excerpt from "Katja's Story" as appeared in *Sojourners Magazine*, June 2006. Used by permission of David Batstone, Cofounder and President, Not For sale Campaign.

392: Susan RoAne, *Face to Face: How to Reclaim the Personal Touch in a Digital World*, pp. 2–3. New York: Simon and Schuster, 2008.

392: Christopher Slobogin, *Privacy at Risk: The New Government Surveillance and the Fourth Amendment*, pp. 3–4. Chicago: University of Chicago Press, 2007.

393: Richard Shenkman, *Legends, Lies, and Cherished Myths of American History*, pp. 37–38. New York: William Morrow, 1988.

394: John Perkins et al., *Attack Proof: The Ultimate Guide to Personal Protection*, p. 7. Champaign, IL: Human Kinetics, 2009.

395: Cathy Greenberg and Barrett S. Avigdor, *What Happy Working Mothers Know: How New Findings in Positive Psychology Can Lead to a Healthy and Happy Work/Life Balance*, p. 97. Hoboken, NJ: John Wiley and Sons, 2009.

396: Lucinda Holdforth, *Why Manners Matter: The Case for Civilized Behavior in a Barbarous World*, pp. 16–17. New York: Amy Enhorn Books/G.P. Putnam's Sons, 2009.

400: Sara King, "Love in the Afternoon-in a Crowded Prison Hall," *Los Angeles Times*, November 5, 1976. Copyright © 1976 Los Angeles Times. Reprinted with permission.

402: Marc Eisenson, excerpt from "Stop Junk Mail Forever" as appeared in *Mother Earth News*, August/September 1994, Copyright 1994 Mother Earth News. Used with permission.

406: Robert Wallace, *Biology: The World of Life*, 6/e, p. 659. © 1992. Reproduced by permission of Pearson Education, Inc., Upper Saddle River, NJ.

406: Marge Thielman Hastreiter, "Not Every Mother Is Glad Kids Are Back in School," *Buffalo Evening News*, 1991.

408: Margaret S. Price, *The Special Needs Child and Divorce: A Practical Guide to Evaluating and Handling Cases*, p. 4. Chicago: American Bar Association, Section of Family Law, 2009.

408: Bess Armstrong, article from *The Choices We Made*, Angela Bonavoglia, ed., p. 165. New York: Random House, 1991.

410: Barry Lopez, "Weekend," *Audubon*, July 1973.

411: John Steinbeck, *America and Indians*, pp. 127–128. New York: Viking Press, 1966.

411: Karen Olson, from "Eat It Raw," *Utne Reader*, March/April 2002. Reprinted by permission of the author and Utne Reader.

416: Rebecca J. Donatelle and Lorraine G. Davis, *Access to Heath (with Interactive Companion CD-ROM)*, 6/e, p. 146. © 2000. Reproduced by permission of Pearson Education, Inc., Upper Saddle River, NJ.

416: Michael Solomon and Elnora Stuart, *The Brave New World of E-Commerce (Supplement to Marketing: Real People, Real Choices)*, p. 17. Upper Saddle River, NJ: Prentice-Hall, 2001.

416: Joe L. Kincheloe et al., *Contextualizing Teaching*, pp. 90–91. Boston: Allyn and Bacon, 2000.

417: Michael R. Solomon et al., *Marketing: Real People, Real Choices*, 2/e, p. 59. Upper Saddle River, NJ: Pearson Education, Inc., 2000.

417: Palmira Brummett et al., *Civilization: Past and Present*, 9/e, p. 578–579. New York: Longman, 2000.

418: Cynthia Audet, "Scar," *The Sun*, Issue 325, January, 2003. Reprinted by permission of the author.

420: Ruth Pennebaker, "The Mediocre Multitasker." From *The New York Times*, August 30, 2009. © 2009 The New York Times. All rights reserved. Used by permission and protected by the Copyright Laws of the United States. The printing, copying, redistribution, or retransmission of the Material without express written permission is prohibited. www.nytimes.com.

Chapter 12

425: Screenshot from Tulsaworld.com. Used by permission of World Publishing Company.

431: Scott Dobson-Mitchell, excerpt from "Beat the Clock," *Maclean's*, November 16, 2009, Vol. 122, Issue 44, p. 114. Used by permission of the author.

431: Yair Amichai-Hamburger, from "Depression Through Technology," *New Scientist*, December 19, 2009, p. 28. By permission of New Scientist, www.newscientist.com.

435: Linda Papadopoulos, *What Men Say, What Women Hear*, p. 22. New York: Simon Spotlight, 2009.

440: Quote from Carol Dweck in Andrew Postman, "Raising a Good Loser," *Good Housekeeping*, January 2010, 250:1, p. 85.

440: Quote from Federal Reserve Chairman Ben S. Bernanke, "Monetary Policy and the Housing Bubble," January, 2010.

440: Edward S. Greenberg and Benjamin I. Page, *The Struggle for Democracy*, 2/e, p. 186. New York: HarperCollins College Publishers, 1995.

441: Arlene Skolnick, *The Intimate Environment: Exploring Marriage and the Family*, 6/e, p. 96. New York: HarperCollins College Publishers, 1996.

444: Studs Terkel, from "Jesusita Novarro" in *Working: People Talk About What They Do All Day*. Reprinted by permission of Donadio and Olson, Inc. Copyright 1980 Studs Terkel.

446: Michael R. Solomon, *Consumer Behavior: Buying, Having, and Being*, 5/e, p. 19. © 2002. Reproduced by permission of Pearson Education, Inc.

451: George C. Edwards III et al., *Government in America: People, Politics, and Policy*, 9/e, p. 685. © 2000. Reproduced by permission of Pearson Education, Inc.

451: George C. Edwards III et al., *Government in America: People, Politics, and Policy*, 9/e, pp. 426-427. © 2000. Reproduced by permission of Pearson Education, Inc.

456: Nathan Harden, "The Generation That Killed Rock 'n 'Roll," *The Huffington Post*, February 1, 2010. Reprinted by permission of the author.

Part 6

462: Kate Chopin, "The Story of an Hour," 1894.

466: Edgar Allen Poe, "The Tell-Tale Heart," 1843.

472: Bruce Holland Rogers, "Little Brother," *Strange Horizons*, October 30, 2000. Reprinted by permission of the author.

478: From *Water for Elephants* by Sara Gruen. © 2006 by Sara Gruen. Reprinted by permission of Algonquin Books of Chapel Hill. All rights reserved.

Part 7

484: John J. Macionis, *Sociology*, 13/e, "The Genetic Crystal Ball: Do We Really Want to Look?" p. 561. © 2010 Pearson Education, Inc. Reproduced by permission of Pearson Education, Inc.

489: Linda T. Sanchez, "New Bullying Technology," *St. Louis Post-Dispatch*, April 5, 2009. Reprinted with permission of The St. Louis Post-Dispatch, copyright 2009.

494: Patrick Welsh, "Txting Away Ur Education" as appeared in *USA Today*, June 23, 2009. Used by permission of the author.

499: Daniel B. Wood, "New No-Smoking Frontier: Condos and Apartments." Reproduced with permission from the February 7, 2007 issue of *The Christian Science Monitor* (www.csmonitor.com). © 2007 The Christian Science Monitor.

504: Steven Reinberg, "Driving While on the Cell Phone Worse Than Driving Drunk," *HealthDay*, June 29, 2006. Copyright © 2006. Reprinted by permission of HealthDay.

509: Holli Riebeek, from "Global Warming," NASA's website *Earth Observatory*, May 11, 2007, http://earthobservatory.nasa.gov/Library/GlobalWarming/global_warming_update.html. Original version by John Weier, April 8, 2002.

PHOTO CREDITS

Index